PARAPSYCHOLOGY,
PHILOSOPHY,
and
SPIRITUALITY

SUNY SERIES IN
CONSTRUCTIVE POSTMODERN THOUGHT
DAVID RAY GRIFFIN, EDITOR

PARAPSYCHOLOGY, PHILOSOPHY,
────────── and ──────────
SPIRITUALITY

A Postmodern Exploration

D AVID R AY G RIFFIN

STATE UNIVERSITY OF NEW YORK PRESS

Published by
State University of New York Press, Albany

© 1997 State University of New York

For information, address the State University of New York Press,
90 State Street, Suite 700, Albany, NY 12207

Production by E Moore
Marketing by Nancy Farrell

Library of Congress Cataloging-in-Publication Data

Griffin, David Ray, 1939–
        Parapsychology, philosophy, and spirituality : a postmodern
exploration / David Ray Griffin.
        p.   cm. — (SUNY series in constructive postmodern thought)
        Includes bibliographical references and index.
        ISBN 0-7914-3315-3 (hc : alk. paper). — ISBN 0-7914-3316-1 (pbk.
: alk. paper)
        1. Parapsychology and philosophy. 2. Spiritual life.
3. Postmodernism. 4. Religion and science. 5. Future life.
I. Title. II. Series.
BF1045.P5G75   1997
133'.01—dc20   96-21472
                                                            CIP

10 9 8 7 6 5 4 3 2 1

This book is dedicated to the memory of Troy Griffin (1913–94),
who would have agreed with some of it,
and to Carolyn Bartell Griffin,
who shared my initial exploration of these strange phenomena.

CONTENTS

ACKNOWLEDGMENTS

My debts in relation to this book are enormous. I will begin by thanking Laurance Rockefeller, who, by providing funding for a conference in 1990, allowed me to get to know and learn from many of the best scientists and philosophers within the parapsychological community. Without the writings of several people fitting that description, this book would have not been possible. Who they are is made clear by the abundant references to them in the notes, but I cannot help mentioning Stephen Braude, Richard Broughton, Alan Gauld, William Roll, Michael Sabom, and Ian Stevenson, upon whose writings I have relied so heavily. I am also grateful to many people for help with specific issues, especially Stephen Braude, Richard Broughton, John Palmer, Gracia Fay Ellwood, Janice Miner Holden, Antonia Mills, Dean Radin, Marilyn Schlitz, Ian Stevenson, Donald Viney, and Rhea White. The library of the American Society for Psychical Research provided prompt help when I needed it. Michael Murphy has been an ongoing source of encouragement. I am grateful to President Robert Edgar, Deans Allen Moore and Marjorie Suchocki, and the Trustees of the School of Theology at Claremont, who have provided the various kinds of support I needed to engage in the quite considerable amount of research that went into this work. I also express my ongoing gratitude to President John Maguire of the Claremont Graduate School. Also essential has been the support of my codirectors at the Center for Process Studies—John Cobb, Mary Elizabeth Moore, Marjorie Suchocki, Jeff Sanders, and John Quiring. I likewise wish to extend public thanks to my new editor at SUNY Press, Clay Morgan, and to my production editor, Elizabeth Moore, with whom it has been a pleasure to work again.

As always, it has been my wife, Ann Jaqua, who has provided the daily environment in which I have been able to engage in this kind of work. This particular volume, however, I dedicate to my first wife, who was with me long ago when I made my initial, short-lived, and entirely unscientific exploration into some of these strange phenomena, and to my father, who died while I was working on this book.

An earlier version of the first part of Chapter 1 has been published as "Why Critical Reflection on the Paranormal is So Important—and So

Difficult," in *Critical Reflections on the Paranormal*, ed. by Michael Stoeber and Hugo Meynell (Albany: State University of New York Press, 1996), 87–117.

An earlier version of the second part of Chapter 1 was published as "Parapsychology and the Need for a Postmodern Philosophy," in *Exceptional Human Experience* 10/2 (December 1992), 155–62. A much earlier and briefer version of Chapter 3, under the title "Life After Death: Religio-Ethical, Philosophical, and Empirical Considerations," was given at a 1991 conference in Dallas sponsored by the Isthmus Institute, "Can Consciousness Survive the Death of the Physical Body?"

Grateful acknowledgment is hereby given to Antonia Mills for permission to quote from personal correspondence; to Ian Stevenson for permission to quote from personal correspondence and from his *Telepathic Impressions: A Review and Report of Thirty-Five New Cases* (Charlottesville: University Press of Virginia, 1970); to Michael Sabom for permission to quote from his *Recollections of Death: A Medical Investigation* (New York: Harper & Row, 1982); to Stephen Braude for permission to quote from his *The Limits of Influence: Psychokinesis and the Philosophy of Science* (New York and London: Routledge & Kegan Paul, 1986); to Random House, Inc. for permission to quote from Richard S. Broughton, *Parapsychology: The Controversial Science* (New York: Ballantine Books, 1991); to Granada Publishing, Ltd., for permission to quote from Alan Gauld, *Mediumship and Survival: A Century of Investigations* (London: Paladin Books, 1983); and to the *Journal of Near-Death Studies* for permission to quote from its Summer 1993 issue.

INTRODUCTION TO
SUNY SERIES IN
CONSTRUCTIVE
POSTMODERN THOUGHT

The rapid spread of the term *postmodern* in recent years witnesses to a growing dissatisfaction with modernity and to an increasing sense that the modern age not only had a beginning but can have an end as well. Whereas the word *modern* was almost always used until quite recently as a word of praise and as a synonym for *contemporary*, a growing sense is now evidenced that we can and should leave modernity behind—in fact, that we *must* if we are to avoid destroying ourselves and most of the life on our planet.

Modernity, rather than being regarded as the norm for human society toward which all history has been aiming and into which all societies should be ushered—forcibly if necessary—is instead increasingly seen as an aberration. A new respect for the wisdom of traditional societies is growing as we realize that they have endured for thousands of years and that, by contrast, the existence of modern society for even another century seems doubtful. Likewise, *modernism* as a worldview is less and less seen as The Final Truth, in comparison with which all divergent worldviews are automatically regarded as "superstitious." The modern worldview is increasingly relativized to the status of one among many, useful for some purposes, inadequate for others.

Although there have been antimodern movements before, beginning perhaps near the outset of the nineteenth century with the Romanticists and the Luddites, the rapidity with which the term postmodern has become widespread in our time suggests that the antimodern sentiment is more extensive and intense than before, and also that it includes the sense that modernity can be successfully overcome only by going beyond it, not by attempting to return to a premodern form of existence. Insofar as a common element is found in the various ways in which the term is used, *postmodernism* refers to a diffuse sentiment rather than to any common set of doctrines—the sentiment that humanity can and must go beyond the modern.

Beyond connoting this sentiment, the term postmodern is used in a confusing variety of ways, some of them contradictory to others. In artistic and literary circles, for example, postmodernism shares in this general sentiment but also involves a specific reaction against "modernism" in the narrow sense of a movement in artistic-literary circles in the late nineteenth and early twentieth centuries. Postmodern architecture is very different from postmodern literary criticism. In some circles, the term postmodern is used in reference to that potpourri of ideas and systems sometimes called *new age metaphysics*, although many of these ideas and systems are more premodern than postmodern. Even in philosophical and theological circles, the term postmodern refers to two quite different positions, one of which is reflected in this series. Each position seeks to transcend both modernism in the sense of the worldview that has developed out of the seventeenth-century Galilean-Cartesian-Baconian-Newtonian science, and modernity in the sense of the world order that both conditioned and was conditioned by this worldview. But the two positions seek to transcend the modern in different ways.

Closely related to literary-artistic postmodernism is a philosophical postmodernism inspired variously by pragmatism, physicalism, Ludwig Wittgenstein, Martin Heidegger, and Jacques Derrida and other recent French thinkers. By the use of terms that arise out of particular segments of this movement, it can be called *deconstructive* or *eliminative postmodernism*. It overcomes the modern worldview through an anti-worldview: it deconstructs or eliminates the ingredients necessary for a worldview, such as god, self, purpose, meaning, a real world, and truth as correspondence. While motivated in some cases by the ethical concern to forestall totalitarian systems, this type of postmodern thought issues in relativism, even nihilism. It could also be called *ultramodernism*, in that its eliminations result from carrying modern premises to their logical conclusions.

The postmodernism of this series can, by contrast, be called *constructive* or *revisionary*. It seeks to overcome the modern worldview not by eliminating the possibility of worldviews as such, but by constructing a postmodern worldview through a revision of modern premises and traditional concepts. This constructive or revisionary postmodernism involves a new unity of scientific, ethical, aesthetic, and religious intuitions. It rejects not science as such but only that scientism in which the data of the modern natural sciences are alone allowed to contribute to the construction of our worldview.

The constructive activity of this type of postmodern thought is not limited to a revised worldview; it is equally concerned with a postmodern world that will support and be supported by the new worldview. A postmodern world will involve postmodern persons, with a postmodern spirituality, on the one hand,

and a postmodern society, ultimately a postmodern global order, on the other. Going beyond the modern world will involve transcending its individualism, anthropocentrism, patriarchy, mechanization, economism, consumerism, nationalism, and militarism. Constructive postmodern thought provides support for the ecology, peace, feminist and other emancipatory movements of our time, while stressing that the inclusive emancipation must be from modernity itself. The term postmodern, however, by contrast with *premodern*, emphasizes that the modern world has produced unparalleled advances that must not be lost in a general revulsion against its negative features.

From the point of view of deconstructive postmodernists, this constructive postmodernism is still hopelessly wedded to outdated concepts, because it wishes to salvage a positive meaning not only for the notions of the human self, historical meaning, and truth as correspondence, which were central to modernity, but also for premodern notions of a divine reality, cosmic meaning, and an enchanted nature. From the point of view of its advocates, however, this revisionary postmodernism is not only more adequate to our experience but also more genuinely postmodern. It does not simply carry the premises of modernity through to their logical conclusions, but criticizes and revises those premises. Through its return to organicism and its acceptance of nonsensory perception, it opens itself to the recovery of truths and values from various forms of premodern thought and practice that had been dogmatically rejected by modernity. This constructive, revisionary postmodernism involves a creative synthesis of modern and premodern truths and values.

This series does not seek to create a movement so much as to help shape and support an already existing movement convinced that modernity can and must be transcended. But those antimodern movements which arose in the past failed to deflect or even retard the onslaught of modernity. What reasons can we have to expect the current movement to be more successful? First, the previous antimodern movements were primarily calls to return to a premodern form of life and thought rather than calls to advance, and the human spirit does not rally to calls to turn back. Second, the previous antimodern movements either rejected modern science, reduced it to a description of mere appearances, or assumed its adequacy in principle; therefore, they could base their calls only on the negative social and spiritual effects of modernity. The current movement draws on natural science itself as a witness against the adequacy of the modern worldview. Third, the present movement has even more evidence than did previous movements of the ways in which modernity and its worldview *are* socially and spiritually destructive. The fourth and probably most decisive difference is that the present movement is based on the awareness that *the continuation of modernity threatens the very survival of life on our planet.* This awareness, combined with the growing knowledge of the interdependence of the modern worldview and the militarism, nuclearism, and ecological devastation of the modern world, is providing an unprecedented impetus for people to see the evidence for a postmodern worldview and to envisage postmodern ways of relating to each other, the rest of nature, and the cosmos as a whole. For these reasons, the failure of the previous antimodern movements says little about the possible success of the current movement.

Advocates of this movement do not hold the naively utopian belief that the success of this movement would bring about a global society of universal and lasting peace, harmony, and happiness, in which all spiritual problems, social conflicts, ecological destruction, and hard choices would vanish. There is, after all, surely a deep truth in the testimony of the world's religions to the presence of a transcultural proclivity to evil deep within the human heart, which no new paradigm, combined with a new economic order, new child-rearing practices, or any other social arrangements, will suddenly eliminate. Furthermore, it has correctly been said that "life is robbery": a strong element of competition is inherent within finite existence, which no social-political-economic-ecological order can overcome. These two truths, especially when contemplated together, should caution us against unrealistic hopes.

However, no such appeal to "universal constants" should reconcile us to the present order, as if this order were thereby uniquely legitimated. The human proclivity to evil in general, and to conflictual competition and ecological destruction in particular, can be greatly exacerbated or greatly mitigated by a world order and its worldview. Modernity exacerbates it about as much as imaginable. We can therefore envision, without being naively utopian, a far better world order, with a far less dangerous trajectory, than the one we now have.

This series, making no pretense of neutrality, is dedicated to the success of this movement toward a postmodern world.

David Ray Griffin
Series Editor

INTRODUCTION:
PARAPSYCHOLOGY, PHILOSOPHY,
AND SPIRITUALITY

The title and contents of this book reflect my conviction that parapsychology is of utmost importance for both philosophy and the spiritual life, especially in the present, as we are being both pushed and lured into a postmodern age.

The potential importance of parapsychology has not been widely recognized. Aside from a few notable exceptions, scientists and philosophers, including philosophers of science, have generally ignored it or treated it with contempt. One of the many reasons for this hostility is a suspicion that parapsychology gives pseudo-scientific support to religion. Yet, in spite of the fact that J. B. Rhine, the most famous of the parapsychologists, many decades ago trumpeted parapsychology as religion's science, philosophers of religion and theologians have shown no more interest, perhaps even less, than scientists, philosophers of science, and other philosophers. In intellectual circles in general, the pervasive state of mind with regard to parapsychology has been characterized by a mutually reinforcing ignorance and disdain.

The main reason that parapsychology, which now has existed as a disciplined field of study for over a century, has been so largely ignored and disdained is that it conflicts with the two worldviews that have been dominant in the modern period. The first of these is the supernaturalistic dualism that was held by most of the founders of modern science, such as Mersenne, Descartes, Boyle, and Newton, and has been presupposed by most conservative-to-fundamentalist Christians and Jews to this day. Because of problems inherent in both the supernaturalism and the dualism of this early modern worldview, it gradually transmuted into an atheistic materialism, which has been dominant in academic circles since the latter part of the nineteenth century (and hence during the entire period of parapsychology's existence).

Although these two worldviews are vastly different in most respects, they have a few commonalities (reflecting the parental relationship of the first

1

to the second). One of these commonalities is lack of room for the three kinds of phenomena studied by parapsychologists: extrasensory perception, psychokinesis, and phenomena suggestive of life after bodily death. Here a distinction must be made: The late modern worldview, with its materialism and atheism, has no room for the phenomena, period. The early modern worldview, with its dualism and supernaturalism, can allow that such phenomena do occur; indeed, it usually insists on the reality of such phenomena under the name of "miracles." What it is hostile to is the naturalistic assumptions that inform the work of parapsychologists, including their terminology. The term "psychokinesis," for example, implies that certain types of events interpreted as (supernatural) miracles in earlier centuries are brought about by power inherent in the human psyche. In any case, in spite of their differing reasons, these two worldviews, which between them have largely informed the modern mind, have conspired to create a formidable prejudice against parapsychology.

Parapsychology's potential importance, especially for making the transition from the modern to a postmodern age, arises, of course, from the same reason that it has been so scorned: It directly challenges the adequacy of both modern worldviews. This should make parapsychology important even apart from any concern with a modern-to-postmodern transition: The fact that parapsychology's data, if genuine, could not be accommodated by the reigning orthodoxies should have led, out of a disinterested concern for truth alone, to its widespread and eager exploration. The concern for truth, however, is rarely disinterested. It is usually informed by our interests (which are reflected in what in Chapter 1 is called "wishful-and-fearful thinking"). Now that there is a widespread interest in moving beyond the modern world and thereby the worldviews that informed it, the time may be ripe for parapsychology to come into its own.

There are, to be sure, many reasons for the widespread conviction that modernity now needs to be transcended. The chief of these is the growing conviction that modernity is simply not sustainable. Because of the late modern lethal mixture of nuclear weapons, polluting and depleting technology, overpopulation, growth economics, and global apartheid, the most urgent decision facing humanity today is that of moving to a postmodern world order, with a new security system, a new economic order, and a new relationship to nature. We are being pushed into a postmodern age simply by the requirements for survival.

Major transitions are usually brought about, however, not only by forces that push from behind, but also by possibilities that attract from ahead. Spiritual aspirations are as important as physical constraints. Modernity, besides having turned out to be socially and ecologically unsustainable, has also been intellectually and spiritually unsatisfactory. The late modern worldview, with its atheism, materialism, and resulting nihilism, has generally been recognized as spiritually unsatisfactory from the outset—even by its proponents, who have said that we had to embrace it nevertheless, putting loyalty to truth above the will to believe. In our time, however, both scientific developments and philosophical considerations have led to the growing realization that this late modern worldview is also inadequate *intellectually*. So now, the ferment to move from the modern to a postmodern world is being fueled by intellectual and spiritual energies as well as by social, political, economic, and ecological pressures.

Parapsychology provides evidence against the intellectual adequacy of the late modern worldview, evidence that is particularly dramatic. This is not to say that the case against the truth of atheistic materialism rests only, or even primarily, on the question of the genuineness of the apparent paranormal interactions investigated by parapsychology. As I argue in Chapter 3, the idea that this worldview is adequate for virtually everything except the (alleged) facts of parapsychology is far from the truth. Nevertheless, parapsychology may turn out to be of decisive importance in moving our culture from a modern to a postmodern outlook. One reason to suspect this is the fact, revealed in recent decades by historians of science, that the early modern worldview was originally formulated to a significant extent precisely to rule out the possibility that paranormal interactions could happen *naturally*. The *late* modern worldview, by rejecting some features of its predecessor but retaining others, ruled out the possibility that they could happen *at all*. It is partly for this reason that, if some of the ostensibly paranormal interactions are genuine, they provide dramatic evidence of the need to revise the prevailing worldviews. Parapsychology, accordingly, should be of special interest to philosophers in our time, at least those philosophers who have not given up on the central task of philosophy: to criticize the prevailing worldview(s) and to suggest a better one.

The best candidate for the worldview of the emerging postmodern age is, in my judgment, one that transcends the dichotomy between supernaturalism and atheism, on the one hand, and the dichotomy between dualism and materialism, on the other. Like supernaturalism, this postmodern philosophy is theistic; but, like atheism, it is naturalistic, rejecting the notion of supernatural origins and interventions. Like dualism, it treats the mind as real and powerful; but, like materialism, it is monistic, rejecting any ontological dualism between mind and matter. The resulting philosophy, with its panexperientialism and naturalistic panentheism, is far more intellectually satisfying than its predecessors. Its greater adequacy includes its consistency with the facts—as I take them to be—of parapsychology.

With regard to spiritual adequacy, it is obvious that this proffered postmodern worldview, by providing naturalism without nihilism, is more satisfying than the late modern worldview. Many would assume, however, that in terms of the spiritual satisfaction to be enjoyed from living in terms of a worldview, the postmodern outlook, given its naturalism, would necessarily pale in comparison with the supernaturalism of the early modern worldview, not to mention its premodern predecessors. That indeed would arguably be the case

were it not for parapsychology. Here we come to its central positive significance (in distinction from its central negative significance of providing dramatic
evidence for the falsity of the modern worldviews). It enables us, within an
entirely naturalistic framework, to form a conception of human life that is spiritually no less satisfying than any theology formulated in terms of some version
of supernaturalism.

Even apart from the additions to this postmodern outlook derived from
parapsychological evidence, there would be much to commend it in relation to
supernaturalistic spiritualities, even in terms of this pragmatic criterion of spiritual satisfaction alone (leaving aside, that is, the issue of intellectual adequacy). For example, the dualism of early modern supernaturalism led to an
alienation from nature that has involved a great spiritual impoverishment. The
patriarchy of premodern and early modern supernaturalisms has been spiritually
crippling—to women most obviously, but also to men. Yet another kind of
spiritual impoverishment is the exclusivism with regard to other religious traditions that has followed almost inevitably from the supernaturalistic view of
divinity. Nevertheless, in spite of all these and other deficiencies, supernaturalistic religion has had a robustness about it that its less ethically and intellectually offensive substitutes, both modern and postmodern, have not had. Thanks
to parapsychology, however, a naturalistic worldview that fulfills our other
criteria can also provide the basis for a robust spirituality.

To give a few examples: The worldview advocated in these pages is
fully naturalistic, so that it does not conflict with the basic presupposition of
natural science that no events lie outside the universal causal nexus. (Science
does not require, I should add for clarification, the deterministic version of
this presupposition, according to which efficient causation from the past is
fully determining of all events, allowing no place for self-determination in the
present.) This worldview, being naturalistic, provides no basis for an exclu-
sivistic view of revelation and salvation; truths and values in all spiritual traditions can be appreciated, perhaps appropriated. This worldview's nondualism
allows humans again to feel kinship with the rest of nature, and it encourages
reverence for life in all its forms. In spite of its naturalism and nondualism,
however, it allows for the genuineness of religious (as well as moral and aesthetic) experience as involving direct infusion by the divine soul of the universe,
and even for the understanding of human life as a spiritual journey that continues beyond bodily death. At the same time, it encourages no escapism, making instead the fate of the earth a matter of utmost religious importance.

This book unfolds in the following manner: In the first chapter, I discuss
the impediments to openminded study of parapsychological evidence in the
modern worldviews and related wishful-and-fearful thinking. I then lay out
briefly how the postmodern philosophy of Alfred North Whitehead creates an
attitude of openness to this evidence. In Chapter 2, some evidence for extrasensory perception and psychokinesis is examined. A discussion of the third major

type of parapsychological evidence, that for life after death, is not begun until Chapter 4, so that I can first discuss, in Chapter 3, the mind-body relation. I there argue that, even apart from parapsychological evidence, the most adequate position is the nondualistic interactionism suggested by Whitehead's philosophy. After making this case, I go on to argue that the evidence for both extrasensory perception and psychokinesis, besides providing further support for this position, also provides indirect evidence for life after death. In Chapters 4 through 8, then, I discuss five kinds of *direct* evidence for life after death: mental mediumship, cases of the possession type, cases of the reincarnation type, apparitions, and out-of-body (including near-death) experiences. (This discussion of the direct evidence for life after death was originally conceived as a single chapter, parallel to Chapter 2, but it became so long it had to be broken up into five chapters.) Finally, in Chapter 9, I sum up the implications of parapsychology, as interpreted through my Whiteheadian lenses, for a postmodern spirituality. I also discuss the connection between such a spirituality and the possibility of a transition to a postmodern world order, which I above called the most urgent need facing the human race today.

1

PARAPSYCHOLOGY AND POSTMODERN PHILOSOPHY

The topic of parapsychology evokes various responses. Ridicule, good-natured or otherwise, is often the first reaction. Several years ago, in Claremont, California, where I teach, I delivered a lecture on which the present chapter is partly based. My then-dean, who has never been shy about expressing his prejudices, sent a note with his apologies for being unable to attend. The note said: "I'm sorry I'll have to miss your talk on Whitehead and the spook world." This friendly critic, furthermore, usually referred to a course of mine titled "Philosophy, Theology, and Parapsychology" as "Griffin's course on magic."

People's tendency to respond to parapsychology with a humorous put-down, however, is often combined with a suspicion that there might be something to it. In some cases, they are not able simply to dismiss all reports of paranormal events because they themselves have had some apparently "psychic" experiences, or they have heard accounts of such from friends whose honesty and sobriety they could not question. For example, my aforementioned dean told me during that same year about a house in Claremont in which, reportedly, the owners would often find a certain picture on the floor in the mornings. They would hang it back up, and the next morning it would be on the floor again. If it had been simply falling down during the night, it would have broken. There was no one else living in the house; and the owners were quite certain that neither of them was sleepwalking. My dean, knowing that the people were neither liars nor crazy, did not know what to make of this.

Most of us have heard stories of this nature, according to which events occur that cannot be explained by "normal" physical causes and that appear, instead, to be the result of intelligent forces producing physical effects without the mediation of a physical body. In the literature, in fact, there are thousands of such stories deriving from every period of history and from every part of the world. If even a few of these stories are true, the implications are enormous.

For example, the presupposition of most modern liberal scholarship on the Hebrew and Christian scriptures has been that events of this kind cannot happen. Accordingly, all the reports in the Bible that we normally classify as "miracles" (except perhaps for those that can be reinterpreted as psychosomatic healing) must be explained away in terms of fraud, primitive credulity, poor observation, mythopoetic license, illustrations of purely spiritual points, and the like. The supposition that such things cannot really happen has been fundamental to "demythologizing" interpretations from David Friedrich Strauss in the middle of the nineteenth century to Rudolf Bultmann in the middle of the twentieth century, and this supposition continues to inform most scholarship today. If, however, we can establish beyond a reasonable doubt that events of this nature happen in our time, the major reason for assuming that they did not happen in biblical times is removed. This removal could lead to a significant change in biblical scholarship and in historiography in general.

That is only one example of the changes that would be implied if that picture in the house in Claremont really was being taken off its hook by an invisible force during the night. Reflecting on the implications of such an event could lead us to revise our views about the nature of the evolutionary process, the possibility of divine influence in the world, the relation between mind and body, the possibility of life after death, and the very meaning of life.

But how many people check out the stories about pictures being moved? How many read the scientific studies that have been carried out in laboratories on the alleged powers of certain people to move physical objects at a distance? Of those few who do some checking, how many then rethink the rest of their beliefs in the light of these facts? Most people, especially highly educated ones, either reject the stories out of hand, assume that there is some "natural" or "rational" explanation for them (taking both "natural" and "rational" to mean "mechanistic"), or else simply put them in that portion of their minds labeled "anomalies."

This last type of response is exemplified by a well-known philosopher of science whose stance and background make him particularly interesting to talk with about the paranormal. On the one hand, he is an avowed materialist; on the other hand, he had, while a graduate student, been closely associated with C. D. Broad, one of the few major philosophers of the twentieth century to have devoted extensive attention to parapsychology.[1]

Shortly after I had learned of an article arguing that, contrary to customary belief, materialism is not necessarily incompatible with belief in paranormal events,[2] I asked this philosopher of science if he agreed. He said no, that it belongs to the very meaning of materialism that paranormal events are deemed impossible. Given that unequivocal response, I asked how he explained the fact that Broad had endorsed the genuineness of certain types of paranormal phenomena, such as telepathy. Did he think Broad engaged in fraud? Absolutely not; Broad was a man of the highest integrity. Did he then suspect that Broad was a poor observer, or had been duped by fraudulent or careless psychical researchers? No, that would have been very unlikely; Broad was an extremely intelligent and circumspect individual. So, how did this philosopher of science reconcile his knowledge that Broad accepted paranormal phenomena with his own belief that such phenomena are impossible? He didn't, he replied; he simply held his own beliefs and his knowledge of Broad's beliefs alongside each other.

In having a worldview that rules out the possibility of paranormal events a priori, this philosopher is not atypical. He is, in fact, unusual only in his acknowledgment that the data for paranormal events are sufficiently impressive to convince some reasonable thinkers. Intellectuals who share this philosopher's materialistic worldview more typically reject the evidence out of hand, either by refusing to examine it or by attacking the credibility of those reporting it—as typified by publications of the Committee for the Scientific Investigation of Claims for the Paranormal. As suggested by their acronym, CSICOP, they exist less to engage in scientific investigation of reports of the paranormal (sometimes called "psi") than to serve as thought-police, blowing the whistle on all claims for psi.*

One member of this committee, C. E. M. Hansel, a British psychologist, refers to his books on parapsychological phenomena as "scientific" and "critical" evaluations,[3] although they are travesties of the scientific approach. He considers that he has disproved a serious study purporting to demonstrate paranormal abilities if he can come up with some other possible explanation for the results, no matter how fanciful, and no matter how insulting to the intelligence and integrity of the experimenters. If Hansel's approach were used with regard to all scientific studies, virtually all of them would have to be thrown out.

---

* This evaluation can be confirmed by examining the official publication of CSICOP, *The Skeptical Inquirer*. The publication of this organization was originally called *The Zetetic Inquirer*. However, sociologist Marcello Truzzi, who was the editor, resigned from the organization, saying that it was interested only in serving as the case for the prosecution, not as an impartial forum in which all sides could be argued. He then began publishing a journal, called *The Zetetic*, to serve this role. For more details about CSICOP, see Richard S. Broughton, *Parapsychology: The Controversial Science* (New York: Ballantine Books, 1991), 81–85, and George P. Hansen, "CSICOP and the Skeptics: An Overview," *Journal of the American Society for Psychical Research* 86 (January 1992), 19–63.

Whether evidence for the paranormal is rejected a priori, however, or simply set aside as anomalous, in neither case is there *philosophical reflection on the paranormal*, by which I mean primarily two things: (1) examining the evidence for paranormal influence open-mindedly, and then, if the evidence is credible, (2) asking how the occurrence of paranormal influence might be compatible with those "normal" causal processes that have in modern times been assumed to rule them out. This latter question involves asking how, if the so-called paranormal were accepted as genuine, the worldview that had ruled them out would need to be revised.

Most intellectuals, however, cannot examine the evidence "open-mindedly" because they have minds that are *not* open, but chock-full with a worldview that says that such things cannot happen. This worldview is usually, as I indicated in the introduction, one of the two versions of the modern worldview.

In the first section of this chapter, I discuss in an elementary way what parapsychology is and the ostensibly paranormal phenomena it studies, indicating what would make events "paranormal." In the second section, I suggest that the main reason for the negative reaction to the possibility of the paranormal in the modern world, especially among intellectuals, is that the modern worldview rules out this possibility, and indeed was formulated in part to rule it out. The topic of the third section is the way in which wishful and fearful thinking interacts with both philosophical paradigms (worldviews) and empirical evidence to help account for the prejudice against the paranormal. In the fourth section, I suggest that parapsychology has shown the need for a *post*modern philosophy. The fifth section suggests that Alfred North Whitehead has filled that need.

1. PARAPSYCHOLOGY AND THE PARANORMAL

In this book the term *parapsychology* is used synonymously with *psychical research*. "Parapsychology" was originally coined to refer only to the portion of psychical research that is carried out under scientifically controlled conditions, usually in a laboratory. Many parapsychologists, understandably, wish to hold fast to this distinction. The term has widely come to be used, however, as a synonym for "psychical research." I am using it in this expanded sense.

Parapsychology or psychical research is sometimes defined as the scientific study of a certain class of events, now widely called "paranormal." These are events in which paranormal influence occurs. (What exactly is distinctive of paranormal influence will be specified in the second section.) It is more accurate, however, to say that parapsychologists study *ostensible* paranormal events, meaning events in which paranormal influence *prima facie* appears to be involved. Adding the word "ostensible" is important: It means that one can be a parapsychologist without necessarily believing in the reality of paranormal influence.* Nevertheless, in the following discussion, I will, for ease of expression, simply speak of paranormal events, assuming that they really do occur, adding the qualifier "ostensible" only when focusing on the issue of genuineness.

Paranormal phenomena are commonly divided into three major types. First, there are events in which a psyche receives influences that are not mediated through its physical senses. The term *extrasensory perception* (ESP) is used to refer to such events.

The two main forms of ESP are telepathy (which means "feeling at a distance"), in which one receives influence from inside another mind, and clairvoyance (sometimes now called "remote viewing"), in which one receives influences, sometimes resulting in sensorylike images, relating to the outer characteristics of things. (So-called precognition, generally classed as a third form of ESP, is better explained in terms of other forms of paranormal influence involving no [unintelligible] "backward causation" from the future to the present. This issue is discussed at the end of Chapter 2.)

Second, there are events in which a psyche produces effects in the world beyond its physical body without using this body to bring about these effects. The term *psychokinesis* (PK) is usually used as a blanket term for events of this type. The most common form of PK is the simple movement of physical objects: Matchsticks may be moved across a table, a string inside a closed bottle may be made to turn, or spoons may be bent, all without being touched. There are also more complex forms of PK, such as materialization and dematerialization, psychic photography, and some types of psychic healing. (Some types of effects brought about *within* one's own body, such as stigmata, might be considered instances of PK, but I leave aside this possible refinement of the definition.)

The third major type of paranormality consists of experiences, such as messages from mediums and near-death out-of-body experiences, that are suggestive of the existence of psyches apart from their physical bodies. Although there are some allusions to evidence for life after death in the present chapter, the discussion of this third type of paranormality is reserved primarily for Chapters 3 through 8.

Parapsychology, then, is the scientific study of events of these three types. The first aim of this study is to determine whether ostensible paranormal events, in which paranormal influence *seems* to occur, are genuine—whether

* Besides implying that parapsychologists necessarily believe in paranormal occurrences, whereas they may not, the definition of parapsychology as simply the study of paranormal interactions also leads skeptics to suspect that parapsychology may well be a subject without a subject matter. Both of these problems are solved by the insertion of the qualifier "ostensible," as suggested by John Palmer in "Progressive Skepticism: A Critical Approach to the Psi Controversy," *Journal of Parapsychology* 50 (1986), 29–42.

they really do, at least in some cases, involve paranormal influence. Does apparent ESP really involve, at least in some cases, the reception of information that does not come through the sensory system? Does apparent PK really involve, at least in some instances, influence of the psyche that is not mediated through the body? Do some apparent communications from physically deceased individuals really involve paranormal communications? If so, is the paranormal communication sometimes best interpreted as deriving from the continued existence of the physically deceased person? The second aim of parapsychology, if the answer to any of these questions is affirmative, is to try to understand *how* these paranormal influences occur. This attempt to understand includes both the *philosophical* effort to understand the nature of this influence and the *scientific* effort to discover what laws, if any, are reflected in the phenomena.

The study of paranormal interactions takes two major forms. First, there is the study of spontaneous events, such as visions or voices that convey information to a person who had no way of acquiring this information from sensory perception. For example, people will sometimes learn through a vision, a voice, or simply a very strong feeling that a relative is in a crisis situation. Second, there are experiments in which subjects are tested for ESP or PK ability under controlled conditions. In these experiments the subjects may demonstrate paranormal abilities by producing scores significantly beyond what would be predicted on the basis of chance, or by producing directly observable effects, such as when someone makes spoons bend simply by thinking about them or by at most stroking them.

This scientific study has been going on in a continuous way for over one hundred years, since the Society for Psychical Research was established in London in 1882. There were some earlier investigations of decent enough quality to merit the term "scientific," such as those of William Crookes, England's leading chemist in the latter half of the nineteenth century. These earlier efforts, however, were by isolated figures or by societies that did not survive. So the founding in London in 1882 of the Society for Psychical Research, which still publishes the *Journal of the Society for Psychical Research*, is usually taken as the beginning of the scientific study of paranormal phenomena. This scientific study goes back almost as far in our own country, as William James and others founded the American branch of the Society for Psychical Research in 1885, which still publishes the *Journal of the American Society for Psychical Research*.[4]

Many people may wince at the use of the term "scientific" for this study. The still-dominant image seems to be of a bunch of "kooks and crackpots" studying phoney mediums in dark séances. A lot of this certainly has gone on. As with other fields, however, we should evaluate psychical research in the light of its best, not only its worst, moments.

With regard to the credibility of the practitioners, the list of well-known people who have become convinced that paranormal events do happen, some of whom were directly involved in psychical research, includes many otherwise reputable figures. Among philosophers, the list includes Henri Bergson, C. D. Broad, Curt Ducasse, William James, Gabriel Marcel, H. H. Price, F. S. C. Schiller, Michael Scriven, and Henry Sidgwick. Among noted psychologists, the list includes Jule Eisenbud, Theodore Flournoy, Sigmund Freud, William James (again), Pierre Janet, Carl Jung, William McDougall, Gardner Murphy, and Rudolf Tischner. Among physicists, we have Sir William Barrett, David Bohm, Sir William Crookes, Thomas Edison, John Hasted, Pascual Jordon, Nobel–Prize winner Brian Josephson, Sir Oliver Lodge, Lord Rayleigh (John William Strutt, who received a Nobel prize in 1904 for his isolation of argon), and Helmut Schmidt. Among astronomers: Camille Flammarion and Sir Arthur Eddington. Among biologists: Alexis Carrel (who won the Nobel prize in 1912), Hans Driesch, Claude Richet (who won the Nobel prize in 1913), and A. R. Wallace (who came up with the natural-selection theory of evolution simultaneously with Darwin). Among literary figures: William Blake, Elizabeth Barrett Browning, Arthur Conan Doyle, Aldous Huxley, Maurice Maeterlinck, Thomas Mann, Gilbert Murray (who often demonstrated his own extrasensory abilities in parlor games), Upton Sinclair (whose book on the subject was recommended by Einstein),* Mark Twain, and W. B. Yeats. Among politicians: Frances P. Bolton (U.S. congresswoman for almost thirty years), Mackenzie King (prime minister of Canada for twenty-two years), and Arthur Balfour (prime minister of England from 1902 to 1905). This is hardly a list of "kooks and crackpots."

In most fields, we take most of our beliefs on authority. We do not demand to look through the telescopes to see the red shift or demand to verify that the Cyclotron is really doing what the scientists say it is doing. We take the word of people who, we assume, are in position to know. Why, then, do we not take the word of at least some of the people listed in the previous paragraph and of the current parapsychologists, whose work is available in scholarly books[5] and journals,[6] that paranormal influence occurs?

It is mainly because we hardly ever hear of these facts. We simply are not informed, in the ways that we are informed about other matters, that these credible people became convinced of the reality of ESP and PK after spending time—in some cases a significant portion of their lives—studying the evidence for them.

---

*Einstein wrote a preface in 1939 for a projected German edition of Upton Sinclair's *Mental Radio*, in which Sinclair reports on successful telepathic experiments with his wife, Mary Craig Kimbrough Sinclair, and which was first published in America in 1931. Although the projected German edition was never published (the publisher went out of business), this preface, in which Einstein says that the book "deserves the most earnest consideration," was included in the revised, second printing of the book (Springfield, Ill.: Charles C. Thomas, 1962). Of special interest is the fact that Einstein, who had witnessed some of the experiments, says that, although the results "stand surely far beyond those which a nature investigator holds to be thinkable," Sinclair's "good faith and dependability are not to be doubted" (ix).

We as a culture do not know of even the most famous spontaneous cases, although in their own time these cases were sometimes well publicized. Take the example of "Patience Worth."[7] During World War I, a woman in St. Louis named Pearl Curran began receiving messages through a ouija board. The source of the messages identified itself as "Patience Worth," saying that she had lived in England in the seventeenth century. After a while Mrs. Curran did not even have to use the ouija board, as she began seeing the words mentally. Works of various sorts were dictated. There were historical novels from various periods. *The Sorry Tale* was a long novel located in Palestine at the time of Jesus. New Testament scholars said that it reflected amazingly accurate information about the ordinary daily practices of the people at that time. The reviewer for the *New York Times* called it "a wonderful, a beautiful, and a noble work." Another large novel was situated in nineteenth-century England, and its knowledge of the language, places, and customs of the time was so exact that it never occurred to a British critic of the book that the author was not British. Then there were hundreds of poems. Some of these were included in books of the outstanding American poetry of the year, with "Patience Worth" sometimes getting more poems chosen than the best-known poets of the time. (Of course, those who chose these poems did not know who "Patience Worth" was; i.e., they did not know how the poems were produced.) There were even debates about whether "Patience" was a better poet than Shakespeare! Besides the quality, magnitude, and variety of the work, all of which was far beyond the capacity of the rather meagerly educated Mrs. Curran, the speed at which the work was dictated was phenomenal. The dictation would come as fast as a stenographer could take it down, and it would go on for hours at a time. Also, "Patience" could go back and forth from one work to another. She would break off in the middle of a long poem to work on a novel for a while; then, perhaps after a week or two, "Patience" would pick up with the poem exactly where she had left off without any hesitation.

Mrs. Curran was studied by various people, including some of the leading psychologists of the day and various skeptics. It was one of the biggest stories of the decade, often getting front-page coverage in Europe as well as America. There has never been any consensus as to how to understand "Patience": Was she a discarnate entity communicating through Mrs. Curran, as she ("Patience") claimed? Or was she an aspect of Mrs. Curran's subconscious? Even if one said the latter, this was one of the most amazing phenomena of all time, with tremendous implications for the nature of human personality and creativity. Few people today, however, have heard of "Patience" and Mrs. Curran, even people in St. Louis, although the story had put St. Louis on the world map in the early part of this century.

There are dozens of other stories of this type, which were closely studied by reputable people and given wide coverage in their own day, but of which most people today are ignorant. Why is this? Mainly because these phenomena lie outside what the modern worldview allows as possible, so they do not get incorporated in the curricular materials of our educational system.

The same ignorance exists about the fact that there are long-established psychical research organizations with reputable journals and rigorous standards. Many people do know that some work on parapsychology was done by J. B. Rhine at Duke University, but that is usually the limit of their information. They do not know that it was the well-known psychologist William McDougall, who left Harvard to go to Duke, who gave Rhine his start at Duke in the 1930s; they do not know that the *Journal of Parapsychology*,[8] which Rhine founded, has existed since 1937; they do not know that many other centers of parapsychological study have existed, with some still going, and that the field has gone through many phases, moving considerably beyond the methods and presuppositions that dominated the work at Duke during the Rhine days; and they do not know that, thanks partly to the intervention of Margaret Mead, the Parapsychological Association has been an affiliate of the American Academy for the Advancement of Science since 1969.

This ignorance exists not only among the general public, but also, and in general probably even more, within the academic world. Most scientists, philosophers, and theologians still write as if ESP and PK were not serious possibilities. I say this not to castigate anyone: I myself was ignorant of the scientific study of these things until 1981, when I stumbled onto it in a book on the mind-body problem.* My point is only that, over a century after the beginning of the scientific study of this potentially most important subject, the ignorance about it in intellectual circles is still widespread.

I have suggested that the major reason for this neglect is that the modern worldview—or, to use the term that philosopher of science Thomas Kuhn popularized, the modern *paradigm*†—does not make room for paranormal influences. It rules them out a priori. By the "modern paradigm," I mean a set of basic beliefs that came to be dominant in connection with the scientific revolution of the seventeenth century. This set of beliefs was associated with the paradigmatic achievements of Descartes, Galileo, Boyle, and Newton, and it was articulated further in the works of Locke, Hobbes, and the eighteenth-century *philosophes*. I turn now to a discussion of this modern worldview and why it has created such prejudice against the reality of the paranormal.

---

* The book was John Beloff's *The Existence of Mind*, which is discussed briefly in Chapter 3. Although, as I indicate there, I disagree with Beloff's (ontological) dualism and also his view that, aside from parapsychological evidence, materialism would be adequate, I will always remain indebted to him for opening me up to this realm of investigation.

† See Thomas Kuhn, *The Structure of Scientific Revolutions*. Although in the second edition, Kuhn drew back from his use of "paradigm" for an all-encompassing worldview (in favor of the more restricted meaning, referring to a paradigmatic experiment or discovery), the widespread use of this larger meaning has been one of the book's lasting legacies.

2. THE PARANORMAL AND THE MODERN WORLDVIEW

Although the discussion in the previous section presupposed a notion of what paranormal influence is, an explicit statement of that notion was postponed until this section. This statement cannot simply be copied from the cover page of a parapsychological journal, however, because the parapsychological community has not yet attained consensus on how to specify what is both distinctive of and common to all the phenomena it studies. There is, however, an implicit consensus: Pervasive of the literature is the presupposition that what is distinctive of the category of the paranormal is the idea of *influence at a distance to or from minds*. Both parts of this definition—"action at a distance" and "to or from minds"—are necessary to account for what is distinctive about paranormal events, as the ensuing discussion will make clear. The presupposition behind this characterization of paranormal influence, obviously, is that "normal" causal influence occurs only between *contiguous* events or things, at least if minds are involved.

It can readily be seen that the two major types of paranormal influence, extrasensory perception and psychokinesis, conform to this characterization. ESP involves a mind's *reception* of influence from a distance. Perception by means of the sensory system, by contrast, involves chains of causal influence between contiguous events. For example, when I see the tree outside the window in my study, the tree image results from chains of photons traveling from the tree to my eye, then chains of neurons from my eye to my brain. Extrasensory perception, if it occurs, is paranormal because it circumvents this system of contiguous causation. If I have a clairvoyant perception of the tree, the tree exerts causal influence directly on my mind. My mind, accordingly, has received causal influence from a distance. This idea is reflected in the terms "telepathy" and "remote viewing."

Psychokinesis (PK) involves the *exertion* of causal influence at a distance by a mind. In what we consider "normal" human action on things beyond the body, by contrast, the mind or psyche directly influences only its own body, usually its motor-muscular system. (I ignore for now the view that equates the mind with the brain and hence with one part of the body.) The body then brings about an extrasomatic effect, such as picking up a matchstick. The mind or psyche thereby brings about extrasomatic effects by means of a contiguous chain of cause-effect relations. In psychokinesis, however, this chain is circumvented, as the psyche brings about extrasomatic effects, such as moving a matchstick, directly, without using the body. That it is causal influence at a distance that makes such an event paranormal was reflected better in the older term *telekinesis*.

That causal influence at a distance to or from minds would be involved in the third type of paranormality, which involves the existence of psyches apart from their (biological) bodies, is not so readily apparent. There are two ways, however, in which it can be subsumed under the general characterization. In the first place, one can describe this third type, as I did earlier, not directly in terms of discarnate existence, but in terms of various *experiences* (such as mediumistic messages and out-of-body experiences) that are suggestive of discarnate existence. These *experiences* all apparently involve influence at a distance to or from minds. Many students of the paranormal, however, think, not without some justification, of the out-of-body state as itself paranormal. Even so, this third type of paranormality arguably fits the general characterization, because the existence of the psyche apart from a physical body would probably involve both extrasensory perception and psychokinesis. I will suggest in Chapter 3 that this is indeed so.

In any case, the crucial question is why this kind of causal influence, involving influence at a distance to or from minds, should be so controversial. Why should modern minds be so convinced that it cannot occur? The answer, I suggest, is primarily that the distinctively modern worldview, sometimes called the "modern scientific worldview," not only excludes this kind of causal influence, but was in part *created to exclude it*. As Brian and Lynne Mackenzie say, the paranormal events studied by parapsychologists are not simply "anomalous" in the sense of being a "specifiable class of events which just happen to conflict with the scientific conception of the world." Rather,

> they were established as paranormal by the genesis of the scientific conception, and are not definable separately from it. The "paranormal" was established as such by being ruled out of nature altogether. . . .
>
> The incompatibility of parapsychology with modern science is neither accidental nor recent, but is built into the assumptive base of modern science itself. It is because the aims and claims of parapsychology clash strongly with this assumptive base that the field attracts such hostility.*

This view, that the worldview associated with modern science was created in part to exclude what we now call the paranormal, is supported by sociologist of science Jerome Ravetz:

> The "scientific revolution" itself becomes comprehensible if we see it as a campaign for a reform of ideas *about* science. . . . Scientific revolution was primarily and essentially about metaphysics; and the various technical studies were largely conceived and received as corroborating statements of a challenging world-view. This consisted essentially of two

---

* Brian Mackenzie and Lynne S. Mackenzie, "Whence the Enchanted Boundary? Sources and Significance of the Parapsychological Tradition," *Journal of Parapsychology* 44 (1980), 125–66, at 143, 153, 135. My agreement with the Mackenzies is, however, only partial; see the next footnote.

Great Denials: the restriction of ordinary faculties such as sympathy and intelligence to humans and to a remote Deity; and *the relegation of extraordinary faculties to the realms of the nonexistent or insignificant.*[9]

What was it about the new metaphysical worldview that ruled out what is now called the paranormal? The Mackenzies point to the central issue by quoting a statement made by scientist George Price in his attack on parapsychology, "Science and the Supernatural." "The essence of science," said Price, "is mechanism. The essence of magic is animism."* The new metaphysics for science introduced in the seventeenth century was called, of course, the "mechanical philosophy." Insofar as we are removed from the debates of the time, we may assume that the chief point at issue in speaking of "mechanism" was an exclusive focus on efficient causes, in distinction from "final causation." The real bite of mechanism, we may suppose, is that, by excluding all self-determination, it entails complete determinism. This was indeed one of the central issues, but not the only one. An at least equally crucial meaning of the "mechanical philosophy" was that action at a distance was proscribed.

Mary Hesse has pointed out, in her study of the idea of action at a distance in physics, that this idea lost favor through the introduction of the mechanical philosophy of nature, according to which its particles were purely material, having no inner, hidden ("occult") qualities that could possibly exert or receive influence at a distance.[10] This philosophy implied that all causation must be *by contact*.

Other historians have added that this implication was not simply an incidental side-effect of the mechanical philosophy but a central intention. Richard Westfall says:

All [mechanical philosophers] agreed on some form of dualism which excluded from nature the possibility of what they called pejoratively "occult agents.". . . All agreed that the program of natural philosophy lay in demonstrating that the phenomena of nature are produced by the mutual interplay of material particles which act on each other by direct contact alone.[11]

"The fundamental tenet of Descartes' mechanical philosophy of nature," Westfall adds, was "that one body can act on another only by direct contact."[12] Brian Easlea has in fact argued, in what is perhaps the best book on the origin of the "scientific revolution," that the desire to rule out the possibility of attrac-

---

*George Price, "Science and the Supernatural," *Philosophy and Parapsychology*, ed. Jan Ludwig (Buffalo: Prometheus Books, 1978), 172–77, at 173. (Price's article was originally published in *Science* 122 [1955], 359–67.) Incidentally, although the Mackenzies quote this statement, they do not make causality at a distance central to their own characterization of the paranormal.

tion at a distance was not simply one of many, but the *central*, motivation behind the mechanical philosophers' denial of all hidden qualities within matter.[13]

The obvious objection to this portrayal is that many considered Isaac Newton the mechanical philosopher par excellence, and yet Newton, with his doctrine of universal gravitation, seems clearly to have been an advocate of action at a distance. Indeed, quite different from Descartes' *kinetic* mechanical philosophy, which mandated causation by contact exclusively, was Newton's *dynamic* mechanical philosophy, which portrayed the ultimate agent in nature as "a force acting between particles rather than a moving particle itself."[14] It was thereby open in principle to the idea of action at a distance. Newton's language of "attractions," in fact, created the suspicion that he affirmed action at a distance. Christiaan Huygens said about Newton: "I don't care that he's not a Cartesian as long as he doesn't serve us up conjectures such as attractions."[15]

The fact that the new worldview banned action at a distance is illustrated, however, not only by the comment of the Cartesian Huygens but also by Newton's own response to the controversy. It was with regard to gravitation that Newton made his famous positivistic reply that he did not "feign hypotheses" about the actual cause but only provided mathematical formulae.[16] In a well-known letter to Richard Bentley, Newton went even further, saying:

> Tis unconceivable that inanimate brute matter should (without the mediation of something else which is not material) operate upon and affect other matter without mutual contact. . . . That gravity should be innate and essential to matter so that one body may act upon another at a distance through a vacuum without the mediation of any thing else by and through which their action or force may be conveyed from one to another is to me so great an absurdity that I believe no man who has in philosophical matters any competent faculty of thinking can ever fall into it.[17]

In these disclaimers, Newton may well, of course, have been hiding his true views. The point, however, is that Newton *as public philosopher* supported the rejection of causal influence at a distance. Furthermore, although the mechanistic worldview is nowadays often called "the Newtonian worldview," Robert Schofield in his study *Mechanism and Materialism* documents the extent to which Newton's ideas were assimilated as much as possible in the eighteenth and nineteenth centuries to the Cartesian form of mechanism.[18] (One manifestation of this development today may be the desire to find explanations of gravitation, such as "curvature of space" and "gravitons," that do not involve attraction at a distance.) According to Richard Westfall, this development had already been anticipated by Newton himself: "In his final years, a growing philosophic caution led Newton to retreat somewhat toward more conventional mechanistic views."[19] In sum, the case of Newton does not significantly weaken the twofold claim that the mechanical philosophy with which science became associated in the latter half of the seventeenth century excluded action at a distance, and that this exclusion was one of the main reasons for its adoption.

Another objection might be that this discussion of physical theory is irrelevant to current attitudes toward the "paranormal," because the paranormal, as it is usually understood and as I have characterized it, involves the causal influence at a distance exerted or received by *minds*, whereas the "mechanical philosophy" dealt exclusively with physical nature from which all mental characteristics were excluded. There is truth in this objection: The dualism between mind and nature, which was adopted by Descartes, Newton, and all the other early leaders of the movement (except Hobbes), did indeed leave open the possibility that the human mind, said to be outside of nature, might be able to act and perceive at a distance; and a few thinkers (such as Joseph Glanvill, one of the founders of the Royal Society) adopted this position.[20]

The dominant position among these dualists, however, as articulated by the "rationalist" Descartes as well as the "empiricist" Locke, was that the mind could perceive and act on the world only through its brain: The sensationist theory of perception said that the mind can perceive only by means of its physical sensory system; the corresponding theory of action said that the mind can act only through its motor-muscular system. Both perception and action, accordingly, occurred only through chains of contiguous causes. There could be no extrasensory knowledge of the world and no psychokinetic action on it.

In the dominant thinking of the time, the connection between the desire to exclude action at a distance in physics, on the one hand, and the desire to rule out all paranormal influence on and by human minds, on the other, was evidently something like this: Given the dualism between (spiritual) mind and (physical) nature, excluding action at a distance from nature did not, strictly speaking, rule out the possibility that human minds might either receive or exert causal influence at a distance. Nevertheless, a philosophy of nature in which all causal influence was by contact created a context in which the idea of causal influence at a distance to or from minds seemed unfitting. In this context, the stipulation (by a Descartes or a Locke) that the mind does not receive or exert any influence at a distance would not seem arbitrary (even though it was). It was for this reason, I suggest, that the issue of action at a distance in physics was so controversial, even though the primary target of the partisans of action-by-contact physics was the belief that the human mind could have "occult" powers.

In any case, a development unforeseen by these partisans overcame the arbitrariness of their argument from nature to mind: Their dualism collapsed into a fully materialistic position. This development occurred in the latter half of the eighteenth century in France and in the latter half of the nineteenth century in the English-speaking world (thanks to a large extent to Darwin). With this development, the "mind" was fully within nature, being purely a function of the brain (as the notorious Hobbes had suggested). It was therefore subject to the same prohibition against action at a distance as the rest of nature.

To speak of this late modern worldview, however, is to get ahead of the story. I have yet to explain why the exclusion of action at a distance was so important to thinkers in the second half of the seventeenth century. We should not suppose, as earlier historians of the history of science and philosophy had naively suggested, that this exclusion resulted solely from a disinterested search for truth. Rather, as historians have been documenting in recent decades, strong theological and social factors were involved.

One of the factors making action at a distance such a controversial issue involved the interpretation of "miracles." The authority of the church was to a great extent based on the assumption that God had endorsed Christianity as the One True Religion by the miracles that occurred in New Testament times (and, for Catholics, in the continuing history of the church, especially in and through the lives of the saints). This interpretation was challenged, however, by advocates of Hermetic and other "magical" philosophies, which allowed influence at a distance, including that to and from minds (perhaps through "sympathy"), as a purely natural occurrence. The "miraculous" healings performed by Jesus, accordingly, required no supernatural intervention and, in fact, were no different from healings performed in other traditions. This view threatened not only the authority of the church but also the stability of the whole social order, insofar as this stability was based on the close relation between church and state.[21] It was in this context that Father Marin Mersenne, Descartes' predecessor, worked to establish the mechanical philosophy in French scientific circles. As shown by Robert Lenoble in his study on "Mersenne or the Origin of Mechanism," the fact that the mechanical philosophy entailed that causal influence at a distance could *not* occur naturally was one of Mersenne's chief motivations for advocating it. The extraordinary events in the New Testament and the ongoing history of the church, accordingly, had to be regarded as genuine miracles, involving supernatural intervention.[22] (Those extraordinary events that occur in non-Christian contexts could conveniently be ascribed to the "preternatural" power of Satan, which could simulate true miracles.)

The issue of action at a distance, especially that form that we now call psychokinesis, was also important because of the "witch craze" of the sixteenth and seventeenth centuries, considered by some historians to have been the major social problem of the era. Estimations of the number of people, usually women, killed in this early modern holocaust run from a few hundred thousand to several million.[23] In any case, the accusations of witchcraft presupposed that the human mind (with Satan's help, to be sure) could cause direct harm to people and their possessions. One of the positive effects of the mechanistic philosophy was that, by discrediting the idea of causal influence at a distance, it undermined the thought-world in which the witch craze had flourished.[24]

Yet another reason for denying the possibility of action at a distance as a natural capacity involved the proper interpretation of gravitation. After receiving the letter from Newton with the above-quoted denial that gravity is "innate and essential to matter," Richard Bentley argued in his Boyle lectures that gravitation provides "a new and invincible argument for the being of God." Newton himself argued that, because the apparent force between things cannot be due to matter, it points to the existence of "immaterial agency," by which he meant, ultimately, God.[25]

Still other theological-social considerations lay behind the adoption of the mechanical philosophy in the late seventeenth and early eighteenth centuries. For example, the idea that the physical world is composed of things that are totally inert, devoid of any capacity for self-motion, was used to support the immortality of the soul and the existence of God.[26] The relevance of the mechanistic view of nature to the question of immortality will be discussed in Chapter 3. With regard to the existence of God, the idea that the physical universe, which is obviously in motion, is comprised of things that are inherently inert was used to argue for the necessity of a First Mover outside the universe. As Robert Boyle put it: "Since motion does not essentially belong to matter, . . . the motions of all bodies . . . were impressed upon them."[27] The considerations mentioned in this paragraph did not directly involve the issue of action at a distance, but, by reinforcing the commitment to the mechanical viewpoint in general, they reinforced the judgment that causal influence between noncontiguous things is not possible.

That is, the contention was that this influence is not *naturally* possible. The idea that the kinds of events in question actually happen was not rejected by most of these thinkers. It was, in fact, important to them that they *did* happen. They were concerned only to stress that they happened because of supernatural agency. The desire to support this supernaturalistic view of God was, in fact, evidently (along with the desire to defend the immortality of the soul) the primary motivation behind the adoption of the mechanical philosophy in the first version of the modern worldview. In any case, this early modern worldview ruled out what we now call paranormal influence, because it is part of the very meaning of "paranormal" that the causal power is a natural, if somewhat extraordinary, power inherent in the finite processes themselves, not a supernatural power lodged in an external deity.

In the *late* modern worldview, by contrast, the kinds of events in question simply cannot happen. Insofar as the dualism of the early modern worldview, by placing the human mind somewhat outside of (mechanical) nature, provided at least a window of opportunity for paranormal events, this window was closed by the transmutation of dualism into the materialism of the late modern worldview, in which the mind is merely a function of, perhaps even identical with, the brain. A central feature of this materialism is its complete ontological reductionism. All "wholes" are assumed to be reducible, at least in principle, to their tiniest parts. Not only, accordingly, is the mind reducible to the brain, meaning that it has no power above and beyond that of its billions of brain cells, but the brain cells are in turn reducible to their organelles, which are reducible to their macromolecules, and so on down. The resulting dogma is that everything that happens in the world is in principle explainable in terms of one or more of the four forces recognized by physics: gravitation, electromagnetism, and the weak and the strong forces in the nucleus of the atom. The compositions of a Mozart, the teaching of a Buddha, the devotion of a Mother Teresa—all of these are said finally to be explainable, in principle, through the interactions of these elementary forces. From such a perspective, the idea that the human mind has power of its own beyond that of the brain, power with which it can directly perceive and directly act on things beyond the body, can scarcely be entertained.

Equally important, the supernaturalistic theism of early modernism transmuted into the naturalistic atheism of late modernism. Accordingly, the mechanical philosophy's implication that events not understandable in terms of action by contact cannot happen *naturally* came to mean that they cannot happen *at all*.

Philosophical reflection on the paranormal is so difficult in our culture because these two versions of the modern worldview are still dominant. The worldview of conservative-to-fundamentalist Christians is, for the most part, a continuation of the early modern worldview. Although in our culture at large, this dualistic supernaturalism is at least as influential as the late modern worldview, in the academy it is primarily the latter that serves to rule out the paranormal as a topic for critical reflection. For this reason, in speaking in this book of "the modern worldview" without a qualifier, I mean primarily the second version of it—the *late* modern worldview—unless I indicate otherwise. I will conclude this section with a couple of illustrations of how effectively this worldview, functioning as a paradigm, is doing its job.

Jane Duran belongs to the tiny minority of philosophers who have published anything whatsoever about the paranormal. However, her acceptance of the modern worldview evidently forestalls any open-minded examination of the evidence. Duran approaches the subject in terms of C. D. Broad's "basic limiting principles," which paranormal events appear to violate.[28] Most crucial for Duran is the principle that "any event that is said to cause another event (the second event being referred to as an 'effect') must be related to the effect through some causal chain." This principle appears to be violated, she says, by telepathy, clairvoyance, and psychokinesis. Broad himself believed the evidence for these phenomena, at least the first two, to be strong enough that this principle should be revised.[29] Duran's view, however, is that

the absence of a specifiable and recognizably causal chain seems to constitute a difficult, if not insurmountable, objection to our giving a coherent account of what it means to make such a claim. As long, at least, as our ordinary notions of causality remain intact, there seem to be strong philosophical reasons for concluding that telepathy [and] clairvoyance . . . are not possible.[30]

She provides as clear an example as one could wish of the belief that action at a distance is probably impossible. Indeed, she seems to think the very idea to be *incoherent*.

Another philosopher who is remarkable for even mentioning the paranormal is Keith Campbell. His dismissal, however, is even more preemptory. While reflecting on the fact that if the occurrence of paranormal events were verified, the philosophical implications would be enormous, he uses the standard Humean argument against all reported evidence for paranormal relations:

The problem of fraud is that we know men can, and do, cheat and dissemble, but we do not know that they have paranormal capacities. On the contrary, the great weight of our fully attested knowledge of man's origin and constitution makes paranormal capacities extremely unlikely. So . . . the explanation by fraud is the more rational one.[31]

Such an a priori rejection may not seem unreasonable in the abstract, given the widespread impression that the only people who have given testimony to the genuineness of paranormal events are "kooks" or at least third-rate minds. As we saw in the first section, however, those who have testified to their belief in the reality of paranormal occurrences include some of the most respected people of our culture, even many Nobel–prize winning scientists. Is it really "more rational" to believe that all of these people, plus many more otherwise trustworthy souls, have been guilty of either engaging in, or being repeatedly taken in by, deception, than to assume that paranormal relations really occur?

Another reason for an a priori rejection of the positive results of parapsychology is contained in William James's acknowledgment that it is "a field in which the sources of deception are extremely numerous."[32] As James also said in this connection, however, it takes only one white crow to prove that not all crows are black.[33] In other words, we need only one case of alleged paranormal influence in which fraud, error, and other "normal" explanations are ruled out to cast doubt on the principle that there is no causal influence at a distance. (James spoke in this context specifically of the sensationist principle that nothing appears in the mind from the outside world that is not derived from the physical senses.)

Campbell's a priori dismissal of the belief in paranormal causal relations on the grounds that such a belief is not "rational," incidentally, is especially interesting in the light of his willingness to countenance other beliefs about causal relations that are by his own admission not rational. That is, he had at one time rejected psychophysical dualism because of the impossibility of understanding how spirit and matter could interact. Now, however, having decided that materialism is inadequate to our obviously nonmaterial experiences, he affirms epiphenomenalism. This view holds that the brain, as a byproduct of its functioning, produces a spiritual mind, but that this mind cannot act back on the brain. Campbell affirms this view even though it faces, he admits, the same "equally embarrassing" questions as did dualism.[34] What is worse, he further admits, it includes an arbitrariness that dualism did not, because it affirms "the action of the material on the spiritual" while denying "the action of spirit on matter."[35] Campbell's response to these difficulties is that

> one who holds to the theory must just grit his teeth and assert that a fundamental, anomalous, causal connection relates some bodily processes to some nonmaterial processes. He must insist that this is a brute fact we must learn to live with, however inconvenient it might be for our tidy world-schemes.[36]

Campbell is *not*, however, willing to "just grit his teeth" and admit that paranormal causal processes occur. It appears that what is wrong with causal influence at a distance is not simply that it is anomalous, and not simply that to affirm it would be irrational, but that it is *taboo*. It is such a strong taboo that it leads him to imply that many otherwise honorable and circumspect fellow human beings, such as William James, have been involved in fraud.

The extreme example of the power of the modern paradigm with respect to the paranormal is provided by the aforementioned Committee for the Scientific Investigation of Claims of the Paranormal (CSICOP). Its publications, including its journal, *The Skeptical Inquirer*, refer to those who accept the paranormal as "believers" while referring to its own members as "skeptics." Skepticism in the true sense of the term, however, refers to an attitude of doubt toward all ideas, *especially* those dominant in one's own society. The prominent members of CSICOP, however, show little skepticism about the late modern worldview: With regard to it, they are true believers.

3. THE INTERACTION OF WORLDVIEW, EVIDENCE, AND WISHFUL THINKING

I have thus far suggested that truly philosophical reflection about the paranormal is difficult in our culture because the occurrence of paranormal events is ruled out by the modern worldview, especially, in the academy, in its late modern guise. Some people, nevertheless, *are* able to reflect open-mindedly about the reality and possible implications of ostensibly paranormal happenings, even though they too have been educated in this same culture. To be adequate, an analysis obviously must be more complex than that suggested so far.

There are, I suggest, three factors involved in the formation of opinions about controversial matters such as the paranormal. Besides the two factors already discussed—one's worldview, which guides one's view of what is possible and impossible, and one's awareness of empirical data, which guides one's view of what is actual—there is also wishful thinking: Our ideas about what is possible and what is actual are also influenced by what we *hope* to be true. Freud used this dynamic to explain (away) belief in an omnipotent God. The influence of wishful thinking is, however, much more pervasive, being evident, for example, even in the formation of Freud's own worldview. The pervasiveness of wishful thinking becomes all the more evident when we realize that it can be negative as well as positive, as our thoughts about philosophical possibility, and our interpretations of empirical data, are sometimes guided by what we hope *not* to be true. This side of the dynamic can be called "fearful thinking."[37] The complete dynamic should, accordingly, be called wishful-and-fearful thinking. To avoid this cumbersome locution, however, I will usually employ one term or the other, using "wishful" as the generic term and "fearful" when that side of the dynamic is especially in view.

Whereas all three of these factors play a role in everyone's thought processes, the weight played by each factor varies from person to person. We can think, however, in terms of three basic types of people: paradigmatic thinkers, data-led thinkers, and wishful thinkers.

Paradigmatic thinkers, or rationalists, are ones for whom the primary consideration is what they consider, on the basis of their general paradigm or worldview, possible and impossible. Their interpretation of, even their interest in, empirical data is largely determined by their prior judgment of what is possible. If their worldview or paradigm says that some alleged phenomenon, such as telepathy, is impossible, no amount of empirical data will change their minds. William James commented: "I believe there is no source of deception in the investigation of nature which can compare with a fixed belief that certain kinds of phenomenon are *impossible*."[38] This is, of course, the dynamic I discussed in the prior section. An example, notorious in parapsychological circles, is provided by Hermann von Helmholtz, one of the great scientists of the nineteenth century. He reportedly said to Sir William F. Barrett—another great scientist (a Fellow of the Royal Society), but one who was open to paranormal events—in a conversation about telepathy:

> I cannot believe it. Neither the testimony of all the Fellows of the Royal Society, nor even the evidence of my own senses would lead me to believe in the transmission of thought from one person to another independently of the recognized channels of sensation. It is clearly impossible.[39]

More in line with the ideal of the scientific or philosophic mind is the fact that the *wishes* of paradigmatic thinkers also take a backseat to their view of possibility. This may mean that they believe things in spite of wishing the truth were otherwise. For example, paradigmatic materialists may be unhappy about the conclusion that there will be no life after death for them and their loved ones, but they will persist in their unsatisfying view of life to the end. Another way, however, for one's wishes to play only a minor role is for them to be brought into line with one's philosophical beliefs: A necessity is turned into a virtue. For example, after deciding that there is no God, one may decide that atheism, besides being true, also has more beneficial consequences than theism. One may decide, perhaps, that belief in God serves as a social opiate, or that it keeps people in an infantile relationship to the universe.

Data-led thinkers, or empiricists, by contrast, wear their paradigms lightly, being ready to change them as soon as the data suggest their inadequacy. For such thinkers, what is possible is settled by what is actual, not vice versa; and, as with the paradigmatic thinker, wishful thinking plays little role in the determination of belief. This account agrees, of course, with the traditional picture of "the scientist." And some thinkers do approximate it. For example, Alfred North Whitehead said of William James: "His intellectual life was one protest against the dismissal of experience in the interest of system."[40] James advocated an empirical, data-led approach not only in general, furthermore, but also with regard to the paranormal in particular, as shown by his white-crow comment, cited earlier, and his statement that "whether supernormal powers of cognition in certain persons may occur is a matter to be decided by evidence."[41] We should not, however, exaggerate: James could be "empirical" about extrasensory perception in part due to the fact that, having a father who was sympathetic to the teachings of Emanuel Swedenborg, he had grown up with a worldview that allowed for it.*

A classic formulation of the different approaches taken by paradigmatic and data-led thinkers is provided by William Crookes, in a statement in which he contrasts his own approach with that of fellow physicist and chemist Michael Faraday:

---

* James's compatriot in both pragmatic philosophy and psychical research, F. S. C. Schiller, provides another example of how one's ability to be open-minded about parapsychological evidence may be due at least as much to philosophical worldview as to temperament. Schiller's attack on James's Harvard colleague Hugo Münsterberg seems, at first glance, to provide a classic example of a futile encounter between a data-led and a paradigmatic mind. Calling Münsterberg "a victim of the Germanic spirit," which he considered "a national infirmity," Schiller said of him: "He cannot be happy until he has convinced himself that [the facts] are *a priori* possible. Before he can be got to admit a fact as a fact, he must be provided with a proof that it is possible." By contrast, Schiller continued, "the British spirit . . . ferret[s] out the facts first of all and postpone[s] to subsequent leisure the task of devising an explanation for them" ("Psychology and Psychical Research," Raymond Van Over, ed., *Psychology and Extrasensory Perception* [New York: New American Library, 1972], 55–79, at 67). Schiller, portraying himself and psychical researchers generally as embodying the second spirit, said: "It is obvious which of these is the more scientific attitude" (66).

Faraday says, "Before we proceed to consider any question involving physical principles, we should set out with clear ideas of the naturally possible and impossible." But this appears like reasoning in a circle: we are to investigate nothing till we know it to be *possible*, whilst we cannot say what is *impossible*, outside pure mathematics, till we know everything. In the present case I prefer to enter upon the enquiry with no preconceived notions whatever as to what can or cannot be.[42]

On the basis of this relative distinction between paradigmatic and data-led minds, we can provide a fuller answer as to why philosophical reflection about the data of parapsychology is so difficult. By philosophical reflection I mean both open-minded examination of the evidence and theoretical reflection about what modifications in the modern worldview this evidence, if found persuasive, would require. Now, on the one hand, those who are prone to engage in this type of theoretical thinking are likely to be paradigmatic thinkers; and, having been educated in the modern world, their worldview is likely to make them far from open-minded about the evidence for the paranormal. On the other hand, data-led minds, who are more likely to be open to the evidence, are, even if they find the evidence persuasive, unlikely to engage in theoretical thinking about the worldview implications of this evidence. That there has been little philosophical reflection on it in the modern world is, accordingly, not surprising.

The difficulties become even more manifest once we bring in the third type of mind, the wishful-and-fearful thinker. For this type, "the wish (or the fear) is the father of the thought." This dynamic can apply to the question of possibility: Such thinkers may construct, or adopt, a philosophical worldview guided primarily by their hopes and fears. For example, they may adopt a philosophical position primarily because it shows life after death to be possible, or—if they intensely fear the prospect of life after death or think the belief in it harmful—impossible. This dynamic can also apply to their attitude toward

---

In partial defense of Münsterberg, one should point out that Einstein, another representative of the "Germanic spirit," is generally thought to have done tolerably good scientific work, even though he notoriously belittled empirical facts in comparison with issues of pure theory. So, even if Schiller was finally right, that theory must bow to fact, the question about the attitude necessary for "good science" is not as clear-cut as he assumed. In any case, the point at hand is that it is futile for data-led minds to berate paradigmatic minds for taking so seriously their ideas about what is and is not possible. A closer reading of Schiller's essay reveals, furthermore, that what at first glance appeared to be a clash between two entirely different types of minds was not so clearly so. Schiller, while presenting himself as the relatively pure empiricist, showed that he was able to accept the facts of psychical research as facts because he had a philosophical position that allowed him to do so. Like Münsterberg, he believed that all events could be fully explained in terms of mechanical causes. He just happened also to believe—which I (like James) do not—that mechanical explanation is compatible with "explanation by higher [meaning teleological] categories" (64, cf. 60). The real difference between Schiller and Münsterberg was perhaps only that Schiller had a worldview that allowed the facts of psychical research to be possible while Münsterberg did not.

available empirical evidence and thus to their view of what actually occurs—or at least to what they are willing publicly to admit. Likewise, many who have a strong will to believe in life after death are extremely credulous with respect to purported evidence for it, not only accepting the evidence uncritically but also ignoring other possible interpretations of the events in question.

The reasons why many people, especially outside the academy, want to believe in the paranormal are fairly obvious. Negatively, for those who dislike the so-called materialistic worldview, the paranormal provides the best evidence that this worldview is false. Positively, the paranormal provides, especially for people estranged from institutional religion, support for the wish that the universe be meaningful, including support for the wish that there be life after death.

By contrast, conservative-to-fundamentalist Christians tend to find purported evidence for the paranormal frightening. Many of the reasons operative in the seventeenth century are still relevant today. For example, the category of the paranormal provides a naturalistic alternative to the category of the miraculous, thereby undermining the supernatural attestation to Christianity as the One True Religion. For many Christians, this more than cancels out any positive value psychical research has in providing evidence for life after death. In fact, many evangelical Christians are *hostile* to this purported evidence, insofar as it suggests that life after death is a natural capacity rather than a supernatural gift of God. Positive near-death experiences, especially if had by non-Christians, are often regarded as the devil's deceit.

Thinkers who see the world in terms of the late modern paradigm, who are our primary concern here, also have reasons for fearing evidence for the paranormal. For some, the victory of "enlightenment" over superstition in our civilization is very precarious, and acceptance of any form of paranormal influence could open the floodgates to "the black mud-tide of occultism" (as Freud reportedly once put it, prior to his own acceptance of telepathy).[43] An example of another common fear is provided in a remark relayed by William James. In answer to his own question, "Why do so few 'scientists' even look at the evidence for telepathy, so-called?," James reported that a leading biologist had once told him:

> Even if such a thing were true, scientists ought to band together to keep it suppressed and concealed. It would undo the uniformity of Nature and all sorts of other things without which scientists cannot carry on their pursuits.[44]

This fear, of course, reflects the common belief that the possibility of science as such is uniquely related to the worldview with which it has been associated in recent times.

There may be a closely related fear connected with cultural prestige and power. Given the materialistic, reductionistic worldview, with its assumption that all causal forces are lodged in atoms and subatomic particles, natural scientists, especially physicists, have the greatest social status in the academy, while those in the humanities have the least, and theologians and philosophers of religion least of all—except for parapsychologists, who are generally considered "beyond the pale." Evidence for the paranormal, which includes evidence not only for nonphysical forms of causation (at least given the usual understanding of "physical") but also for downward causation from mind to matter, is arguably seen as a threat by some intellectuals with a vested interest in the status quo.*

More generally, the paranormal is emotionally threatening to those who are strongly attached to the modern worldview simply because the paranormal suggests the need for more or less radical revision. Most human beings find challenges to their beliefs threatening. This is especially the case with worldview beliefs, because one's very sense of identity is involved. It has been suggested that religious beliefs should be called *convictions* to bring out the intensity, and oft-times tenacity, with which they are held.[45] But this same dynamic occurs as well with worldview beliefs that we do not readily characterize as religious and may in fact call *anti*religious, such as atheistic materialism: The discussion of "paradigms" in recent decades has brought out the similarity between religious worldviews and worldviews in general in this respect. This dynamic occurs especially in those whose professional identity is closely bound up with their worldview, such as philosophers, theologians, and the ideological leaders of the scientific community.

Besides these paradigm-related reasons for finding the paranormal threatening, there are also more personal, psychological reasons. Many people find it threatening to think that others might be able to "read their minds." Even more threatening, of course, is the idea of psychokinesis, as it reopens the specter of "black magic" or "witchcraft," which the modern worldview was adopted in part to exclude. If, in particular, there can be large-scale psychokinesis, then—I have heard this fear expressed more than once—airplanes could be brought down simply by the power of thought. Many people intensely want the world to be free from this kind of danger, and this wishing affects their beliefs about the way the world actually is. Psychoanalyst Jule Eisenbud, whom Stephen Braude calls parapsychology's "premier theoretician," has suggested that much of Western religious, philosophical, and scientific thought has been motivated, in part, by the desire to rule out the possibility that human thoughts can have direct effects.[46]

This third variable, wishful thinking, complicates enormously the possibilities for philosophical reflection about parapsychology. Many philosophers

---

*Colin A. Russell has suggested that "Scientific Naturalism—the view that nature's activity can be interpreted without recourse to God, spirits, etc.," was advanced by some to help the scientific community achieve cultural hegemony (*Science and Social Change 1700–1900* [London: Macmillan, 1983], 256, 258.

who appear, even to themselves, to be rationalists, may actually be wishful thinkers. The attempt to change their minds about the paranormal by means of rational argument will, accordingly, be frustrating, because the primary reasons for the positions they are maintaining will not be addressed. Likewise, many apparent empiricists may be closet wishful thinkers, so that no amount of evidence, however impressive to the presenter, will make a difference.

The situation, furthermore, is even more complicated than I have suggested thus far. We do not simply have three basic kinds of thinkers, plus the confusion as to which kind a particular person really is. In some individuals, two of the three factors share dominance. For example, paradigmatic and empirical concerns may predominate, with little deflection from wishes. The "rational empiricist" is nowadays widely considered the ideal in scientific and philosophical circles. Probably at least equally present in those populations, however, are individuals with the other combinations: There are "wishful empiricists," who base their opinions primarily on their wishes and the relevant data, with little consideration for questions of philosophical possibility, and there are "wishful rationalists," whose worldview is primarily a product of their wishes and their views as to what is possible, being little affected by attention to empirical evidence. The fields of philosophy and theology seem to attract wishful rationalists to a disproportionate extent, which, if true, would help explain why thinkers in these fields have been especially closed to the paranormal (even though one might suspect, apart from these considerations, that they would be the most open). But wishful rationalists are probably well represented in the scientific community as well.

A particularly poignant instance is provided by John G. Taylor, a mathematical physicist at the University of London. His encounter with Uri Geller on a BBC television show led him to explore the phenomenon of metal bending. Besides becoming convinced that Geller's feats were authentic cases of psychokinesis, Taylor also came into contact with several boys and girls, some as young as ten years old, who evidently could bend things by thought almost as effectively as Geller. On the basis of his adventures, Taylor wrote a book called *Superminds*,[47] complete with dozens of pictures, in which he assured his readers that the phenomenon was genuine, that there was no possibility that he was duped. For one thing, he argued, whatever one's suspicions might be about Geller, who had been a stage magician, it is impossible to believe that these young boys and girls could have mastered the extremely complicated tricks it would take to create those effects by fraud under controlled circumstances. Taylor also assured his readers that it would be possible to explain this phenomenon on the basis of the principles of physics. Fully accepting the reductionism of the late modern worldview, Taylor explained that there are only four possible forces that could account for PK: gravitation, the weak force, the strong force, and electromagnetism. Then, having ruled out the first three forces, he explained that so-called psychokinesis must be explainable in terms of electromagnetism. Taylor then set out to do this, in preparation for his next book.

Taylor soon learned, however, that this issue had been discussed for several decades by parapsychologists, most of whom had long since come to the conclusion that something other than the four forces of physics had to be operating. In particular, some Russian parapsychologists, given their Marxian materialistic orthodoxy, had devised experiments explicitly designed to show ESP and PK to be electromagnetic phenomena. Their experiments suggested otherwise. The presence of barriers that cut the subjects off from most of the electromagnetic spectrum either had no effect or else actually improved the psi performance. On the basis of these and other considerations, Taylor came to the conclusion that PK simply could not be reconciled with modern physics. Maintaining his position that to accept things physics could not explain would be to accept irrational, supernatural beliefs, he entitled his next book *Science and the Supernatural*. In it he declared that all reports of ESP and PK must be due to hallucination, trickery, credulity, the fear of death, and the like. "Such an explanation," he said, "is the only one which seems to fit in with a scientific view of the world."[48] He did not, however, explain how those ten-year-old boys and girls had duped him. (Further, he did not, as far as I know, turn back the royalties he had earned from his first book.)

This account could make Taylor appear to be a pure example of the paradigmatic mind. The role played by wishful-and-fearful thinking, however, is made clear by Taylor himself. Having said that he could not see how fraud could have been involved in Geller's demonstration of key-bending right in front of him and the television cameras, Taylor then added:

But this made my faith in science even more at risk, for I just could not see how there could be even a glimmer of a scientific explanation for these phenomena. The scientific framework with which I had viewed the world up till then was crumbling about my ears.[49]

Although Taylor at one place says that he began his investigations with an open mind,[50] he elsewhere admitted that open-mindedness is not easy "if the facts that are staring you in the face will totally destroy your understanding of the world."[51]

The fact that wishful-and-fearful thinking plays an important role in seemingly paradigmatic thinkers in no way, however, reduces the importance of the paradigm, or worldview, out of which they work. As Taylor's example shows, his wishful-and-fearful thinking was oriented primarily around the late modern worldview, with which he had equated scientific rationality itself and in relation to which his own sense of professional identity had been shaped.

In sum, philosophical reflection on the evidence for paranormal influence is so difficult not only because the modern worldview rules it out as impossible but also because intellectuals, like other people, are influenced in their judgments by what they wish to be the case, and there are powerful reasons, both professional and personal, leading modern individuals to want the paranormal to be a null category. On the other side, positive wishes about the paranormal often make critical reflection about it, as distinct from credulous acceptance, difficult. The primary problem within the academy, however, has been excessive credulity not toward the paranormal, but toward the modern.

Near the beginning of the twentieth century, William James paraphrased with approval the moral philosopher Henry Sidgwick's complaint, with regard to claims about the paranormal, that

> the divided state of public opinion on all these matters was a scandal to science, absolute disdain on *a priori* grounds characterizing what may be called professional opinion, whilst completely uncritical and indiscriminate credulity was too often found amongst those who pretended to have a first-hand acquaintance with the facts.[52]

Today, approximately a century later, the situation is little changed. The reflections in this section are meant to cast light on the reason that a movement toward consensus on this issue has been so difficult. The main problem, to repeat, has been the pervasiveness in intellectual circles of a worldview that makes examination of the evidence, let alone *open-minded* examination, very difficult. Because of the resulting "absolute disdain on *a priori* grounds," the leaders of the scientific, philosophical, and theological communities have been in no position to do anything to mitigate the "indiscriminate credulity" that often abounds in other circles. If a new worldview is now emerging, however, we may do better in the coming century.

4. THE NEED FOR A POSTMODERN WORLDVIEW

The evidence for the genuineness of interactions that are now called paranormal points to the need for a postmodern philosophy. On the one hand, we have overwhelming evidence that influence at a distance to and from minds does occur. We have testimony from every period of history and from every culture,* including the testimony of various religious saints whose integrity is other-

---

* Although James Frazer considered all this testimony to be superstitious, his *Golden Bough* remains the most extensive survey of the beliefs in paranormal phenomena from various cultures. For one who provided a survey of such beliefs on the assumption that, "however erroneous, however darkened by fraud and fancy," they nevertheless "repose on a basis of real observation of actual phenomena," see Andrew Lang, *The Making of Religion*, 2nd ed. (London: Longmans Green, 1900); quotation from page 45. More recently, see the important book *Wondrous Events: Foundations of Religious Belief* by James McClenon (Philadelphia: University of Pennsylvania Press, 1994).

wise undoubted.[53] We have a one-hundred-year tradition of often rigorous scientific investigation that has validated the reality of psi phenomena time and time again; summaries of these results are readily available.[54] Many of the people involved in these investigations, furthermore, have been otherwise regarded as among the most honest and intelligent in our culture. On the other hand, the paradigm that has been used in the remainder of our scientific investigation, and that has increasingly come to dominate our culture as a whole, rules out the possibility of paranormal phenomena. The result is a classic example of what Thomas Kuhn has called a "paradigm crisis." It is quite usual for there to be anomalies that do not fit the paradigm used in a certain area of research. The scientist is often well advised simply to let these recalcitrant data stand *as anomalies* for a period, with the expectation that they will eventually be incorporated into the existing paradigm. When, however, the anomalies continue to build up and continue to resist explanation in terms of the present paradigm, a crisis is reached. This crisis necessitates the emergence of a new paradigm.

This is where we are now—not simply with regard to one of the special paradigms relevant only to a particular science, such as physics or psychology, but with regard to the general paradigm or worldview that has undergirded all of our sciences and increasingly our intellectual culture as a whole in the late modern period. The late modern worldview is arguably as inadequate as the early modern worldview it replaced; I will give several reasons for thinking this in Chapter 3. The evidence for this inadequacy that is provided by parapsychology is, however, perhaps the most dramatic. It seems long past time to rethink this worldview in the light of the evidence from parapsychology, along with other anomalous facts. This idea was expressed, in fact, by William James, long before the idea of "paradigms" and "anomalies" was popularized by Kuhn. James in a lecture put it this way:

> "The great field for new discoveries," said a scientific friend to me the other day, "is always the unclassified residuum." . . . No part of the unclassified residuum has usually been treated with a more contemptuous scientific disregard than the mass of phenomena generally called *mystical* [by which James meant phenomena now generally called *paranormal*].[55]

Many people have, to be sure, been calling for a rejection of the modern worldview for some time. Many of these calls, however, have been to return to something premodern. The call for a *post*modern worldview, by contrast, is a call for one that would keep the gains of modernity while overcoming some restrictions within the modern paradigm that were not essential to those gains. In brief, a postmodern outlook would retain that peculiar combination of empiricism and rationality that has been fundamental to the scientific progress that has distinguished the modern West from other cultures. It would retain this rational empiricism, however, while overcoming those assumptions—such as the equation of perception with *sense*-perception and the more general belief that all causal influence is between contiguous events—that have led defenders of the modern worldview dogmatically to deny well-attested facts, such as those of parapsychology.

The retention of rational coherence as an ideal needs to be emphasized. Many devotees of the late modern worldview have not only thought of it as *the* scientific worldview but have also virtually identified it with rationality itself. They have tended to believe, accordingly, that those who advocate acceptance of extrasensory perception or psychokinesis are out to destroy science, even rationality. But such an intention need not be involved, and usually is not. For example, William James, having said that science, so far as it denies paranormal occurrences, "lies prostrate in the dust for me," added: "the most urgent intellectual need which I feel at present is that science be built up again in a form in which such things may have a positive place."[56] C. D. Broad suggested how to go about this: We need, he said, to "revise . . . fundamental concepts and basic limiting principles in such a way as to include the old and new facts in a single coherent system."[57] In other words, increased adequacy to the facts would not necessarily be at the expense of rational coherence. The new worldview might, in fact, be *more* coherent. A widespread assumption—one that lies behind much of the resistance to the paranormal—is that the late modern worldview, with its materialistic ontology and sensationist theory of perception, works quite well for virtually everything except paranormal data.[58] I will argue in Chapter 3 that this assumption is far from true, that the inadequacy to parapsychology is simply part of a much more general inadequacy and incoherence.

One good reason for assuming that the acceptance of paranormal influence necessarily implies an antiscientific worldview—good because it can be based on statements from many parapsychologists and philosophical fellow travelers—is the belief that its acceptance requires us to give up the notion that the cause-effect relation goes only from the past to the present. One form of paranormal interaction, so-called precognition, is said to involve the reverse relationship: A future event causes a present cognition.[59] If belief in paranormal influence really did entail acceptance of this "backward causation," then the worldview suggested by the evidence from parapsychology would be antiscientific, even antirational. As I will point out in Chapter 2, however, one can well accept extrasensory perception and psychokinesis without accepting the idea of true precognition. The experiences that have been interpreted as precognitive can better be interpreted in other ways.

Yet another good reason for suspecting that an acceptance of the positive claims of parapsychology will take us backward, rather than forward, is the assumption that these claims entail a return to the (Cartesian) dualism of the early modern worldview. The good reason for this suspicion is that most parapsychologists and their philosophical supporters have argued that the evidence for both ESP and PK (not to mention out-of-body existence) implies mind-body dualism. This view, however, involves a fundamental confusion, as I will explain at length in Chapter 3. Suffice it here to say that parapsychological evidence (as well as much else) does indeed imply a distinction between the mind and the body (which allows for interaction), but not an ontological (Cartesian) dualism.

Having argued that we need a postmodern worldview, and having indicated abstractly some of the features such a worldview, to be adequate to the evidence for what has in modern times been considered paranormal influence, would and would not involve, I turn now to the philosophy that, in my opinion, provides the best basis for such a worldview, the philosophy of Alfred North Whitehead (1861–1947). I will in the remainder of this chapter simply provide an introductory sketch of a few salient features of his philosophy. A more complete picture will emerge in the subsequent discussion.

5. WHITEHEAD'S POSTMODERN PHILOSOPHY
AND THE PARANORMAL

Whitehead turned to philosophy in the sense of metaphysical cosmology only late in life. Early in his career he had focused on mathematics (having, among other things, coauthored *Principia Mathematica* with Bertrand Russell) and mathematical physics (his dissertation had dealt with Maxwell's work on electromagnetism). In the second period of his career, he wrote several books on "natural philosophy," one of which provided an alternative to Einstein's formulation of relativity theory.* In these books, and in the first of the books of his final, metaphysical period, *Science and the Modern World* (1925), he argued that the supposed basis in science for mechanistic materialism as a worldview had been completely undermined by developments in science itself, including evolutionary theory, relativity theory, and quantum theory.[60] In his several metaphysical books, preeminently in *Process and Reality*, he developed a "philosophy of organism."[61] His major concern was to provide a viewpoint that is adequate both to science and to our moral, aesthetic, and religious intuitions.[62] He does mention telepathy positively a few times in passing and, even though he himself evidently did not believe in life after death, points out that his philosophy does allow for its possibility. But in no way could it be said that it was

---

* Alfred North Whitehead, *The Principle of Relativity* (Cambridge: Cambridge University Press, 1922). Although Whitehead's theory has generally been dismissed as falsified, a more recent interpretation has shown that those criticisms were based mainly on misunderstandings. See Robert John Russell, "Whitehead, Einstein and the Newtonian Legacy," in *Newton and the New Direction in Science*, ed. G. V. Coyne, S. J. M. Heller, and J. Zycinski (Vatican City: Specola Vaticana, 1988), 176–92. The other books by Whitehead in this middle period were *The Concept of Nature* (Cambridge: Cambridge University Press, 1920) and *An Enquiry Concerning the Principles of Natural Knowledge* (Cambridge: Cambridge University Press, 1919).

a primary or even secondary concern of his to reconcile parapsychology and normal science, paranormal influence with "normal" causation. His philosophy does, nevertheless, provide the basis for such a reconciliation. Although Whitehead does not use the term "postmodern" (no one did in those days), the *idea* is implicit in his critique of several central features of distinctively modern science and philosophy. His philosophy is, furthermore, de facto postmodern in just the ways necessary if the evidence provided by parapsychology is to be appropriated.[63]

I will discuss some ways in which Whitehead's philosophy is postmodern both formally and substantively, indicating in both cases how this postmodernism creates openness to evidence for paranormal phenomena.

Whitehead's philosophy is postmodern, in the first place, in its general attitude. One aspect of this attitude is an appreciation of the complexity of the universe such as to forbid the dogmatic assumption that we already have all the answers. For example, in a passage that anticipates Kuhn's distinction between progress within a paradigm and a shift to a fundamentally new paradigm, Whitehead says:

> The Universe is vast. Nothing is more curious than the self-satisfied dogmatism with which mankind at each period of its history cherishes the delusion of the finality of its existing modes of knowledge. Sceptics and believers are all alike. At this moment scientists and sceptics are the leading dogmatists. Advance in detail is admitted: fundamental novelty is barred. This dogmatic common sense is the death of philosophic adventure. The Universe is vast.[64]

Whitehead's experience with quantum and relativity physics had made him keenly aware that our judgments based on inherited common sense* are hardly an adequate index of likely truth. He said:

> The eighteenth century opened with the quiet confidence that at last nonsense had been got rid of. To-day we are at the opposite pole of thought. Heaven knows what seeming nonsense may not to-morrow be demonstrated truth.[65]

A further aspect of Whitehead's general attitude was his belief that philosophy needs to be open to every available type of evidence: "The rejection of any source of evidence is treason to that ultimate rationalism which urges forward science and philosophy alike."[66] Particularly pertinent to the current situ-

---

* In Chapter 3, I distinguish between "soft-core common sense," which can intelligibly be rejected, and "hard-core common sense," which cannot. In speaking of "inherited common sense," I refer to the former type.

ation, in which defenders of the modern paradigm condemn all beliefs in paranormal phenomena as occult nonsense and some advocates of occult knowledge urge us to reject science, is Whitehead's statement that "it is fatal to dismiss antagonistic doctrines, supported by any body of evidence, as simply wrong."[67] Whitehead urges us not to regard a clash of doctrines as a disaster, but as an opportunity, because the clash can be a stimulus to attempt to develop a more inclusive view.[68] His postmodern attitude is expressed in a statement about his own attempt, in which he says: "I have endeavored to outline an alternative cosmological doctrine, which shall be wide enough to include what is fundamental both for science and for its critics."[69]

Whitehead's general attitude differs from that typical of modern philosophy in at least one more way: In contrasting ancient philosophers favorably with modern ones, Whitehead said: "The ancients asked what have we experienced, and the moderns asked what can we experience."[70] The point is that modern philosophy began not with a truly empirical examination of what we *do* experience, but with an a priori notion of what we *can* experience, dismissing as impossible the various other things people have claimed to experience. The problem with modern epistemology, furthermore, is that it has asked the question of what we can experience on the basis of the assumption that we have only "a few definite avenues of communication with the external world, the five sense-organs."[71]

This formal point leads to the first *substantive* difference between Whitehead and modern philosophy. He does not believe that sensory perception is our only, or even our primary, means of receiving information about the world beyond ourselves. Rather, he says, "sense-perception, despite its prominence in consciousness, belongs to the superficialities of experience."[72] What is primary is a nonsensuous perception of the surrounding world, which Whitehead coined the term "prehension" to express. When he speaks of nonsensuous perception, he generally does not have in mind what is normally meant by extrasensory perception. He is usually speaking, instead, of our perception (prehension) of our own past, which we call "memory," and our direct perception (prehension) of our own bodies, especially our brain cells. In a few places, however, he does mention telepathy. In one of these places he says:

> [W]e must allow for the possibility that we can detect in ourselves direct aspects of the mentalities of higher organisms. The claim that the cognition of alien mentalities must necessarily be by means of indirect inferences from aspects of shape and of sense-objects is wholly unwarranted by this philosophy of organism. The fundamental principle is that whatever merges into actuality, implants its aspects in every individual event.[73]

Whitehead had many reasons for thinking that modern philosophy's ideas about perception are "topsy-turvy,"[74] and that sense-perception, far from being our only access to the world of actualities beyond ourselves, is a late, derivative feature of some experiences, which lifts certain aspects of them into prominence. He did not develop this epistemology primarily to handle the data from psychical research. His position that nonsensuous perception is our fundamental mode of apprehending other realities does, however, provide a basis for investigating reports of extrasensory perception with an open mind.

A more general point underlying Whitehead's doctrine of nonsensory perception is his allowance for action at a distance. It is a fundamental feature of his philosophy that each event is a product of its whole past world and in some limited respect incorporates this entire past. This doctrine *could* be interpreted so as to be compatible with the view that all causation is between contiguous events. That is, one could hold that event D incorporates event A only as mediated through events B and C. Whitehead, however, does not limit the causal influence of the past to that which occurs between contiguous events, saying instead that his philosophy leads to the expectation of action at a distance. He explicitly cites telepathy as providing some empirical support for this doctrine.[75]

Whitehead does not mention psychokinesis. He probably got most of whatever knowledge he had of the field from the British psychical researchers, who were biased against psychokinesis, and from William James, who also makes little positive reference to it. Whitehead's allowance for action at a distance does, however, provide one of the conditions necessary for conceiving of psychokinesis as a possibility. Another of his doctrines is also directly relevant.

Whitehead does not limit the causal power in the universe to the energy recognized by contemporary physics. He says that all actualities, which he calls "actual occasions," embody creativity. This creativity involves a twofold power: the power to determine oneself, then the power to influence others. Energy as it is described by mathematical physics (Whitehead's own former field) is merely an abstraction from this "full-blooded creativity."[76] There exists, accordingly, causal power beyond that recognized by current physics, so that all events need not be explained in terms of its four forces. It is thinkable, for example, that the occasions of experience constituting a human psyche could have power by which spoons could be directly bent. (If they do, John Taylor need not feel guilty about the royalties he received from his earlier book, *Superminds*.)

Whitehead's view that energy as studied by physics is merely an abstraction from the creativity of the universe is part of his more general rejection of the reductionism of modern thought. This rejection is also directly related to the issue of psychokinesis. Psychokinetic phenomena are almost exclusively reported in connection with human minds. Some effects detectable by statistical analysis have been found in relation to other animals, to be sure, but all the well-attested *dramatic* effects have been associated with humans. This is significant: Whereas the late modern paradigm suggests that all causal power is lodged in the simplest entities, here is a kind of effect that is associated only with the beings at the top of the evolutionary scale. I mentioned earlier that Whitehead's philosophy turns the epistemology of modernity upside down, making sensory perception derivative instead of basic. He does something similar with the ontology of modernity. In place of its reductionism, according to which all power is located at the lowest level, Whitehead suggests a multi-leveled view, in which the higher-level actualities have more power than the lower ones. Atomic actual occasions, far from being simply the product of their electronic, protonic, and neutronic occasions, not only have their own creativity, but have *more* than any of their constituents. The same is true for the molecule in relation to its constituent atoms and for the cell in relation to its molecules. Furthermore, the series of occasions of experience constituting the psyche of the animal has more creative power than any of the cells of the brain, and the psyche of human beings has more power than that of the other animals. This doctrine fits with the fact that strong psychokinetic effects are apparently produced only by human minds.

This point would lead naturally into yet another way in which Whitehead's postmodern philosophy,* if widely accepted, would create openness to the various types of ostensible paranormal occurrences: Its position on the mind-body relation allows for the possibility of life after death. This is such a complex and controversial issue, however, that it will be best to set Whitehead's position, which in general terms he shares with some other thinkers, in the context of the recent discussion. Chapter 3 is devoted to this issue. First, however, I will examine the evidence for extrasensory perception and psychokinesis.

---

*For a more extensive and technical discussion of the ways in which Whitehead's philosophy allows for various types of paranormal phenomena, see my "Parapsychology and Philosophy: A Whiteheadian Postmodern Approach," *Journal of the American Society for Psychical Research* 86/3 (July 1993), 217–88. Further discussion is found in my replies to two responses to that essay in "Dualism, Materialism, Idealism, and Psi: A Reply to John Palmer," in JASPR 88/1 (January 1994), 23–39, and "Parapsychology, Psychokinesis, Survival, and Whitehead: A Reply to Frederick Ferré," JASPR 88/3 (July 1994), 255–74.

2

WHITE CROWS ABOUNDING: EVIDENCE FOR THE PARANORMAL

Having said that one's attitude toward the occurrence of paranormal events will be shaped by the interplay of three factors—philosophical beliefs as to what is possible, wishful-and-fearful thinking, and empirical data—I dealt in Chapter 1 with the first two factors. In the present chapter, I examine various kinds of empirical evidence for paranormal events. For data-led minds, the question of the reality of paranormal events will be settled primarily by the quantity and quality of this evidence. Even for those for whom paradigmatic or wishful thinking is primary, the empirical evidence is, at least usually, not without importance. In many cases we can be led, by the weight of evidence, to believe things that we had strongly believed to be impossible, undesirable, or both.

The title of this chapter involves an allusion to William James's famous statement to the effect that it takes only one white crow to prove that all crows are not black. This statement was made, as mentioned earlier, in relation to the doctrine that rules out extrasensory perception, namely, "the orthodox belief that there can be nothing in any one's intellect that has not come in through ordinary experiences of sense."[1] James's point was that, to undermine this belief, we need only one counterexample:

If you will let me use the language of the professional logic-shop, a universal proposition can be made untrue by a particular instance. If you wish to upset the law that all crows are black, you mustn't seek to show that no crows are; it is enough if you prove one single crow to be white.[2]

Logically, what James says is certainly true. *Psychologically*, however, most of us do not operate in this way. If we knew of only one putative instance of extrasensory perception, we would most likely reject the evidence for it, or simply put it aside as anomalous. We, indeed, have another avian proverb: "One swallow does not a summer make." To be convinced, we need some kind of replication. We need, in other words, *repeatable* white crows.

Although the term repeatability, or replicability, is usually used with regard to laboratory experiments, there are really at least four relevant kinds of repeatability. Besides the belief that parapsychologists have no repeatable laboratory experiments, there are three other widespread beliefs about parapsychological evidence: that alleged spontaneous paranormal events are not repeatable, that there have been no subjects who could reproduce paranormal phenomena on a regular basis under tightly controlled conditions, and that the only people who have reported and accepted the occurrence of paranormal phenomena are deficient in intelligence, critical acumen, competence, or integrity. Responding to these beliefs in reverse order, I will suggest that we have repeatable white crows of all four types. That is: (1) Since the beginning of the scientific study of ostensible paranormal phenomena in the late nineteenth century, there have repeatedly been persons of otherwise undoubted intelligence, honesty, and competence who have accepted the occurrence of paranormal events, often on the basis of firsthand experience. (2) There have repeatedly been individuals who could repeatedly demonstrate ESP abilities, PK abilities, or both in tightly controlled situations, many of whom were never detected in any kind of fraudulent activity. (3) There are types of spontaneous paranormal phenomena that occur repeatedly in various times and places. (4) There have been a wide range of controlled experiments, both with and without exceptional people, that have produced positive results significantly above chance on a repeatable basis.

This fourth assertion is perhaps the one that will cause the most raised eyebrows among critical readers, at least those who have not followed the fortunes of parapsychology since the mid-1980s. Until that time, it was regularly said that parapsychology had no repeatable experiments, or at least that those that it had produced could be challenged in terms of methodology, experimenter bias, or statistical interpretation. Even many parapsychologists accepted this evaluation. But this situation has dramatically changed, thanks in part to a new experimental approach called the *ganzfeld* and in part to the application of the new social-science technique of "meta-analysis" to a large number of parapsychological experiments. A number of turnabouts have resulted. Erstwhile critics have looked on the evidence for paranormal effects with new respect. Mainline journals are accepting parapsychological articles reporting positive results, and at least one prestigious psychology textbook now includes a section on "Psi Phenomena." What meta-analysis of the ganzfeld and other experiments has demonstrated is *statistical* repeatability, and because it also points the way to even more repeatable research in the future, a 1991 survey of parapsychology, written from the viewpoint of an experimentalist, says that "parapsychology is incomparably stronger today than it was just five or six years ago."[3] Accordingly, negative attitudes toward paranormal influence in general formed on the basis of earlier periods of parapsychological experimentation, to whatever extent they were then justifiable, now need to be reconsidered.

Much of this chapter will be devoted to some of the kinds of repeatable evidence, both spontaneous and experimental, that are now available for two of the three major types of paranormal events, extrasensory perception and psychokinesis (leaving for Chapters 4–8 evidence suggesting the mind's separability from its physical body). Before turning to this evidence, however, I will discuss the two other kinds of white crows: people who disprove the assumption that few if any credible intellectuals have accepted the reality of paranormal occurrences, and people who disprove the assumption that no claims about extraordinary paranormal abilities could be sustained under carefully controlled conditions.

1. WHITE CROWS OF THE FIRST KIND

In referring to intellectuals who are "credible," I mean ones whose intelligence, honesty, and competence (e.g., to conduct well-controlled experiments and to prevent or detect fraud) would not otherwise be questioned—that is, *if* they had not testified to their belief in paranormal occurrences. The fact that there is a large number of such intellectuals is important, because the main way of rejecting the evidence for paranormal influence, both spontaneous and experimental, has been to cast aspersions on the intelligence, competence, or honesty of the intellectuals who have reported this evidence. The very fact that they have so testified usually means, in the eyes of critics who consider paranormal events impossible, that they are *not* credible. As one of the early psychical researchers, Edmund Gurney, parodied the position of these critics with regard to reported evidence for some paranormal occurrence:

> The fact is so improbable that extremely good evidence is needed to make us believe it; and *this* evidence is not good, for how can you trust people who believe such absurdities?[4]

In other words, when some counterinstance is provided to the claim that no credible people have reported paranormal events, the very fact that the person in question has reported such events is taken as proof that he or she is not credible. This strategy can work with regard to ordinary people, whose general credibility is not well known. And it can even work in relation to a *few* intellectuals, such as scientists and philosophers, whose credibility is generally known. But this strategy itself loses credibility when it has to be used in relation to a large number of such intellectuals.

The rejection of reports of paranormal events usually comes down to the charge of fraud—either fraud on the part of the intellectual, or fraud by the subject that the intellectual was too incompetent to detect. The fact that the rejection of the evidence so often rests upon the charge of fraud is, in a sense, a victory for the parapsychological community. Henry Sigdwick, the first president of the Society for Psychical Research (SPR), said in his opening presidential address in 1882:

> We must drive the objector into the position of being forced either to admit the phenomena as inexplicable, at least by him, or to accuse the investigators either of lying or cheating or of a blindness or forgetfulness incompatible with any intellectual condition except absolute idiocy. . . . We have done all that we can when the critic has nothing left to allege except that the investigator is in the trick. But, when he has nothing else left to allege, he will allege that.[5]

It is in relation to these allegations, which have indeed been repeatedly made, more or less directly, that the number of credible intellectuals involved becomes important. A large number of uncritical individuals could surely be fooled repeatedly. And any given individual, no matter how critical normally, might be duped now and then. But the charge that *all* reports of paranormal occurrences result from tricks perpetrated on the investigators become increasingly implausible when the number of credible investigators is increased. The same is true for the charge of fraud on the part of the investigators. A number of scientists who have generally been assumed to be honest, including a few parapsychologists, have been caught in fraud. But the charge becomes increasingly implausible as the number of otherwise credible intellectuals is increased. A partial list of such credible intellectuals was provided in Chapter 1. I will here discuss only a few of them.

Henry Sidgwick

We can begin with the person I have just quoted, Henry Sidgwick (1838–1900), who was professor of Moral Philosophy at Trinity College at the University of Cambridge, and who is probably best known for his book titled *The Methods of Ethics*.[6] When a meeting was held early in 1882 to discuss the idea of forming the Society for Psychical Research, some of the participants made it a condition of their membership that Sidgwick consent to be the president, which he did after considerable hesitation. This was an important decision. As C. D. Broad has said, the reason that the Society for Psychical Research, in spite of its controversial subject-matter, came to enjoy the status of "at least semi-respectability in scientific circles" was due largely to Sidgwick.[7] In Broad's words:

> [T]he fact that Sidgwick, whose reputation for sanity, truthfulness, and fairness was well known to everyone who mattered in England, was at the head of the Society gave it an intellectual and moral status which was invaluable at the time. It was hardly possible to maintain, without writing oneself down as an ass, that a society over which Sidgwick presided and in whose work he was actively interested consisted of knaves and fools concealing superstition under the cloak of scientific verbiage.[8]

Testimony as to Broad's own credibility, incidentally, was cited near the outset of the first chapter.

Sidgwick's integrity was illustrated by his behavior with respect to his appointment as a Fellow at Trinity, which meant a teaching position with a good income. At that time it was a condition of such fellowships that each holder declare himself a "*bona fide* member of the Church of England." Although this obligation was not usually taken seriously, Sidgwick decided that, because he did not accept some features of orthodox dogma, especially regarding the miraculous origins of Christianity, he should resign his fellowship. This decision resulted in a considerable loss, both of income and amenities.[9]

Although Sidgwick did not consider himself particularly good at psychical research as such, in the sense of conducting and evaluating experiments, he was involved in many investigations of Spiritualism and decided that most of the phenomena were fraudulent, or at least too ambiguous to pronounce authentic. Although he had deeply hoped to be able to find convincing evidence for life after death, he wrote, a few years before his own death in 1900: "I am drifting steadily to the conclusion that we have not and are not likely to have empirical evidence of the existence of the individual after death."[10] Wishful thinking, in other words, did not make him uncritical with regard to empirical data. Broad, in fact, suggests that it was the importance the issue of human survival held for Sidgwick that led him "to weight the scales against *prima facie* evidence for it [rather] than to accept such evidence lightly."[11] Sidgwick did, however, come to the conclusion that there was sufficient evidence for the reality of telepathy. Indeed, much of the *prima facie* evidence for survival provided by mediumistic communications could be discounted only by appeal to telepathy as an alternative explanation.[12]

William James said of Sidgwick that what had held the SPR together in its early years was primarily "Sidgwick's extraordinary gift of inspiring confidence in diverse sorts of people." James continued:

Such tenacity of interest in the result and such absolute impartiality in discussing the evidence are not once in a century found in an individual. His obstinate belief that there is something yet to be brought to light communicates patience to the discouraged; his constitutional inability to draw any precipitate conclusion reassures those who are afraid of being dupes.[13]

William James

William James himself (1842–1910), from whom the metaphor of the "white crow" derives, is another white crow of the first kind. His own conclusions were similar to those of Sidgwick. In fact, with regard to Sidgwick's statement shortly before his (Sidgwick's) death that after twenty years he was "in the same identical state of doubt and balance that he started with," James says that the same is true for him after twenty-five years, adding: "I confess that at times I have been tempted to believe that the Creator has eternally intended this department of nature to remain *baffling*."[14]

Like Sidgwick, however, James was referring to the question of life after death. Like Sidgwick, he had no doubts about the reality of telepathy. The various kinds of evidence for it form, he suggests, not a chain (which would depend upon its weakest link) but a "fagot," meaning that while no one item depends on the others, "taken together the items have a certain general consistency," so that they have a cumulative force.[15] However, he adds, his own conviction about telepathy does not rest solely on such presumptive evidence, but upon a "decisive thunderbolt." It is at this point that he makes his statement about the white crow, cited above, followed by this declaration:

My own white crow is Mrs. Piper. In the trances of this medium, I cannot resist the conviction that knowledge appears which she has never gained by the ordinary waking use of her eyes and ears and wits. What the source of this knowledge may be I know not, and have not the glimmer of an explanatory suggestion to make; but from admitting the fact of such knowledge I can see no escape.[16]

While this medium, Leonora Piper, was in a trance state, communications would be delivered by various personalities claiming to be "spirits" of deceased individuals. James did not accept these personalities at face value and was convinced that most of them, at least, were simply products of Mrs. Piper's subconscious mind. His conviction was only that paranormal (which he called "supernormal") knowledge was manifested. In his "Final Impressions of a Psychical Researcher," written shortly before his death, he said of the communications of mediums:

When imposture has been checked off as far as possible, when chance coincidence has been allowed for, when opportunities for normal knowledge on the part of the subject have been noted, and skill in "fishing" and following clues unwittingly furnished by the voice or face of bystanders have been counted in, those who have the fullest acquaintance with the phenomena admit that in good mediums *there is a residuum of knowledge displayed* that can only be called supernormal: the medium taps some source of information not open to ordinary people. . . .I wish to go on record for . . . *the presence*, in the midst of all the humbug, *of really supernormal knowledge.*[17]

The *kinds* of material James found convincing are indicated in the following excerpts from his accounts of Mrs. Piper:

My mother-in-law, on her return from Europe, spent a morning vainly seeking for her bankbook. Mrs. Piper, on being shortly afterwards asked where this book was, described the place so exactly that it was instantly found. . . . [O]n my mother-in-law's second visit to the medium she was told that one of her daughters was suffering from a severe pain in her back on that day. This altogether unusual occurrence, unknown to the sitter, proved to be true. The announcement to my wife and brother of my aunt's death in New York before we had received the telegram . . . is a 'test' of the sort which one readily quotes; but to my mind it was far less convincing than the innumerable small domestic matters of which Mrs. Piper incessantly talked in her sittings with members of my family. With the affairs of my wife's maternal kinsfolk in particular her acquaintance in trances was most intimate. Some of them were dead, some in California, some in the State of Maine. She characterized them all . . . spoke of their relations to each other, of their likes and dislikes, of their as yet unpublished practical plans, and hardly ever made a mistake. . . . The most convincing things said about my own immediate household were either very intimate or very trivial. Unfortunately the former things cannot well be published. Of the trivial things . . . the following . . . may serve as samples of their class: . . . She told of my killing a gray-and-white cat, with ether, and described how it had "spun round and round" before dying. She told how my New York aunt had written a letter to my wife, warning her against all mediums. . . . (Of course no one but my wife and I knew the existence of the letter in question.) She was strong on the events in our nursery, and gave striking advice during our first visit to her about the way to deal with certain "tantrums" of our second child, "little Billy-boy," as she called him, reproducing his nursery name. She told how the crib creaked at night, how a certain rocking chair creaked mysteriously, how my wife had heard footsteps on the stairs, etc., etc. Insignificant as these things sound when read, the accumulation of a large number of them has an irresistible effect.[18]

In citing such things, James was simply telling why *he* believed that Mrs. Piper manifested paranormal knowledge. He was not trying to give evidence that others would find convincing, at least not without much more information about his reason for confidence that Mrs. Piper was not obtaining all this information from normal means. I will mention some of these reasons in the discussion of Mrs. Piper in the next section.

Whereas James was convinced that telepathy had been proven, he thought more evidence was needed on other matters. With regard to psychokinesis, he said:

> I find myself believing that there is "something in" these never ending reports of physical phenomena, although I haven't yet the least positive notion of the something. It becomes to my mind simply a very worthy problem for investigation. Either I or the (orthodox) scientist is of course a fool, with our opposite views of probability here; and I only wish he might feel the liability, as cordially as I do, to pertain to both of us.[19]

With regard to the possibility that some apparent communications from spirits of the dead might be genuine, he said: "I remain uncertain and await more facts, facts which may not point clearly to a conclusion for fifty or a hundred years."[20] That statement, in fact, expressed James's considered judgment about the field as a whole. In his "Final Impressions of a Psychical Researcher," he said that, in spite of his occasional feeling that these phenomena would remain permanently baffling, his "deeper belief is that we psychical researchers have been too precipitate with our hopes, and that we must expect to mark progress not by quarter-centuries, but by half-centuries or whole centuries."[21] Some would think that James's statement, cautious as it was intended to be, was still too optimistic. Others would say that this statement, written in 1909, was accurate, that we are only now, about a century later, approaching some definitive results.

Eleanor Sidgwick

Eleanor Mildred Balfour Sidgwick (1845–1936), Henry's wife, was the niece of one prime minister of England, the sister of another (Arthur Balfour), and sister-in-law of the wife of the Archbishop of Canterbury. She was also the sister-in-law of Lord Rayleigh, with whom she conducted some electrical experiments and jointly authored three papers published in the *Philosophical Transactions of the Royal Society*. She, furthermore, was president of Newnham

College in Cambridge from 1892 to 1910. Being very precise, methodical, and hard-working, she did most of the actual editing of the Society's *Journal* and *Proceedings* after Henry was made the editor in 1888. She was also the principal author of the Society's 1894 "Report on the Census of Hallucinations." Outliving her husband thirty-six years, she continued the work on evidence suggestive of life after death, publishing a 657-page "Contribution to the Study of the Psychology of Mrs. Piper's Trance Phenomena" in 1915, then participated in the analysis of the "cross-correspondences case," which will be discussed in Chapter 4. On the basis of these studies she gradually came to believe in the survival of death.[22]

Sir William Crookes

Another intellectual white crow from the early days of psychical research was the physicist and chemist (Sir) William Crookes (1832–1919). Early in his career, in 1861, he discovered the element thallium. He was elected a Fellow of the Royal Society at the age of thirty-one, soon thereafter becoming the editor of the *Quarterly Journal of Science*. In 1870, he began investigating paranormal phenomena, believing it his public duty as a scientist:

> I consider it the duty of scientific men who have learnt exact modes of working, to examine phenomena which attract the attention of the public, in order to confirm their genuineness, or to explain, if possible, the delusions of the honest and to expose the tricks of the deceivers.[23]

Initially, Crookes was skeptical, but his investigations convinced him that some of the phenomena were genuine, leading him to continue those investigations for fourteen years. Afterwards, in 1876, he invented the radiometer and the device that bears his name, the Crookes tube, used to study cathode rays (which suggests that the years of psychical research had not followed on, or resulted in, a loss of scientific capacity). He was very famous, receiving honors from universities around the world, being knighted in 1897, and receiving the Order of Merit, the highest honor that can be conveyed by the English monarch. The results of some of his investigations of D. D. Home will be mentioned in the next section.

From my list of white crows of the first kind in the first chapter, I have lifted up here only four, and all of them are long deceased. The list does include, however, many contemporary examples, such as Stephen Braude, whose rigorous mind is amply demonstrated in his books (*ESP and Psychokinesis: A Philosophical Examination, The Limits of Influence: Psychokinesis and the Philosophy of Science,* and *First-Person Plural: A Philosophical Examination of Multiple Personality*); Jule Eisenbud, a psychiatrist whose books (such as *Parapsychology and the Unconscious* and *The World of Ted Serios*) leave no doubt as to his philosophical and psychological profundity, and whose experimental work (with Ted Serios) will be examined in the next section; Robert Jahn, who was dean of the School of Engineering and Applied Science at Princeton University and a recognized authority on aerospace engineering, who had done much work for NASA and the Department of Defense, before he became interested in parapsychological research; and Helmut Schmidt, whose position before turning to full-time parapsychological research was that of senior research scientist at the Boeing Scientific Research Laboratories, whose integrity has never been challenged by anyone knowing him, and whose rigor has led one well-known critic of parapsychology to say: "By almost any standard, Schmidt's work is the most challenging ever to confront critics such as myself. His approach makes many of the earlier criticisms of parapsychological research obsolete."[24]

2. WHITE CROWS OF THE SECOND KIND

It was the second kind of white crow to which James himself applied the term: a person who can demonstrate paranormal capacities on a regular, repeatable basis. This repeatability need not be, and usually is not, 100 percent. But the paranormal capacity is manifested in a far more regular fashion than in ordinary persons, and in some cases does approach "repeatability on demand."

History provides accounts of numerous individuals who evidently had such abilities. Some of these, such as Jesus, Gotama, and a contemporary, Sathya Sai Baba, have resulted in new religious movements. Many others, while not founding new movements, are revered as saints of their respective traditions. Still others, such as oracles and shamans, have specific religious offices connected with their special abilities.

Until a few decades ago, it was almost universally assumed in intellectual circles that all these accounts were false. Recently, however, a new attitude has been emerging. Shamans, previously referred to contemptuously as "witch doctors," have become figures of respect in some circles, partly because of testimony by anthropologists that some of them seem to have genuinely paranormal powers.[25] The alleged miracles of the saints of the Catholic Church—beatification required two verified miracles, canonization required two more—had long been thought by Protestants and secularists to epitomize "medieval superstition." But recently the actual study of the testimony, and of the skeptical attitude employed in the verification process,[26] has led some (non-Catholic) students of these matters to accept the events.[27] (Of course, acceptance of the genuineness of the events does not entail acceptance of the Catholic Church's insistence that they were supernatural, as distinct from merely "preternatural" [paranormal], events.) And, although the so-called miracle stories told about

Jesus and Gotama are beyond the possibility of verification, analogous phenomena are now reported in connection with Sathya Sai Baba in India, and a well-respected parapsychologist, after intensive investigation, has been convinced that the phenomena are genuinely paranormal.[28] The conviction that such events are occurring today would, of course, remove the main reason for supposing that they had not happened two thousand years ago or so in Israel and India.

Not all white crows of the second kind, however, are especially religious, a fact that is consistent with the view that their powers, while extraordinary, are not supernatural. And some of these individuals have been willing to subject themselves to the tests of parapsychologists. This section is devoted to individuals of this type.

Leonora Piper*

It is appropriate to begin with Leonora Piper (1857–1950), because she is the one to whom the term "white crow" was originally applied and because some of her results have already been mentioned. Also, she was the first subject to provide members of the SPR, both in England and America, with convincing evidence for paranormal abilities, and the records made of her "mediumship" are still, in terms of both quantity and detail, the best we have.[29] Several things, aside from her convincing messages, made her an ideal subject: She was not highly educated, so could not be suspected of being the source of much of the information she conveyed; she was not wealthy, so could not have had a vast number of detectives on her payroll; she was fully cooperative with all the measures imposed by the investigators; and she was studied for over twenty-five years.

She was, as I reported above, discovered for psychical research by William James. After his initial studies, however, the investigation of her powers was taken over by Richard Hodgson, an Australian who came to Boston in 1887 to become the secretary of the American Society for Psychical Research. Hodgson had a reputation for detecting fraud, which he and others assumed he would do in this case.[30]

Hodgson's skepticism was shaken at his first sitting, which was anonymous, as Mrs. Piper while in trance conveyed intimate details about his relatives and friends in Australia, which he could see no way she would have known through ordinary means. The following extract is from his notes at

---

* Although her first name is often spelled Leonore, the fact that the correct spelling is Leonora has been established beyond doubt by James G. Matlock, "Leonora or Leonore? A Note on Mrs. Piper's First Name," *Journal of the American Society for Psychical Research* 82 (July 1988), 281–90.

that first sitting. ("Phinuit" was the "control" personality* who was dominant in those days. The comments in square brackets are Hodgson's own
responses.)

> Phinuit began . . . by describing members of my family. "Mother living,
> father dead, little brother dead." [True.] Father and mother described
> correctly. . . . Phinuit tried to get a name beginning with "R," but failed.
> [A little sister of mine, named Rebecca, died when I was very young. . . .]
> "Four of you living besides mother." [True.] Phinuit mentioned the name
> "Fred.". . . "He says you went to school together. He goes on jumping-
> frogs, and laughs. He had convulsive movements before his death, strug-
> gles. He went off in a sort of spasm. . . . [My cousin Fred far excelled any
> other person that I have seen in the games of leap-frog, fly the garter,
> &c. . . . He injured his spine in a gymnasium . . . and was carried to the
> hospital, where he lingered for a fortnight, with occasional spasmodic
> convulsions, in one of which he died.][31]

Deciding that Mrs. Piper was worthy of further study, Hodgson took great
precautions to prevent any possible fraud. He made tests to see if her trance
was genuine, finding that she was not disturbed by being pricked, cut, burned, or
having ammonia held under her nose.[32] Sitters were introduced to her anonymously or with pseudonyms and were drawn from a wide range of people. Mrs.
Piper and her family were followed by detectives for several weeks to make sure
that they were not making inquiries about people, and letters were checked to
guarantee that she was not receiving information from agents. She was never, in
all the years she was studied, detected doing anything suspicious.

Deciding that the possibility of fraud could be ruled out even more completely if Mrs. Piper were away from Boston, Hodgson took her to England in
the winter of 1889–1890, in what would be the first of many extended visits during which she would be studied by the British investigators. For a while she
stayed with the physicist Oliver Lodge, who was then teaching at Liverpool.
Lodge, who was to have twenty-one sittings with her, found them evidential, in
part because of various factors that lessened the chance that she could have
learned intimate details about him, his family, and his friends from ordinary
means: The household had new servants, who would have known little about the
family; the family Bible and photograph albums were locked up; Mrs. Piper
allowed her baggage to be searched and her mail examined; and sitters were
introduced anonymously. Here is part of Lodge's summary of one sitting:

---

* A "control" is a personality presenting itself as a deceased individual who is now speaking through the body of the medium, although it may in fact be simply a secondary personality of
the medium. In any case, the control is something like a master of ceremonies, introducing and
describing other purported deceased personalities and then either relaying their messages or allowing them to communicate through the medium's body.

It happens that an uncle of mine in London, now quite an old man, had a twin brother who died some twenty or more years ago. I . . . wrote to ask if he would lend me some relic of his brother. By morning post on a certain day I received a curious old gold watch, which his brother had worn and been fond of; and that same morning, no one in the house having seen it or knowing anything about it, I handed it to Mrs. Piper when in a state of trance.

I was told almost immediately that it had belonged to one of my uncles—one that had been very fond of Uncle Robert, the name of the survivor—that the watch was now in possession of this same Uncle Robert, with whom he was anxious to communicate. After some difficulty and many wrong attempts Dr. Phinuit caught the name, Jerry, short for Jeremiah, and said emphatically, as if a third person was speaking, "This is my watch, and Robert is my brother, and I am here. Uncle Jerry, my watch.". . . . I pointed out to him that to make Uncle Robert aware of his presence it would be well to recall trivial details of their boyhood. . . .

"Uncle Jerry" recalled episodes such as swimming the creek when they were boys together, and running some risk of getting drowned; killing a cat in Smith's field; the possession of a small rifle, and of a long peculiar skin, like a snake-skin, which he thought was now in the possession of Uncle Robert. All of these facts have been more or less completely verified. . . .[33]

This verification, as the continuation of Lodge's summary reveals, was interesting. Although Uncle Robert recalled the snake-skin, he said he had only *watched* the swimming of the creek. He, furthermore, could not remember "Smith's field" and denied killing a cat. But then another living brother, Frank, was contacted. He vindicated the existence of "Smith's field," recalled the killing of a cat by another brother, and gave full details of the swimming of the creek, in which only he and Jerry had participated. (Lodge, deciding to test the possibility that an agent for Mrs. Piper might have discovered this information about his uncles, sent his own agent to the area to see how much could be learned about the matters in question. After several days of investigation, during which this agent looked up records, quizzed old inhabitants, and so on, he discovered no more than the probable location of "Smith's field.")[34]

In the examples I have cited, there is clear evidence of paranormal knowledge (assuming, of course, that fraud on the part of Mrs. Piper was ruled out, and that a large number of people of the caliber of James, Lodge, and the Sidgwicks were not involved in a massive fraudulent undertaking). Mrs. Piper did, to be sure, have bad days, in which the control personality would fish for information, babble on inanely, make manifold false assertions, try to cover up "his" mistakes, and so on. But the good days were many, and on those days Mrs. Piper provided copious amounts of information about large numbers of people she had never seen before, and whose relatives were scattered around the globe. This information was usually not the type that could be learned from public records, gravestones, and gossip (she was generally weak on names and dates), but usually involved trivial and intimate matters. A few people who caught her on bad days and never returned were unimpressed. But almost everyone who worked with her extensively—some of them off and on for twenty-five years—became convinced that she truly had paranormal powers.[35]

The only real question in their minds was how to interpret these powers. Most of the evidential sessions suggested that she was in touch with, perhaps even being momentarily controlled by, spirits of the dead. One thing that led many sitters to this conclusion was that, besides often speaking of matters from the viewpoint of the deceased individuals, she would even embody their tone of voice and bodily gestures. However, in Richard Hodgson's first paper about Mrs. Piper, in 1892, he rejected this interpretation, holding instead that all of her information was obtained through telepathy and clairvoyance. In the case of Oliver Lodge's uncles, for example, she could have received part of the information telepathically from Lodge himself, some of it from Uncle Robert, and the remainder from Uncle Frank. Indeed, allowing for retrocognition, she could have derived it all from Uncle Jerry prior to his death.

Later, however, Hodgson changed his mind, partly because of the emergence of a new "control" with a fuller personality. That is, although Phinuit claimed to have been a real person who had lived in France, no one took this idea seriously: There was no record of such a person, and "he" could not speak or even understand French. But in 1892, a control personality calling himself "George Pelham" emerged. There really had been such a person, a young man, named George Pellew, from a well-known Washington family who had been killed in a riding accident a few weeks earlier. Pellew had known Hodgson, although not intimately, and had had one anonymous sitting with Mrs. Piper five years earlier. The control personality demonstrated a very intimate knowledge of George Pellew's life. In one test, he recognized, out of 150 sitters, the 30 (and only those) that Pellew had known, and demonstrated awareness of their concerns.[36]

The emergence of this personality brought with it an additional mode of communication: automatic writing. Sometimes, in fact, two ostensible spirits would communicate through Mrs. Piper at the same time, one by voice and one by hand.[37] It was as an automatic writer that Mrs. Piper would play a role in one of the most fascinating and lengthy cases of all time, the "cross correspondences," which I will discuss in Chapter 4. She continued her trance mediumship until 1911 and her automatic writing even longer. Never was any fraud, or even any suspicious behavior, detected. Even the severest critic in the SPR, Frank Podmore, became convinced of her paranormal powers.[38] This is not to say, of course, that debunking accounts have not been written, such as that by C. E. M. Hansel. But his account, which is based on two other unreliable sources, has been shown to be riddled with errors.[39]

Gladys Osborne Leonard

A British trance medium of comparable ability was Gladys Osborne Leonard (1882–1968), who was made famous by Oliver Lodge's book *Raymond* (1916). In this book, Lodge explained his reasons for believing that his son Raymond, who had been killed in World War I, had communicated to him through Mrs. Leonard. Even most of those who did not accept this interpretation agreed that she had genuinely paranormal powers. Like Mrs. Piper, she was willing to cooperate fully with investigators, was shadowed by detectives, and was never detected doing anything suspicious.

She specialized somewhat in "book tests," which were meant to prove that the personality communicating through her was indeed the deceased person it claimed to be. In the following example, the supposed communicator was "Bim" Tennant, who had been killed in World War I. ("Feda" is the name of Mrs. Leonard's control.)

> *Feda*: "Bim now wants to send a message to his Father. *This book is particularly for his Father.* . . . It is the ninth book on the shelf counting from left to right in the bookcase on the right of the door in the drawing-room as you enter; take the title, and look at page 37."
>
> We found the ninth book in the shelf indicated was: *Trees*.
>
> And on page 36, quite at the bottom and leading on to page 37, we read:
>
> *Sometimes you will see curious marks in the wood; these are caused by a tunnelling beetle, very injurious to the trees.* . . ."

The reason that this message seemed evidential was that Bim's father was very interested in forestry, and his obsession with beetles was a family joke.[40] In 1921, Eleanor Sidgwick analyzed 532 of these book tests, classifying 92 (17%) as successful, 100 (19%) as somewhat successful, 96 as dubious, 40 as almost complete failures, and 204 as complete failures. At least 36 percent, in other words, could be considered successes. A control experiment, involving 1,800 simulated book tests, indicated that under 5 percent of the successes could be attributed to chance.[41]

Daniel Dunglas Home

Mrs. Piper and Mrs. Leonard were primarily "mental mediums," meaning that their paranormal abilities were exclusively (Mrs. Piper), or at least primarily (Mrs. Leonard), in the area of extrasensory perception. The central figures of the SPR liked it that way, as they were quite uncomfortable with so-called physical mediums, who purportedly had psychokinetic powers. The Society might well have not come into existence, however, if it had not been for one such medium, Daniel Dunglas Home (1833–1886). It was William Crookes's reports of experiments with Home (pronounced Hume) that created the interest out of which the Society was formed.

The types of physical phenomena credited to Home are so astounding, to at least most of us, that considerable preparation should probably be given before any of the phenomena are mentioned. Such preparation would need to be so extensive, however, that I cannot provide it here. I can, instead, only refer the reader to the first seventy pages of Stephen Braude's *The Limits of Influence*, a book of great courage as well as acumen (on which my own summary of Home's feats is based). In this discussion, Braude not only answers the various a priori arguments that are usually made against such phenomena, but also points to the kinds of fears that generally keep people, even most parapsychologists (including Braude himself until recently), from confronting the strong evidence that such phenomena have really occurred. At least one of those fears among intellectuals—that of being scorned by one's colleagues if one even takes reports of such phenomena seriously enough to investigate them—is, Braude points out, well founded. But, he also points out, devotion to truth requires that even this fear be surmounted—at least after one has tenure! He reports that, when he reached this point:

> I started with the expectation that the received wisdom would be supported, and that my belief in the relative worthlessness of the material would merely be better-informed. But the evidence bowled me over. The more I learned about it, the weaker the traditional skeptical counter-hypotheses seemed, and the more clearly I realized to what extent skepticism may be fueled by ignorance. I was forced to confront the fact that I could find no decent reasons for doubting a great deal of strange testimony.[42]

Although Braude fully recognized that it is difficult to read these accounts without supposing that fraud *must* have occurred somehow, even if one cannot imagine how, he "argue[s] that—at least for the best cases—the skeptic's charge of fraud is forceful only so long as one remains ignorant of the facts."[43] With this very minimal preparation, I turn now to turn to D. D. Home, probably the most powerful white crow of his type to appear in modern times (at least, perhaps, prior to Sathya Sai Baba).

Shortly after his birth in Edinburgh in 1833, Home was adopted by a maternal aunt, with whom he moved to New England when he was nine. Although he evidently had paranormal visions throughout his teens, and perhaps even earlier, physical phenomena did not begin occurring in his presence until he was seventeen, shortly after his mother's death. Whereas Daniel took these occurrences (raps and moving objects) as expressions of God's goodness, his aunt regarded them as manifestations of the devil and, when he was eighteen, turned him out of the house. From then on, he lived on the hospitality of those who were intrigued by his abilities, although he evidently never asked for or received money. He would have preferred to have become a physician, and was sent to medical school by one of his benefactors, but poor health forced him to withdraw.

The first good description we have of Home's phenomena is based on an investigation carried out in 1852 by two experienced investigators of alleged spiritualist phenomena—the journalist William Cullen Bryant and Professor David Wells of Harvard—who came, along with two other Harvard professors, with the intention of exposing Home's trickery. The sitting took place in a well-lit room (which became Home's custom), and the investigators were allowed to inspect everything, including the table that would be involved. Instead of reporting trickery, however, the investigators wrote and signed the following statement:

> The table was moved in every possible direction, and with great force, when we could not perceive any cause of motion. It (the table) was forced against each one of us so powerfully as to move us from our positions. . . . Mr. Wells seated himself on the table, which was rocked for some time with great violence, and at length, it poised itself on the two legs, and remained in this position for some thirty seconds, when no other person was in contact with it. . . . Three persons, Messrs. Wells, Bliss and Edwards, assumed positions on the table at the same time, and while thus seated the table was moved in various directions. . . . In conclusion, we may observe, that Mr. D. D. Home frequently urged us to hold his hands and feet. During these occurrences the room was well lighted, the lamp was frequently placed on and under the table, and every possible opportunity was afforded us for the closest inspection, and we admit this one emphatic declaration: *We know that we were not imposed upon nor deceived.*[44]

In 1855, Home moved to England (having been advised to do so, for some strange reason, by his doctors), after which his career as a medium really took off. He became an international celebrity, demonstrating his abilities before thousands of people over twenty-five years (except for one year in which he lost his powers). Unlike most physical mediums, he did not operate in the dark. His performances were often carried out on the spur of the moment in places (including royal palaces) where he had never been before (so that no advance preparation would have been possible). In all this period, no fraud of any sort on his part was ever detected. He had, to be sure, detractors, but even some of them became, unwittingly, witnesses to the authenticity of his powers.

One such hostile witness was the poet Robert Browning. Within a month after a séance he attended in 1855 in Ealing, Browning was arguing passionately that Home had cheated. He later used Home as the model for the charlatan in *Mr. Sludge the Medium*. However, in a letter dated only two days after the séance, Browning had written a detailed account that differed greatly from his later allegations. He described seeing Home, in good light, levitate a table, stating that Home's hands were above the table and that he was not using his legs or feet. He also described the playing of an accordion that nobody was touching, which was one of Home's standard feats, and the materialization of a garland that settled on the head of his wife, Elizabeth Barrett Browning.[45] What led Browning later to change his story and to begin attacking Home savagely was not some later observation, as he did not attend another Home séance. Indeed, it was perhaps the very fact that the host at Ealing refused to invite him to a second séance. Or perhaps Browning felt that his wife, with whom he wanted complete spiritual union, had become too preoccupied with Home. Or perhaps, like many people who have given testimonials of belief shortly after witnessing such events, he later decided that fraud simply *had* to be the explanation. In any case, the extant letter shows that, shortly after observing Home's demonstration, he believed the phenomena to be genuine.

A second hostile witness was Sir David Brewster, a Scottish physicist who was considered one of the leading scientists of his day. Brewster attended two séances with Home in 1855, one at Ealing and one at the home of a William Cox. After the latter session, Home wrote a letter to a friend in America, stating that Brewster and the others had admitted that they could provide no normal explanations for his feats. This letter found its way back to England and was published in a London newspaper, evidently causing some embarrassment. Brewster wrote a letter to the editor, denying the claim, saying instead that he not only had seen how all the phenomena *could* have been produced by hands and feet, but that he had also proved that some of them were indeed thus caused. In the exchange of letters that followed, Cox reported that Brewster at the time had declared, "This upsets the philosophy of 50 years." Cox also contradicted Brewster's claim that he had not been allowed to look under the table, as did the novelist Anthony Trollope, who added that, at the Ealing séance, Brewster admitted seeing the table move *while* he was looking under it.[46]

Brewster refused to retract his denials, but, like Browning, he had written an account shortly after the séances. This account was published in 1869, the year after his death, by his daughter in *The Home Life of Sir David Brewster*. (As Braude points out, the revelation of her father's dishonesty in this affair, as well as the pun in the title, was surely unintended.)[47] Here is Brewster's private account of the seance at Cox's house, to which he had been invited by Lord Brougham "in order to assist in finding out the trick":

> We four sat down at a moderately-sized table, the structure of which we were invited to examine. In a short time the table shuddered, and a tremulous motion ran up all our arms; at our bidding these motions ceased, and

returned. The most unaccountable rappings were produced in various parts of the table; and the table actually rose from the ground when no hand was upon it. A larger table was produced, and exhibited similar movements. . . . [A] small hand-bell was then laid down with its mouth on the carpet, and, after lying for some time, it actually rang when nothing could have touched it. The bell was then placed on the other side, still upon the carpet, and it came over to me and placed itself in my hand. It did the same to Lord Brougham.

These were the principle experiments; we could give no explanation of them, and could not conjecture how they could be produced by any kind of mechanism.[48]

With regard to the tension between Brewster's private and public accounts, the *Spectator* remarked: "The hero of science does not acquit himself as we could wish or expect."[49]

The Home-Brewster episode illustrates the truth of a point made by the philosopher C. J. Ducasse with regard to wishful thinking and dishonesty, with which believers in paranormal phenomena are regularly suspected. As Ducasse points out, we should be at least equally suspicious about testimonials on the other side:

[A]llegations of detection of fraud, or of malobservation, or of misinterpretation of what was observed, or of hypnotically induced hallucination, have to be scrutinized *as closely and as critically* as must testimony *for* the reality of the phenomena. For there is likely to be just as much wishful thinking, prejudice, emotion, snap judgment, naiveté, and intellectual dishonesty on the side of orthodoxy, of skepticism, and of conservatism, as on the side of hunger for and of belief in the marvelous. The emotional motivation for irresponsible disbelief is, in fact, probably even stronger—especially in scientifically educated persons whose pride of knowledge is at stake—than is in other persons the motivation for irresponsible belief.[50]

Ducasse's final sentence is especially important. David Hume argued that, when it is a choice between believing that the normal order of nature has been violated or that human beings have lied, we should always adopt the latter hypothesis, because we *know* that human beings sometimes do such things, whereas we do not know that the normal order of nature is ever violated. However, besides adding the elementary point that we do not, even now, know all the variables in the "normal order of nature," we also need to add more about what we do know about human motivation. On the one hand, we can easily think of several reasons why intellectuals would decline any opportunity to witness paranormal occurrences, or, if they did witness them, why they would later deny that they had. On the other hand, it is hard to imagine why people of the stature of William James, Henry and Eleanor Sidgwick, Oliver Lodge, and William Crookes would testify to the occurrence of paranormal events if they were not certain that they had occurred. They would know that giving such testimony would do nothing to help their careers and reputations and, if anything, would harm them.

Having paused to consider that point, I turn now to Crookes's reports of his investigations of Home. I quoted earlier Crookes's statement as to why he thought it his public duty as a scientist to investigate Home's alleged powers. He was not precipitate: Stories about Home, including reports of levitation in broad daylight, had been circulating in England for fifteen years prior to Crookes's invitation to Home, in 1870, to submit himself to investigation.

Initially, Crookes simply observed séances, during which he saw the standard phenomena, such as accordion playing, table levitations, and demonstrations of incombustibility. The latter was something of a specialty for Home (perhaps because of identification with the Book of Daniel, with its story of three men who were thrown into a fiery furnace but remained unsinged, because they were protected by an angel of God [Daniel 3:19–28]). Here is part of Crookes's account of one such occasion:

> Mr. Home again went to the fire, and after stirring the hot coals about with his hand, took out a red-hot piece nearly as big as an orange, and putting it on his right hand, covered it over with his left hand so as to almost completely enclose it, and then blew into the small furnace thus extemporized until the lump of charcoal was nearly white-hot, and then drew my attention to the lambent flame which was flickering over the coal and licking round his fingers; he fell on his knees, looked up in a reverent manner, held up the coal in front and said, "Is not God good? Are not His laws wonderful?"[51]

Not content, however, simply to observe, Crookes later conducted some experiments. The first involved table-tilting involving a thirty-two-pound table. Using a spring balance, Crookes established that it normally required eight pounds of force to make the table tilt. Then, when Home told the table to "be light," it required only two pounds to lift one of the feet off the floor; after the command to "be heavy," thirty-six pounds were required. One might well suspect that the latter figure could be explained by the fact that the sitters, who were supposed to have their hands lightly resting on the table, were unconsciously exerting downward force. However, in another "heavy" trial, in which the force required to lift a leg was forty-five pounds, the hands of the sitters were *under* the tabletop. Home, of course, was carefully watched to make sure he was not using his feet.[52]

In another test, Crookes had Home place his fingers on one end of a board, then try to make the other end, which was supported by a spring balance, heavier. The board was set up so that, had Home been pushing on his end, it ·would have made the other end lighter, not heavier. And yet the weight of the other end increased from 3½ pounds to 9 pounds. Also participating in this experiment was William Huggins, a prominent physicist and astronomer and, like Crookes, a Fellow of the Royal Society.[53]

Still another test involved the accordion. Crookes bought a new accordion for the test, to dispel suspicion that Home's own accordion was somehow rigged. He also observed Home dressing for the occasion, noting that Home had no hidden apparatus on him. Crookes had brought a cage, furthermore, in which to place the accordion so that Home could not possibly be touching it except with the one hand that he used to hold it, with his thumb and middle finger, at the end opposite the keyboard. Home's other hand rested on the table, and his feet were being held. Nevertheless, Crookes reports, the accordion expanded and contracted, and music was played. Then Home removed his hand from the accordion altogether, placing it in the hand of the person next to him, and yet the accordion continued to play while it floated about in the cage. Running an electric current to the insulated copper wire, which Crookes had wound around the cage, made no difference.[54]

With only a few exceptions, Crookes was not able to get other scientists to come to observe and test these phenomena for themselves. George Stokes, an officer of the Royal Society, declined an invitation to meet Home with these words: "I don't want to meet anyone; my object being to scrutinize the apparatus, not to witness the effects."[55] Stokes later decided that he was too busy even to examine the apparatus—although he was *not* too busy to write Crookes a long letter explaining what *must* have been wrong with his experiments. Then, when Crookes submitted a paper about his investigations of Home to the Royal Society, Stokes took it upon himself to reject the paper without any referees, evidently without even reading the paper himself.[56]

Another example of the treatment accorded to Crookes by orthodox scientists is provided by an episode involving William Benjamin Carpenter, who published an article about Crookes and others titled "Spiritualism and Its Recent Converts" in the Royal Society's *Quarterly Review of Science.* Besides being published anonymously, the article was full of distortions and even dishonest statements. The Council of the Royal Society, in a special resolution, admitted that statements in the article were false, but Carpenter was not censured by the scientific community. In fact, the following year he was elected president of the British Association for the Advancement of Science.[57]

After a few years of such responses, Crookes gave up trying to communicate with members of the scientific community about Home. In a letter to Lodge in 1894, he said:

It seems a cruel thing that Home was about London for years, asking for scientific men to come and investigate, and offering himself freely for any experiments they liked, and with one or two exceptions no one would take advantage of the offer. I tried my best to get men of science to look into it, but all I got for my pains was a suggestion of lunacy for myself and insults for Home.[58]

Those today, accordingly, wishing to cast doubt on the authenticity of Home's phenomena, cannot refer back to any scientific studies of the day that discredited them. The scientists who actually investigated the phenomena pronounced them genuine. These scientists included (besides Crookes himself) David Wells, David Brewster (reluctantly and posthumously), William Huggins, Alfred Russel Wallace (codiscoverer of Darwinian evolutionary theory), and Francis Galton (who, in a letter to Darwin in 1872, referred to the openness of Home to investigation and said that he considered Crookes "thoroughly scientific in his procedure"[59]). Accordingly, today's critics of Home's phenomena can do little more than repeat the argument of the critics of the time who felt free to reject the phenomena without empirical investigation: The events as reported by Crookes and others did not occur because they could *not* have occurred.[60]

This episode illustrates with special clarity the point that the evaluation of empirical evidence is inseparable from the philosophical issue of possibility, and therefore worldview, and from concomitant wishful-and-fearful thinking. For those today with philosophical perspectives that do *not* rule out such phenomena, there is no good reason to deny that, as astounding as Home's reported feats seem in comparison with the ordinary course of events, they really did occur.

Of course, the mere absence of a philosophical perspective that rules out such phenomena, combined with the strength of the testimony of the day, would not be enough for most of us if the reports of Home's phenomena were completely without parallel. They, however, are not. In the first place, there is laboratory evidence of psychokinesis, which will be discussed below. Most of it, to be sure, is on a vastly smaller scale than that reported of Home, but the crucial barrier would be crossed if psychokinesis of any type were demonstrated. The report of a major psychokinetic event may, psychologically speaking, evoke much greater incredulity than that of a minor one. Philosophically speaking, however, it raises no new problems. In any case, even Home-like phenomena were not unique to him. There are credible reports of at least most of his phenomena in relation to other people. One of these phenomena, levitation (of his own body), has been extensively documented in relation to St. Joseph of Copertino, St. Teresa of Avila, and several others.[61] Movements of pieces of furniture have been documented in relation to a number of other physical mediums.[62] Large-scale physical phenomena have repeatedly been documented in relation to so-called poltergeist cases (to be discussed below). And deliberately produced physical phenomena on the same scale as Home's have been documented in relation to Sathya Sai Baba.

Although there is impressive testimony from many credible witnesses as to the authenticity of Sai Baba's paranormal powers, incidentally, I have not included him as one of the white crows of the second type because he has not been willing to submit himself to experimental testing. He has been studied extensively, however, by one of the premier parapsychologists, Erlendur Haraldsson. In *Modern Miracles: An Investigative Report on Psychic Phenomena Associated with Sathya Sai Baba* (1987), Haraldsson writes this summary statement:

> What then is our conclusion about the physical phenomena? For lack of experimental evidence it can only be somewhat tentative, though the testimony is extensive and consistent over four decades. Whether some of the physical productions, in some periods of Baba's life, may have been produced by sleight of hand, we cannot, of course, ascertain. What we can, however, squarely state is that in spite of a longlasting and painstaking effort, we found no direct evidence of fraud.[63]

So, in response to the complaint that all the examples of white crows of the second major type are in the past, where they cannot be observed, Haraldsson's book provides good *prima facie* evidence that such a white crow is active today.

Ted Serios

It would be a cause for suspicion, of course, if all *prima facie* white crows of the second kind in recent years had refused to submit to testing. That, however, is not the case. One person with ostensible psychokinetic powers who submitted himself, with enthusiasm, to experimental testing is Ted Serios (b. 1918), mentioned earlier in relation to psychiatrist Jule Eisenbud, who studied Serios extensively for several years.

Serios' special ability was in paranormal photography, claims about which have been made for almost as long as photography itself has existed. Numerous experiments were carried out and reported in Japan (Tomokichi Fukurai, *Clairvoyance and Thoughtography*, 1931 [originally published in Japanese in 1913]), America, France, and England in the early part of the twentieth century. The Society for the Study of Supernormal Pictures in England stated that "after many tests and after the examination of thousands of pictures, they are unanimously of the opinion that results have been obtained excluding the possibility of fraud."[64] After an exposé of "spirit photography" in the *Proceedings of the Society for Psychical Research* in 1933, however, the subject fell into disrepute and was not revived until Ted Serios came to Eisenbud's attention.

The first paranormal photographs occurred while Serios, in his mid-thirties, was working in a Chicago hotel as an elevator operator. A fellow employee who practiced hypnotism, having discovered that Serios was a good subject, had suggested that he (Serios) use "traveling clairvoyance" to locate hidden treasures. The hypnotist's suggestion was that Serios try to get pictures of the places that he claimed to see paranormally. When the film came back one day with a couple of pictures on it, Serios assumed that the hypnotist had played a trick on him. But when he got paranormal pictures on a Polaroid camera, he and several other people as well were convinced. In 1962, Pauline Oehler, vice-president of the Illinois Society for Psychical Research, published an article in *Fate* magazine. When Eisenbud received a copy of this article from the publisher, Curtis Fuller, he threw it away with this rationale:

> I had seen enough of this sort of stuff to know that despite the precautionary measures allegedly taken there must obviously be something fishy somewhere. I had no reason to doubt Mrs. Oehler's veracity and sincerity . . . but I thought I had every reason to entertain doubts of her (and Mr. Curtis Fuller's) scientific acumen, or at least training and competence in the elementary but absolutely indispensable techniques of differentiating genuine psi phenomena from very trickily produced normal (that is, fraudulently produced) phenomena giving the appearance of the same.[65]

Eventually Eisenbud was persuaded to conduct his own experiments with Serios and became convinced that his abilities were genuinely paranormal. As a result, Eisenbud would have the above-quoted reasoning employed time and time again in the coming years in relation to *his* reports about Serios.

Eisenbud has written several of these reports, the most extensive being a book, *The World of Ted Serios: "Thoughtographic" Studies of an Extraordinary Mind*. In this book, Eisenbud provides many examples of the pictures Serios has produced, accompanied at times with psychological analyses of the Freudian "primary process" thinking evidently involved in some of them. He also describes at considerable length the only conceivable ways that the photographs could have been produced fraudulently and the precautions taken to prevent such fraud. Without the photos themselves and Eisenbud's own commentary, a bare summary of the results will surely not be terribly impressive. My hope, however, is that it will lead readers to Eisenbud's own book, which is one of the most profound as well as one of the most fascinating ever written.

Eisenbud studied Serios intensively from 1964 to 1967. During this period Serios produced over 400 photographic images that could not be explained through ordinary means. He was observed by over three dozen trained observers.[66] Many of these signed observer statements asserting that they had witnessed the production of the pictures under conditions in which no normal explanations were conceivable. The signatories included conjurors, photographers, psychiatrists, physicists, engineers, and other scientists.[67]

Eisenbud reports that no one who had observed Serios in action ever refused to sign such a statement.[68]

Various aspects of the experiments militate against the suspicion that the pictures were produced fraudulently: Witnesses brought their own cameras and their own film and were instructed never to let these out of their own possession. These were Polaroid cameras, which ruled out any alterations in the developing room. The films were pulled and developed in front of everyone. Serios was not allowed to come into contact with the camera or the prints during this process. And witnesses were allowed to inspect anything at any time.

The normal procedure was for the witnesses to aim their cameras at Serios, who would say "Now" when they were to push the button. Normally, of course, they would simply get a picture of him. Sometimes, however, they would get either a "whitie" or a "blackie." More surprisingly, they would sometimes get a picture of something that Serios was imagining, such as a building. These pictures might be based on pictures that Serios himself had seen (although there would often be distortions, such as a word misspelled). Sometimes, however, one of the witnesses would have brought target pictures and kept them locked in a briefcase, so that Serios had to learn what the picture was clairvoyantly before impressing it psychokinetically on the film. Even some of these tests were successful.

One theory as to how fraud could have occurred depends on the fact that Serios was not always successful, and that, even when he was, the success may have come after an hour or two of unsuccessful attempts. Perhaps, the theory is, the witnesses became bored and distracted, thereby allowing Serios to engage in trickery undetected. However, Eisenbud counters, the production of images would usually be preceded by a progressive darkening of the prints, leading up to complete blackies, which brought the witnesses to a highly concentrated state. Also, Serios would often produce many images in a session—at his peak producing 50 images in 60 to 80 trials.[69]

Likewise, it is hard to see how any gimmick could have been employed. Serios held, or had someone else hold, a little "gizmo" in front of the camera, but it could be inspected by anyone to see that it had no pictures in it. Furthermore, it was often fashioned on the spot out of the black paper that came with the film. Also, Serios often produced various types of images in one session, which would have required that several gimmicks go undetected by people who had come precisely to detect such things. Finally, Serios sometimes produced his pictures while being away from the camera, even as far as sixty-six feet.[70]

There was, to be sure, an article that came to be known as an exposé, although it was nothing of the sort.[71] And there is a magician, CSICOP's James ("The Amazing") Randi, who has claimed to be able to duplicate the Serios phenomena. But he has never done so, and he has repeatedly refused Eisenbud's challenges to produce such photographic images under similar conditions in the presence of scientific observers, even when he was offered $10,000 if he could do so.[72] One magician who was not content to speculate at a distance, but came to observe Serios, said: "No conjuring techniques are remotely conceivable under the conditions."[73]

Nina Kulagina

Yet another person who has recently demonstrated psychokinetic powers under experimental conditions is Nina Kulagina (1925–1990). She had served with distinction as a senior sergeant in the defense of Leningrad in World War II, and lived in Leningrad with her husband, a marine engineer, until her death. She was discovered in 1963 by Leonid Vasiliev, the Soviet Union's best-known parapsychologist, who ran tests with her until his death in 1966. Research on her was then taken over by Adenek Rejdak, a scientist at the Prague Military Institute, Genady Sergeyev, a physiologist and mathematician at the Uktomskii Physiological Institute in Leningrad, and other parapsychologists, who prepared a film about her that was shown at an international parapsychological conference in Moscow in 1968.

This film, which brought Kulagina to the attention of Western parapsychologists, showed her producing various kinds of paranormal movement, such as moving a cigar tube inside a closed plastic case, moving several objects simultaneously in various directions, and selectively moving one or two matchsticks among several scattered on a table.[74]

Although the film and the other Soviet reports were impressive, Western parapsychologists were anxious to study her themselves. In 1970, J. Gaither Pratt, who had long worked with J. B. Rhine at Duke, came to Leningrad and made his own films of Kulagina moving objects. Then in 1973, Benson Herbert and Manfred Cassirer from England set up a kind of paraphysics laboratory in a Leningrad hotel. Although Kulagina was weak from illness, they found that she could move a hydrometer in a saline solution from several feet away. Besides checking for strings or wires, they had the whole system surrounded by an electrically grounded screen.[75] In another test, she was to rotate a compass needle. After only marginal success, she sat back in her chair, exhausted. As she sat there motionless, the whole compass began moving about the table.[76]

Although further visits by Western scientists were eventually discouraged, she continued to be studied by Soviet scientists, both those with and those without interest in paranormal phenomena. She was typically searched for strings, magnets (even by X ray), and anything else that could simulate PK, and often moved nonmagnetic objects in sealed containers. In 1978 the scientists at the USSR Academy of Sciences who had studied her drew up an official document testifying to the authenticity of her psychokinetic abilities.[77] Sustained work with her ceased in the mid-1980s due to her ill health. Although Kulagina never exploited her abilities for gain, and although no sign of fraud was ever detected, the Soviet journal *Man and Law* published an article in 1986 that accused her of trickery. When she sued the journal, two members of the Soviet Academy of Sciences testified on her behalf, and the court in 1988 ordered the journal to reprint a retraction, which it did.[78]

3. WHITE CROWS OF THE THIRD KIND

A third kind of repeatability in psychical research arises from the fact that various kinds of ostensibly paranormal phenomena of a spontaneous nature have been repeatedly reported in various times and places throughout recorded history. It is true, to be sure, that some kinds of paranormal events are unique to a particular tradition, such as stigmata in the Christian tradition.[79] But various broad categories of paranormal phenomena, such as telepathy, clairvoyance, psychokinesis, and out-of-body experiences, have been reported in many, perhaps all, traditions. This fact suggests that they are "natural kinds." It is probably also the case that fraudulent claims about all these types of phenomena have also occurred in many, and perhaps all, traditions. But this would appear to be "imitative fraud," based on the real thing. If that were not the case, it would be difficult to understand why the same general kinds of claims have been made in widely separated societies.

In this chapter, the discussion is limited to two types of recurrent spontaneous paranormal phenomena: telepathic impressions and poltergeist activity.

Telepathic Impressions

Probably the most common type of spontaneous paranormal experience is telepathic impressions, in which people, without having any clear sensorylike perception, have a strong feeling about a distant person that turns out to be veridical. Most such cases are crisis cases, in which the distant person has died, is dying, has had an accident, or is in danger. In a 1970 book entitled *Telepathic Impressions*, Ian Stevenson published an analysis of 160 previously published cases followed by reports of 35 new cases. The criteria for inclusion were the following: (1) The percipient has a strong feeling about a distant person that closely corresponds to that person's situation at that time, without any normal way of knowing about it. (2) The percipient reports this feeling to someone else or takes some appropriate action, and this fact is independently corroborated. (3) The percipient's statement or action was unusual, thereby not interpretable as simply one of many that happened this time to correspond to reality.[80] As illustrations, I have chosen two cases involving Joicey Acker Hurth of Cedarburg, Wisconsin. I have chosen these cases in part because, unlike many of the others, the participants allowed their real names to be used.

The first reported event occurred in 1949, three months after Joicey and her husband had been married. They were in Cedarburg temporarily living with his parents, Dr. and Mrs. O. J. Hurth. Although Joicey was about a thousand miles from her own home in Anderson, South Carolina, she did not feel lonely or homesick, as she was very close to her new family, and her sister, who was married to her husband's brother, lived nearby. I will pick up her own account:

> It must have been sometime after midnight, January 23 [1949] when I awakened with a feeling of deep sadness, an impression that something was wrong. I did not want to disturb my husband, so for a long while I stared wide-eyed at the ceiling. . . . I remember the terrible ache in my heart. I started to cry and sobbed softly into my pillow. My husband was immediately awake and asked many questions to which I had no answers. I repeated over and over to him that I had a feeling that something was wrong. His efforts to console me were futile and I did not sleep the rest of the night.
>
> The next morning when we went downstairs to breakfast my in-laws were shocked at my appearance—swollen red eyes and haggard expression. They accused us of having had a "lovers' quarrel," but I assured them that this was not the case. I told them I had no explanation for my mood of depression. They were much concerned.
>
> I put bread into the toaster and while waiting for it I suddenly wheeled around and exclaimed, "It's my father! Something is terribly wrong with my father!"
>
> I had no reason for my statement. My father was a man of robust health for his sixty-nine years and had known little illness in his entire life.
>
> Each one speaking in turn tried to tell me that it was my imagination. My mother-in-law reminded me of the letter I had received from my father only a few days before and he had made no mention of an illness.
>
> "No," I said. "I'm sure. I must go home!"
>
> The telephone rang while I was speaking, and although this was a doctor's home where the telephone rang constantly, I knew this call was for me and answered it.
>
> My aunt spoke first, telling me that my father was in a coma and was dying. Then my mother took the phone and asked, "Didn't you receive my letter? I wrote you that your father was very ill."
>
> I told her I had received no letter from her. (I later learned that all planes had been grounded because of bad weather and the mail was held up.)

She then learned that he had taken a sulfa drug for a backache. The drug was not given to him by his regular physician, who was out of the office, but by a male nurse, who had failed to caution him to take it with plenty of water. The drug caused crystallization in the kidneys, so that they could not function properly, and he died within the week. Joicey and her sister, who had to take a train instead of a plane because of the weather, arrived at the Anderson County Hospital on January 25, just before their father, who awoke briefly from his coma, expired.

Stevenson received written corroboration of these events from Joicey's husband (R. P. Hurth) and her mother-in-law (Mrs. Oscar J. Hurth, who had written the corroborating letter to Joicey in 1964).[81]

Joicey Hurth reports that she has had a total of six experiences of this type, five of which have been verified by others and four of which Stevenson includes in his book.[82] I will give one other, which occurred six years later, in 1955. It involved her then five-year-old daughter, also named Joicey, who, on returning home from a birthday party, discovered that her father and brother had already left for the Walt Disney movie without her. Her mother told her that they expected her to join them at the theater, which was only a block and a half away; "so she waved goodbye and skipped towards the corner." Mrs. Hurth then continues:

> I returned to the dinner dishes still unwashed in the kitchen sink. Quite suddenly while I held a plate in my hand an awesome feeling came over me. I dropped the plate, turned my eyes towards heaven and prayed aloud, "Oh, God, don't let her get killed!"
>
> For some unexplainable reason I knew Joicey had been hit by a car or was going to be. I was quite conscious of her involvement in an accident. I immediately went to the telephone, looked up a number, and shakily dialed the theater. I gave my name and said, "My little girl was on the way to the theater. She has had an accident. Is she badly hurt?"
>
> The girl answering the telephone stammered, "How did you know? It—the accident—just happened. Hold the phone please!"
>
> While I held the receiver, waiting, the siren sounded and an ambulance went out. I was frantic. Soon a very calm voice, that of the manager, Ray Nichols, spoke, "Mrs. Hurth, your little girl was struck by a car, but she is all right. Your husband is with her now. She appears to be in good shape, only stunned. Your husband is taking her to Dr. Hurth [little Joicey's uncle] now for an examination. Incidentally, Mrs. Hurth, how did you know?"
>
> I don't remember my reply to this question; probably I said that I had a strong feeling that something had happened.
>
> Another call to Dr. Hurth's home assured me that Joicey had not been seriously hurt. She had run into a moving car, was bounced off the front left fender to the pavement, had gotten up herself and run back to the same side of the street from which she started and sat on the curb until someone came. . . .

Joicey remembers that at the time she was hit she called, "Mama." She remembers sitting on the curb crying and calling "Mama, Mama, I want my Mama."

Stevenson has letters of corroboration from Mr. Hurth and from little Joicey (written in 1967 and 1968, respectively). He also, during a visit to Cedarburg, had a conversation with the theater manager, Ray Nichols, who confirmed that Mrs. Hurth had telephoned the theater right after the accident, too soon for anyone to have run to tell her about it. Nichols also thought it highly unlikely that Mrs. Hurth might have heard screeching brakes, given the distance and the fact that, due to the narrowness of the street, cars always go slowly along it.[83] (The fact that little Joicey was not badly hurt also suggests that the car was not going very fast.)

Although both of these cases are recent and corroborated (and not anonymous, so that anyone could check up on them), those who are convinced that extrasensory impressions are impossible could, of course, find reason to reject them, or simply dismiss them as anomalies. The point of this section, however, is that these experiences are *repeatable*, in the sense that large numbers of people from different times and places have reported similar experiences (and sometimes, as the present cases illustrate, one person may have two or more such experiences). Stevenson has assembled 195 verified cases, and Louisa Rhine's collection of (unverified) spontaneous paranormal experiences included 1,839 impression cases.[84] Stevenson's reflections about his own collection are to the point:

It is . . . possible that I have overlooked some important details in one or more cases which, if known about, would disqualify a paranormal interpretation. But as the number of cases grows, this possibility becomes less and less reasonable as grounds for dismissing all of them. . . . [W]e have 195 cases in all. For most of these there are at least two witnesses and for many, three or more witnesses. The cases have had many different and independent investigators. It seems to me most improbable that all these informants would have mixed up their observations and memories or that all these investigators would have been completely misled. It is surely much more likely that at least in some cases the main events corresponded closely enough with the reports published so that the one represents the other accurately enough for judgment and interpretation. If so, we can regard at least some of these cases as being examples of extrasensory perception.[85]

I turn now to a second form of repeated spontaneous paranormal experience.

Poltergeist Phenomena

As the second example of these white crows of a third kind, I will use a particularly bizarre type that is popularly known by the German term *poltergeist*, which means noisy ghost (or spirit). This term reflects the earlier belief that the phenomena are caused by a discarnate spirit. More recently, parapsychologists seek to avoid implying this theory by speaking instead of *poltergeist phenomena, poltergeist incidents*, or the like. Still more recently, some parapsychologists have spoken of *recurrent spontaneous psychokinesis* (RSPK). Although this term is unlikely to replace expressions using the term *poltergeist*, it does bring out an important feature of these phenomena, which is that they generally recur many times during the period of activity. This is important for psychical research because most large-scale spontaneous phenomena happen only once, or only sporadically, making study of them impossible, except retrospectively. Due to the recurrent nature of most poltergeist incidents, however, it is sometimes possible for parapsychologists to arrive in time to observe them, and even to engage in experimentation.

It is not simply the recurrent nature of poltergeist phenomena that makes them apt for scientific study. Apparitions and hauntings also often involve recurrent phenomena, but in such cases the phenomena may recur only occasionally over very long periods of time. In poltergeist cases, by contrast, the period of activity is usually much shorter, typically a couple of months or even less, and the phenomena may recur daily. Because poltergeist phenomena thereby lend themselves to sustained observation and experimentation, they are, in spite of their bizarre and seeming incredible nature, especially well documented.

The Rosenheim Poltergeist

One of the best-documented cases occurred in 1967 in Germany, in the Bavarian town of Rosenheim, in the law office of Sigmund Adam. In November, various disturbing events began to occur regularly. The fluorescent lights on the ceiling went out repeatedly, sometimes following a loud bang. (On one such occasion, the electrician, climbing a ladder to check out the lights, discovered that they had been twisted in their sockets so as to break the connection. Shortly after he fixed them, they went out again, following another loud bang.) The incandescent light bulbs would explode, sometimes when they were not on, and often the filaments would still be intact. Electrical fuses blew for no apparent reason. And the telephones acted up in various ways: All four phones would ring simultaneously, but no one would be on the line; calls would be cut off; and the telephone company registered a great number of calls that no one had evidently made, sending the phone bills soaring. These calls continued to be registered even after all the telephones except one were disconnected, to prevent any surreptitious use.

With business grinding to a halt, Sigmund Adam was desperate to discover the cause. Suspecting the electrical supply, Adam called in the Rosenheim Maintenance Department, whose assistant, Herr Brunner, fully expected to discover a normal explanation. Having discovered large deflections, Brunner brought in an emergency power unit. But the deflections and the strange phenomena continued.[86] Adam also brought in officials from the post office (which is there in charge of the telephone system). When recording equipment was installed, calls were registered almost immediately, although no phone was being used. Calls to the time-of-day number (which are not free) were made as often as six times a minute. Two German television companies, having heard of the events, came in and produced documentaries, showing some of the phenomena. Finally, Adam filed criminal charges, which meant that the Rosenheim Police were put in charge of the investigation. At this point, Hans Bender, Germany's best-known parapsychologist, was brought in. He in turn invited two physicists, F. Karger of the Max Planck Institute for Plasma Physics and G. Zicha of the Technical University in Munich.

Installing even more monitors, Karga and Zicha ruled out the possibility that the phenomena were caused by variations in the voltage, demodulated high-frequency voltage, electrostatic charging, external static magnetic fields, ultrasonic and infrasonic effects, loose contacts, mechanical defects in the recorder, or any other known physical cause, including trickery.[87] They also quickly discovered that the phenomena occurred only during office hours, and, in particular, only when one particular employee, Annemarie Schneider, was present. Annemarie, an eighteen-year-old secretary, was a fairly new employee. The first deflection in the power was registered the moment she crossed the threshold.[88] This evidence fit with the fact that, on previous occasions, fellow employees had observed that lamps would begin swinging and bulbs exploding shortly after her arrival.[89]

After Bender shared his belief that the phenomena were caused by psychokinesis, the disturbances intensified, and new types of phenomena arose. Decorative plates jumped off the wall; paintings began to turn over on their hooks; drawers would open by themselves; and a filing cabinet weighing almost 400 pounds twice moved about a foot. These phenomena were observed by the police officers, the power-company engineers, Bender and the physicists, and others. Some banging sounds, the swinging of the lamps, and the rotation of a picture (320 degrees) were captured on videotape, this evidently being the first time that poltergeist activity had been visually recorded.[90]

As these phenomena were occurring, Annemarie became visibly nervous and eventually developed hysterical contractions in her limbs. When she went on leave, the disturbances stopped. Some similar disturbances occurred at her next place of employment, but they were less intense and eventually ceased.[91]

Because city officials as well as parapsychologists were brought in, the documentation of this case was particularly good. Otherwise, however, this case was fairly typical of poltergeist incidents reported down through the centuries. The fact that some of the phenomena involved modern technology, such as telephones and electric lights, did, of course, distinguish the case from those in earlier centuries. But in terms of more general characteristics, it was not uncommon.

Typical Features of Poltergeist Cases

A useful survey of 116 cases by William Roll in 1978[92] helpfully summarizes several of the features that are typically found in poltergeist cases. Other surveys provide even more cases. For example, Alan Gauld and Anthony Cornell's *Poltergeists* (1979) includes 500 poltergeist and haunting cases since 1525, even though they limited their selection to cases that had been reported in detail (in diaries, published investigations, or court records). Roll's criteria of inclusion, however, were even more restrictive, as he included only cases in which (a) the account appeared in print (in a professional parapsychological journal if the case occurred after 1850), (b) the author witnessed the phenomena or interviewed witnesses who did, (c) the author was generally known to be credible, and (d) phenomena occurred that could not be explained by witnesses in ordinary terms. In 105 of the 116 cases, there were witnesses from outside the family involved, and in 73 of these there were witnesses with training in observing, reporting, and evaluating events, such as parapsychologists, police officers, government officials, psychologists, physicians, scientists, lawyers, clergymen, and teachers. The majority of the cases came from the United States and Europe. For comparative purposes, the 116 were divided into four periods: 1612–1849 (19 cases), 1850–1899 (25), 1900–1949 (38), and 1950–1974 (34).

With regard to duration, the disturbances have lasted from one day to six years. The median duration, however, is two months, with little difference among the four historical periods. One of the most common features of poltergeist cases is the association of the phenomena with a particular person. This is true of 92 of the 116 cases, with no statistically significant difference among the four periods. In 39 of these 92 cases, the phenomena followed the focal person to locations other than that of the primary disturbances. There are generally no disturbances when the focal person is sleeping.[93] The focal person seems equally likely to be male or female. The median ages for females in the four periods are 12, 13½, 15, and 13, and that for males 14, 12, 15, and 14.[94] Of these 92 focal persons, 49 evidently had fairly severe medical problems, psychological problems, or both, with 22 having seizures or disassociative states. Of the 29 focal persons in the fourth period, 13 underwent psychological examinations and were found to be characterized by high irritability and repressed aggression.[95]

This identification of a focal person in most cases, along with attention to the characteristics of such persons, reflects the dominant theory among contemporary parapsychologists: that the phenomena are produced psychokinetically, usually unconsciously, by the focal person, who is generally called, accordingly, the "poltergeist agent." Some prominent parapsychologists who have studied the cases, however, think otherwise, believing that we must separate them into two types: those that can be explained by the dominant theory, and those in which the phenomena must be ascribed to discarnate agents— that is, to *real* "poltergeists."[96]

However that may be, the most common ostensibly paranormal phenomenon has been the recurrent movement of objects, which has been involved in 105 of the 116 cases. In 63 of the 116 cases, there were sounds, either percussive (knocks or raps) or explosive. In 55 of the cases, there were both movements *and* sounds. The proportions are about the same in the four time periods.[97]

A particularly interesting feature of many of the movements is the unusual trajectory taken by the flying objects. For example, an object may move very rapidly toward something, such as a wall or a human body, but then strike it very gently. Or an object may float very slowly through the air. It may even change speeds in midflight, or hover, or move around corners. Of the 105 cases with moving objects, 43 have one or more of these unusual kinds of movement, with the proportion remaining the same in the four periods.[98]

A still more bizarre feature that sometimes occurs is teleportation, in which an object seems to be instantly transferred from one place to another in a normally inexplicable way, perhaps even through a wall. For example, Sigmund Adam, the lawyer in whose office the Rosenheim case occurred, investigated a case in a town ten miles away the following year. He was told by the family that objects that had disappeared from the house would sometimes be seen falling to the ground outside. Adam then placed perfume and tablet bottles on the kitchen table, sent everyone outside, closed all the doors and windows, then went outside himself. According to Hans Bender's report: "After a short time, the perfume bottle appeared in the air outside the house, and a bit later on, the bottle of tablets appeared in the air at the height of the roof and fell to the ground in a zigzag manner."[99] Reports of teleportation are contained in 18 of the 105 cases that had moving objects.[100]

The Miami Poltergeist Case

A case that occurred in Miami in 1967, the same year as the Rosenheim case, contained at least most of these features. What was particularly notable about this Miami case, however, is that it was the first poltergeist case in which parapsychologists performed experiments.

The location was Tropication Arts, a wholesale business for novelty items managed and partly owned by Alvin Laubheim. Beginning in December of 1966, there was an increase in breakage in the warehouse, which Laubheim attributed to carelessness by the two shipping clerks, Julio, a nineteen-year-old

Cuban refugee, and Curt Hagemeyer, an older man. In the second week of January, beer mugs, boxes, and other items started falling off the shelves. Laubheim and his workers tried to keep quiet about the disturbances, fearing that publicity would hurt business, but delivery men, customers, and even a reporter witnessed events, so word did get out. On January 13, the other owner, Glen Lewis, who had not been present very much and was skeptical of the reports, saw things falling just after he had placed them securely on the shelves.[101] The same day, the company's insurance agent, having witnessed an event, satisfied himself that the shelves were so substantial that nothing but a very strong tremor could cause things to fall off of them.[102]

The next day, the police were called. The officer who came, William Killin, assumed that Laubheim had to be "a nut." After Killin himself witnessed the falling of a few things, however, he asked his sergeant to come over, fearing that, if he simply submitted his report, *he* would be considered crazy. When the sergeant and two other officers arrived, they all witnessed further events. They then found that they could not make anything fall from the shelves by shaking them.[103]

Laubheim also brought in a friend, Howard Brooks, a professional magician. Brooks at first discounted the reports, and even played a practical joke. But after he and a policeman both saw two cartons fall, they performed some experiments in an area that they roped off as a target area. In one experiment, two beer mugs that they had placed on the shelves fell. The second one, which fell about an hour after the first one, did not break. No employees were nearby.

Another investigator was Susy Smith, a writer of popular books about parapsychology. While she was giving a radio interview on January 12, one of the artists at Tropication Arts called in and reported the strange breakages. Smith brought with her an Eastern Airlines pilot, Sinclair Buntin. After an ashtray fell to the floor, Buntin checked the shelves, making sure that everything was back from the edges. After a box fell in an area where no one was present, he made sure there were "no contraptions, or strings, or wires or anything that could cause it to move." And Julio was far away.[104] In one of the six incidents that occurred while Buntin was there, he saw the object in motion: A box about fifteen feet from him fell at "about a 30-degree angle out away from the shelf," an angle at which it could not have fallen "if it had just been pushed off." This observation fit with that of Mrs. Joyce George, Laubheim's sister, who witnessed the moving of a mug that had been placed on a shelf by Howard Brooks and a television crewman (who was there trying to capture some movement on film). Mrs. George said that while she was looking at the mug, "it scooted off the shelf and moved straight out into the air, then dropped straight down."[105]

The parapsychologist William Roll, having been called by Susy Smith, arrived on January 19. Roll's presence at first had an inhibitory effect (which had been true in some prior investigations as well).[106] Enough events occurred, however, to convince him that further investigation was warranted. Roll then had to go to Durham to attend a meeting of the Board of Directors of the Psychical Research Foundation on January 23. As it happened, that Monday was the biggest day of the entire episode, with 52 incidents, almost a quarter of the total of 224 events that were recorded altogether.[107] This fact would support the notion that Roll's presence had had an inhibitory effect.

On Roll's first day back, January 25, he established a target area, which could be kept under close observation and could be examined for any strings, chemicals, or anything else that could provide a normal explanation for the movements. Having such an area, where all the objects had been placed by Roll himself, also removed any doubt about where the fallen objects had come from and how far they had moved. (Some of the previously fallen items had evidently ended up quite a distance, in one case about twenty-two feet, from where they had been resting.)

On this day, however, nothing happened. This was not surprising— although not because of the presence of Roll, but because of the absence of Julio, who was home with a cold. It had long been clear that he was the center of the disturbances, which fellow workers suspected he was causing by means of trickery. Care was taken by Roll, accordingly, to keep Julio under observation, without being obvious about it. In any case, the next day, when Julio returned, items began falling again. In one experiment, Susy Smith placed an alligator ashtray in the target area, and Julio placed a cowbell directly in front of it. Roll then checked to make sure that nothing was attached that could simulate an incident. A few hours later, while Julio was involved in a argument with another employee at some distance from the target area, and while Roll was observing him, the alligator ashtray fell to the floor—even though the cowbell had remained in place. Some twenty minutes later, when Roll asked Julio how he felt, he said: "I feel happy: that thing [the breakage] makes me feel happy; I don't know how."[108]

On January 27, Roll was joined by fellow parapsychologist Gaither Pratt. To guard against the possibility that Pratt, too, might have an inhibitory effect, Roll introduced him to Julio simply as an interested friend. During the four days that Roll and Pratt were both there (although Roll often left the warehouse to remove his inhibitory presence), ten target objects fell. After Pratt had to return to Durham, Roll remained two more days. By then his presence had become less inhibiting, and twenty-eight more incidents occurred, thirteen in his presence. In one case he directly observed three boxes suddenly fall into the aisle while Julio was standing behind him and no one else was nearby.[109] Ten more target objects moved. One of these was a beer mug that was placed behind two small cartons and between a Fanta bottle and a cowbell, so that it presumably would have had to move up into the air to clear the obstacles. Julio was walking toward Roll with a broom in his hand at the time that the mug fell.[110]

In this case, as with the one in Rosenheim, there was little doubt that the disturbances were related to one individual, in this case Julio. In Roll's first visit, after a long period when nothing happened, he asked Julio how he felt. Julio replied, "Now I am nervous because nothing happens." After several incidents had occurred on January 27, he replied to Roll's query: "I feel good. I really miss the ghost—I mean—not the ghost, but I miss it when something doesn't happen."[111] Roll, drawing on Gardner Murphy's ideas, speculates that the breakages were a way of releasing tension. This speculation was based in part on later psychological studies, which indicated that Julio was deeply troubled, having aggressive feelings and impulses that he found unacceptable, so that he could not express them directly.[112] Shortly before the incidents began, furthermore, Julio's stepmother had told him that he had to move out of the house, which he did at the end of December. After he left Tropication Arts, reports came back about moving objects in his subsequent places of work.[113]

In conclusion: Whether parapsychologists think that all poltergeist phenomena can be attributed to psychokinesis by living agents usually depends on two things: the extent to which they are willing to attribute psychokinetic powers to the unconscious dimension of the human psyche, and their belief regarding the possibility of discarnate agency. In any case, the phenomena, given their similarity in various places and times, provide a kind of repeatability that allows us to think of them as constituting a white crow of the third kind. Given the spontaneous nature of the phenomena, of course, this repeatability is not that of the laboratory sciences, such as physics and chemistry. But it is not totally unlike some phenomena of the science of meteorology, such as tornadoes: Although the actual occurrence is unpredictable, we can say something about the kinds of conditions likely to bring on such an occurrence, and the occurrence, when it comes, will have various predictable features. Even though poltergeist outbreaks are not as common as tornadoes and their effects are neither as publicly observable nor as lawlike, they too appear to be "natural kinds." Although my summary was intended to bring out this point, the strange similarity that runs through these cases can be appreciated only be reading accounts of dozens of such cases, which can be found in the book by Roll or that by Gauld and Cornell.[114] It is probably only through this means—unless one has been directly involved in such a case—that one can become convinced that poltergeist cases do indeed constitute a white crow of the third kind.

4. White Crows of the Fourth Kind

Whereas white crows of the third kind involved spontaneous phenomena, those of the fourth kind involve *paranormal effects repeatedly produced in laboratory experiments.* The phenomena that occur under such conditions are usually far less robust. Any ostensible paranormal functioning is often not conspicuous: That anything other than chance is occurring can sometimes only be detected by means of statistical analysis. Nevertheless, this kind of parapsychological evidence is of great importance for two reasons. First, it alone has been produced under conditions that are (1) tightly controlled and (2) widely replicable. For many people, especially scientists, only evidence produced under such conditions could be acceptable. Second, this evidence, because it has mostly been derived from ordinary and nearly ordinary individuals, supports the view that the paranormal powers possessed by the white crows of the second kind are simply extreme versions of extrasensory and/or psychokinetic powers that are widely distributed, and that may even be universal. Third, this evidence, in spite of typically indicating only very weak paranormal powers, lends credibility to the evidence for much greater paranormal powers possessed by a few individuals.

To expand on this third point: The primary philosophical reason for rejecting all reports of paranormal perception and influence is simply the belief that such perception and influence are impossible. If *any* such paranormal functioning is established, that belief is shown to be false. The decisive barrier has thereby been overcome. The difference between inconspicuous paranormal functioning, which can only be detected by means of statistics, and directly observable paranormal functioning, such as that of Daniel Home, is important, of course, in all sorts of ways. But in terms of the philosophical question of possibility, the former kind is as good as the latter. I will begin with experimental evidence for extrasensory perception, then turn to that for psychokinesis.

Experimental Evidence for Extrasensory Perception

Laboratory tests for extrasensory perception have been of two types: restricted-choice and free-response. One of the most popular restricted-choice experiments has involved a 25-card deck of ESP (or Zener) cards, each of which contains five sets of cards with standard symbols (circle, cross, star, wavy lines, square). By pure chance a person should average five correct guesses ("hits") per run. Some subjects, however, have consistently scored higher.

One such subject in the early days of J. B. Rhine's work at Duke was Hubert Pearce, a divinity student. The experiments were conducted by Rhine's assistant, Gaither Pratt. In one run, Pratt was in the physics building, while Pearce was in the library, about a hundred yards away. The test was for clairvoyance: Once a minute Pratt took a card from the (preshuffled) deck and, without looking at it, placed it facedown. Pearce, who had a synchronized watch, was then to record what he thought the card was. In 12 runs, he averaged 9.9 hits per run. Another set was conducted with Pearce in the medical school, over 250 yards away. All in all, there were 74 runs, which means a total of 1,850 guesses. Pearce had a total of 558 hits (instead of the 370 predicted by chance), for an average of 7.1 hits per session. The odds against this occurring by chance are calculated to be one in 22 billion.[115]

Another restricted-choice experiment restricts the subject to only two options. Pavel Stepanek, a library clerk from Czechoslovakia, was regularly successful in such experiments involving cards that were green on one side and white on the other. These cards were placed inside envelopes, which in turn were placed inside opaque covers. The cards were randomly inserted in a way that the researchers themselves did not know which way the cards were facing. In an experiment involving 500 runs, Stepanek was correct 53.9 percent of the time, the odds against which are a million to one. Stepanek was studied for ten years, from 1961 to 1971, by eighteen investigators from various countries, and was the subject of twenty-seven research reports. He continually scored significantly above chance.[116]

In another forced-option experiment, involving ordinary playing cards, the subject tries to guess both the suit and denomination. One successful subject was Bill Delmore, who was a Yale law student in the early 1970s when the experiments with him were conducted at Duke. In a total of 46 runs (of 52 guesses each), Delmore had exact hits (correctly naming both the suit and the denomination) 6 percent of the time (compared with the less than 2% that would be expected by chance). The odds against this occurring by chance are a million trillion trillion (10^{30}) to one. Especially remarkable was Delmore's success on "confidence calls," which are those in which he was most confident that he was correct. On these, he was indeed correct 14 out of 20 times.[117]

In free-response experiments for ESP, the distinction between a "hit" and a "miss" is not so cut-and-dried, and statistical evaluations are more complex, involving subjective judgments. These experiments, however, do more nearly approximate the way ESP seems to operate in ordinary life. And it is not impossible to determine that something other than chance is operating, as the following examples show.

During the 1960s, a series of experiments was carried out at the "dream laboratory" at the Maimonides Medical Center in New York. While the subject was sleeping in one room, an agent in another room would seek to convey images from randomly selected pictures. Electrodes were attached to monitor the brain waves and eye movements of the subject. When the recordings indicated that the subject had begun to dream, a buzzer would tell the agent that it was time to begin "sending." After the subject had been dreaming for several minutes, he or she would be awakened and asked for a description of the dream, which would be tape-recorded and then transcribed. Outside judges, who did not know which of the several possible pictures was actually chosen, would then rank the transcript against the possible targets.

One successful subject was William Erwin, a Manhattan psychoanalyst. The target picture for one session was *Zapatistas*, a painting by Carlos Orozco Romero depicting Emiliano Zapata's Mexican-Indian followers, who traced their ancestry to the Mayans and Aztecs. The painting shows armed marching men and horseman on the move, with dark mountains and ominous clouds in the background. In his description of his dream, Erwin said:

A storm. Rainstorm. It reminds me of traveling—a trip—traveling one time in Oklahoma, approaching a rainstorm, thundercloud. . . . I got a feeling of memory, now, of New Mexico, when I lived there. There are a lot of mountains around New Mexico, Indians, Pueblos. . . .

The next morning, when Erwin was asked to mention anything more about his dreams that came to mind, his description of the dream in question included the following comment:

Here it gets into this epic type of thing . . . a DeMille super-type colossal production. I would carry along with it such ideas as the Pueblo going down to the Mayan-Aztec type of civilization.[118]

On another night, the target picture was Max Beckmann's *The Descent from the Cross*, which depicts Jesus being taken down from the cross by two men while two women are kneeling and other figures are looking on. The next morning, in describing a theme common to two dreams, one involving a speech by Winston Churchill and the other a native ceremony, Erwin said:

In the Churchill thing there was a ceremonial thing going on, and in the native dream there was a type of ceremony going on . . . leading to whatever the ceremonial would be to sacrificing two victims. . . . It believed in the god-authority . . . no god was speaking. It was the use of the fear of this, or the awe of god idea, that was to bring about the control. Not that (the) god spoke. . . .[119]

This is a rather remarkable "hit," especially if we take "Churchill" as a "primary process" word-play connecting Golgotha, the hill where Jesus is said to have been crucified, and the later history and dogma of the church. In any case, Erwin was the subject of 16 sessions, 14 of which were scored as hits.[120]

Another type of free-response experiment is called "remote viewing" (which some prefer to the older term "clairvoyance"). Remote-viewing experiments were first carried out in the 1970s at the Stanford Research Institute by two physicists, Hal Puthoff and Russell Targ. One of their first subjects was Patrick Price, who had formerly been the police commissioner in Burbank, California. (Having thought that his psychic abilities had helped in his police work, Price volunteered his services after hearing about the SRI research.) Normally, Puthoff would receive from the division director a sealed envelope, which had been chosen randomly from a pool of 100. After leaving the SRI premises, he would open the envelope and drive to the location described therein, where he would then spend fifteen minutes observing what was there. Back at SRI, Price would be in an electrically shielded room with Targ, who did not know the target location. At the preassigned time, Price would try to describe the location. On one day, the division director, having been surprised at the positive results that had been reported, himself drove Puthoff to a location that he had not chosen in advance but reached simply by driving as he felt. At this location, which turned out to be the Redwood City Marina, Puthoff looked at the scene for fifteen minutes, gazing both at the sailboats and at the marina's restaurant, the stepped roof of which gives it an Oriental appearance. Back at SRI, Price said:

> What I'm looking at is a little boat jetty or dock, along the bay. . . . Yeah, I see little boats, some motor launches, some little sailing ships, sails all furled, some with the masts stepped and others are up. Little jetty or little dock there. . . . Funny thing—this flashed in—kinda looks like a Chinese or Japanese pagoda effect. It's a definite feeling of Oriental architecture that seems to be fairly adjacent to where they are.[121]

Not all of Price's descriptions were such clear hits. But in a total of nine trials, independent judges, who compared the nine transcripts with the nine target pictures, ranked seven of the nine transcripts first at the correct site. Although a failure to randomize the transcripts before giving them to the judges in the first series of experiments allowed for a non-ESP explanation, the results remained about the same when this problem was eliminated, and Targ and Puthoff have published additional successful studies after correcting this problem.[122]

Other experimenters, furthermore, have been able to replicate the results. In one test the subject was Marilyn Schlitz, an anthropologist turned parapsychologist. She was in Michigan, while German parapsychologist Elmar Gruber was in Rome. He went to a randomly selected place out of forty possible target sites (which were unknown to Schlitz). One day the place was a hill beside Rome International Airport, from which he could see the terminal and the planes taking off. The hill had many holes, which had been dug by people looking for Roman coins. Schlitz, back in Michigan, wrote:

> Flight path? Red lights. Strong depth of field . . . A hole in the ground, a candle-shaped thing . . . Outdoors. See sky dark. Windy and cold. Something shooting upward . . . The impressions that I had were of outdoors and Elmar was at some type of—I don't know if institution is the right word—but some place. Not a private home or anything like that— something—a public facility. He was standing away from the main structure, although he could see it. . . . I want to say an airport but that just seems too specific. There was activity and people but no one real close to Elmar.[123]

This was one of 10 trials. According to the five judges who compared Schlitz's transcripts with the target sites, 6 of the 10 trials were direct hits, compared with the 2½ that would be expected by chance. The odds are less than one in 200,000 that this result would occur by chance.[124]

Ganzfeld Experiments

Although these results are impressive, the experiments that have done the most to change attitudes of scientists outside the parapsychological community are the *ganzfeld* (meaning "whole field") experiments. They are based on the idea (which my own Whiteheadian perspective supports) that extrasensory perceptions, while perhaps occurring regularly, seldom make it into conscious awareness because, being rather weak compared with sensory perceptions, they are usually overwhelmed by the latter. In the ganzfeld experiments, various means are used to minimize sensory input: Halved Ping-Pong balls are placed over the eyes; white noise is played through headphones; and subjects lie down or sit in a comfortable reclining chair. A soothing voice may lead the subject into relaxation exercises.[125] After the subject is in a relaxed state, a sender in another room concentrates on a picture, which had been selected randomly by means of a computer program. (The program first selects a set of four pictures out of thirty-six sets, then selects one of the four pictures.)

In one experiment, the target picture was a *National Geographic* photo, in which a pickup truck is traveling down a curving country road. (The other three pictures were of a Chinese nobleman, flowers, and rows of automobiles snowbound in a parking lot.) The subject said:

> I kept picking up something about horses. . . . There was a road . . . a hard-packed pebble road. . . . And, there was a very fleeting image of being inside of a car and I could see just the rearview mirror. . . . A feeling of going very rapidly, everything was like if you are in a car or train and you are going very fast . . . Also, at one point, the feeling of being out in the country and wide open spaces. . . . I had the feeling of driving out in the country.

At the end of a session, a duplicate set of pictures is taken to the subject, who is to say which of the four pictures was being sent. (A duplicate set is used to ensure that no sensory cues, such as fingerprints from the sender, could contaminate the results.) In this particular experiment, the subject had no doubt as to which of the four was the target picture, saying, "That's it—that's what I've been seeing."[126]

In other cases, the subject is not so sure, or chooses the wrong picture. The results with many subjects, however, have been statistically quite significant. Charles Honorton, the leading pioneer of these studies, calculated in 1978 that 23 of 42, or 55 percent, of the experiments had statistically significant results, whereas only 5 percent would be anticipated by chance.[127] Subsequent discussion with critics led this figure to be reduced to 45 percent, which is still highly significant. When attention was limited to the twenty-eight studies that used the "direct hit" method of scoring (in which the target picture was rated first), the success rate was 43 percent. The odds against this occurring by chance are over a billion to one.[128]

Meta-Analysis

The debate about the ganzfeld results led to the use in parapsychology of "meta-analysis," which had been employed in various social sciences, with Robert Rosenthal of Harvard being its most well-known proponent. Meta-analysis couples certain statistical procedures with rules for combining studies carried out with somewhat different procedures. It thereby allows results from a much larger pool of experiments to be quantified. One aspect of meta-analysis involves coding each set of experiments in terms of quality, so that the likelihood that positive results were due to fraud, incompetence, or statistical flukes can be rated. Meta-analysis also deals with the "file-drawer problem," by calculating how many unreported, nonsignificant studies would have to exist in order to bring the positive results of the reported studies down below the level of statistical significance.

The results have proved convincing to many. After Honorton had applied meta-analysis to the ganzfeld studies in a debate with CSICOP member Ray Hyman, British mathematician Christopher Scott, another well-known critic of parapsychology, called Honorton's reasoning "the most convincing argument for the existence of ESP that I have yet encountered."[129] Robert Rosenthal, after analyzing the twenty-eight direct hit studies, estimated that, whereas by chance a subject would select the correct picture 25 percent of the time, subjects in the ganzfeld experiments were likely to do so 33 percent of the time. While recognizing that "more nearly perfect studies" might allow for a more accurate judgment, Rosenthal (who had previously taken no public position on parapsychology) said that it would be "implausible" to conclude either that still more data were needed or that the results should be attributed to chance.[130]

Rosenthal, incidentally, would not be likely to attribute the results to fraud or incompetence: In a report he coauthored for a committee of the National Research Council (of the National Academy of Sciences) on a U.S. Army-funded study of techniques said to enhance human abilities beyond normal ranges, parapsychology was rated more highly with regard to "research quality" than all the other areas. The ganzfeld research in particular was given a rating of 19 (out of 25), while the nonparapsychological areas received ratings ranging from 3 to 13.[131] (Given these positive comments, Rosenthal was—outrageously but predictably—asked to withdraw the parapsychology section of his report by the chairman of the committee, John Swets. [Swets had refused to put any parapsychologists on the parapsychology subcommittee, choosing instead as the chair Ray Hyman, who could hardly be considered a neutral judge.* Another member of CSICOP, James Alcock, who has publicly declared that science is necessarily materialistic so that parapsychology could not possibly be scientific,[132] was chosen as the "outside expert" on parapsychology.] Although Rosenthal refused to withdraw his report, the parapsychology section of the final document, *Enhancing Human Performance*, makes no reference to Rosenthal's report, citing instead the "conclusions" of the CSICOP members.[133])

One of the most important turnabouts in the scientific community brought about by the ganzfeld experiments, especially in the light of the meta-analysis, is that the authors of the standard *Introduction to Psychology*, long known as "Hilgard and Atkinson," included a section on "Psi Phenomena" for the first time in the 1990 edition, crediting their change of mind to "the recent work on telepathy using the Ganzfeld procedure."[†]

Yet a further result of the 1986 debate between Honorton and Hyman was "A Joint Communique," in which the two authors agreed on a set of methodological standards for future research. In 1989 Honorton and his colleagues presented 11 new ganzfeld studies that conformed to these standards, 10 of which had positive results. The overall success rate for direct hits in these "more nearly perfect" studies, which Rosenthal had anticipated, was 34 percent—which is virtually (only one percent higher than) what Rosenthal had calculated from the earlier studies. The odds against this result being due to chance are more than 20,000 to one. When combined with the results of the previous 28 studies using the direct-hit method, the odds against chance are over 10 trillion to one. Richard Broughton concludes that although not everyone can do it, *"in the hands of a competent experimenter* the ganzfeld-ESP *is* a repeatable experiment."[134]

One interesting aspect of this repeatability is Honorton's three-factor analysis of persons likely to do well with the ganzfeld in their first try. These are

---

* Hyman had written that parapsychology should be considered a "pathological science" ("Pathological Science," in R. A. McConnell, ed., *Encounters with Parapsychology* [R. A. McConnell, 1982], 156–64). At first, Hyman makes pathological science inclusive not only of "bizarre claims" made by scientists (such as the claim of "scientific evidence for the ability of certain individuals to project thoughts upon camera film") but also of irrational responses by other scientists to these claims (157, 161). By the end of the article, however, pathological science is equated only with the "bizarre claims," which are referred to as the "failures" and "follies" of otherwise accomplished scientists (161, 163). (This article has been reprinted, with critical responses, in Ray Hyman, *The Elusive Quarry: A Scientific Appraisal of Psychical Research* [Buffalo: Prometheus Books, 1989], 243–51.)

† Rita Atkinson, Richard C. Atkinson, Edward E. Smith, and Daryl J. Bem, *Introduction to Psychology* 10th ed. (San Diego and New York: Harcourt Brace Jovanovich, 1990), vi. Illustrating the data-led or empirical attitude, these authors criticize those who reject psi phenomena on the grounds of impossibility, saying that "such a priori judgments are out of place in science; the real question is whether the empirical evidence is acceptable by scientific standards" (235).

persons who (1) believe that they have had psychic experiences, (2) have practiced some form of mental discipline, and (3) come out as Feeling and Perceiving types on the Myers-Briggs Type Indicator (which is based on Jung's personality theory). The twenty-eight subjects with this profile were found by Honorton to have a success rate of 64 percent (in comparison with the 25 percent that would be expected by chance).[135] In an attempt to duplicate this result, the Institute for Parapsychology in Durham found that those first-time ganzfeld subjects who fit the three-factor model had a success rate of 43 percent, which, while not as astounding as the earlier results, is still far above the normal success rate.[136]

We can conclude, then, that telepathy and clairvoyance, which have been reported throughout history and were verified by tests with mediums and other people in the early days of psychical research, have now been verified in strictly controlled experiments in laboratories. The extrasensory perception revealed by these laboratory experiments is generally much weaker than that which sometimes occurs spontaneously and in trance-conditions. But by verifying that even a minimal degree of extrasensory perception can and does occur under such conditions and therefore is not impossible, this laboratory work lends credibility to the reports of the more robust occurrences.

It might be expected, incidentally, that this section on extrasensory perception should also deal with precognition, not simply telepathy and clairvoyance. True precognition, however *is* impossible (in my opinion and in the opinion of many others, including several parapsychologists). The phenomena that are often called "precognitive" can all, furthermore, be accounted for in terms of clairvoyance, telepathy, and/or psychokinesis. I will give the reasons for considering true precognition (and therefore retrocausation) impossible,* along with some alternative interpretations of the phenomena, at the end of this chapter, after dealing with psychokinesis.

Experimental Evidence for Psychokinesis

With regard to ESP, as we have seen, there were various types of experiments prior to the laboratory tests instituted by Rhine at Duke. The history of research on psychokinesis is similar. After many decades of study of spontaneous and mediumistic physical phenomena, experimental parapsychologists wanted PK experiments that, like the card-guessing experiments, could be statistically analyzed as well as rigorously controlled. The type of test first instituted at Duke involved the attempt to affect falling dice. These tests never resulted in the very high scores that were occasionally forthcoming in the ESP tests, and

---

*This claim is not, incidentally, an example of the kind of a priori judgment criticized in the previous footnote. The reason that that kind of judgment was said to be out of place in science is that it involves an a priori rejection of the phenomena. The judgment here about precognition involves a rejection not of phenomena but only of a prevalent *interpretation* of them.

the overall positive effect, while evident, was very weak. It was possible, therefore, for critics to dismiss the results as due to inaccurate recording, defects in experimental design, or as statistical flukes.

More recently, however, meta-analysis has been applied to these old experiments. In an essay on "Effects of Consciousness on the Fall of Dice: A Meta-analysis," Dean Radin and Diane Ferrari examine 148 studies in which subjects were trying psychokinetically to cause a certain die face to come up. These studies involved over 2,500 subjects and over 2.5 million dice throws. Radin and Ferrari found that, whereas 5 percent of the studies should be significant by chance, in fact 44 percent were significant. (A set of 31 control studies had nonsignificant results.) The odds against this result occurring by chance are calculated to be about 10^{70} to one. Even after coding each study with regard to various criteria related to methodological quality, the effect size was still extremely significant.[137] For the results to be discounted because of the "file-drawer problem," the ratio of unreported to reported studies would have to be 121 to 1, far beyond the 5-to-1 ratio that Rosenthal considers safe.[138]

A more recent type of PK experiment involves the attempt to influence microelectronic systems. In the early experiments in the 1970s by Helmut Schmidt (who was briefly discussed at the end of the first section of this chapter), for example, a binary random event generator (REG) based on the emission of electrons from radioactive strontium-90 was used. A ring of lights attached to the machine indicated in which of the two possible positions the arrival of an electron had stopped the oscillator: One of the positions would move the light clockwise, the other, counterclockwise. By chance there would be roughly equal numbers of steps in each direction. The subject's task was to try to make the light move more in one direction than the other. Some individuals were able to shift the probabilities from 50 percent to between 51 and 52 percent, and a few have shifted them to over 54 percent.[139] Since its rise in the 1970s, experiments using REGs have been central to PK research, and this for a number of reasons:

> These machines eliminate target bias, recording errors, and opportunities for fraud by a subject. They readily provide control runs; in fact, these are routinely produced for randomicity checks. In some experiments the REG is coupled to a computer that runs the experiment and processes the data. If the experimental procedure is properly designed, it leaves little to criticize.[140]

The other reason for the popularity of these tests is, as already mentioned, that they have rather consistently produced significant results.

The fact that these positive results have been so consistently significant has led to criticism even though, as the quotation above says, there was "little to criticize." One charge is that the results are not in general repeatable, and that repeatable results have been reported only by a few experimenters, which suggests fraud or incompetence. (These vague charges were all made in the influential report of the National Research Council, *Enhancing Human Performance*, mentioned earlier.[141]) These charges were directly refuted by a meta-analysis of PK studies involving microelectronic systems, which was published in 1989 in *Foundations of Physics*. This article, "Evidence for Consciousness-Related Anomalies in Random Physical Systems," by Dean Radin and Roger Nelson, analyzed 152 reports that described 597 experimental studies (and 235 control studies) carried out by 68 investigators. By Radin and Nelson's calculations, there is about one chance in 10^{35} that the positive effects arose by chance.[142]

Radin and Nelson's meta-analysis involved an assessment of the factors involved in the standard criticisms. One such criticism has always been that positive results disappear to the extent that experiments are carefully performed. Doing a "quality analysis" in terms of the four factors usually mentioned in criticisms—procedures, statistics, integrity of data, and the REG device—Radin and Nelson found that there was no relationship between the quality of the study and the likelihood of evidence for PK. With regard to the charge that the positive effects were due to only a few researchers, they found that eliminating the 17 percent of the studies with the most extreme results made little difference. With regard to the file-drawer problem, they found that there would have to be 90 unreported unsuccessful studies to every known study to reduce the results to nonsignificance. "Radin and Nelson's meta-analysis demonstrates," concludes Richard Broughton, "that the micro-PK results are *robust* and *repeatable*."[143]

Macro-Pk and Bio-PK

While this new work, and reevaluation of old work, on micro-PK has been proceeding, some parapsychologists have turned back to macro-PK, meaning directly observable psychokinesis. I have already described the experiments with Daniel Home, Nina Kulagina, Ted Serios, and the Miami poltergeist. Having given so many examples of macro-PK already, I will here describe some studies that are somewhere in between the PK that is directly observable and that which can only be detected statistically.

One such kind of experiment involves "bio-PK," or psychokinesis on living systems. Bernard Grad, a psychologist at McGill University in Montreal, carried out some experiments of this type with Oskar Estebany, a healer. In one experiment, mice were put on a diet that induced enlarged thyroid glands. They were then divided into three groups. Estebany would hold the cages of the experimental group in his hands, seeking to induce healing. The cages of one control group were heated to simulate the heating effect of Estebany's hands, while nothing was done for the other control group. There was no difference in the growth rate of the thyroid glands in the two control groups, but the growth rate in the mice treated by Estebany was significantly slower.[144]

In a second test, Grad had a small (1.9 square centimeters) oval patch of skin removed from the backs of 300 mice (who had been anesthetized for the operation). The mice were then randomly placed into three groups. Estebany sought to accelerate the healing of one group, putting his hands around the cages for fifteen minutes twice a day. For the second group of mice, medical students carried out the same activity, while the cages of the mice in the third group were simply placed on a table for fifteen minutes twice daily. After fifteen days, when measurements were made, there was no difference between the mice in the two control groups, but the wounds of Estebany's mice were significantly smaller.[145]

Grad also tested Estebany's ability to make water healthier for plants. Estebany would "treat" bottles of saline solution by holding them between his hands. Then two sets of barley seedlings were watered, one with the treated solution, the other with untreated. (Those doing the watering did not know which was which.) The barley seeds watered with the treated solution grew significantly faster. Several later experiments confirmed this effect.[146] One reason that Grad prefers carrying out the "healing" experiments on animals, plants, and even nonliving things is that a common view, that the results are due to hypnosis or some other form of suggestion, is thereby effectively ruled out.[147]

PK Experiments in China

A related finding by Grad, that Estebany's treatment of the saline solutions changed their absorption spectrum for infrared radiation, connects his research with some that has been reported in China. Lu Zuyin, who was previously in the chemistry and biology department at Qinghua University but in 1990 moved to the Institute of High-Energy Physics in Beijing, has carried out a series of experiments with Yan Xin, a well-known qigong master and healer. Yan Xin's task was to try to produce effects in various biological and chemical preparations at a distance, usually from seven to ten kilometers. Here is Broughton's summary of the results:

> Using a U.S.-made Laser Raman Spectrometer, Lu's team observed dramatic shifts in the spectral characteristics of ordinary tap water. A huge peak in the spectrograph appeared at 1970 cm^{-1} wavelength immediately after treatment. . . . Physiological saline (0.9%) normally shows a characteristic peak at 246 cm^{-1}, but shortly after treatment this peak disappeared or was shifted to 237 cm^{-1}. . . . Yan's treatment of a 50% glucose solution produced an elimination of one normally occurring peak and the intensification of others. All the experiments have been repeated several times. The researchers interpret these findings as signs that the mol-

ecular structure of the solutions is being temporarily altered. . . . Using similar methods, Lu's team have reported that Yan . . . can produce certain chemical reactions under conditions in which they should not occur, as well as alter the ultraviolet-absorption characteristics of DNA and RNA preparations.[148]

Some other PK experiments in China involve Zhang Baosheng, a man in his late thirties who has been studied by scientists in Beijing since 1982. Unfortunately, however, western parapsychologists have not been allowed to study him, and since 1984 he has not even been accessible to Chinese scientists outside the military-controlled Institute of Space-Medico Engineering in Beijing. The reports we do have, however, suggest that he may well be another contemporary "white crow of the second kind."

One of Zhang's feats evidently involves moving small objects in and out of sealed containers. Lin Shuhuang of the physics department of Beijing Teachers' College, who headed a group of nineteen scientists who studied Zhang for six months in 1983, described experiments in which small pieces of chemically treated paper were placed in an irreversibly sealed test tube. After five minutes, during which experimenters were watching Zhang from various angles, the pieces of paper were lying outside the tube, although its seal was undamaged. In a second experiment Zhang reportedly did the same thing with a live insect. In 1987, the team studying Zhang at the Institute of Space-Medico Engineering finally made public some of their work with him in the form of a film (for which they received that year's Scientific Research Achievement Prize from the spaceflight department). According to reports, the film shows a medicine pill moving through an irreversibly sealed glass vial, with this movement occurring in three frames of the 400-frame-per-second film. (This rapid movement would explain why for observers the objects seem not to move through the glass but instead to be inside one moment and outside the next.) In 1990 the *Chinese Journal of Somatic Science* contained a report of new experiments with Zhang, complete with photos (perhaps from the film) showing a pill exiting from the bottom of a bottle being held by Zhang.[149]

Conclusion with Regard to ESP and PK

The evidence for ESP and for PK—and I have presented only brief summaries of a few examples of it—seems to be adequate. Serious attention to the evidence should be convincing to all except those who are irreversibly committed to the worldview of materialism and sensationism, according to which ESP and PK are impossible in principle. I have, however, given reasons in the previous chapter, other than ESP and PK themselves, for being skeptical of the truth of this worldview. I will give further reasons for this skepticism in the following chapter. Before concluding the present chapter, however, I need to address the type of paranormality that I have put off until now, apparent precognition.

Apparent Precognition

I add the qualifier "apparent" because, as mentioned earlier, I hold, with many others, that literal precognition is impossible. Literal precognition would mean that a person *knew*, in the full sense of that term, an event prior to its occurrence, in the same way in which one can know a past event. Because knowledge of events is based on perception, literal precognition would mean that the person had perceived the event prior to its occurrence. Those who accept the idea of literal precognition, in fact, usually classify it as a form of extrasensory perception. On this basis, J. B. Rhine argued that, just as telepathy and clairvoyance show ESP to transcend the limits of space, precognition shows that it transcends the limits of time as well. Rhine realized that, because perception and causation are two sides of the same relationship, to speak of perceiving a future event means saying that the future event has caused the present perception, which involves "a reversal of the principle of causation, getting the cart before the horse, the effect before the cause." This idea of a reversal in the causal order, so that causation goes "backward in time," has come to be known as "retrocausation." Such a reversal, Rhine admitted, seems impossible:

> It is hard to understand how the act of perception, which is the result, could occur before its cause. . . . If there were ever an occasion in science on which it would be proper to use the word impossible, it would be when the hypothesis of prophecy is advanced.[150]

However, Rhine immediately added, "'science knows no impossibles' and theory must conform to evidence." Accordingly, arguing that ESP of future events has been demonstrated experimentally, he concluded that we had to revise our worldview so as to allow literal perception of future events.

Rhine was mistaken, however, to say that scientists should not exclude anything as impossible a priori. He was certainly right to say that no one, be they scientists or philosophers, should ignore evidence for extrasensory perception and psychokinesis on the grounds that they are impossible, because, prior to examining the evidence, we have no good reasons for considering them impossible. The case is different, however, with regard to the idea of precognition, as the reasons for considering it impossible are different in kind from the kinds of reasons often given for considering ESP and PK impossible.

This distinction has been stated clearly by philosopher Antony Flew, who rejects all of these alleged phenomena. While considering ESP and PK "just plumb impossible,"[151] he points out that this is a judgment of *contingent* impossibility.[152] Such judgments are generalizations based on experience and can, accordingly, be revised on the basis of further experience. The reason for considering PK contingently impossible, for example, is the following general principle (as formulated by C. D. Broad): "It is impossible for an event in a person's mind to produce directly any change in the material world except certain changes in his own brain."[153] If there is good evidence that minds sometimes produce changes in the outer world directly, without employing the brain, then we could revise the general principle. Flew would agree that such a change could intelligibly be made. With regard to literal precognition, however, the problem is "an altogether different kind, and totally decisive."[154] This problem is that the notion of precognition involves a self-contradiction and is therefore a *logical* impossibility.[155]

> Because causes necessarily and always bring about their effects, it must be irredeemably self-contradictory to suggest that the (later) fulfillments might cause the (earlier) anticipations. By the time the fulfillments are occurring the anticipations already have occurred. It would, therefore, be futile to labor either to bring about or to undo what is already unalterably past and done.[156]

On this philosophical point, Flew is right and Rhine was wrong: No amount of empirical evidence can turn nonsense into sense. No data can count as evidence for the self-contradictory. This conclusion does not mean that we are to reject the data. It means only that we need to find some self-consistent way or ways to take account of the data.

Before turning to this issue, however, we should note that there are other reasons to reject the notion of retrocausation, besides the fact that it is self-contradictory. Another reason for considering the notion incoherent has been given by Stephen Braude:[157] Although the term "retrocausation" suggests a type of causation that is the mirror image of ordinary efficient causation except for going in the opposite direction, it is not in fact portrayed in this way. That is, in ordinary causation, every effect itself becomes a cause with effects spreading out into the indefinite future. The presumed effects of the imagined retrocausation, however, are not themselves portrayed as having effects extending into the indefinite past. So, even if retrocausation were not logically impossible, it would not be just like ordinary causation except for going backwards. We have at least two reasons, accordingly, for considering retrocausation, and thereby (true) precognition, to be incoherent.

Still another reason for rejecting literal precognition is that it contradicts our presupposition about freedom. That is, besides presupposing that the past is settled (as Flew pointed out), we also presuppose that the future is not yet fully settled, so that what actually occurs will be finally settled in part by our decisions. The idea of literal precognition, however, means that one now *knows* what is going to occur in the future. If this is true knowledge, it cannot be wrong, which means that what is going to occur is now already fully settled. This conclusion is reinforced by the idea that precognition involves a present *perception* of a future event: For such a perception to be possible, the "future" event would necessarily already exist *now*. If what seem to be future events already exist in the present, then both time and freedom are illusory. Freedom, however, belongs to that very special class of notions which, in the next chapter, I call "hard-core commonsense notions." These are notions that we all inevitably presuppose in practice, which means that we cannot reject them in theory while remaining self-consistent. Accordingly, far from being a negotiable item to be adjusted in the name of science, freedom is one of the criteria to which any theory, whether called philosophical, theological, or scientific, must conform to be intelligible. Rhine himself, incidentally, recognized the incompatibility of precognition with freedom. He thought, however, that the incompatibility would obtain only if "precognition ever is or could be 100 per cent accurate."[158] But the conceptual problem would exist whether or not we could *know* the future with perfect accuracy. The conceptual problem would exist if we assumed "future events" already to exist, so that they would be knowable in principle, even if they were not knowable in fact. In any case, the fact that literal precognition contradicts one of our inescapable presuppositions provides an additional reason for rejecting it.

To be sure, given the fact that the belief in precognition has been based on real evidence, both spontaneous and experimental, we would face a real dilemma if this evidence were interpretable only as true precognition. We would be forced to choose between dogmatically denying the evidence or accepting a radically incoherent theory. That, fortunately, is not the case, because there are numerous alternative explanations for those experiences that have led people to the idea of precognition. I have, in fact, elsewhere discussed 13 alternative explanations,[159] all of which are "real time" explanations, meaning that they involve the kind of causal relationships we presuppose in general: from the past to the present and from the present to the future. I will here discuss only the four most important of these alternative explanations.

Quite often, when people speak casually of precognition, or knowing the future, they mean only knowledge of the *probable* future—especially of what will probably occur unless remedial action is taken. This is usually, for example, the message of "fortune tellers": that such and such will happen unless you do something to avert it. In so-called precognition of this sort, there is no claim to knowledge of the *actual* future, as if the foreseen event were absolutely predetermined by the present configuration of events or were already actual in some eternal, tenseless realm. If that were the case, it would be impossible to take any action to avert it. The claim is only about certain probabilities built into the current state of the world, given its various trajectories. The "cognition," in other words, is really about present probabilities, not about the actual future as such. Thus understood, so-called precognition does not imply the unreality of time, or the reality of reverse causation.

In many cases that are usually classed as instances of precognition, the best explanation is really in terms of clairvoyance of present conditions combined with an unconscious inference and perhaps dramatization. For example, a person may learn unconsciously, through clairvoyance, that a mountain near a school is structurally unsound, so that a landslide is imminent. The person may then bring this knowledge to consciousness by means of a dream, in which the school building is crushed by a landslide and many children and teachers are killed. When the event then occurs as seen in the dream, the person may speak of precognition, as if somehow the tragic event had caused the dream. One could then either speak of "retrocausation," as if the future event had exerted causation back on the earlier experience, or of some kind of timeless connection. But that is not the only, or even the best, explanation. (For one thing, the landslide might have come on a Sunday, when no one was in the school building. Or the person might have told officials about the dream, and those officials, taking it as a true warning, might have closed the school, in which case the part of the dream about the landslide would have "come true," but not the part about the deaths of the students and teachers.) We can simply say that the mountain, a few days prior to the landslide, evoked a clairvoyant prehension of it by the person. The causal process, in other words, worked as it normally does in perception. The perception, to be sure, was *para*normal in one sense, in that sensory perception was not involved. But the cause (the change in the mountain making a landslide imminent), as always, was prior to the effect (the perception that resulted in the dream). This kind of explanation can, of course, be generalized to all sorts of so-called precognitive visions of events, such as ships sinking, airplanes crashing, and buildings collapsing.

A third alternative explanation, applicable to some cases that are often classified as precognition, involves the same dynamics, except that the paranormal perception involved is telepathy rather than clairvoyance. For example, a woman may have a dream that her brother, who is incommunicado continents away, commits suicide. She learns later that, a week after she had her dream, he indeed did commit suicide. She might then believe that the act of suicide was what caused her dream. A real-time explanation, however, is ready to hand: He was planning, consciously or at least unconsciously, to commit suicide for some time before the actual event, and she telepathically learned of this intention a week before he acted upon it. No violation of the normal order of causal influence, from the present to the future, need be supposed. This kind of explanation, based on telepathic knowledge of other people's intentions, conscious or unconscious, can be used to explain a wide range of apparently precognitive experiences.

A fourth explanation, which is based on psychokinesis, has probably been the most discussed of the alternative explanations.[160] (It should be recalled that I use "psychokinesis" broadly, to include all paranormal influence exerted by the psyche, whether it be on inanimate matter, biological systems, or other minds.) For example, a man who now lives in Santa Barbara may dream of seeing a French female friend, with whom he had lost contact after leaving Paris several years earlier, at the Palace Cafe, where he often eats lunch. The next week, while eating lunch at the Palace Cafe, he, to his great surprise, sees her. The explanation could well be something like the following: His dream was evoked in part by his learning unconsciously, through telepathy, of her decision to come to the United States for a vacation and to include Santa Barbara in her itinerary. But then her decision to have lunch at the Palace Cafe, which she had not heard of prior to her arrival in Santa Barbara, was causally influenced by his dream that she would be there. That is, out of a list of restaurants provided to her by her travel guide, she chose the Palace Cafe because of his dream's psychokinetic influence on her. In other words, when a dream is followed by an event that closely resembles the dream, we need not assume that the event caused the dream. It is more natural, given the direction causal influence otherwise works, to assume that the dream caused the event. Such an explanation, at least for some apparent instances of precognition, is more plausible to the extent that one is aware of the following: the power of unconscious images and intentions (including those in dreams) to bring about extraordinary psychokinetic effects (such as in poltergeist cases); the power of suggestion under hypnosis and in posthypnotic conditions to cause people to do things they otherwise would not; and the capacity to induce hypnotic states at a distance psychokinetically.

Many people find this psychokinetic interpretation objectionable. This is, to some extent, understandable: It *does* suggest that we may be more responsible for some events than we would like to think, and it suggests that other people, quite removed physically from us, may have more power over our fates, for good and for ill, than we would like to think. Also, if this psychokinetic explanation is proffered as the *only* alternative to true precognition, it suggests a degree of psychokinetic power in a considerable percentage of the population (the power, for example, to produce airplane crashes and landslides) that is both frightening and incredible. However, with regard to the first objection: The fact that this explanation implies that we may be more responsible for some events than we might like to think and that, contrariwise, other people may be more responsible for some of "our" decisions than we might like to think is no argument against the truth of this view. Here no more than in general should we allow wishful-and-fearful thinking to control (even if it inevitably influences) our view as to what is really the case. With regard to the second objection: There is no need, as I have indicated, to assume that, if this explanation is applied to some cases, it must be applied to all. It is, in my own list, merely one of thirteen of the real-time explanations. I myself assume that the explanation in terms of clairvoyance (or occasionally telepathy) is generally the correct one in cases involving large-scale physical events.

All of my examples, incidentally, are of spontaneous events that might be interpreted as precognition. Much of the discussion among parapsychologists about precognition and retrocausation, of course, is related to experiments. Can the experimental data that are sometimes adduced as evidence for the reality of precognition and retrocausation be handled by one or more of these real-time explanations? In "Assessing Experimental Support for True Precognition," Robert Morris, an experimental parapsychologist, has said "alternative, on-line [real-time] interpretations do exist for all studies that offer evidence for retroactive influence."[161]

I have here given only four of my alternative interpretations. With regard to the others, some of them, such as those based on subliminal sensory perception and mere coincidence, are quite prosaic. Others are quite fanciful, such as the idea that a discarnate spirit, having learned of a person's dream telepathically, then brings about its fulfillment. But, however fanciful some of the real-time explanations might be, they are at least possible, whereas true precognition is not. So, if it were ever necessary to resort to them (which it probably is not), this would be preferable to speaking nonsense. This point is of utmost importance: If the parapsychological community would agree to cease speaking of (true) precognition, it would remove the one justified basis for the criticism that its alleged phenomena are impossible.*

In the next chapter, I begin the discussion of the third major concern of parapsychology, life after death. As with extrasensory perception and psychokinesis, however, I begin not with a discussion of the empirical evidence but with a philosophical discussion of possibility.

---

* I should add that the difficulties involved in the idea of precognition do not apply to *retrocognition*, which is direct, noninferential knowledge of the more or less remote past other than one's own personal past. Sometimes retrocognition is said to be just as problematic as precognition on the grounds that, just as the future does not yet exist, the past *no longer* exists. In Whiteheadian process philosophy, however, past actual occasions are as fully actual as present ones, and the remote past exists as objectively as does the immediate past (even if its causal efficacy is, at least usually, far less insistent). And, if the idea of the past existing in itself, as past, is considered problematic, process philosophy also portrays the past as existing in the divine awareness. There is no difficulty, then, in the idea of retrocognition—which, under the name "retroprehensive inclusion," will play a central role in Chapters 4–8. The term "retroprehension," incidentally, is in one sense redundant, because *all* prehensions are of the past: there can be no prehensions of future occasions or even of those that are strictly contemporary with the prehending occasion. The term is used here, however, to signify a direct prehension of occasions of experience belonging to the life of another person.

3

THE MIND-BODY RELATION
AND THE POSSIBILITY
OF LIFE AFTER DEATH

1. INTRODUCTION: DIFFICULTIES AND APPROACH

The question of life after death is one about which most people care deeply.
It evokes very passionate feelings, both of attraction and of repulsion. Some
people are convinced that life after death is both desirable and actual. Others
are equally convinced that it is both undesirable and impossible. Still others,
tragically, find it desirable but impossible. It is no cause for surprise, then,
that properly philosophical discussion about life after death—about its possibility and the evidence for it—is even more difficult than is such discussion
in relation to extrasensory perception and psychokinesis. In fact, they are
often regarded, by both opponents and proponents, as important mainly in
relation to their implications for the power of the mind or soul to survive
bodily death. This was certainly true of the founders of the Society for
Psychical Research, most of whose activities bore more or less directly on
this question. For example, the major work of Frederick Myers, one of the
most influential of these founders, is titled *Human Personality and Its
Survival of Bodily Death.*[1] On the other side, much of the animosity toward

parapsychology is generated by the suspicion, sometimes but not always justified, that the main purpose of its proponents is to support belief in life after death.

Because of these deep passions on both sides about both the possibility of life after death and the desirability of belief in it, the open-minded consideration of evidence for and against it is especially difficult. A priori judgments based on paradigm-convictions and wishful-and-fearful thinking play an even stronger role, if possible, than they do in relation to extrasensory perception and psychokinesis as such.

For example, paradigmatic minds, if they believe that life after death is not possible, may quickly conclude that there is no good evidence for it. They will perhaps reach this conclusion in a largely a priori way, by simply refusing to look at the evidence, as William James learned when he tried to get some of his Harvard colleagues to observe Mrs. Piper.* Or, if they do deign to look at some of the evidence, they will either explain it away, giving alternative explanations, or simply set it aside as "anomalous." For example, philosopher Kai Nielsen, who espouses an atheistic and materialistic philosophy,[2] says forthrightly that no amount of evidence could change his mind:

> If . . . we think that the concept of disembodied existence makes no sense . . . then we will interpret the data differently. . . . [W]e will say, and reasonably so, even if we do not have a good alternative explanation for it, that [disembodied existence] cannot be the correct description of what went on. . . . We have rather some anomalous phenomena for which we cannot, for a given time, give a proper account. . . . If there are good theoretical arguments for thinking that the concept of an immaterial soul is problematic . . . then some anomalous data . . . should be treated as just that.[3]

---

* In speaking of the prejudices that scientists obey, James wrote: "For instance, I invite eight of my scientific colleagues severally to come to my house at their own time, and sit with a medium for whom the evidence published in our *Proceedings* has been most noteworthy. Although it means at most the waste of the hour for each, five of them decline the adventure. . . . I advise another psychological friend of mine to look into this medium's case, but he replies that it is useless, for if he should get such results as I report, he would (being suggestible) simply believe himself hallucinated. When I propose as a remedy that he should remain in the background and take notes, while his wife has the sitting, he explains that he can never consent to his wife's presence at such performances. This friend of mine writes *ex cathedra* on the subject of psychical research, declaring (I need hardly add) that there is nothing in it; . . . and one of the five colleagues who declined my invitation is widely quoted as an effective critic of our evidence. So runs the world away! I should not indulge in the personality and triviality of such anecdotes, were it not that they paint the temper of our time" (William James, *Essays in Psychical Research* [Cambridge, Mass. and London: Harvard University Press, 1986], 194–95). James went on to predict that that temper would be impossible in future generations. On that point, alas, he was wrong; the temper in intellectual circles is little changed today.

In any case, having concluded that life after death is impossible and that there is no good evidence for it either, paradigmatic minds will then often bring their wishes into line, saying that belief in life after death is generally harmful anyway, so that it is better for people not to believe in it. A necessity is turned into a virtue.

Contrariwise, those paradigmatic minds who think that belief in life after death is both desirable and possible are often less than fully critical about the empirical data. They often conclude all too quickly that the evidence is sufficient, failing to consider the fact that alternative interpretations of the evidence are possible, especially if strong manifestations of extrasensory perception and psychokinesis are allowed.

Wishful-thinking minds, of course, tend to assume that the world is the way it ought to be. Accordingly, if life after death would be a good thing, then it must be true. Insofar as such thinkers develop philosophical systems with which to gauge the possibility of life after death, the argument tends to be circular, because the system was originally constructed, at least in part, precisely to demonstrate this possibility. If wishful-thinkers hold, instead, that belief in life after death is a bad thing, then the philosophical system may be developed, at least in part, to rule out the possibility. Furthermore, be they for or against belief in life after death, wishful-thinkers will tend to be very critical of all data that would contradict their point of view while accepting with considerable naïveté evidence and arguments based thereon that support their point of view.

Those people with what I have called data-led minds are able to consider the evidence more objectively. Accordingly, data-led people who think that belief in life after death is a good thing *could* come to the conclusion that the evidence does not strongly support it. Likewise, data-led minds who find the idea of survival distasteful might well conclude that it is, nevertheless, possibly true. This attitude characterized the philosopher C. D. Broad, who said that, if after death he found himself still conscious, he would be "slightly more annoyed than surprised."[4]

Primarily empirical or data-led minds, however, seem to be few and far between. In most of us, philosophical preconceptions of possibility and/or strong hopes or fears significantly color our response to whatever relevant evidence is available, often determining whether or not we will even study it. For this reason, it is, in relation to most people, futile to begin with a discussion of the evidence. The issues of possibility and desirability need to be treated first. In line with my conviction that, of these two issues, that of philosophical possibility has a certain priority (in that a culture's worldview tends to shape its adherents' view of what is desirable), this chapter on life after death deals only with the issue of its philosophical conceivability, or possibility. (The issue of desirability, which I have treated elsewhere,[5] will be addressed briefly in Chapter 9.)

This issue of the philosophical conceivability of life after death comes down primarily to the mind-body relation: Survival of the personality will be deemed possible only if we hold that what is normally called the "mind," the "soul," or the "self" is related to the physical body in such a way that it could conceivably exist apart from it.

In discussing this issue of possibility, a naturalistic rather than a supernaturalistic framework is here presupposed. If, instead, the existence of a supernatural deity were presupposed, then a discussion of the mind-body relation would not be necessary. One could hold a materialistic view of the human person, according to which the mind could not conceivably exist apart from the physical body, and yet simply say that God, being deterred by nothing but logical impossibility, will give us life after death by recreating our physical bodies. For example, Bruce Reichenbach, without endorsing materialistic monism, says that life after death would be possible even if it were true. It would be possible because

> it is not self-contradictory that an individual could be physically re-created . . . such that he would look identical. . . . And since consciousness is a brain process, his brain could be so re-created and programmed as to have neural and chemical components and structures identical to the deceased, such that he would have the same memories, ideas, perspectives, and personality traits. . . . This is possible . . . because God is omnipotent; that is, he can perform any action which does not entail a self-contradiction.[6]

The acceptance of a naturalistic worldview, by contrast, means that life after death will seem possible only if it seems possible apart from supernatural intervention. Naturalism need not entail that all divine influence is excluded. It entails only that any divine influence must be part of the normal causal processes, not an interruption of them.

The rejection of supernaturalism is not as innocuous as it may at first glance seem, because the stipulation that a framework for affirming life after death must be naturalistic rules out not only materialism but also dualism, which has been the worldview of choice for most believers in life after death. This fact, given the way the options are generally presented, makes life after death seem impossible.

In this chapter, I will review some of the recent discussion regarding the mind-body problem, which has revolved primarily around the relative merits of dualism and materialism. After arguing that neither position is tenable, I will point to an important development within the past few years: the acknowledgment by both dualists and materialists that their own positions are seriously inadequate. I will then present a third alternative, panexperientialism, which avoids the various problems that plague dualism and materialism. The central point of this chapter is that the one position that can do justice to the mind-body relation also allows for life after death within a naturalistic worldview.

2. THE PRIMARY CRITERION FOR ADEQUACY: HARD-CORE COMMON SENSE

One of the reasons why discussion of the mind-body relation has been so inadequate and seemingly interminable is the same reason that most modern philosophy has been inadequate: It has not realized that common sense must be its ultimate criterion of adequacy. The general assumption has been that "common sense," far from being such a criterion, is something that must always give way when it conflicts with the "scientific worldview," that is, the materialistic worldview of late modernity. As John Searle says, "the general form of the mind-body problem has been the problem of accommodating our common sense and prescientific belief about the mind to our general scientific conception of reality."[7] Our commonsense intuitions, in fact, not only are not taken seriously; they are actively derided by some philosophers. As Searle complains, "The fact that the views in question are implausible and counterintuitive does not count against them"; indeed, "it can even seem a great merit . . . that they run dead counter to our intuitions."[8] Searle then brings out the reasoning behind this view:

> For is this not the very feature that makes the physical sciences so dazzling? Our ordinary intuitions about . . . the solidity of the table . . . have been shown to be mere illusions. . . . Could not a great breakthrough in the study of the mind similarly show that our most firmly held beliefs about our mental states are equally illusory? Can we not reasonably expect great discoveries that will overthrow our commonsense assumptions?[9]

Searle is here explicating the position of those "eliminative materialists" who, having realized that conscious states such as beliefs cannot be reduced to physical-chemical descriptions, take the drastic step of simply denying that we really have such states.

How could such an aberration, such a rejection of common sense, have come about? The answer is that "common sense" is a radically ambiguous notion, which can be given two quite different meanings. The distinction between the two meanings is implicit in Searle's complaint that eliminative materialists "claim that giving up the belief that we have beliefs is analogous to giving up the belief in a flat earth or sunsets."[10]

I have coined the distinction between "soft-core common sense" and "hard-core common sense" to emphasize the radical difference between these two meanings.* The term "common sense" is nowadays widely used to refer to ideas that, while commonly accepted at a certain time and place, are not necessarily shared by all human beings in all times and places. Such "common sense" often turns out to be false. Searle's statement alludes, for example, to the fact that it was once (soft-core) common sense that the earth was flat and that the sun moved around the earth. His earlier statement alluded to the fact that it once belonged to (soft-core) common sense that tables were solid. Those who point out that common sense of this soft-core variety can, and often should, be given up are right.

Hard-core common sense, however, is something quite different. It refers to various assumptions that *we all inevitably presuppose in practice, even if we deny them verbally.* For example, solipsists deny that we have any knowledge that there is an actual world, with its own reality, beyond our own experience. For all we know, they say, everything else may be illusions, figments of our imagination, no more real than the things and people in our dreams. But, whereas people may espouse solipsism theoretically, they cannot live it out in practice. We all presuppose the existence of other things and people that are just as real as we are and that have their own power to produce effects on us—for good or for ill. We are not content with imagined food, but look for the real thing, and we get out of the way of moving automobiles.

This belief in the reality of the "external world" is so deeply presupposed, furthermore, that the very attempt to refute it presupposes it. This fact is brought out by an old joke: A philosopher announced in the midst of a lecture that he was a solipsist. "Thank God," said a voice from the audience, "I was afraid I was the only one!" The point, of course, is that both the philosopher and the person in the audience, in telling other people that they were solipsists, were contradicting their theory with their practice, for in practice they were presupposing that those other people existed.

The idea that the ultimate criterion for judging a philosophy's adequacy should be these hard-core commonsense presuppositions, such as the reality of the world beyond ourselves, has been enunciated by Whitehead. The "metaphysical rule of evidence," he says, is "that we must bow to those presumptions which, in despite of criticism, we still employ for the regulation of our lives."[11] One may ask why this criterion should be accepted. One answer is that the first rule of reason is the principle of noncontradiction: A position that is self-contradictory cannot be true. And if we reject in our explicit philosophy any of those ideas that we inevitably presuppose in practice, we are necessarily engaged in self-contradiction between our explicit and our implicit ideas. Also, if we cannot help but presuppose certain ideas, this fact provides overwhelming

---

* My most careful formulation of hard-core common sense, partly with Charles Peirce's "critical common-sensism" in view, is in the introduction to Griffin et al., *Founders of Constructive Postmodern Philosophy*, 23–29.

reason to consider those ideas to be true. We have, in other words, more reason to be confident of these ideas than we do of any other ideas from which the falsity of these hard-core commonsense ideas might be deduced.

To announce this criterion of adequacy is to reject a strong tradition of modern philosophy going back to David Hume. Having realized the implications of the sensationist theory of perception, which he accepted, Hume realized that various things that we inevitably presuppose in practice cannot be included in an *empiricist philosophy*, meaning one in which all elements must be based on direct perceptual experience. The reality of the external world was one such belief; the reality of causation as real influence was another. Hume's solution was a radical bifurcation between philosophical "theory" and everyday "practice," according to which we must continue to presuppose various things in practice that we cannot defend in theory. Proposing his criterion as a direct rejection of this Humean bifurcation of theory and practice, Whitehead says:

> Whatever is found in "practice" must lie within the scope of the metaphysical description. When the description fails to include the "practice," the metaphysics is inadequate and requires revision.[12]

Since the time of Hume, most mainline philosophy has not held itself accountable to this standard. Eliminative materialism is only the most extreme example of this dualism between theory and the universal presuppositions of practice. Overcoming this dualism is the first step toward arriving at a satisfactory solution to the mind-body problem.

Once we have in principle accepted hard-core commonsense presuppositions as the ultimate standard, we then need to assemble a list of the presuppositions of this type that are most important in relation to the mind-body problem. We can then use these presuppositions for evaluating various proposals. We can even use them to eliminate some solutions from the outset. I will now briefly indicate what some of these ultimate presuppositions are, indicating in some cases the philosophical positions that they rule out.

1. *The reality of conscious experience, with its emotions, memories, beliefs, and purposes*: Descartes was right about at least one thing: One cannot deny the existence of one's conscious experience without self-contradiction. As Searle says, "If your theory results in the view that consciousness does not exist, you have simply produced a *reductio ad absurdum* of the theory."[13] We should, accordingly, eliminate eliminative materialism from the positions to be taken seriously.

2. *The reality of the "external world"*: I have already pointed out that this presupposition rules out solipsism. I will now extend the implications of this presupposition to rule out all phenomenalisms and idealisms that deny, or at least fail to assert, that "nature" or "the physical world" is as actual as we are. This acceptance of realism need not mean a "naive realism," according to

which the world exists in itself *just as* it appears to our sensory perception or *just as* it is conceived in sensory-based conceptions. What is denied is only the idea that the very reality of what is normally called "the physical world" depends on its being perceived or conceived.

3. *The reality of efficient causation as real influence:* What is ruled out by this presupposition is the idea that efficient causation does not exist, or that it is, as Hume suggested, to be understood as nothing but the regularity of sequence (the "constant conjunction" of certain types of events).

4. *The causal efficacy of our bodies for our conscious experience:* This presupposition, in fact, is one of the strongest bases for our knowledge of efficient causation as real influence, because we directly experience our bodies as causing pains, pleasures, and sensory perceptions.

5. *Freedom in the sense of partial self-determination in the moment:* This presupposition limits the scope of the previous one, saying that no matter how much our conscious experience is influenced by our bodies, it is not totally determined by them. Our bodies, for example, can cause us to feel extreme hunger pangs, but they cannot dictate what we will eat or, indeed, whether we will eat at all. This presupposition of freedom rules out all deterministic philosophies. That we really do in practice presuppose that *we ourselves* are free is shown by various reactions that we have to our own actions, such as feelings of obligation, shame, guilt, and remorse. That we presuppose that *other people* are not totally determined is shown by reactions such as gratitude, anger, and condemnation. Freedom in the sense of partial self-determination is the hard-core commonsense idea that is most widely rejected by philosophers. But, as Whitehead says: "This element in experience is too large to be put aside merely as misconstruction. It governs the whole tone of human life."[14]

6. *The efficacy of conscious experience for bodily behavior:* Besides presupposing that our experience is causally influenced but not totally determined by our bodies, we also presuppose that our partially free decisions influence our bodily behavior in return.

7. *The reality and efficacy of values:* This presupposition is closely related to our presupposition about freedom. That is, in presupposing partial freedom, we are presupposing that our purposes and decisions are not totally determined by the power of the past (efficient causation), but are partly drawn by the attraction of realizing some possible value (final causation). That such values are inevitably presupposed in practice can be shown by the philosopher who says: "Although determinism may be an unpleasant philosophy, we have to accept it because it's true." This philosopher is presupposing that there is such a thing as truth and that it (rightly) exerts a pull on our experience.

Given this list of a few of our hard-core commonsense ideas (which I have discussed at greater length elsewhere[15]), I turn now to a discussion of the two most common positions taken on the mind-body relation in our time, dualism and materialism. Although there have been other positions taken in modern philosophy, the exclusion of most of them is justified by the limitation of the discussion, stated in the second principle above, to *realistic* philosophies, meaning ones that accept the full-fledged actuality of the physical world. Dualism and materialism (as distinct from various phenomenalisms and idealisms) are realistic in this sense. There is also a third form of realism, which is usually ignored. Before turning to it, however, we need to see why neither dualism nor materialism is adequate.

Given this chapter's concern with the possibility of life after death, I will begin with the inadequacy of dualism, because it is the position that is usually endorsed by those who believe in life after death. This endorsement, with the resulting association of belief in life after death with dualism, makes it very unlikely that the philosophical and scientific communities will ever be won over to the acceptance of life after death, no matter how much empirical evidence is presented.

This is so because, as Daniel Dennett reported in a survey of "Current Issues in the Philosophy of Mind," it is widely agreed among philosophers that dualism is not a serious view to contend with,* and also because this agreement exists for good reason. That is, dualism really is extremely problematic, especially if one adheres consistently to the implications of the rejection of supernaturalism. When materialists dismiss dualism with dispatch, they do so justifiably, because dualism is incoherent.

However, to agree with materialists that dualism is incoherent is not to agree with them that materialism should be accepted, because materialism, as we will see, has even more defects than does dualism. Besides sharing many of the same problems that dualism faces, it has some more of its own. In the next section, I will discuss the problems that are unique to dualism. In the following section, I will turn to those problems that are unique to materialism. Finally, I will discuss those problems that dualism and materialism share. The main point of these sections is to drive home the need to consider the form of realistic philosophy that has been, thus far, virtually ignored.

3. DUALISM AND ITS UNIQUE PROBLEMS

Of the various problems with metaphysical dualism, the most commonly mentioned is the problem of interaction. How can two things that are totally unlike be thought to interact causally with each other? The classical discussion of this problem occurred in relation to the dualism formulated by Descartes. Mind

---

* Daniel C. Dennett, "Current Issues in the Philosophy of Mind," *American Philosophical Quarterly* 15/4 (October 1978), 249–59. In a more recent statement, in a section titled "Why Dualism Is Forlorn," Dennett says: "*[D]ualism* . . . is deservedly in disrepute today. . . . [T]he prevailing wisdom, variously expressed and argued for, is *materialism*" (*Consciousness Explained* [Boston: Little, Brown and Co., 1991], 33).

and body were said to be different in virtually every conceivable way. The body, being composed of matter, was spatially extended, whereas the mind was not. The mind's essence consisted of cogitations—thoughts, feelings, perceptions, willings—while the body's matter was totally insentient and passive. The mind acted in terms of final causes, or purposes, being led to make decisions on the basis of the attractiveness of ideals, whereas matter, being insentient, could be moved only by mechanistic impact. As John Passmore has put it, according to dualism "the only force the mind has at its disposal is spiritual force, the power of rational persuasion," whereas a body "can only push."[16] Philosopher Gilbert Ryle highlighted the problem created by Descartes' dualism by speaking of the Cartesian mind as the "ghost in the machine."[17] How could a ghost, conceived as a purely nonphysical entity, possibly interact with a body, understood as a machine composed of purely physical nuts and bolts?

It is sometimes said that Descartes sought to solve the problem by proposing the pineal gland as a mediator between mind and body. According to this view, this gland could, on the one hand, affect and be affected by other physical substances in the body, because it is itself a physical substance. On the other hand, because its matter was so ethereal, it could also interact with the nonphysical mind. This would have clearly been an illegitimate, ad hoc move on Descartes' part. After saying that the world consisted entirely of two types of substances, physical and mental ones, he would then have introduced a *tertium quid*, a third type of thing, by implying that the pineal gland is halfway between a physical and a mental substance.

This, however, was not Descartes' position. He meant his discussion of the pineal gland to be purely *empirical*, a suggestion of the *place* where mind and body interacted. With regard to the *philosophical* question as to how mind and body, being wholly unlike each other, could interact, he finally admitted, in response to questioning, that he had no answer. He was content to say that obviously mind and matter *can* interact because mind and body so obviously *do*.[18] Descartes evidently did not see that he was begging the question, which is whether his philosophical account of the *nature* of mind (as purely mental) and the *nature* of the body (as purely material) was correct.

In any case, two of Descartes' followers, Geulincx and Malebranche, believing that his account *was* philosophically correct, said that we must simply admit that mind and body, being completely different, cannot possibly interact. These thinkers, accordingly, had to come up with a way to explain their *apparent* interaction. Their solution was the doctrine of "occasionalism." According to this doctrine, on the occasion of my hand's being on a hot stove, God causes my mind to feel pain, which leads me to decide to move my hand. My mind, unfortunately, cannot cause my body to move any more than my body could cause my mind to feel pain. On the occasion of my deciding to move my hand, accordingly, God obliges, moving it for me. All apparent interaction between mind and body is said to require this constant supernatural intervention.

This appeal to God to solve the mind-body problem was commonplace. Leibniz, for example, rejected Malebranche's occasionalism because it impugned God's omnipotence, suggesting that God could not make a world-machine that did not need continuous adjustment.* Leibniz proposed instead that God had, at the beginning of creation, built in a preestablished harmony between minds and bodies so that they would, like two clocks, run along parallel with each other without really influencing each other.† Bishop Berkeley said that, because mind and matter, being unlikes, cannot interact, the truth must be that matter does not actually exist, that matter *appears* to exist only because God impresses sensory data on our minds.[19] Scottish philosopher Thomas Reid said that if God wants minds and bodies to interact, God, being omnipotent, can simply *make* them interact, regardless of how different they are from each other.[20] This same assumption probably lay behind the complacency about the problem evidenced by Descartes, who had one of the most extreme views of divine omnipotence in the history of thought, doubting whether even the *logically* impossible was beyond divine power.

Since about the middle of the eighteenth century, thinkers have been increasingly reluctant to appeal to supernatural intervention to explain the relation between body and mind. This reluctance has been one of the factors leading a growing number of thinkers to follow Hobbes and Spinoza in trying to avoid the Cartesian problem of interaction by denying that mind and body are two different things. The idea that the mind is somehow identical with the brain, or with certain of its functions or properties, does at least seem to avoid the interactionist question.

Some thinkers, finding this materialistic view implausible, have, in spite of their naturalism, reaffirmed dualistic interaction. Not being able to appeal to God, however, they are left with no solution to the problem of how the interaction between mind and body is conceivable. An eighteenth-century example is provided by French *philosoph* Diderot. In an article on the soul-body relation in his *Encyclopaedia*, he dismissed as "pure imagination" Descartes' theory, as he understood it, of the pineal gland as an intermediary. But he offered no alternative explanation of the relation of soul and body, saying simply that it is

---

* Actually, Malebranche, being a staunch Augustinian, held God to be immutable and considered God's action in the world, accordingly, to be timeless. Speaking as if God responded to temporal events was only a popular way of explaining it. His philosophical view, accordingly, did not really differ from that of Leibniz on this point.

† As will be mentioned later, Leibniz was not an ontological dualist, holding mind and matter to be different kinds of substances. He was, instead, a pluralistic monistic of the panpsychist variety, holding that the world is comprised of "monads," all of which enjoy experience to some degree. Given this position, he should not have had a problem with real interaction between mind and body—except for one other feature of his position: He, for metaphysical reasons of his own, defined his monads as "windowless," meaning they had no way to perceive each other, which is to say, no way to receive causal influence from each other. He, accordingly, had to appeal to God to explain the correlations between mind and body, just as if he had been a dualist.

a "fact which we cannot put in question but whose details are completely hidden from us."[21] This inability to explain dualistic interaction, once an interventionist *deus ex machina* could no longer be called on, has led many dualists either to belittle the problem or simply to ignore it.

One recent dualist who has sought to belittle the problem is Karl Popper. He had not always done so. In a book published in 1966, he thought a solution to dualistic interaction was essential. He said: "What we want is to understand how such nonphysical things as *purposes, deliberations, plans, decisions, theories, tensions*, and *values* can play a part in bringing about physical changes in the physical world."[22] A decade later, however, when he and John Eccles published *The Self and Its Brain*, Popper had evidently decided that no solution was possible, so he belittled the problem. He still affirmed strong dualism, according to which causal relations go both ways between mind and brain (the subtitle of the book is *An Argument for Interactionism*). He even accepted Gilbert Ryle's pejorative language of the "ghost in the machine" as descriptive of his position.[23] But the problem of how to *conceive* of the interaction of mind and brain—arguably the *chief* problem of modern philosophy—is dismissed. "Complete understanding," says Popper, "like complete knowledge, is unlikely to be achieved."[24] What this attempted parallelism between (empirical) knowledge and (philosophical) understanding obscures, of course, is the fact that lack of knowledge is a *natural* lack, due to the finiteness of our minds and the vastness and complexity of the universe. By contrast, the failure to understand the interaction of mind and body, understood as totally unlike things, is an *artificial* problem, created solely by the human decision to define them as totally unlike things.

Popper does seek to mitigate the problem by saying that quantum physics has superseded Descartes' idea of causation, according to which bodies push each other around.[25] But then, in explaining what he means by the "ghost in the machine," he says: "I think that the self in a sense plays on the brain, as a pianist plays a piano."[26] How a physical-physical (finger–piano key) relation can be used as an analogy for the psychical-physical (mind-brain) relation, however, is not cleared up by telling us that physical-physical relations are not as pushy as Descartes thought they were.

Popper's coauthor, John Eccles, also a dualist, has said that "conscious experiences . . . are quite different in kind from any goings-on in the neuronal machinery."[27] He formulates his dualism as that between "the world of conscious experience" and "the matter-energy world."[28] Unlike Popper, Eccles affirms belief in God, but, unlike the Cartesians after Descartes, he does not appeal to God to solve the problem of interaction. Nor is he as content as Popper with confessing ignorance. Rather, he suggests a neo-Cartesian solution, pointing to a very subtle intermediary between mind and brain.

One contemporary way to phrase the mind-body problem is in terms of physical energy: If the mind, being nonphysical, by definition embodies no physical energy, how can it affect the physical brain? Besides being inconceivable, this type of causation, many thinkers fear, would violate the law of the conservation of energy. In response, Eccles suggests that the brain contains "critically poised" neurons, which would require only a "vanishingly small" amount of energy to make them go this way or that. Conscious decisions could, by affecting them, bring about physical changes in the body.[29] The idea seems to be that, just as the Cartesian pineal gland, on the popular interpretation, was so ethereal that the nonphysical mind could make it flutter by creating an ever-so-light breeze, so certain neurons in the brain, being so critically poised, can be moved by the mind even though, being "different in kind from any goings-on in the neuronal machinery," it is totally devoid of physical energy.

As Wade Savage has argued in "An Old Ghost in a New Body," this solution is no advance upon Descartes. Savage says:

> Does the soul act on a neuron in the way that one neuron acts on another? . . . Does the soul act on a neuron in the way that a cosmic ray might act on a neuron . . . ? If so, the soul is something like a [neuron or] a cosmic ray . . . and is a material, spatial entity. Does the soul act on a neuron in a manner quite unlike those mentioned? If so, the action of the soul is utterly mysterious and inexplicable. This is precisely the unsatisfactory state in which Descartes left the problem of interaction.[30]

Indeed, Eccles elsewhere admits that he has not really solved the conceptual problem, saying: "When thought leads to action, I am constrained, as a neuroscientist, to postulate that in some way, *completely beyond my understanding*, my thinking changes the operative patterns of neuronal activities in my brain."[31]*

If this is the best dualism can do, then it would seem to provide a very poor basis from which to argue that the mind's existence apart from the body is conceivable. We have hardly shown that survival of bodily death is conceivable if we argue that it is conceivable on the assumption that interactionism is true, but then admit that interactionism is itself not conceivable!

Some thinkers believe that dualism *can* do better than this, that there is a more effective way to belittle the problem of dualistic interaction. This approach goes back to Hume, who argued, like his Scottish contemporary Reid—except without appeal to God—that causal relations can obtain between minds and bodies. Hume's claim depends on his purely phenomenal account of

---

* In *How the Self Controls Its Brain* (Berlin & New York: Springer, 1994), Eccles claims finally to have solved the "how" question (181). His focus, however, is on *empirical* issues— which part of the brain the mind directly influences and how this influence can occur without violating the conservation of energy. Failing to address the *conceptual* problem of how interaction is possible between "two authentic orders of existents with completely independent ontologies" (167), he still does not answer the most difficult "how" question.

efficient causation. Claiming, as an empiricist, that all concepts must be based on experience, and claiming further, as a *sensationist* empiricist, that we have no direct experience of causation in the sense of one thing's bringing about another thing, Hume said, as I mentioned above, that the only empirical meaning for causation is "constant conjunction." To say that A causes B *means*, and means *only*, that we have learned from multiple experiences that, when B happens, it is preceded by A, and that when A happens, it is followed by B. To say that clapping your hands causes a noise means only that, in our experience, the two things, hand-clapping and a noise of a particular sort, constantly go together. Likewise, to say that my clapping was caused by my decision to clap means only that I have observed many times that my decision to clap is followed by my actual clapping. On this basis, Hume denies that Descartes, Locke, and other dualists had a problem, certainly not a problem that had to be resolved by Berkeley's resort to God and idealism. Because causality means nothing other than a constant conjunction of two types of events in our experience, Hume says, there is no a priori reason to say that there can be no causation of mind on matter or of matter on mind. The only way to decide what kinds of things interact is to consult our experience.

It would be problematic for a dualist to appropriate Hume's position, however, because part of the price tag is accepting Hume's purely phenomenalistic account of substances, which effectively undermines dualism. Also, Hume's phenomenalistic account of causation undermines most forms of rational inference. The Humean notion of causation as constant conjunction would be particularly problematic for believers in extrasensory perception, psychokinesis, and other psi phenomena, because these phenomena are notoriously *un*constant.

Some dualists, nevertheless, have tried to use part of Hume's position to get around the problem of interaction. An example is the philosopher C. J. Ducasse, who wrote one of the most extensive examinations of our topic in the twentieth century, *A Critical Examination of the Belief in a Life after Death.* Ducasse clearly affirms a form of Cartesian dualism, referring to his position variously as "interactionistic dualism," "psychophysical dualism," and "ontological dualism."[32] He claims, however, that the fact that mind and body are ontologically "heterogeneous" (different in kind) creates no problem of interaction. With an appeal to Hume's analysis of causation, Ducasse says that

> an event, of no matter what kind (that is, whether it be a physical or a mental event), can, without contradiction or incongruity, be conceived to cause an event of no matter what other kind. Only experience can tell us what in fact can or cannot cause what.[33]

Elsewhere, Ducasse says: "The Causality relation is wholly neutral as to whether the cause-event and the effect-event are both physical, or both psychical, or either of them physical and the other psychical."[34] Thus far, this sounds like straight Hume.

There is, however, a crucial difference. Ducasse *rejects* Hume's analysis of causality as merely constant conjunction, or empirical regularity of sequence, as "patently invalid." The term causation *means*, Ducasse insists, that the event called the cause *etiologically necessitates* the effect.[35] Ducasse is correct that this, or at least something close to it, is what we all mean by causation. But how can Ducasse legitimately appeal to Hume's conclusion that mind and body can causally interact while giving up the Humean analysis of causation on which that conclusion depends? He, of course, cannot. Ducasse's whole defense of the philosophical conceivability of the survival of the mind thus collapses, because he has not shown how dualistic interaction is conceivable.

Popper, Eccles, and Ducasse, in trying to belittle the problem of dualistic interaction, at least face up to it. Most other dualists, including the majority of those who use the results of psychical research to argue for the possibility of life after death, simply ignore the problem. They thereby fail even to address the major reason for the collapse of early modern dualism into late modern materialism. With this central problem ignored, one cannot expect other philosophers and scientists to give serious attention to the empirical data said to show the reality of life after death. In a recent essay, for example, Paul Badham offers empirical evidence, such as out-of-body experiences, for life after death, but, while endorsing dualism, does not address the problem of dualistic interaction.[36] It was this essay by Badham that evoked the above-quoted (at note 3) statement by Kai Nielsen, who calls dualism "an utter non-starter." If we do not show how the existence of the mind beyond the body is conceivable, we should not be surprised that most thinkers will not take seriously the evidence that it actually occurs.

A second objection often raised against dualism is that it violates the law of the conservation of energy. However, although Eccles, as we saw, has devoted his attention to getting around it, this objection does not seem insuperable. For one thing, we have no exact knowledge that energy is always absolutely conserved. Also, even assuming that it is, the interaction of mind and body would not necessarily involve an exception. For example, a dualist could suppose that the notion of "psychic energy" should be taken literally—that pyschic energy is simply one more form of energy into which other forms of energy (such as mechanical, electrodynamic, chemical, and thermodynamic) can be transformed.[37] However, even if we dismiss the objection based on the conservation law, dualism is problematic enough to send us on a search for a more viable alternative. The problem of dualistic interaction is formidable enough by itself, and the inadequacy of dualism is even more apparent when those problems that it shares with materialism are added. First, however, we will look at materialism and the problems that are unique to it.

4. MATERIALISM AND ITS UNIQUE PROBLEMS

Due to its problem with interaction, dualism has been widely rejected in favor of materialism. Of course, the preference for materialism over dualism may be partly due to other reasons, perhaps of the type mentioned in the discussion of wishful thinking, such as the desire to see the world as wholly predictable in principle (hence as containing no partly self-determining minds) and the desire to rule out paranormal influence and life after death. But the fact that dualism is unintelligible is the usual basis publicly offered as to why it should be rejected.

From the fact that dualism is unintelligible, however, it does not immediately follow that materialism should be embraced. The question should be: Which of the several positions other than dualism is the best, in terms of self-consistency and adequacy to the various facts of experience? Advocates of materialism, however, usually skip quickly over these other possibilities, indicating that they are not really worth taking seriously. The reason for this (aside from impatience to get on with the task of articulating and defending some particular form of materialism) is evidently that these philosophers themselves cannot take these other possibilities seriously. This seems to be due to one feature that they all—the various idealisms, phenomenalisms, positivisms, and panpsychisms—have in common: *They reject, or at least fail to endorse, the idea of "matter."* This is the twofold idea that (1) what we call the physical world is composed of stuff that is *real* in itself, apart from any mind's perception or conception of it, and (2) *that it itself is devoid of anything "mindful," that is, any experience.* The first part of this idea is simply realism, which I have already said to be required by our hard-core common sense. This realism does rule out phenomenalism, positivism, and most forms of idealism. But the second part of this idea goes beyond realism to uphold the notion of matter as insentient.

For most materialists, the idea that matter in this sense exists seems to be virtually self-evident. Because dualism, for all its problems, at least affirms the existence of matter in this sense, it can be taken seriously. (Of course, we usually do take our parents seriously, even if we disagree violently with them. The similarity between dualism and materialism is no accident. The latter is simply a decapitated version of the former, having retained the former's "nature" while lopping off its "mind.") The views that do not affirm matter in this sense seem so obviously false that they can be quickly dismissed.

From this perspective, it *does* follow that, if dualism is false, materialism must be true, because it is the only serious alternative. This perspective allows materialistic philosophers to be relatively sanguine about problems in their own position. The problems can be admitted because they seem not nearly as severe as those plaguing dualists. I will later come back to the question of "matter" and thereby whether one of the other alternatives might be preferable to both dualism and materialism. First, however, I will look at materialism's claim to be more problem-free than dualism. I argue that it is not.

This discussion of its problems serves two purposes. The first is to deal with the widely held view that almost all empirical considerations support the materialistic, identist view, with the only possible evidence supporting inter-actionism being that of parapsychology. Not surprisingly, many materialists hold this view, concluding from it, of course, that the evidence from parapsy-chology must somehow be dismissed.[38] Somewhat surprisingly, however, even some supporters of interactionism have accepted this view. John Beloff, for example, has said that identism accords better than interactionism with most scientific knowledge, and adds: "If parapsychology were to fizzle out there would be little reason to jib at a monistic [meaning materialistic] or dual aspect theory of the mind-body relationship."* Paul Badham says that "a thorough-going interactionist dualist and an exponent of brain-mind identity will be in complete agreement about how they see the world 99.9 percent of the time," because "all the 'normal' data of human experiencing will be equally compat-ible with brain-mind identity and brain-soul interaction." The only data sup-portive of belief in the reality of the soul, he says, "are the data from religious experience . . . and the data from telepathy."[39] Even the acute philosopher H.H. Price, who devoted much attention to parapsychological issues, accepted the view that normal experience supports the identist view, so that without para-normal experience the interactionist view would have little if any experiential support.[40]

However, if all the evidence aside from paranormal phenomena, such as extrasensory perception, supported the materialistic view, that would provide a good (even if not quite sufficient) reason to follow the materialists in doubt-ing the authenticity of these phenomena or simply putting them aside as anom-alies. One of the purposes of this examination of materialism is to show how far from the truth is this view that most empirical considerations support, or are at least consistent with, materialistic identism.

The second purpose follows from the fact that, once one accepts the notion of "matter" as defined above and hence the mechanistic view of nature, materialism and dualism are the only options. By demonstrating that material-ism is at least as problematic as dualism, this discussion will show how neces-sary it is, even aside from parapsychological concerns, to rethink the nature of matter.

---

*John Beloff, *The Existence of Mind* (London: MacGibbon and Kee, 1962), 257–58. Beloff qualifies his statement by adding "apart from certain metaphysical considerations which would carry little weight in a scientific civilization." He does not explain what he means by "metaphysi-cal considerations," so I do not know whether he would consider the arguments I have presented against sensationism and identism to be "metaphysical." In any case, because these arguments involve presuppositions involved in the very practice of science, I do not consider them impotent in a "scientific civilization." Some scientists, in fact, when presented with these considerations, have found them persuasive.

With regard to the relation of mind and brain, materialism implies that, in some sense, the mind simply *is* the brain. This claim sometimes takes the form of identism in the strictest sense, according to which what we call the mind is said to be simply identical in every sense with the brain (with the brain, of course, understood to be nothing but a very complex arrangement of matter, in accord with the ontological reductionism summarized in Chapter 1). One analogy has it that the mind is identical with the brain just as the morning star is identical with the evening star.

The problems with identism in this strictest sense have proved so formidable that many materialists have moved to "functionalism," according to which the actual material of which the brain is composed is irrelevant. Only organization is important. Functionalism thinks of the relation between mind and brain as analogous to that between the software (program) and the hardware in a computer. This analogy is not meant, however, to allow a return to dualism or even epiphenomenalism, according to which the mind is a real entity distinct from the brain. While rejecting identism in the strict sense, functionalism still holds that the mind is *in some sense* identical with the brain. For example, while calling his own position "a version of functionalism," Daniel Dennett, in *Consciousness Explained*, says: "Somehow the brain must be the mind."[41] In referring to materialism as identism, I am using "identism" in this broader way. This view that the mind is somehow identical with the brain is what leads to the problems that are unique to the materialist's view of the mind-body relation. I turn now to a brief discussion of these.

Inadequacy to the Unity of Conscious Experience

Implicit in the mention (in the above discussion of hard-core commonsense presuppositions) of the reality of conscious experience is the unity of this experience. Our experience is not simply an aggregation of bits of data but a unification of a vast amount of data into an experiential unity. John Searle, who includes "unity" as one of the structures of consciousness to which any theory of the mind-brain relation must do justice,[42] points out that one simultaneously experiences sights, sounds, smells, tastes, touches, memories, pains, pleasures, and hungers, while simultaneously feeling desires and emotions, anticipating the future, making decisions, and so on. Given the fact that the brain is composed of at least 100 billion neurons, this unity of experience is hard to square with the idea that mind and brain are one and the same thing. Even allowing for the distinction between conscious and unconscious dimensions of experience, the bifurcation between experiences of different types in split-brain patients, and for multiple personalities, a person's experience has a unity that seems radically inconsistent with the thesis that this experience is in any sense identical with the brain. As Thomas Nagel—who has been frank about physicalism's problems without rejecting it— has said: "[T]he unity of consciousness, even if it is not complete, poses a problem for the theory that mental states are states of something as complex as a brain."[43] Daniel Dennett tries to avoid the problem by taking the eliminative approach, saying that the unity of experience is mere appearance.[44] He says that, in reality, there are billions of "miniagents and microagents (with no single Boss)." But if "that's all that's going on," as he says, then the very *appearance* of unity is utterly mysterious. More candid is Searle, who, after describing the remarkable unity of conscious experience, says: "We have little understanding of how the brain achieves this unity."[45] Dualism, which distinguishes between the mind and the brain, saying that the unity is achieved not by the brain but by the mind, seems more adequate to this fact about our experience.

Inadequacy to the Unity of Our Bodily Behavior

The question here is, for example, how I can drive an automobile while talking to my wife (about the mind-body problem, of course), while smiling, while turning the dial on the radio, while remembering a childhood event, and so on. If there is "no single Boss," but merely a vast aggregation of microagents, how is this coordination achieved? Again, dualism, with its distinction between mind and brain, seems more adequate.

Difficulty Acknowledging the Efficacy of Consciousness
   for Bodily Behavior

The issue here is epiphenomenalism, the doctrine that consciousness is merely a nonefficacious by-product of the brain. For many materialists, epiphenomenalism has been part and parcel of the materialistic approach to the mind-body relation. But the denial that our conscious experience affects our bodily behavior seems to conflict with our hard-core common sense. As William Seager says in *Metaphysics of Consciousness*, the "efficacy of consciousness . . . presents the aspect of a datum rather than a disputable hypothesis."[46] John Searle includes "the reality and causal efficacy of consciousness" among the obvious facts about our minds, adding that it is "crazy to say that . . . my beliefs and desires don't play any role in my behavior."[47] In *Consciousness Reconsidered*, Owen Flanagan, another materialist, rejects what he calls "conscious inessentialism," which is the view that any intelligent activity that is done *with* consciousness could in principle be done *without* it. He insists instead that our bodily actions are "individuated in part by the intentions and motives that constitute them."[48] This new breed of materialism is certainly more adequate to our experience than the epiphenomenalist form. But this adequacy brings with it the problem that was crucial to the rejection of dualism: How can conscious experience affect the physical world? The verbal insistence that consciousness is somehow "identical" with a portion of the physical world in no way removes that problem. With this point, we anticipate the fact, to be discussed below, that many of the problems used by materialists to reject dualism are, in fact, shared by materialism itself.

Inadequacy to Freedom

The hard-core commonsense presupposition most consistently denied by materialists is the partial freedom of conscious experience, along with the consequent partial freedom of our bodily behavior (which follows from the efficacy of consciousness for our bodily behavior). Nagel is again forthright in pointing out the problem. On the one hand, he agrees that freedom is a presupposition of human practice, saying, "I can no more help holding myself and others responsible in ordinary life than I can help feeling that my actions originate with me."[49] On the other hand, Nagel, who as a physicalist rejects the idea of a mind or soul distinct from the brain,[50] says that he can find no way to give a coherent account of freedom. Being thus drawn in two contradictory directions, Nagel says candidly: "I change my mind about the problem of free will every time I think about it."[51]

The reason that freedom cannot be espoused in theory by materialists, although they presuppose it in practice, is that for them the "mind" is in no sense an actuality in its own right, distinct from the brain, which might have some autonomous power of its own. Our experience must be thought to be entirely a product of the brain, with no power of self-determination. This notion is illustrated in John Searle's description of the sense in which consciousness "emerges" from the brain. He affirms emergence in the weak sense, according to which, crudely put, "consciousness gets squirted out by the behavior of the brain." But he rejects emergence in a stronger sense, according to which "once it has been squirted out, it then has a life of its own." If emergence in that stronger sense were true, then "consciousness could cause things that could not be explained by the causal behavior of the neurons."[52] Searle's denial that our conscious experience has any degree of autonomy, any power of self-determination, throws into question whether he has really rejected epiphenomenalism, as the quotations in the previous point seemed to indicate. There he was quoted as saying that it is "crazy to say that . . . my beliefs and desires don't play any role in my behavior." But now we see that he says that our beliefs and desires are totally produced by the brain, so that they are not at all something for which our conscious experience is responsible. We see, accordingly, that he has not really done justice to our hard-core commonsense belief about this matter. We presuppose that we are responsible for our bodily behavior because it results in large part from our conscious beliefs, desires, and especially our purposes, which are to some degree freely formed in our conscious experience. But Searle is saying that our desires and purposes are simply products of the deterministic functioning of the brain: There is downward causation from conscious experience to the brain, but everything sent down from consciousness to the brain had been previously sent up from the brain, so that consciousness is simply one more link in the deterministic chain of cause and effect. On this view, to say that our beliefs, desires, and purposes affect our bodily behavior does not imply that we are any more responsible for our actions than a billiard ball is for its movements. Searle's materialism has led him to violate his own dictum that we should not deny obvious facts of experience.

Colin McGinn, in *The Problem of Consciousness*, also illustrates materialism's difficulty in affirming freedom. Like Searle, he rejects as obviously false the denial by eliminative materialists that consciousness exists. But he is more sympathetic with their denial of freedom, saying that "it is much more reasonable to be an eliminativist about free will than about consciousness."[53] It is certainly true that the denial of freedom is not *as* obviously false as is the denial that consciousness is real. Freedom is, nevertheless, one of those ideas that we all inevitably presuppose in practice, so that materialism's inability to accept it is another sign of its inadequacy.

Since the discovery of quantum indeterminacy, it is true, materialism need not hold that the behavior of humans (or anything else) is absolutely predictable in principle. Many thinkers still do, however, hold this deterministic assumption about humans and all other large objects. They argue that, by the "law of large numbers," any ontological indeterminacy that may exist in relation to individual particles at the quantum level is canceled out when there are large numbers of particles. Just as the behavior of a billiard ball, with its billions of molecules, is completely deterministic, even though that of its subatomic particles is not, so is the behavior of a human being. But materialists are also free to reject this line of reasoning, even arguing instead that certain organizational structures, such as the human organism, are such as to magnify the indeterminacy that obtains at the quantum level. This move can make materialism somewhat less counterintuitive and self-refuting.

Nevertheless, materialism cannot affirm the kind of freedom that is presupposed in our notions of human responsibility. It cannot speak of a center or self that is capable of self-determination, a self that, in a given situation, could have chosen to act differently than it did. The denial of such a self is, of course, part of the point of the denial of a "mind" or "soul" that is distinct from the brain. Materialists can, to be sure, acknowledge that we engage in an activity that we *call* decision-making. But they have to regard decision-making as an effect (or better, a concomitant) of the physical processes constituting the brain, not as an activity that is partly autonomous and that can exert influence back on those brain processes, thereby directing the activities of one's limbs, tongue, and larynx.

Inadequacy to Values

Materialism entails the denial of yet another hard-core commonsense notion. Insofar as materialism is a theory not simply about human beings but about the universe as a whole, it maintains that nothing but material things exist. This doctrine rules out not only a (nonmaterial) mind but also those things often called "values," such as truth, beauty, and goodness. Whatever be the referent for these words, it is not, according to materialism, a set of nonmaterial entities existing somehow prior to, and hence objectively to, human experience. Yet we all presuppose that such values do in some sense objectively exist. The materialist, for example, sometimes says that the materialistic worldview may be unpleasant, but that we should embrace it anyway, because it is true. Here we have truth presupposed as an objective value, good in itself, acting as an attractor, a final cause. Of course, one can propose reductionistic accounts of values, saying, for example, that they were not in any sense "discovered" but were "created" and then "selected" because of their survival value. If we observe our own behavior and that of others, however, we will see that these attempts fail. We inevitably presuppose that truth, goodness, and beauty are valuable apart from, and in fact often in tension with, what is useful for survival, whether of the individual or of the group. Materialism's reductionistic account of values inevitably creates an opposition between theory and practice. This tension is closely related to that created by the denial of freedom, because the presupposition that objective values exist involves the presupposition that we are moved not only by efficient causes but also by final causes that elicit our self-determining response.

Epistemological Inadequacy

Still another problem of materialism is that it entails a sensationist doctrine of perception, according to which we can perceive only by means of our physical sense organs. This doctrine implies that we should not be able to know all sorts of things that we do, in fact, know. One of these is the "external world," knowledge of which is among the hard-core commonsense notions mentioned at the outset of this chapter. As Hume saw, sense-perception as such gives us nothing but sense-data, and these are universals, or abstractions, such as colors and shapes. Sense-perception as such, in other words, gives us no knowledge of the existence of *other actual things*. This means that the sensationist doctrine of perception leads, *in theory*, to solipsism, the doctrine that I do not really *know* that anything actually exists except myself. *In practice*, however, we are all realists, as Hume agreed: We all live as if we knew that other things are real in the same sense that we are. Various accounts have been offered to account for this practical realism. One account is that it results from an intellectual judgment, but this account fails to explain why cats and mice are as realistic as we are. Santayana remedied this weakness by attributing our realism to "animal faith."[54] But the term "faith" is too weak: We show by our behavior that we *know*, in the strongest sense of the term, that we live in a world of other actual things. The fact that we know this suggests that we somehow directly perceive it. The fact that the sensationist theory of perception cannot do justice to this truth suggests its inadequacy. The fact that materialism entails sensationism is one more count against materialism.

The sensationist theory of perception, as Santayana saw, implies not simply solipsism, but "solipsism of the present moment."[55] Sense-perception, in other words, conveys no knowledge of the past—that is, that there has even been a world prior to the present moment. We do not see, hear, smell, taste, or touch the past. We do, to be sure, perceive things with our senses that we believe to have originated in the past. For example, we often say that, in seeing the stars in the sky at night, we are seeing the past, because it has taken many years for that light to reach us. But what we directly *see* are the colored shapes, which are immediately present to our conscious experience. That this light originated in the past is an interpretation (however well founded). The philosophical problem is: How do we know that there *was* a past? Bertrand Russell once claimed that we do not know this, that for all we know the present moment might be the first moment in the history of the universe. But Russell later wrote an autobiography, showing that, in practice, he had no real doubts.

The problem can be put even more starkly: Where do we even get the idea of "the past," given the fact that sense-perception gives us nothing but data, such as colored shapes in the case of vision, that are immediately present to our experience? The obvious answer to these questions, of course, is that we both have the idea of "the past" and know that there *was* a past because we *remember* the past. To appeal to memory, however, sounds suspiciously like appealing to some other, nonsensory, form of perception. And so it is, a fact to which I will return later. For now, the point is that if sensory perception were our only means for perceiving the realities that lie beyond our present experience, we would have no conception of the temporal structure of reality—which would be a significant oversight. Darwinism is considered a materialistic theory; but if materialism were true, we should have no idea of evolution through past aeons.

Yet another notion that we all presuppose in practice, but that sensationism cannot account for, is the notion of causation as real influence. When we say that A causes B, we may sometimes mean that B was completely determined in all its details by A (perhaps in conjunction with A_1, A_2, A_3, etc.), as when we say that the cue-ball caused the 8-ball to go into the corner pocket. But we do not, as determinists suppose, always mean this. For example, if I say, "Your scream caused me to miss the shot," I mean, or at least should mean, only that the scream was a contributing factor. In either case, however, in speaking of "causation" we refer to *real influence*. But sense-perception, as Hume pointed out, provides no basis for this idea. The only empirical meaning we can give to the term causation, he said, is "constant conjunction" understood as regularity of sequence—that the two things we refer to as "cause" and "effect" regularly appear together, and in that order. This analysis is clearly inadequate. When we say A caused B, we mean that A exerted real influence on B, and if sensationism cannot do justice to this fact, then so much the worse for sensationism—and for the materialistic ontology that entails it.

For a final contradiction between the sensationist theory of perception and the presuppositions in practice of everyone, including sensationists, we can return to the issue of values. I pointed out above that the materialistic universe has no place for values, given their notorious nonmateriality. One might suppose, however, that the materialistic worldview could be loosened up enough to allow some objective status for truth, beauty, and goodness. Even if this were so, however, the materialist, qua sensationist, would have no legitimate way of knowing the reality of these values: The physical sense-organs are capable, by definition, of perceiving only physical things. This point, of course, involves no criticism of materialists and other sensationists as people: They are often in practice the most devoted to truth, beauty, and goodness. The criticism is directed purely at their theory, the fact that it stands in tension with the presuppositions of their practice.

The sensationist doctrine of perception, to be sure, has been held by most modern philosophers, and thereby by dualists as well as materialists. The origin of modern sensationism, in fact, is often traced to the dualist John Locke. It might be thought, accordingly, that the problems arising from sensationism should be included under the problems shared by materialists and dualists alike. However, whereas many dualists have indeed affirmed sensationism, this doctrine of perception is not required by their ontology. Having a distinction between the mind and the brain, they are free to affirm the reality of a nonsensory form of perception. Indeed, most philosophers and scientists who have accepted the reality of extrasensory perception have been dualists. Given the acceptance of that one type of nonsensory perception, they *could* expand it to explain our knowledge of the external world, causation, values, and the past (and therefore time). Materialism, by contrast, virtually *entails* sensationism: If the mind simply is the brain, then it can have, almost all materialists agree, no power to perceive except through the brain's sensory system. It is appropriate, accordingly, to consider these epistemological difficulties as uniquely problematic for materialism.

The Meaning of Mind-Brain Identity

A final problem unique to materialism, and the one to which materialists themselves have given the most attention, is the fundamental problem raised by the claim that the mind is in some sense identical with the brain: What can this *mean*? How is this claim even *intelligible*? The problem is created primarily by the materialist's assumption that the "gray matter" of the brain is also "matter" in the philosophical sense—namely, that it is devoid of all experience. Materialists typically speak of the brain as composed of "insentient neurons." What can it mean to say that our mind is identical with the brain—that is, that our *experience* is somehow *identical* with a large *aggregation of nonexperiencing things*? After several decades of failed attempts to make sense of this assertion, many materialists have concluded that the task is impossible. That conclusion is what has led many materialists to favor eliminating consciousness from our vocabulary.

But some materialists, such as John Searle, still believe that a conceptual reduction of the mind to the brain is possible. Searle argues that consciousness can be understood to be simply one more "material property" of the brain,[56] one that "supervenes" upon the brain. To help us understand how consciousness could be "supervenient" upon the brain, he uses the analogies of the liquidity of water and the solidity of ice. The point of the analogies is that a macrostate (liquidity or solidity) is a property that is supervenient upon the microphenomena (the molecules) when they are in a particular state. When the H_2O molecules are in the state of "rolling around on each other," the property of liquidity supervenes, being both produced by and identical with the molecules in that state; when the molecules are in a lattice structure, solidity supervenes. In the same way, Searle argues, consciousness is a supervenient property of the brain in certain states.[57]

This analogy is problematic, however, as even fellow materialists have pointed out. In the case of the liquidity of water and the solidity of ice, says William Seager, we can understand, given what we know about the properties of the molecules in question, why the joint activity of the molecules would give rise to these properties. With regard to the neurons making up the brain, however, this is not the case. Nothing that we know about these neurons from biology and brain physiology explains why the joint activity of such entities should give rise to conscious experience.[58] (The assumption here, of course is that the neurons are individually insentient.) In reply to such criticisms, Searle has admitted that there is a difference between the type of supervenience that is said to occur in the brain and the type that is involved in all the other examples he cites, such as liquidity and solidity. That is, in all the other cases there is *constitutive* supervenience in which the microphenomena cause the macrophenomenon by constituting it.[59] In the case of the brain-mind relation, however, there is merely *causal* supervenience, meaning that the microphenomena cause the macrophenomenon without being constitutive of it. By making this distinction, Searle has, in effect, admitted that his analogies provide no help whatsoever in explaining how our conscious experience can be said to be a "property" or "feature" of the brain or in any other way identical with it. The relationship remains a complete mystery.

The fact that materialism cannot explain the mind-body relation has long been maintained by dualists. Today, however, a number of materialists are coming to agree. Seeing that neither elimination nor reduction seems possible, they admit to mystery. Thomas Nagel says that "physicalism is a position we cannot understand because we do not at present have any conception of how it might be true."[60] Whereas Nagel does think that philosophers might overcome the mystery in two or three centuries, Colin McGinn argues that our present perplexity is terminal, that the mystery will never be resolved.[61] William S. Robinson, in *Brains and People*, is equally pessimistic, saying that there is no imaginable story that leads from descriptions of neurons in the brain to "our seeing why *such* a collection of neurons has to be a pain." This lack, he adds, "is not merely a temporary limitation."[62] William Seager, while not declaring the mystery to be permanent, suspects that it may be, saying that "it remains true, and may forever remain true, that we have no idea whatsoever of *how* the physical states of a brain can constitute consciousness."[63]

This despair among physicalists with regard to the alleged identity of mind and brain might well seem a basis for cheer to those who wish to make the idea of life after death philosophically intelligible. That is, if materialism is so obviously inadequate that leading philosophers in the physicalist camp are now admitting it, the conclusion might seem to be that dualism, in spite of its problems, should be embraced. Before rushing to that conclusion, however, we need to remind ourselves just how problematic dualism itself is. Although in terms of the problems that are unique to each of them, materialism does exceed dualism by a score of seven to one (or at most two), dualism's problem of interaction is formidable, as we have seen. Furthermore, there are still further problems to be mentioned. To be sure, these further problems are shared by materialism as well, so they do not greatly affect the question of the *relative* inadequacy of dualism vis-à-vis materialism. But they do constitute further reasons to consider dualism inadequate *absolutely*. They thereby count against the adequacy of both dualism and materialism relative to some other possible version of realism, if such there be. I turn now to these further problems.

5. PROBLEMS SHARED BY DUALISM AND MATERIALISM

Although the five problems to be discussed here have usually been discussed as problems for dualism, they really apply to materialism as well. The reason that materialism shares so many problems with dualism is that, although materialism sees itself as a form of monism, holding that there is only one kind of reality (namely, matter), it is really dualism in disguise.[64] This cryptodualism follows from the fact that materialists, on the one hand, think of matter as wholly devoid of experience, and yet, on the other hand, cannot help but believe, through self-knowledge, that things with experience also exist. Just like *avowed* dualists, accordingly, they see the world as composed of experiencing and nonexperiencing things. That is, the alleged identity of matter and experience does not go both ways: Materialists do not say that all matter has experience. For example, Herbert Feigl said that, in his identism, "nothing in the least like a psyche is ascribed to lifeless matter," which implies that the language of psychology is applicable "only to an extremely small part of the world."[65] The resulting cryptodualism means that materialists have many of the same problems that the avowed dualists have.

It is true, however, that these problems are *more obviously* problems for dualism than for materialism (which is why materialists often get away with citing them as reasons to reject dualism in favor of materialism). I will, accordingly, first discuss each of them as a problem for dualism, then point out that it is a problem for materialism as well.

The Problem of Discontinuity

There are two dimensions of this problem, the empirical and the metaphysical. The metaphysical aspect will be discussed below as "the problem of emergence." The empirical problem is that the evolutionary account of the world, which in most general terms is now beyond reasonable doubt, suggests what can be called the principle of continuity, which means that we should not expect any absolute jumps in the evolutionary process. This principle has been increasingly confirmed with further scientific discoveries. For example, the total gap once assumed between the human mind and that of other creatures has been greatly modified with further research into the linguistic capacities of dolphins and primates. Likewise, the once-imagined gap between living cells and inorganic molecules has now been filled with intermediaries such as macromolecules, viruses, and organelles. The dualistic view, however, posits an absolute difference in kind between entities that experience and those that do not. The former have an "inside" and exercise final causation, whereas purely material entities are all "outside" and operate entirely by efficient causation. The speculation that such a discontinuity exists is out of step with the continuity that the empirical study of the world has increasingly revealed.

While more obviously a problem for dualism, this discontinuity is also a problem for materialism, because it also posits that, at some point in the evolutionary process, entities with an inside as well as an outside emerged. Dualism does compound the problem by speaking of experience as a new kind of *substance*, or at least *actuality*; but the problem still exists for materialism as well.

The Problem of Where to Draw the Line

A second problem for dualists, given their absolute line between mental and physical things, is exactly where to draw that line. Descartes, notoriously, drew it below the human mind, from which it followed that dogs (including his own dog, Monsieur Grat) were mere machines, with no feelings. Most dualists have found this complete dualism between humans and the rest of the animal world implausible.[66] Accordingly, some have attributed experience to all animals with central nervous systems. This is problematic, however, because having such a system is not an all-or-nothing affair. Others, often called vitalists, have said that where there is life there is experience. But where exactly does "life" begin? Are we to say that bacteria are alive, and therefore sentient, while viruses, which have some but not all the properties usually said to characterize living things, are not? Or, if we include viruses, are we going to exclude macromolecules, such as DNA, RNA, and protein molecules, in spite of their remarkable abilities? If we do include them, however, will not a line drawn below them be just as arbitrary as a line drawn above them? Wherever dualism draws its line between experiencing and nonexperiencing entities will be arbitrary. This problem, however, cannot comfort materialists. Because of their cryptodualism, it equally applies to them.

How Could There Have Been Time for Experience to Emerge?

A third problem for dualists, at least for those who accept evolution, is this: After having decided at about what point in the evolutionary process mind arose, they must explain how evolution could have had the time—literally—to have gotten to that stage. The reason this problem exists is that, as most of those who have thought about it have seen, time presupposes experience, because without experience there would be no "now," therefore no distinction between past and future.[67] Dualists, accordingly, must hold that time itself arose sometime in the course of the evolutionary process. This is the view of J. T. Fraser, as reflected in the title of one of his books, *The Genesis and Evolution of Time*. The problem with this view, of course, is that evolution itself presupposes the existence of time. The paradox is explicitly expressed by Fraser's assertion that, although we cannot help thinking of several billion years passing between the Big Bang and the rise of life (which is when Fraser thinks time in the real sense of the word arose), we must actually say that all the events "prior" to the rise of life were all "contiguous with the instant of Creation."[68] Something must be amiss! I am uncertain whether Fraser considers himself a dualist or a materialist. The problem, in any case, exists equally for materialism, insofar as it, as a form of cryptodualism, also says that aeons of evolution occurred prior to the rise of experience.

The Problem of the Great Exception

This is most clearly a problem for dualism. If minds with their experiences are real things with their own power, not simply functions of physical things, then they cannot be subsumed under the explanatory laws that account for most things (given the dualist's account of "most things" as devoid of experience). They are the great exception. One who cannot accept this view is J. J. C. Smart. He says that, although states of consciousness do seem to be the one sort of thing left outside the physicalist picture, . . . I just cannot believe that this can be so. That everything should be explicable in terms of physics . . . except the occurrence of [states of consciousness] seems to me to be frankly unbelievable.[69]

Michael Levin, in his book, *Metaphysics and the Mind-Body Problem*, expresses a similar sentiment:

So far as we know, everything, except possibly the psychological states of sentient beings, is physical. . . . [Against dualism] it is simply more reasonable to think that the properties expressed by psychological predicates will turn out to be physical. Given that most of the universe is explicable physicalistically, the view which least multiplies independent principles is that the entire universe is explicable physicalistically.[70]

Levin, in fact, makes this consideration "the main positive evidence for materialism," even more important than the problem of dualistic interactionism.[71]

Unfortunately for Smart, Levin, and other materialists, however, the problem of the Great Exception counts equally against *their* worldview, especially in the light of the agreement by Nagel, McGinn, Seager, and Searle, not to mention countless dualists, that conscious experience is *not* "explicable physicalistically," meaning in purely externalistic categories.[72] That is, experience *cannot* be described in purely objective or "third-person" terms, such as chemical transactions, neuron-firings, and the like; subjective or "first-person" categories, such as feelings, emotions, and purposes, are necessary. On this basis, we can turn the Great Exception argument around, saying: Given the fact that human beings (and at least many animals) are *not* fully explicable physicalistically, would it not be strange if the rest of the universe *were*? This counterargument points ahead to a third form of realism, beyond both dualism and materialism. Before moving to it, however, we need to look at one further problem shared by these more common positions.

The Problem of Emergence

Alongside the problem of dualistic interaction—in fact, as an evolutionary form of this problem—dualists today have the problem of explaining how conscious experience emerged out of insentient matter in the first place. This was not a problem for the supernaturalistic dualists of the seventeenth century, such as Descartes, because they could simply assume that God created both minds and matter at the origin of the world. It is not even an insuperable problem for contemporary dualists who are supernaturalists, even if they think in evolutionary terms. For example, John Eccles can explain the origin of the soul as a "special creation by God."[73] But it presents an enormous problem for dualists who are naturalists (whether theistic or nontheistic). For example, Karl Popper thinks of consciousness as an emergent property of animals arising under the pressure of natural selection.[74] He believes, however, that the elements from which conscious experience emerges are totally devoid of sentience of any sort.[75] How could bits of matter (or matter-energy) that are wholly devoid of experience of any sort give rise to conscious experience? As J. J. C. Smart puts it in explaining one of his reasons for rejecting dualism in favor of materialism:

> How could a non-physical property or entity suddenly arise in the course of animal evolution? . . . [W]hat sort of chemical process could lead to the springing into existence of something non-physical? No enzyme can catalyze the production of a spook![76]

Thomas Nagel, in his well-known essay "What Is It Like to Be a Bat?," says:

> One cannot derive a *pour soi* [something that exists *for* itself] from an *en soi* [something that does not]. . . . This gap is logically unbridgeable. If a bodiless god wanted to create a conscious being, he could not expect to do it by combining together in organic form a lot of particles with none but physical properties.[77]

Evolutionary biologist Sewall Wright says simply: "Emergence of mind from no mind at all is sheer magic."[78]

Dualists typically try to finesse this problem by likening the alleged emergence of mind out of insentient matter to noncontroversial examples of emergence. For example, Eccles, when not explaining the emergence of the human mind supernaturally, says:

> Just as in biology there are new emergent properties of matter, so at the extreme level of organized complexity of the cerebral cortex, there arises still further emergence, namely the property of being associated with conscious experiences.[79]

This attempted analogy involves a category mistake. All the other emergent properties, such as wetness, hair, and feathers, are *external* properties, properties of things as they appear to the sensory experience of others. Experience, however, is what something is *for itself*, not what it is for others. To say that scales might evolve into feathers is completely different from saying that things that are totally devoid of any experience for themselves might evolve into things that do exist for themselves. Popper gives half-recognition to this point, saying that the "incredible" invention of animal consciousness out of nonconsciousness "is much more incredible than, for example, the invention of flight."[80] This recognition that the alleged fact at issue is so incredible does not, however, lead Popper to be incredulous. It should have. As Nagel says, it is inconceivable that a *pour soi* could emerge out of an *en soi* even with the aid of a creative deity—unless, of course, that deity has supernatural interventionist powers. Popper and most other dualists nowadays, however, refuse to resort to this type of explanation—which leaves them with *no* explanation.

This problem of emergence, however, is equally a problem for the materialist. The alleged emergence of matter with experience, out of matter that is wholly devoid of experience, is different in kind from any of the examples of emergence that are often suggested as analogous. Accordingly, J. J. C. Smart's criticism of the dualistic doctrine of emergence can be turned against his own materialistic position. He is right to say that "no enzyme can catalyze the production of a spook." What he fails to explain, however, is how chemical processes, assuming that cells and molecules are wholly devoid of experience, can catalyze even the production of an *apparent* spook. That is, whether the "mind" is considered a fully actual thing, as by dualists, or only a "property" or even a mere "appearance" of matter, as by materialists, is irrelevant with respect to the problem at hand. Both positions have the problem of how experience can arise out of wholly insentient things.

That this is a problem for materialism has been stressed by Colin McGinn, who explicitly discusses this problem in terms of the issue of naturalism versus supernaturalism. "It is a condition of adequacy upon any account of the mind-body relation," says McGinn, "that it avoid assuming theism" [by which he means supernaturalistic theism].[81] But, he says, no naturalistic explanation of the emergence of sentience out of "insensate matter" is possible.[82] Although we must assume that, just as there is a "basic continuity between the inorganic and the organic," there is also such a "basic continuity" between the insentient and the sentient. The problem, however, is that this latter continuity cannot be demonstrated or even understood:

> Somehow or other sentience sprang from pulpy matter, giving matter an inner aspect, but we have no idea how this leap was propelled. . . . One is tempted, however reluctantly, to turn to divine assistance: for only a kind of miracle could produce *this* from *that*. It would take a supernatural magician to extract consciousness from matter, even living matter. Consciousness appears to introduce a sharp break in the natural order—a point at which scientific naturalism runs out of steam.[83]

With this point, we have in effect returned to the problem, discussed above as a problem unique to materialism, as to how the mind can in any sense be identical with the brain, given the assumption that the brain is composed of insentient bits of matter. Nagel's statement quoted above, that we cannot understand how a *pour soi* can be derived from an *en soi*, was in fact directed more at himself and fellow materialists than at dualists. And McGinn's reason for thinking the mind-body problem permanently insoluble is stated in exactly these terms, as he says that "we have no understanding of how consciousness could emerge from an aggregation of non-conscious elements."[84]

I wish to note, at the end of this review of the problems of dualism and materialism, that I did not even include, as a problem unique to materialism, the fact that it cannot be adequate to the evidence for the paranormal interactions provided by parapsychology. (Its inability to account for extrasensory perception would be a further consequence of its sensationistic doctrine of perception. Its difficulty with psychokinesis would be a further consequence of its inability to assign any autonomous power to the psyche in distinction from the brain, which I discussed in relation to the problems of freedom and the efficacy of consciousness.) The fact that materialism's list of insuperable difficulties is long enough without including its difficulties with paranormal data shows how baseless is the widespread conviction, shared even by many dualists in parapsychological circles, that most of our experience, aside from paranormal experience, can be adequately handled from a materialistic perspective. That conviction, as we have seen, is far from the truth, and is even rejected by many materialists. We emphatically do *not* have to appeal to parapsychological evidence to show that materialism cannot do justice to our experience.

To summarize and conclude this section: The main argument for materialism has always been that, whatever its problems, it is not as bad as dualism, with its insuperable problems. The main argument for dualism has always been that, whatever its problems, they are at least not as severe as those of materialism. This at-least-not-as-bad-as-the-alternative argument has become especially prevalent in recent years. As we have seen, physicalists such as McGinn, Nagel, Robinson, and Seager say forthrightly that we cannot understand how materialism can be true. They assume that it is true only because the only rival taken seriously, dualism, must be false. John Searle puts the point even more strongly, seeing the "deepest motivation of materialism" to be "simply a terror of consciousness."[85] He says:

> [O]ne of the unstated assumptions behind the current batch of views is that they represent the only scientifically acceptable alternatives to the antiscientism that went with traditional dualism, the belief in the immortality of the soul, spiritualism, and so on. Acceptance of the current views is motivated not so much by an independent conviction of their truth as by a terror of what are apparently the only alternatives.[86]

On the dualist side of the argument, Geoffrey Madell begins his defense of dualism in *Mind and Materialism* by frankly admitting "the difficulties which any dualist position confronts."[87] He concedes in particular that "the nature of the causal connection between the mental and the physical, as the

Cartesian conceives of it, is utterly mysterious."[88] He also admits the "inexplicability" of the emergence of consciousness at some point in evolution and in the development of each embryo, given the assumption that prior to that point everything was understandable in terms of physical laws alone.[89] Nevertheless, after going through the various insuperable problems faced by materialism, he concludes that "interactionist dualism looks to be by far the only plausible framework in which the facts of our experience can be fitted."[90]

My discussion above supports his conclusion that dualism is less problematic than materialism: By my count, there are seven problems that are unique to materialism compared to one that is unique to dualism. However, given the fact that there are five that are common to them both, so that the final tally is twelve to six, Madell's statement that dualism is "by far" more plausible than materialism seems a bit of an exaggeration. In any case, what is really questionable is his conclusion that dualism is therefore "the only plausible framework." Even if dualism has fewer insuperable problems than does materialism, a total of six such problems should not leave one sanguine. Madell is, in fact, far less complacent than most dualists, offering, in the light of its many problems, only "a limited and qualified defense of dualism."[91] Instead of resting content with such an unsatisfactory position, however, should we not ask whether we might have overlooked another possibility? Perhaps the assumption that dualism and materialism are the only possibilities, even if all nonrealistic positions are excluded, is false.

That that is indeed the case will be argued in the next section. At the root of the mind-body problem is the idea of "matter" that was originally proposed by dualists and then taken over by materialists. That a reconsideration of the nature of matter is necessary to solve the mind-body problem has been suggested by Searle. After the long period in which neither side has been able to solve the problem, Searle suggests, "one might suppose that the materialists and the dualists would think there is something wrong with the terms of the debate."[92] What needs rethinking, Searle adds, is the Cartesian assumption that if something is "physical" it cannot be "mental," and if something is "mental" it cannot also be "physical."[93] I agree; I will, however, take this rethinking further than does Searle, who has remained content with a form of materialism.

6. RETHINKING MATTER AND INTERACTIONISM

If we had to accept the usual presentation of the realistic options—taking "realism" in the philosophical sense of accepting the reality of "nature" or "the physical world" independently of its being perceived and conceived—so that we had to choose between dualistic interactionism and materialistic identism, we would be in a sorry state.

Perhaps, however, as I have intimated above, not all the realistic views of the mind-body relation *have* been examined. To see that this is indeed the case, we need only to look at a "catch-22" built into the usual presentation of the interactionist position. The introduction to a book on *The Mind-Brain Identity Theory* provides a particularly clear example. In explaining why one should adopt mind-brain identity rather than an interactionist (or causal) view, the author says:

> Since it only makes sense to speak of causal transactions between onto-logically distinct phenomena, the result is a dualist point of view. The difficulties of attempting to explain the causal interaction of fundamentally unlike phenomena have, notoriously, led to various psychophysical parallelist doctrines.[94]

This argument could be paraphrased thus: "To hold an interactionist view, one must distinguish between mind and brain, because if they were identical they obviously could not causally interact. Interactionism thus requires dualism. But if dualism is affirmed, then mind and brain are ontologically unlike and hence *cannot* interact. An interactionist view is therefore impossible."

When the dilemma is stated so baldly, the dubious hidden assumption becomes visible. This assumption is that, if mind and brain are *numerically distinct* from each other, rather than simply identical, then they must also be *ontologically different* kinds of things. That, however, does not necessarily follow. The mind might be only different in degree from the brain cells—even if *greatly* different in degree—rather than absolutely different in kind.

In other words, most presentations of interactionism smuggle in, under the cover of the ambiguous term "dualism," two very different meanings. One meaning is a purely *numerical* one: The mind is, contrary to the identist view, not numerically the same thing as the brain. This is the meaning that is essential to interactionism. The other meaning is a metaphysical, *ontological* meaning: The mind is not only distinct from the brain but also, as Descartes said, an ontologically different *kind* of thing. This meaning, far from being essential to interactionism, makes interaction between mind and brain unintelligible.

The widespread use of the word "dualism" for any position that affirms interactionism, and thereby distinguishes numerically between mind and brain, has been the source of endless confusion. Once this problem has been recognized, what we should do is clear. We should henceforth not use the term "dualism" as a synonym for interactionism. We should use it only to refer to *Cartesian* dualism, or some variant thereof, according to which mind and matter are said to be ontologically different in kind. In other words, "dualism" should be used only as shorthand for "ontological dualism." Then, rather than taking "dualism" and "interactionism" to be synonymous, we would distinguish between two types of interactionism: dualistic interactionism and non-dualistic interactionism.

Although this distinction is obvious once it is seen, one will look in vain in most presentations for any recognition of it. The two issues are collapsed into one under the weight of that heaviest of all words, *dualism*. Almost all writers, whether they themselves be for or against dualism, assume that, to affirm that mind and brain are not the same thing is to affirm that they are ontologically different types of things.

For example, Daniel Dennett's conclusion that materialism must be true is based on this assumption. The only alternative he evidently sees to materialism is the dualistic view that "conscious thoughts and experiences cannot be brain happenings, but must be . . . something in addition, made of different stuff." Dennett makes the transition from numerical distinctness ("something in addition") to ontological difference ("made of different stuff") with no comment.*

For an example of an advocate of dualism as a support for belief in life after death, we can cite John Hick, who begins a chapter on "Mind and Body" in this way:

> We have the two concepts of body and mind, and various rival views of the relation between them. According to the . . . mind/brain identity theory the two concepts refer to the same entity. This is the monistic option; all the others are dualist, regarding body and mind as *distinct* entities, and indeed entities of *basically different kinds* [italics added].[95]

Hick's discussion at least has the virtue of seeing that two different meanings are connoted by the word "dualism." But this recognition seems to disappear a few pages later in the book, as Hick says:

> In rejecting the mind/brain identity, then, we accept mind/brain dualism. We accept, that is to say, that mind is a reality of a different kind from matter.[†]

---

*Dennett, *Consciousness Explained*, 29. That this was not simply a slip on Dennett's part is shown by statements on later pages: "If the self is distinct from the brain, it seems that it must be made of mind stuff. . . . The idea of mind as distinct in this way from the brain, composed not of ordinary matter but of some other, special kind of stuff, is *dualism*" (29, 31).

[†]John H. Hick, *Death and Eternal Life* (San Francisco: Harper, 1976), 120. Hick recognizes that it is difficult to understand how interaction between two different kinds of things can occur. This difficulty, however, does not lead him to question whether the interactionist view requires ontological dualism. As did Descartes three centuries earlier, Hick simply assures his readers that, because "the evidence for this mysterious reciprocal causality is overwhelming," we can accept the fact that this interaction between basically different kinds of things does occur. What the evidence shows, of course, is only that mind and brain interact, not that mind and brain as *ontologically different kinds of things* interact. The idea that the brain cells are ontologically different in kind from our conscious experiences is pure supposition. A position similar to Hick's can be found in Hywel D. Lewis, *The Elusive Self* (London: Macmillan, 1982), 1–18, 33–34, 38–39, and *The Elusive Mind* (London: George Allen and Unwin, 1969), 26, 123–25, 173–74.

Why is this transition so natural? Why does almost everyone assume that, if the mind is not simply identical with the body, or some part of it, it must be different in kind? The reason is that the body is composed of what we call matter, and that *almost all modern thinkers assume that matter is devoid of the characteristics that are basic to minds, namely, experience and self-determination.* But why do they assume that? Primarily because, as citizens of the modern world, they have been *taught* to assume it. As we saw in Chapter 1, the mechanistic idea of nature, according to which its elementary units are completely devoid of experience and spontaneity, is one of the pillars of the modern worldview. It is common to the early modern worldview, with its dualism and supernaturalism, and to the late modern worldview, with its materialism and atheism. To question this mechanistic view of nature would be to question part of the essence of modernity. Perhaps, however, it is time to question it.

One basis for questioning the idea that the basic units of nature are devoid of experience and spontaneity is that, contrary to what has generally been assumed, this idea was adopted in the seventeenth century not primarily because of empirical discoveries but more for theological and sociological motives. Several of these motives, having to do with the desire to support belief in a supernatural creator and miracles and to forestall charges of witchcraft, were discussed in Chapter 1. Another of these motives had to do precisely with our topic, the possibility of life after death.

Some freethinkers who wanted to undermine the power of the church were doing so by arguing for "mortalism," the heretical idea that when the body dies, so does the soul. One basis for this heresy was a view of matter deriving from some of the Renaissance philosophies according to which all matter has the power of self-motion. These mortalists were saying that the fact that the soul is a self-moving thing, as Plato said, does not prove that the soul is incorruptible, because matter is self-moving and yet the body clearly decays.

Against this mortalist argument, Descartes, Mersenne, Boyle, and others argued that matter does *not* have the power of self-movement: It is purely passive, not moving unless it is moved by another. Accordingly, the fact that *we* are self-moving individuals shows that we have something in us, a soul, that is different in kind from matter. Because the soul is different in kind from the body, the fact that the body dies is no reason to suspect that the soul dies, too.[96]

This argument is still used today. For example, in discussing the relation between the interactionist view and life after death, John Hick says:

Intuitively, it seems odd that of two realities whose careers have been carried on in continuous interaction, one should be mortal and the other immortal. But it also seems, intuitively, odd to deny that of two independent realities of basically different kinds, one might be capable of surviving the other.[97]

In the seventeenth century, this advocacy of dualism may have helped belief in life after death more than it undermined it, because then the appeal to God, whether explicit or implicit, could solve the problem of interaction created by dualism. Today, however, the situation is quite different. In any case, the mechanistic view of nature was originally adopted primarily for reasons of this type. There is no reason today to continue to accept it on the basis of the authority of the seventeenth-century giants.

Besides that historical argument for rethinking the nature of matter, there is what may be called a scientific-philosophical argument. This argument builds on the fact, noted above, that nature as portrayed by modern science not only does not suggest a clear place to draw a line between sentient and insentient things, but also suggests, with its evolutionary continuities, the probability that no such place exists. This suggestion, that experience and spontaneity may go all the way down, has been increasingly supported as the scientific study of nature has become increasingly subtle. To give only a few examples: More and more ethologists are rejecting a behavioristic approach to nonhuman animals, saying that experience must be attributed to even quite low-level animals, such as bees, to make sense of their behavior.[98] Researchers have even found evidence that bacteria, the lowest forms of life, make decisions based on memory.[99] Going still lower, there is no absolute line to be drawn, as argued earlier, between low forms of life such as bacteria, on the one hand, and viruses and even macromolecules, such as DNA and RNA, on the other; they all show signs of spontaneity and self-organization.* Going all the way down to the world of quantum physics: The indeterminacy at this level can be interpreted as betokening an iota of self-determinacy.

The view that actual things at every level enjoy experience, analogous to our own, has usually been called panpsychism. The word "psyche," however, suggests a rather high level of experience. The term "panexperientialism" is better. Even it, nevertheless, can be misleading. The "pan" could be taken to mean literally everything, which would mean that sticks, stones, telephones, and typewriters would all have a unified experience, analogous to that of a human being. The assumption that panexperientialism necessarily implies this implausible idea has often been used to dismiss it. Karl Popper and John Eccles, for example, have dismissed panpsychism for implying that telephones have experience.[100] It is true that some panexperientialists, usually ones who have held a parallelist rather than interactionist version of panexperientialism,† have taken the "pan" to mean

---

*The work of Barbara McClintock has been instrumental in showing that DNA molecules should be thought of not as machines but as organisms. See Evelyn Fox Keller, *A Feeling for the Organism: The Life and Work of Barbara McClintock* (New York: Freeman, 1983).

†The criticisms by Karl Popper and John Eccles of panexperientialism (under the name "panpsychism") do not apply to the version being advocated here. They falsely assume that all versions would, like that of Spinoza, entail that mind and brain, being simply two aspects of the same thing, would run parallel with each other, rather than causally interacting (*The Self and Its Brain*, 53–55, 71, 516).

all things absolutely, so that things such as rocks and telephones would have experience. Panexperientialism as such does not require this conclusion, however, and many panexperientialists have not affirmed it. In fact, some panexperientialists, beginning with Leibniz, have pointedly rejected it.

In Whitehead's philosophy in particular, a distinction is made between two basic ways in which a multiplicity of experiencing individuals can be ordered (a distinction that goes back to Leibniz). On the one hand, a multiplicity of individuals at one level can be subordinated to a "dominant" individual with a higher level of experience and greater power. (Leibniz had spoken of the "dominant monad.") If this is the case, then the thing as a whole has experience by virtue of its dominant member. Examples would be humans, other animals, cells, bacteria, molecules, and atoms. These things are "compound individuals," to use Charles Hartshorne's word,[101] because a higher-level individual has been compounded out of lower-level individuals. On the other hand, there may be no dominant individual, but merely a multiplicity of individuals, much as molecules, with equal power and experience. Examples would be rocks, shingles, typewriters, oceans, and stars. Such things are aggregational societies of individuals, not true individuals themselves. These nonindividuated societies have no experience as such. For example, although the molecules making up a rock all have their own lowly experiences, the rock itself has no unified experience over and above that of its members, just as the United States has no unified experience over and above that of its individual citizens: There is no "Uncle Sam," no literal "soul of the nation." In the same way, most plants probably differ from most animals in having no unified experience. Accordingly, we have the word "animal" from anima, or soul, and we speak of a person who appears to have no mind left as a "vegetable."

In short, the "pan" in panexperientialism refers not literally to all things, but only to *all individuals*. This is a metaphysical point. The empirical question, as to which things are to be considered true individuals, should be settled in terms of evidence of spontaneity or self-determination. To have a unified experience is also to be capable of a self-determining response to one's environment. We should posit a soul, a unity of experience, only where we see signs of this capacity. Until the rock begins climbing the hill on its own, we should not suppose it to be analogous to Sisyphus.

Modern science, with its increasingly subtle analysis of matter, has been crucial in establishing the plausibility of the distinction between compound individuals and nonindividuated aggregations of individuals. This distinction was first enunciated, as mentioned earlier, by Leibniz, in what Charles Hartshorne calls one of the most important, if still largely ignored, insights in the history of philosophy.[102] Prior to the twentieth century, science-based thinkers could not be blamed for ignoring Leibniz's suggestion that a molecule in a rock, which one throws at a rat, is more analogous to the rat than to the rock. It was easy to assume, with Descartes and Newton, that the molecules were inert, hard, and impenetrable, thereby more analogous to the rock than to the rat. Given twentieth-century science, however, this idea has lost its scientific support. The most important philosophical implication of quantum physics, philosopher of science Milič Čapek has argued, is that it has shown the falsity of the analogy assumed by Descartes and Newton between inert matter as it appears to our senses and the ultimate units of which it is composed.[103] Dualists and materialists, nevertheless, continue to presuppose the old view, according to which the elementary constituents of inert material bodies are essentially more like those bodies than like animals. Karl Popper, defending his dualism against panexperientialism, says that he "share[s] with old-fashioned material-ists the view . . . that solid material bodies are the paradigms of reality."[104] Old paradigms die hard.

A third argument for panexperientialism, which is strictly philosophi-cal, was implicit in the criticism of materialism for being insufficiently empir-ical. Our own conscious experience, as I argued earlier, is not only the reality in the universe that we know most immediately. It is also the only thing whose nature we know from inside. As such, we know what it is *in itself* in a way that we do not of anything else. What we know about what it is in itself, further-more, is that it is something *for itself*. Of other things, be they other people, squirrels, amoeba, or DNA molecules, we have no such privileged information. (The idea that we have "privileged access" to our own experience has been crit-icized by Wittgenstein and his followers. But the fact that these thinkers, with their behaviorist leanings, have criticized this idea is no reason to reject it, given its obviousness.) We do not know directly whether they do or do not have experience; we can only speculate. Either opinion, that they either are or are not analogous to us in having experience, is speculative.

There is a sense, however, in which the idea that they do not have expe-rience is *more* speculative, because it involves two levels of speculation. It involves not only the speculation that these other individuals are not analo-gous to us. It also involves the speculation that *there can be individuals* that are *actual and yet devoid of experience*. This is a speculative hypothesis that is not grounded in experience, because we have no direct experience of individuals as being both actual and devoid of experience. The panexperientialist hypothesis, by contrast, involves only a single speculation—namely, that all individuals have experience. It does, to be sure, also involve the idea that there can be *individuals who are actual and have experience*. But this idea involves no speculation: We know that it is true by knowing ourselves as actual individuals with experience. On this basis alone, the panexperientialist hypothesis should be preferred to both the dualistic and the materialistic forms of realism.

This argument can be made even stronger with an appeal to Bishop Berkeley. He argued, of course, that we should base the meaning of "to exist" on experience. If we do, we have two and only two ideas of what it means to exist: to perceive (*percepere*) and to be perceived (*percipi*). To exist in the latter sense, however, is not to exist as actual, but only as an *idea* in an actual being's perception. The only meaning we have for *actual* existence is to perceive, to be a perceiver. Berkeley himself used this argument to support a form of personal idealism, according to which nature exists only as an idea impressed on our minds by God; this *use* of his argument has led many realists to reject or ignore the argument itself. But the argument as such is sound, and it can be used to support a panexperientialist form of realism in place of Berkeley's own nonrealistic idealism, once we reject Berkeley's assumption that only God and human souls can be "perceivers." (The argument does require acceptance of the experiential criterion of meaning. But it is difficult to see why we should not seek to hold to this criterion, apart from notorious problems created by trying to do so on the basis of a *sensationist* empiricism, which, as we have seen, cannot provide us with an empirical meaning for the most basic terms. If a nonsensationist empiricism is accepted, those notorious problems disappear.) This argument supports panexperientialism over against the dualistic and materialistic versions of realism, because it suggests that these latter two versions involve an idea of dubious meaning. That is, having had no direct experience of an individual as both actual and devoid of experience, we do not really have any clear idea of what we *mean* by a "nonexperiencing actual individual." Even if this argument is not taken as conclusive, it should add some additional presumptive weight to the case for panexperientialism.

If every individual has experience and is thereby analogous to our own minds, has the term "matter" lost all meaning? No. On the one hand, the dualistic meaning of "matter," according to which it refers to a kind of substance that is ontologically different from minds, is to be rejected. On the other hand, the term "matter" is still meaningfully contrasted with mind. In the first place, with reference to an individual, the term "mind" (or "experience") refers to what it is *for itself*, while "matter" refers to its appearance to the sensory perception of others. We can begin with the double perspective we have of ourselves when we look in the mirror—as matter from without but experience from within—and generalize it to all other true individuals. In the second place, the contrast between "mind" and "matter" has an even stronger meaning when nonindividuated aggregations are brought into view: "Mind" refers to what an individual is for itself, "matter" to what such an aggregation (such as a rock) is to the sensory perception of others. This latter meaning comes close to the old dualistic meaning. But by recognizing (1) the role that sensory perception plays in creating the idea of matter, (2) the difference of the inner and outer views, and (3) the organizational duality between compound individuals and nonindividuated societies, it avoids the disastrous ontological dualism of that old view.

A fourth reason to favor the panexperientist starting point is pragmatic: It works. That is, by beginning with the working hypothesis that at least some iota of spontaneous experience characterizes individuals at every level of nature, we can affirm nondualistic interactionism, in which all the ontological problems of dualistic interactionism are avoided: Interaction between mind and brain is no longer counterintuitive, because the mind and the brain cells are said to be qualitatively similar, only greatly different in degree. There is no absolute discontinuity and therefore no problem of where to draw an absolute line in the evolutionary process between sentience and insentience. There is no problem of emergence, because conscious experience is said to emerge not out of insentient matter but out of things with less sophisticated experience. There is no problem of how time existed before experience did or, alternatively, how several billion years of evolution could have occurred before time arose. The experience and freedom of humans, or of humans and other animals, is not thought to be the great exception; spontaneous experience is characteristic of every level of nature.

It is not the case, as my discussion has largely implied thus far, that panexperientialism has been totally ignored by mainline philosophers. What is true is that it has not been *seriously* considered, and that what little attention has been devoted to it has been to forms of it that are far less defensible than the Whiteheadian form. I already mentioned that Popper and Eccles tend to equate panpsychism with the parallelism of Spinoza. The same is true for Thomas Nagel, who has given more attention to panpsychism than has any other contemporary mainline philosopher.[105] That Spinozistic, parallelist kind of panpsychism, however, not only (incredibly) assigns experience to all things whatsoever, including aggregates such as rocks and telephones that show no sign of spontaneity. It also, by not having a doctrine of compound individuals, provides no basis for mind-brain interaction and therefore for freedom. Some other philosophers have, thanks evidently to Nagel's treatment of panpsychism, at least mentioned it as a possible alternative. William Seager, for example, says in a note that panpsychism *might* make sense of the relation between mind and brain. But on the basis of a very brief discussion of one kind of panpsychism, he dismisses it as "implausible."[106] Colin McGinn correctly notes that panpsychism "is not supernatural in the way postulating immaterial substances or divine interventions is."[107] He even comments that panpsychism could solve the mind-body problem: If neurons had conscious or protoconscious states, he says, it would be "easy enough to see how neurons could generate consciousness."[108] Given McGinn's conclusion that neither dualism nor physicalism will *ever* be able to solve the mind-body problem, one would think that the realization that panpsychism might solve it would lead him to examine the various forms of panpsychism to see if one of them is adequate, or if an adequate form could be developed. But he does not. He simply dismisses it (in a footnote) as "extravagant," saying that he will be "assuming" its inadequacy.[109] Most other philosophers dismiss panpsychism even more casually, if they consider it at all.[110]

We see here the tremendous power of paradigmatic thinking. At the root of the modern worldview, established by the supernaturalistic dualists of the seventeenth century, was the notion of matter as, in Whitehead's phrase, "vacuous actuality": It was as actual as our own minds, yet completely devoid of experience. Materialistic philosophers, while rejecting the idea of God that this view of matter presupposed and was used to buttress, uncritically retained this view of matter. And, irony of ironies, they even, in its name, rejected the actuality of their own minds or souls, although that view of matter had originally been accepted in part to defend the idea that those souls were so actual as to be immortal. Even today that view of matter is so deeply accepted that few philosophers can bring themselves to take seriously the panexperientialist challenge to it, even if they realize that neither dualism nor materialism, each of which presupposes that view of matter, can ever resolve the mind-body problem. Even if they see that panexperientialism is the one hope for doing justice to the mind-body relation, they casually dismiss it, because their commitment to the modern view of matter makes it seem "implausible," even "extravagant." (McGinn's dismissal of it as extravagant, incidentally, occurs on the same page in which he says that "something pretty remarkable is needed if the mind-body relation is to be made sense of.")[111]

Readers can be assured, accordingly, that the claim I am making here—that panexperientialism works—is not one that has been extensively examined and refuted in mainline philosophy books and journals. The power of paradigmatic thinking, probably along with wishful-and-fearful thinking, has simply prevented this solution to the mind-body problem from being seriously considered. Although I cannot here develop this solution in any detail, thereby fleshing out my claim that it works, I have done this elsewhere.[112]

In any case, I have already pointed out how this type of panexperientialism overcomes the various *ontological* problems that have plagued dualism and materialism. Implicit in this panexperientialist ontology is also a solution to the various *epistemological* problems of materialism that derive from its sensationist doctrine of perception: If all individuals, even those without sensory organs, can have experiences of other things, then obviously some form of nonsensory perception preceded sensory perception. This is one of the bases for the Whiteheadian doctrine, introduced in Chapter 1, of a nonsensory "prehension" that is enjoyed by all individuals and that in us is more basic than, because presupposed by, our sensory perception. It is through this more basic mode of perception that we perceive other actualities directly (which grounds our realism) and perceive them as exerting causal influence on us. This is why we have the idea of causation as real influence—because we directly perceive (prehend) such influence. Whitehead, in fact, refers to prehension as "perception in the mode of causal efficacy." The "intuition" of values, such as truth, beauty, and goodness, also occurs through this nonsensory mode of perception. Likewise, our knowledge of the past arises from the fact that our present moment of experience directly prehends our own past moments of experience, this being the form of nonsensory prehension that we call "memory" (although, of course, what we think of as "memories" always involve more or less creative reconstructions as well as prehensions of the past events as they really happened). This doctrine of perception also not only allows, as discussed in Chapter 1, for that form of nonsensory perception that is usually called "extrasensory." This doctrine also shows this extrasensory perception not to be an exception to the general nature of perception.

The point of this section has been that panexperientialism commends itself as the best solution to the mind-body problem on purely philosophical grounds. This is true apart from any concern to be adequate to evidence suggestive of life after death. It is even true apart from any concern to be adequate to parapsychological evidence in general. However—and this is the relevance of this section to the concern of this chapter as a whole—this same view, while commending itself in terms of other considerations alone, does also allow for paranormal phenomena in general and life after death in particular. And, because it does this without dualism's problems, which are insoluble within a naturalistic worldview, panexperientialism provides a much stronger philosophical basis for thinking about these matters.

7. PANEXPERIENTIALISM IN THE PARAPSYCHOLOGICAL TRADITION

Although, as I have said, most advocates of paranormal interaction in general, and of life after death in particular, have adopted a dualistic philosophy, there is some precedent within the parapsychological tradition for the nondualistic interactionism I am recommending.

Henri Bergson, one-time president of the Society for Psychical Research, was a panexperientialist, after overcoming his early dualism. This early dualism of Bergson's had been a dualism of the temporal and the timeless. He had come to a clear realization that time, in the sense of an absolute difference between the past and the future, depended on freedom or creativity, the ability to make decisions and to introduce novelty in the present. In his first book, *Time and Free Will*,[113] he attributed this power only to the mind. This meant, he said, that there is literally no time, no temporality in any real sense, in the physical world, including the human body. This position, he came to see, created a problem for interaction between mind and body that was even more intolerable than that created by Descartes' dualism. How could that which is essentially temporal have daily intercourse with that which is outside of time? This realization led him in later writings to attribute a degree of self-determination, and thereby experience, to matter.[114] This doctrine perhaps led him to be more open to parapsychological phenomena than he otherwise would have been.

William James, a founder of the American Society for Psychical Research, accepted, after some wavering, a panpsychist view. Besides explicitly saying that "pluralistic panpsychism" was his view,[115] James said:

a concrete bit of personal experience . . . is a *full* fact . . . ; it is of the *kind* to which all realities whatsoever must belong; the motor currents of the world run through the like of it. . . . That unsharable feeling which each one of us has of the pinch of his individual destiny as he privately feels it . . . is the one thing that fills up the measure of our concrete actuality, and any would-be existent that should lack such a feeling, or its analogue, would be a piece of reality only half made up.[116]

In a footnote on that page, James added: "Compare Lotze's doctrine that the only meaning we can attach to the notion of a thing as it is 'in itself' is by conceiving it as it is *for* itself."

William McDougall, James's successor at Harvard and the founder of the parapsychological laboratory at Duke, was at least open to the panexperientialist position. McDougall strongly defended the view that the mind is distinct from the brain and interacts with it—the view that he called "animism," which refers to having souls. It has often been said, accordingly, that McDougall was a dualist. But he deliberately used the word "animism" instead of "dualism" to prevent this misunderstanding, saying that "the word Dualism is apt to be taken to imply metaphysical Dualism, an implication which I am anxious to avoid: for Animism does not necessarily imply metaphysical Dualism."[117] When McDougall did use the term "dualism," he explicitly distinguished between "psycho-physical dualism," which insists simply on the (numerical) distinction between mind and body, and "metaphysical dualism."

> It is true that Descartes' psycho-physical Dualism was made by him a metaphysical Dualism; for he taught that matter and soul are two ultimately different kinds of reality. But scientific Animism is under no obligation to accept Descartes' ontological dogma.[118]

If all the philosophers who have written on this topic had been as clear about this distinction as the psychologist McDougall, there would be far less confusion and irrelevant argumentation. In any case, McDougall added that animism is compatible with "metaphysical monism." The form of metaphysical monism he had in mind is panexperientialism, as made clear by a passage in which he says: "It may be that the soul that thinks in each of us is but the chief of a hierarchy of similar beings," after which he has a footnote that reads: "I remind the reader of the metaphysical doctrine (of Leibniz, Lotze, and others) that the body is in its real nature an organized system of beings of like nature with the soul."[119]

The intelligibility of interactionism, especially of an interactionism that makes life after death conceivable, would be greatly increased if its defenders would adopt a panexperientialist form of interactionism. Interactionists who for some reason do not want to commit themselves to panexperientialism should at least follow McDougall's good judgment in not committing themselves to ontological dualism. Better yet would be to follow James and Bergson in supporting interactionism by explicitly affirming panexperientialism.

Although an intelligible form of interactionism is a necessary condition for the conceivability of life after death, it is not a *sufficient* condition, at least for a form of continued existence worth anticipating. If one's version of interactionism excludes the possibility of perception and action in this continued existence, most of us would probably just as soon stay in the grave. In fact, it is arguably true—my version of interactionism holds that it *is* true—that actual existence necessarily involves both perception and action. To show that perception and action are both conceivable in a discarnate state, accordingly, is a necessary part of showing the conceivability of life after death as such.

8. THE POSSIBILITY OF DISCARNATE PERCEPTION AND ACTION

In this discussion, I will be showing how parapsychological evidence and the philosophical doctrine of nondualistic interactionism, based on panexperientialism, are mutually supportive. In the previous discussion, by contrast, I had not appealed to parapsychological evidence, because part of the thesis to be established was that an interactionist position, if it is not dualistic, is much more consistent with the various kinds of relevant experience than is materialistic identism, even apart from evidence for extrasensory perception and psychokinesis. Having argued that case, I will now show how this special empirical evidence and the panexperientialist philosophical perspective support each other, thereby providing a stronger case for the possibility of life after death than either could supply on its own.

As I stated in the introductory section of this chapter, I do not deal here with the *direct* evidence for life after death. The evidence to which I appeal in this chapter is solely for extrasensory perception and psychokinesis. It provides *indirect* evidence for life after death by buttressing the case for its possibility.

To begin with the question of perception: The dominant view has been that, if a human mind found itself existing apart from its physical body, it would not be able to perceive. This view is based on the assumption that perception by means of the physical senses is the mind's basic and only mode of perception of things beyond itself. If while in the body the mind can perceive nothing beyond itself except by means of its bodily sensory organs, then it would be highly improbable that a mind separated from these organs would be able to perceive anything. If such a mind could in some sense survive apart from the physical body, it would have a completely autistic experience: Memory and imagination would be its only sources. A discarnate mind might, however, be able to perceive if, while still incarnate, sensory perception had not been its only means of perception. The case for postcarnate perception would be even stronger if, besides not having been its *only* mode of perception, sensory perception had not even been the incarnate soul's *basic* mode of perception.

The fact that sensory perception is not our only mode of perception was shown by the discussion of sensationism in the section on materialism. There we saw that we know all sorts of things that we could not know if the sensationist theory of perception were true: We know that there is an actual world beyond our own experience, that there has been a past, that causality as real influence occurs, and that (nonmaterial) values exist. Whitehead accounts for our knowledge of such things, as we saw, through a nonsensory mode of perception, or "prehension."

One of the clearest everyday examples of this nonsensory mode of perception is our perception of our own bodies. I do not mean, to be sure, when we look at our hands or look at our eyes in the mirror: These are ordinary instances of sensory perception. I mean when we feel our bodies from the inside—for instance, when we feel pain in them, or when we become aware that we see *by means of* our eyes. In seeing the paper, I am not also seeing the eye. I am seeing the paper by means of the causal efficacy of the eye. Accordingly, I have a (sensory) perception of the paper by means of a (nonsensory) perception of my eye. In such instances our minds are aware of both the actuality and the causal efficacy of something beyond themselves, even though this something is part of that portion of nature that is our own body. Of course, we perceive bodily pains and organs (such as eyes) by means of routes of nerve cells running from the brain to various parts of the body. We learn of the data from these routes of influence, however, through the mind's (nonsensory) prehension of its brain. More on this subject will follow.

The other everyday example of nonsensory perception is memory. We tend to take it for granted because it is so commonplace and because we have a name for it. Yet when we think about it, we see that it should, given modern presuppositions, be a source of wonder: In remembering something, we have a direct, nonsensory apprehension of an event in the past! Of course, modern thought tends to interpret it otherwise, saying that we are really only perceiving present things, perhaps "memory traces" in the brain. Aside from other problems, however, that line of thought, pushed to the hilt, would have no explanation as to why we have the very conception of "past events" as ones that happened "before" our present experience. Unless we experience the past *as* past, we have no explanation for this conception.

Not only does nonsensory as well as sensory perception exist. It is also the case that the nonsensory mode is more fundamental, with sensory perception being derivative. We can see this by analyzing what goes on in sensory perception. (This analysis presupposes that the truth of interactionism, according to which mind and brain are distinct and interact with each other, has already been accepted.) In vision, for example, photons travel from the external object to the eye, and then the information travels up the optic nerve to the brain. For the *mind* to perceive the outer object, however, the relevant part of the brain must first affect the mind, which means—to say the same thing from the other perspective—that the mind must perceive the brain cells. Now, the mind obviously does not *see* the brain, as if the mind had eyes of its own. Rather, the mind directly perceives the brain in a nonsensory mode. The mind prehends or directly grasps the relevant brain cells, thereby receiving the information that *they* had received from the cells in the optic nerve. Sensory perception occurs when the mind receives diffuse, emotion-laden feelings from contiguous organisms (brain cells) through nonsensory perception, then turns some of the information latent in these feelings into rather clear and distinct information about noncontiguous things. For example, in seeing a tree, I receive information from my brain cells, which are contiguous to my mind, but I turn some of this information into a clear and distinct image of a tree some distance from my body. In terms of this analysis, we can see that sensory perception presupposes nonsensory perception. Nonsensory perception is, accordingly, not, as some assume, a mode of perception *higher* than sensory perception (as the term "extrasensory perception" might suggest), but a more fundamental mode.

The fact that nonsensory perception is the more fundamental mode is also implied by the panexperientialist ontology, as I suggested earlier. To say that all individuals have experience implies that even single-celled organisms such as amoeba and bacteria, which are devoid of sensory organs, have some type of perceptual experience, a supposition that is consistent with their behavior. The panexperientialist solution to the mind-body problem, furthermore, implies that those single-celled organisms that are our brain cells can receive influence from the mind because they can perceive, in a nonsensory way, the feelings and intentions of the mind. According to this panexperientialist ontology, in fact, the causal interconnectedness of the world is constituted by an infinitely complex web of nonsensory perceptions. Sensory perception is a rather rare form of perception, being exemplified only by the minds of animals with central nervous systems. Our nonsensory perception, accordingly, is not a higher, more evolved mode of perception, but a more fundamental mode, which we share with all other organisms.

Having argued that sensory perception is not our only or even our basic mode of perception, I now suggest that in nonsensory perception we are always directly perceiving not only contiguous events, meaning our brain cells and our immediately past moments of experience, but also remote events. That is, perception at a distance is going on all the time. For the most part, however, this direct nonsensory perception of remote events remains in what we call the "unconscious" portion of our minds. This nonsensory perception of remote events usually does not have sufficient intensity to rise to the level of conscious awareness. For example, when we watch and listen to a speaker, we are also receiving, at the same time, telepathic and clairvoyant impressions from her or him. Most of us, most of the time, however, are conscious only of the visual and auditory impressions.

This position is a variant of the position taken by Henri Bergson, F. S. C. Schiller, and William James. I am *not* suggesting, however, the view that the purpose of the brain with regard to perception is not to generate perceptions but to block most of them out—that is, to block out most nonsensory perceptions, which would otherwise flood our consciousness. Rather, I suggest that the function of the brain, with regard to perception, is to give us rather clear and distinct sensory perceptions with sufficient intensity to rise to consciousness, so that we can be conscious of certain dominant aspects of the physical world around us. A *side-effect* of this function is that most nonsensory perceptions, especially direct nonsensory perceptions of remote events, are blocked out. The brain's activity does not keep these nonsensory perceptions from reaching the psyche. It does, however, by providing more intense sensory data, prevent most of the nonsensory perceptions from rising to the conscious portion of the psyche's experience. So, although blocking most nonsensory perceptions from reaching consciousness is not directly the "purpose" of the brain, it is an effect.

This position is consistent with the experimental and spontaneous evidence for extrasensory perception. Telepathy provides empirical evidence that perception is not dependent solely on our sensory organs, and clairvoyance (taken broadly to include clairaudience, and so on) and out-of-body experiences (to be discussed in Chapter 8) show that even sensorylike perceptions that correspond to the facts do not require sensory organs.

There is also considerable evidence, both spontaneous and experimental, to support the notion that extrasensory perception occurs primarily at the unconscious level of experience and that conscious ESP is unusual only by being conscious. This view has been widely held by those conversant with the evidence. It is at least consistent, furthermore, with the hypothesis that extrasensory perception is going on at the unconscious level all the time.

There is also considerable support for the view that sensory perception serves to prevent extrasensory perceptions from becoming conscious. Conscious extrasensory perceptions are more likely to occur, for example, during sleep, both in spontaneous and in experimental situations, as illustrated by the "dream telepathy" experiments discussed in Chapter 2. Sensory deprivation experiments have been successful, furthermore, in increasing the consciousness of extrasensory perceptions, as illustrated by the *ganzfeld* experiments discussed in Chapter 2. The idea that the intensity of a perception determines, or at least is a crucial factor in determining, whether or not it rises to consciousness is supported by the fact that spontaneous cases of conscious telepathy are most likely to occur when there is an intense personal relation between the parties involved and/or when the "sender" is having a crisis or some other intense experience.

Accordingly, there are mutually supporting theoretical and empirical reasons for the following three propositions: First, if we were to find ourselves existing apart from our physical bodies, we would not be wholly devoid of perceptions. Second, we also would not be limited to the rather vague intuitions that are characteristic of most extrasensory perception documented in experimental situations. Third, the clear and distinct telepathic and clairvoyant perceptions sometimes experienced by people while embodied would, in the disembodied state, occur regularly, not only occasionally.

I move now to the second question, whether a soul would be able to *act* apart from its physical body. The widespread modern view is that it would not. The person acts, it is widely thought, only by means of the physical body. For the identist view, this statement is a virtual tautology, because the person *is* his or her body, at least certain parts or functions of it. But even many interactionists assume that the mind can act on the world beyond itself only by means of its body. In particular, they have assumed that we can act voluntarily only through our motor system (which consists of nerves that carry impulses to the muscles). Just as sensationism implies that we would not be able to perceive apart from our sensory system, what can be called "motorism" implies that we would not be able to act apart from our motor system.

Two qualifications of the motorist position have, however, already been widely accepted. In the first place, for the mind to act *through* the body it must first act *on* the body. (I am, of course, still presupposing the interactionist position that mind and body are distinct.) Just as we must speak of nonsensory perception *of* our own bodies in order to understand sensory perception, we must speak of a nonmotor action *on* our bodies to understand motor action. Philosophers have come to call this direct action of the mind on the body, in which there are no intermediary instruments, "basic actions."[120] The second qualification is that this nonmotor basic action on the body is not limited to action on the motor system: Through psychosomatic studies we in the modern West now know what many other peoples have known all along.

Having thus acknowledged a type of nonmotor direct action of the mind on the body, and that this action affects parts of the body other than the motor system, the next question is whether this "basic action" can be exerted only on our bodies, or whether it can be exerted on other things as well. This raises the question of action at a distance. Can this basic action be exerted only on contiguous events, namely, the nerve cells in the brain, or can it be exerted at a distance too? It may be, of course, that some forms of psychosomatic effects, such as stigmata, already involve action at a distance, meaning the direct action of the mind on some portion of the body other than the brain. We can, however, assume for the sake of argument that all psychosomatic influences may be mediated through the brain. To ask about action that is clearly at a distance, accordingly, is to ask whether there can be direct extrasomatic causal influence.

Theoretically, according to the philosophical position sketched earlier, this causal influence at a distance is possible. From the panexperientialist point of view, causation and perception are simply two sides of the same process. To perceive something is to be causally influenced by it; to exert causal influence on something is to be perceived (prehended) by it. Accordingly, to say that perception at a distance is possible, as we did earlier, is to imply that it is possible to exert causal influence at a distance. For example, if my wife perceives me telepathically, then I have exerted causal influence on her at a distance, whether I meant to or not. According to panexperientialism, this capacity for perception, including perception at a distance, goes all the way down. My psyche can exert direct influence on a plant, because the cells in the plant can perceive my feelings; the same is true for the molecules in a matchstick. The psyche's action on the world beyond its body, therefore, should not be limited to the actions it performs indirectly, through its body. The psyche should be able to act directly not only *on* its brain but also *around* it. It should be able, in other words, to exert extrasomatic basic actions.

This theoretical position is supported, again, by empirical evidence, meaning, of course, the evidence for psychokinesis, broadly understood. The term "psychokinesis" is often narrowly defined as the direct influence of the psyche on "inanimate matter." This definition, however, implies a metaphysical dualism. By "psychokinesis, broadly understood," I mean direct influence of the psyche on any noncontiguous thing or event, whether it be thought to be animate or inanimate. Thought transference is, accordingly, a form of psychokinesis. In any case, as we saw in Chapter 2, people do sometimes exercise direct mind-to-mind influence on other people. People do sometimes, furthermore, exert detectable influence on plants and animals—perhaps accelerating or retarding their growth—and on so-called inanimate objects, such as matchsticks and tables.

Accordingly, if the soul can *now*, while associated with a brain, act on other things without using the brain as an instrument, we have some reason to believe that a soul apart from its brain would still be able to exert influence on things beyond itself.

One point to bring out explicitly here is that psychokinesis, understood broadly, is as important for the possibility of life after death as is extrasensory perception. This point is not always acknowledged. Many writers on the topic have assumed that extrasensory perception is very important for establishing the possibility of life after death, while giving little if any attention to psychokinesis. This has perhaps been due in part to thinking of it narrowly as the influence of psyche on matter and assuming that there would be no "matter" in a postmortem environment. If we think of psychokinesis broadly, however, as any form of extrasomatic basic action, then it is equally important for the issue of life after death, because "life" involves acting as much as receiving. We would not consider postmortem existence *life* in the full sense if we could only receive influence, not being able to exercise any influence in return.

Through a combination of the nondualistic interactionism afforded by panexperientialism and the supporting evidence from parapsychology, accordingly, we can see that the human mind or soul might be capable of both per-

ceiving and acting apart from its physical body. This combination of philosophical theory and empirical evidence will be used in the next section to deal
with still another question.

9. WHY MIGHT ONLY THE HUMAN SOUL BE CAPABLE OF SURVIVAL?

The assumption within the Western tradition has been that only the human
soul, not also the souls of other animals, will experience life after death. Why
this was the case raised no real questions. The assumption was that God had
freely created the human soul alone with the capacity to survive bodily death, or
that God had chosen to sustain human souls after the death of their bodies
and/or to resurrect those bodies. The twentieth-century Swiss theologian Karl
Barth expressed this idea by saying that God did not create heaven for geese.
The early modern assumption that the human soul is ontologically different
from the rest of creation, as we have seen, gave an additional reason as to why
humans alone should enjoy (or suffer) life after death.

If we presuppose a naturalistic, nondualistic worldview, however, what
reason would there be to believe that human souls alone can live apart from
their organic base? The human soul is not different in kind from other animal
souls; and there is no supernatural God with the power arbitrarily to sustain
the existence of things that are not otherwise capable of continued existence.
Why might it be, then, that the human soul among all creatures would continue its journey beyond bodily death? Do we not have to follow the suggestion (made by Darwin, among others) that, within a naturalistic evolutionary
perspective, we are constrained by logic to say either that the souls of all
animals, including oysters, survive, or else that no souls, including those of
human beings, do?[121] Of course, some people, especially some reincarnation-
ists, do not limit survival to the human soul, extending it instead to the souls
of all higher animals, perhaps to all animals whatsoever. This position, however, would still have the same problem, only at a lower level: If the animal
psyche is not different in kind from the cells of the body (or, for that matter,
the molecules within the cells), why should that stream of experience that we
call the animal psyche survive but not the streams of experience in the cells
and the molecules? We can continue to pose our question in its original form,
then, as to why human souls alone might survive. One reason to favor this
formulation is that virtually all of the direct evidence that we have for life
after death is evidence for the postcarnate existence of human (or at least
humanlike) beings. Neither Descartes' dogs nor Barth's geese have supplied
much if any reason to believe that they continue to experience after the death
of their bodies.

In any case, however we pose the question, we seem to be faced with a dilemma: Either draw an arbitrary line somewhere or else say that all streams of experience whatsoever survive, including those of atoms, thereby leaving both plausibility and empirical evidence far behind. The only way to avoid this dilemma might seem to be to say that nothing, not even the human soul, survives.

There is, however, another option. The human soul, although not different in kind from the souls of other animals, may have developed, in the evolutionary process, the power to survive apart from the body. This idea, like the previous ones, is somewhat supported by both theoretical and empirical considerations.

On the theoretical side, Whiteheadian panexperientialism, as we have seen, rejects the reductionism of the materialistic worldview, according to which all the power in the world is located at the subatomic realm. This reductionism says not only that the activity of the "mind" is reducible to that of the brain (which is the claim of identism), we recall, but also that the activity of the brain cells is reducible to that of their macromolecules, which is reducible in turn to that of their ordinary molecules and atoms, and so on, so that everything is finally said to be explainable (in principle) in terms of the four forces of physics. The panexperientialist philosophy, by contrast, says that individuals at every level have their own power, so that, although much of the power of the atom is found in its subatomic particles, the atom as a centered whole has power that is not reducible to that of its parts. The same is said of, for example, ordinary molecules, macromolecules, cells, and animals, with the power of the animal as a whole being that of its soul.

Furthermore, besides the fact that the higher individuals have their own power, they have *more* power than the individuals at lower levels. Although much of the power of a cell is contained in its molecules, it has billions of molecules. Any one molecule would have a trivial degree of power compared with the power of the central organizing activity of the cell as a whole. Likewise, the brain of an animal is composed of billions of cells, whereas its psyche is a single individual. To get some idea of the power of the animal psyche, we might suppose that it affects the brain about as strongly as the brain affects it. Accordingly, it would seem that the animal psyche would be billions of times more powerful than any individual brain cell. So, far from accepting reductionism, the panexperientialist philosophy suggests that the evolutionary process has brought forth higher and higher individuals with more and more of the twofold power to determine themselves and to exert influence on others.

These increases in power continued, furthermore, within the evolution of animals, with the most powerful psyche to emerge thus far, at least on our planet, being the human psyche. The distinctive powers of the human psyche, which greatly exceed those of other primates (which are genetically very similar), seem to be associated primarily with the tremendous increase in the capacity for symbolic language. We certainly have good reason to believe that we have much more freedom—that is, much more power of self-determination—than do other animals, thanks to a capacity for symbolic language far beyond that of other animals. We also have much greater power to bring about effects beyond our own psyche. The fact that human beings have changed the face of the earth in the past few thousand years more drastically than any other species has over millions of years is one sign of this power. Another sign is our power, evidently fairly distinctive, to produce psychosomatic effects. Psychokinesis provides a third sign.

Although nonhuman animals are evidently capable of psychokinesis, this "animal PK" seems always to be very weak. Strong psychokinesis, capable of moving heavy objects, seems to be a prerogative of human souls alone. For example, poltergeist cases, in which the effects requiring the greatest force have occurred, seem to be associated with the presence of a particular human being. In some cases, to be sure, some parapsychologists, as I mentioned in Chapter 2, believe that a discarnate humanlike agent must be responsible. In any event, there are no validated cases, to my knowledge, in which the poltergeist activity seemed to be due to a nonhuman animal. Significant power to produce effects psychokinetically, among earthly creatures at least, seems limited to human souls.

My proposal is that the distinctive powers of the human soul, which emerged along with the distinctively human capacity to use symbolic language, may include yet one more power: the power of the soul to survive separation from the kind of body that was originally necessary to bring it forth. Perhaps the very power of human souls to ask, "When we die, will we live again?" (Job 14:14), brought with it the power to do just that. Accordingly, we can retain a naturalistic view, according to which human souls are not different in kind from other souls and according to which there is no supernatural intervention, without saying either that all souls survive or that none do. We can suppose that the capacity of the human soul to survive death is a fully natural, emergent property, analogous to the other distinctive powers of the human soul.

This position does not necessarily imply that the soul has developed this power apart from divine influence. My view, in fact, is that divine influence was necessary. Nevertheless, the position is still naturalistic, involving a naturalistic rather than a supernaturalistic theism, because the kind of divine influence that resulted in the first emergence of this power was not formally different from the divine influence in other cases of the emergence of novelty, and in fact in all other events whatsoever.

10. SURVIVAL AND THE EVIDENCE FOR THE BRAIN-DEPENDENCE OF CONSCIOUSNESS

Although I have addressed at least most of the reasons for the *a priori* dismissal of the possibility of life after bodily death, I have not yet dealt with the fact that has probably been most fundamental throughout the ages: the fact that consciousness seems to depend upon the state of the brain. This is true of the very fact of consciousness: If we get hit on the head with considerable force, we lose consciousness. And it is true of the nature of our consciousness: If the brain is affected with a virus or becomes chemically unbalanced, our thinking may become confused, even delusional. Other brain problems may result in more or less complete loss of memory. And so on.

I can here, at the conclusion of this already too-long chapter, indicate only the direction my response would take. From the point of view of the Whiteheadian understanding of the mind-body relation, although the mind is distinct from the brain, it is intimately related to it. The general principle involved is that any occasion of experience is internally related to its environment, in the sense of being largely constituted by its reception of influences from the events in its immediate vicinity. Although an experience is directly influenced to some degree by the entire past, being directly as well as indirectly influenced by noncontiguous events, it is most intensely influenced by contiguous events. It is to be expected, then, that the mind would be heavily conditioned by the state of the brain, so long as the brain constitutes its immediate environment. Seen from this perspective, the commonplace experiences of the brain-dependent nature of consciousness are compatible with the belief that the mind, when no longer contiguous with the brain, would be free from brain-related debilities.

In this chapter, I have addressed only the question of whether, in the light of a view of the mind-body relation that does justice to our normal experience of mind-body interaction, life after death seems possible. I have not addressed the question as to whether there is any good reason, given the possibility, to believe that people really do survive bodily death. An answer to this question, whether positive or negative, should be made in the light of the various types of experiences that have been taken as evidence of the reality of life after death. I turn now to the study of these experiences.

4

EVIDENCE FOR
LIFE AFTER DEATH:
MEDIUMISTIC MESSAGES

Wishful-and-fearful thinking aside, the two major considerations with regard to the question of life after death are antecedent probability and empirical evidence. For late modern thinkers, the empirical evidence is seldom examined, at least with anything approaching an open mind, because the antecedent probability of life after death is considered so low. Materialists with strongly paradigmatic minds, indeed, would tend to place it at zero.

The previous chapter addressed this issue of antecedent probability. I argued, first, that by far the most adequate view of the mind-body relation is nondualistic interactionism, according to which the mind is numerically distinct from the brain although not ontologically different in kind from the brain's constituents. This is true, I stressed, even apart from any consideration of paranormal functioning. I then suggested that the evidence for extrasensory perception and psychokinesis, besides bolstering the case for the mind's distinctness from the brain, also provides indirect evidence for the mind's capacity to exist, perceive, and act apart from its physical body. These considerations, I suggest, balance off all those facts that point out the great extent to which the mind seems to be dependent on the brain for its ability to perceive, to act, and even to be conscious.

The result, I conclude, is to place the antecedent probability of the human mind's survival of bodily death at about 50 percent (insofar as assigning a numerical figure makes sense at all). In other words, the panexperientialist view of the mind-body relation, especially insofar as it incorporates the parapsychological evidence for ESP and PK, is *neutral* with regard to the idea of life after death: On the one hand, this view does not define the human mind or soul in such a way as to make life after death necessary. On the other hand, this view does not make survival of death a priori impossible or even improbable. The twofold implication of this paradigmatic neutrality is that beliefs about life after death should be based primarily on an evaluation of the ostensible evidence for it, and that such evidence should be examined, insofar as possible (given inevitable wishful-or-fearful thinking), without prejudice, whether negative or positive.

Experiences that are *prima facie* suggestive of life after death constitute the third major kind of ostensibly paranormal occurrences, alongside those suggestive of extrasensory perception and psychokinesis. I did, to be sure, already bring parapsychological evidence to bear on the question of life after death at the end of the previous chapter. There, however, I limited the discussion to the *indirect* evidence, meaning that which suggests the *possibility* of life after death. The present chapter begins a discussion, continued in the four following chapters, of various types of *direct* evidence—that which suggests that human minds or souls *actually do* continue to live after bodily death.

Ironically, the indirect and the direct kinds of evidence are somewhat in tension with each other. That is, experiences that would otherwise seem to produce virtual proof of life after death can, if one posits extensive extrasensory powers, psychokinetic powers, or both, be given alternative explanations. These are, to be sure, still *paranormal* explanations; but they count against the kind of paranormal explanation that has been the uppermost concern of many psychical researchers: that which posits the soul's survival of death. For example, in Chapter 2 we examined some of the communications of Mrs. Piper and Mrs. Leonard that *prima facie* suggest communications from spirits of the dead. But an alternative explanation, I pointed out, is that these mediums, while in trance, had extraordinary extrasensory powers through which they acquired all the paranormal information. This has been called the "super-ESP hypothesis." Likewise, some of the phenomena that occurred in the presence of Daniel Home, such as the accordion-playing, and some of the poltergeist phenomena, such as flying objects with curved trajectories, have been taken by many as evidence of discarnate agency. All such events, however, can alternatively be attributed to extraordinary psychokinetic powers on the part of a living person (a Daniel Home or a "poltergeist teenager"). This is called the "super-PK hypothesis." Given the fact that the word "psi" is now widely used to cover both ESP and PK, this alternative paranormal way of explaining all data *prima facie* suggestive of life after death is sometimes referred to simply as the "superpsi hypothesis." The explanation in terms of the agency of a discarnate mind is, by contrast, often called the "survivalist hypothesis." (The reference to a mind as "discarnate" means only that the mind is apart from its physical, biological body; it need not mean that the mind has no type of body whatsoever. Some survivalists think in terms of some kind of "spiritual" or "astral" body.)

This tension between the survivalist and superpsi hypotheses has become the central issue with regard to the evidence for life after death. For example, Alan Gauld, in discussing the super-ESP hypothesis, says that it provides survivalists with the following dilemma:

> If a piece of putative evidence for survival is to be of use, it must be verifiable—we must be able to check by consulting records or surviving friends that the information given by the ostensible communicator was correct. But if the sources for checking it are extant, they might in theory be telepathically or clairvoyantly accessible to the medium or percipient. Since we do not know the limits of ESP we can never say for certain that ESP of the extraordinary extent that would often be necessary—"super-ESP"—is actually impossible. This is the central dilemma in the interpretation of ostensible evidence for survival.[1]

This dilemma, in fact, leads Gauld to the extreme statement that, "if there were *no evidence at all* for ESP, the 'case for survival' could well be *much stronger than it is.*"[2]

To look at the issue in this way, however, is to ignore or minimize the fact that the *primary* reason for the widespread rejection of life after death among intellectuals in our time is not an alternative interpretation of the putative evidence, but a view of the mind-body relation that makes the antecedent probability of survival seem so close to zero as to make the examination of this evidence seem unnecessary, even a waste of time. In particular, even if a strict identism is not held, it is widely thought that a mind could not possibly perceive, act, or even be conscious apart from a central nervous system. Accordingly, the *indirect* evidence for life after death provided by ESP and PK (in conjunction with more general philosophical considerations) is at least as important as the direct evidence. And this indirect evidence is stronger to the extent that it points to the reality of superpsi. Those who favor survivalist interpretations, accordingly, should not regard the possibility of superpsi with hostility: Whatever the difficulties created for the survivalist hypothesis by the possibility of superpsi interpretations of the direct evidence for life after death, these difficulties are more than compensated for by the support such interpretations give to the antecedent probability of life after death.

In other words, antisurvivalists also have a dilemma: On the one hand, the more they reject or belittle ESP and PK, thereby portraying the human mind as incapable of surviving apart from the physical body, the more they render a straightforward interpretation of the *prima facie* evidence for life after death necessary. On the other hand, the more they urge superpsi interpretations of that evidence, the more they portray the human mind as having the capacities necessary to survive bodily death. From this standpoint, those who consider belief in life after death desirable should be relatively free from the temptation to minimize the likelihood of superpsi interpretations of the putative evidence. The question is whether, after superpsi explanations have been pushed to the hilt, there are still facts that cannot be explained, at least plausibly, without positing postcarnate existence.

The reader, to be sure, will understandably suspect that I do not approach the evidence with complete neutrality. And that is true of my state of mind today. When I first examined the evidence in 1981, however, I approached it with the assumption that all the direct evidence that could not be explained away in normal terms could indeed be explained away in superpsi terms. This initial assumption stood up for some time, in part because my Whiteheadian worldview allows for some possibilities that go even beyond the usual superpsi explanations. Even today, furthermore, I find myself becoming resistant when reading survivalist authors who, to my mind, too quickly conclude that superpsi explanations of various phenomena are too farfetched to be taken seriously. In any case, it was finally the quality of some of the evidence that overwhelmed my initial assumption, leading me to conclude that the survivalist hypothesis is more plausible, at least with regard to some of the evidence. As I make the argument with regard to this evidence, many readers, no doubt, will find their own resistance rising. My purpose, however, is less to try to convince others of the reality of life after death than to show that there is evidence that is worthy of serious study, and to explain why I, at least, have concluded that it is best interpreted as pointing to the reality of life after death.

With those introductory comments, I turn now to some of the evidence. I will begin with mediumistic evidence, some of which was already mentioned in Chapter 2. I will then, in the four subsequent chapters, look at cases of the possession type, cases of the reincarnation type, apparitions, and out-of-body experiences (including near-death out-of-body experiences).

An examination of recent surveys of evidence for life after death would seem to suggest that the importance of messages from mediums is variously rated. On the one hand, Alan Gauld, in *Mediumship and Survival*, says: "By far the greater part of the ostensible evidence for survival comes from the phenomena of mental mediumship."[3] John Hick, in a chapter on "The Contribution of Parapsychology" in *Death and Eternal Life*, in fact limits the discussion to mental mediumship.[4] On the other hand, many surveys, such as David Lorimer's *Survival?*,[5] devote no attention whatsoever to mediumistic communications. A reconciling explanation is provided in Richard Broughton's chapter on "Life after Death?" Broughton himself devotes no space to mediumistic evidence, concentrating instead on out-of-body, near-death, and reincarnation experiences, which have been at the center of research in recent decades. He adds, however, that the reason there have been no recent studies of mediumistic communications, as well as of apparitions, is not that the older evidence was not good, but only that the research was no longer progressing. "[T]hose who take the trouble to examine the best of this work," he says, "would find it an impressive achievement."[6] We will here look at some of this older work, following Gauld's lead.

There is certainly much *prima facie* evidence for survival in the records of mediumistic recordings. Some of this *prima facie* evidence is provided by the *method* of communication, in that the medium will sometimes speak with the vocabulary, inflection, pitch, and tone of the deceased person who is ostensibly speaking through the medium. (In other cases, the medium's "control" will simply report what he or she is ostensibly learning from the deceased individual. In still other cases, the communication may come through automatic writing.) Most of the evidence, however, is usually provided by the *content* of the communication, which often contains information that, seemingly, only the deceased individual could have known. The task of evaluating this *prima facie* evidence is that of deciding whether it indeed points to the survival of the deceased individual's mind. To have good evidence for ongoing individuality, Gauld plausibly suggests, we would need evidence for memories, intellectual skills, mannerisms, and purposes recognizably continuous with those of the deceased.[7] All four of these criteria are certainly fulfilled by many mediumistic communications. The difficult part of the task, however, is to decide whether they could all be explained in terms of super-ESP plus the dramatic skills of the medium's unconscious mind (or alternate personality).

1. MEMORIES

The mere fact that a message contains information not knowable by normal means does not provide good evidence for survival. As we saw in Chapter 2, Mrs. Piper certainly produced enough information of this sort to convince William James that something paranormal was going on. As James was aware, however, she could have been acquiring most of this information telepathically from him or the other sitters. To eliminate this possibility, there were often "proxy sittings," in which the person wanting a message from beyond would send a third party. This third party would know little if anything about the other two individuals and would simply bring the name (and perhaps a relic) of the deceased individual. However, given the super-ESP hypothesis, these precautions would not rule out telepathy from the living: For all we know, simply the name of the deceased individual might be sufficient to connect the medium's mind, in the ESP-enhanced state of trance, with the mind of the person who sent the proxy.

Gauld believes that this type of explanation becomes strained when information is forthcoming that could not have been derived from simply one living person. Such information was produced, for example, in the case reported in Chapter 2 involving Oliver Lodge and his three uncles. When Uncle Jerry, who had died some twenty years earlier, purportedly began communicating through Mrs. Piper, "he" recalled some childhood incidents (swimming the creek, killing a cat in Smith's field) that were not recalled by Uncle Robert, from whom Lodge had received Jerry's watch, but were only later confirmed by Uncle Frank, who did not recall one of the items that Robert did remember. Gauld concludes that "if Mrs. Piper got all this information by telepathy, she must have ransacked the memory stores of two separate individuals and collated the results."[8] Given the possibility of super-ESP, however, that would not be a particularly difficult task.

There is, moreover, a simpler possibility: The medium could have acquired all of the information directly from the past mind of the deceased individual, Jerry. Curt Ducasse mentions this alternative in passing, speaking of the possibility that "Mrs. Piper has powers of retrocognitive clairvoyance so extensive as to enable her to observe the past life on earth of a deceased person."[9] Ducasse should have, more precisely, spoken of "retrocognitive telepathy," because he was referring to the acquisition of the information directly from the past mind of the deceased individual, not from a clairvoyant observation of the external facts of that individual's life. In any event, seldom if ever does one see this possibility discussed in relation to the concrete cases, even by Ducasse himself. And it does make the super-ESP hypothesis much less complex. In the present case, Mrs. Piper, while entranced, would have directly prehended the past mind of Jerry, with all its memories. She then, through unconscious dramatization, would have recalled the events from Jerry's perspective. There would have been no need to assemble the account from the minds of the two surviving brothers.

2. THE THEORY OF RETROPREHENSIVE INCLUSION

Whitehead's philosophy, furthermore, allows for an even stronger grasp of the past mind than the term "retrocognitive telepathy" suggests. In this philosophy, what we think of as the enduring mind or soul is in reality a series of momentary "occasions of experience." Each such occasion begins by prehending prior occasions of experience. The most important of these prior occasions are usually our own past experiences. Our prehension of these past occasions accounts for what we call memory and personal identity. These prehensions of our own past occasions, while obviously very different from our prehensions of other past experiences, are not absolutely different in kind. There seems to be the possibility, accordingly, that one might prehend the prior experiences of others *as if they were one's own*. If this were the case, then one might feel, think, and act in the present on the basis of memories, purposes, skills, and personality characteristics that had constituted a past life. That prior personality might have ended at the time of that person's biological death. There would, accordingly, be no memories of events between that person's death and the present. And yet that person would in a sense momentarily come to life again in the medium by being prehensively incorporated into the medium's own mind. I will refer to this idea as the hypothesis of "retroprehensive inclusion." Retro*prehension* is better than retro*cognition*, because what is suggested is not a mere knowing about, from the outside, but an appropriation that includes the prior soul, similarly to the way in which our present experience includes our own past history.

3. INTELLECTUAL SKILLS AND RESPONSIVE INTERACTION

If retroprehensive inclusion is a real possibility, then much of the *prima facie* evidence for survival loses some of its evidential force. Mere memories of the past, no matter how accurate and no matter how many presently existing sources would have to be located to confirm them, would not provide unambiguous evidence for survival. The same might even be true for the intellectual skill manifested by ability to respond in situations as that previous person, if still alive, would respond.

I will illustrate this last point by using a particularly impressive case cited by Gauld. It involved some sittings with Mrs. Piper had by Reverend and Mrs. Sutton, whose daughter Katherine, nicknamed Kakie, was the last of three children who had died. (In these sittings, "Phinuit," Mrs. Piper's control personality, does all the speaking, sometimes speaking and adding gestures on behalf of the ostensible child communicator. The words in square brackets are Mrs. Sutton's annotations.)

> Phinuit said . . . A little child is coming to you. . . . He reaches out his hands as to a child, and says coaxingly: . . . Come, darling, here is your mother. He describes the child and her "lovely curls." Where is Papa? Want Papa. [He (i.e. Phinuit) takes from the table a silver medal.] I want this—want to bite it. [She used to bite it.] [Reaches for a string of buttons.] Quick! I want to put them in my mouth. [The buttons also. To bite the buttons was forbidden. He exactly imitated her arch manner.] . . . Who is Dodo? [Her name for her brother, George.] . . . I want you to call Dodo. Tell Dodo I am happy. Cry for me no more. [Puts hands to throat.] No sore throat any more. [She had pain and distress of the throat and tongue.] Papa, speak to me. Can you not see me? I am not dead, I am living. I am happy with Grandma. [My mother had been dead many years.]

Phinuit says: Here are two more. One, two, three here—one older and one younger than Kakie. [Correct.] Was this little one's tongue very dry? She keeps showing me her tongue. [Her tongue was paralysed, and she suffered much with it to the end.] Her name is Katherine. [Correct.] She calls herself Kakie. She passed out last. [Correct.][10]

All of the information in this transcript, as Gauld points out, was available from the minds of the sitters. Gauld suggests, however, that "the flow of paranormally acquired information [was] so quick, so copious, and so free from error" that it could only with great difficulty be attributable to ESP, even super-ESP.[11] This is true of super-ESP as usually understood. But the extraordinary kind of super-ESP that I have called retroprehensive inclusion might be up to the task.

More difficult to explain, to be sure, would be responsive interaction, especially when it involves associations on the part of the purported communicator that contradict the associations in the sitters' own minds. This occurred in the next part of the transcript:

Where is horsey? [I gave him a little horse.] Big horsey, not this little one. [Probably refers to a toy cart-horse she used to like.] Papa, want to go wide [ride] horsey. [She plead this all through her illness.]

It turned out that "Kakie" had in mind a horse different not only from the one that Mrs. Sutton had initially surmised, but even from the toy cart-horse she then mentioned. In the next sitting, "Kakie" again asked for the horse and, when given the little horse again, said:

No, that is not the one. The big horse—so big. [Phinuit shows how large.] Eleanor's horse. Eleanor used to put it in Kakie's lap. She loved that horsey.[12]

Only then did Mrs. Sutton recall the intended horse, which belonged to Kakie's sister Eleanor and was packed away in another city and forgotten. In a parallel misunderstanding, "Kakie" asked for "the little book," which Mrs. Sutton supposed to mean a linen picture book. At the second sitting it became clear that "Kakie" meant a little prayer book that had been read to Kakie just before her death. Gauld concludes:

If we are to say that Mrs. Piper could select from the sitters' minds associations conflicting with the ones consciously present and utilize them in order to create the impression that the communicator's thoughts moved along lines distinctively different from the sitter's, we are beginning to attribute to her not just super-ESP but super-artistry as well.[13]

We do know from our own dream life, however, that our minds, in altered states, *are* capable of "super-artistry." And with the hypothesis of retroprehensive inclusion, we would not need to suppose that some of the information (about two of the horses and one of the little books) was drawn from the *conscious* mind of the sitter and the remainder (about the other horse and the other little book) from the sitter's *unconscious* mind. We could simply assume that all the information, including that about Kakie's preferences and attachments, was drawn directly from Kakie's own past experiences, which were retroprehensively included in Mrs. Piper's own mind, as a transitory alternate personality, while entranced during those sittings.

4. Manifestation of Mannerisms

There is more, however, to the "super-artistry" that must be attributed to the medium if some version of the super-ESP hypothesis is preferred to that of contemporary influence from the surviving mind of the deceased: Besides presenting the information from the point of view of the deceased individual, as illustrated in the above transcription, the medium sometimes delivers the material with that individual's characteristic mannerisms. Although there was some of this in the above case, it is sometimes much more dramatic, with the individual's vocabulary and even voice being exactly reproduced. (In some cases, a deep baritone voice will come through the female medium.) This feature of some mediumistic messages has been taken as decisive evidence in favor of the survivalist hypothesis by some psychical researchers, such as James Hyslop (1854–1920)—William James's good friend, professor of logic and ethics at Columbia University, and mainstay of the American Society for Psychical Research in its early years. In reflecting on sittings with Mrs. Piper in which his own father was the purported communicator, Hyslop said that the only alternative to believing that his father was really communicating was that

> we have a most extraordinary impersonation of him, involving a combination of telepathic powers and secondary personality with its dramatic play that should as much try our skepticism as the belief in spirits. . . . When I look over the whole of the phenomena and consider the suppositions that must be made to escape spiritism, which not only one aspect of the case but every incidental feature of it strengthens, such as the dramatic interplay of different personalities, the personal traits of the communicator, the emotional tone that was natural to the same, the proper appreciation of a situation or a question, and the unity of consciousness displayed throughout, I see no reason except the suspicions of my neighbours for withholding assent.[14]

Richard Hodgson, Mrs. Piper's chief investigator (who was introduced in Chapter 2), drew a similar conclusion in reflecting on the personality of "George Pelham" (also mentioned in Chapter 2):

> The continual manifestation of this personality—so different from Phinuit or other communicators—with its own reservoir of memories, with its swift appreciation of any reference to friends of G.P., with its "give-and-take" in little incidental conversations with myself, has helped largely in producing a conviction of the actual presence of the G.P personality which it would be quite impossible to impart by any mere enumeration of verifiable statements.[15]

However, as impressive as these apparent manifestations of living personalities are, it does seem possible that even this feature of the mediumistic messages could be explainable in terms of the super-ESP hypothesis, given the addition to it of the idea of retroprehensive inclusion. If in the trance state the medium's own past has in a sense been replaced by the past of the deceased individual, then the present experiences of the entranced medium would be drawing on not only all the memories of that prior person but also all the causal powers of that person's mind, both conscious and unconscious. From this perspective it is not so amazing that the medium might speak and gesture in the ways characteristic of that person.

5. MANIFESTATION OF STILL-LIVING PERSONALITIES

This theory of retroprehensive inclusion would, incidentally, explain one of the otherwise most puzzling of the mediumistic phenomena—the manifestation of the personalities of people who turn out to be still living. The most famous instance, usually called the Gordon Davis case, involved G. S. Soal (1889–1975), a British mathematician who was also one of Britain's best-known parapsychologists. In a report published in 1926, Soal tells of a communication that he received through a medium, Mrs. Blanche Cooper, from Gordon Davis, with whom he had attended school when they were boys. Since that time Soal had talked with him only once, about service matters, when they had met by chance on a railroad platform. Sometime after that meeting Soal had heard that Davis had been killed in the war. The personality that came through Mrs. Cooper, presenting itself as Gordon Davis, was able to describe his childhood interests, schoolteachers they had both had, and their last conversation. All of this, plus the assumption that Davis had died, could have been derived telepathically from Soal. But the Davis personality also spoke in the first person and, although Mrs. Cooper herself had not known Gordon Davis, the language and even the accent were recognizably those of Davis. In a second sitting, furthermore, "Davis" told about the house in which he was living. Afterwards, when it was learned that Davis was in fact still very much alive, it was also learned that the house was one in which Davis and his wife were about to move into.[16]

If this was an illustration of retroprehensive inclusion, the explanation would be that Mrs. Cooper in trance prehended Gordon Davis's mind up to the time that Soal assumed he was killed, so that that mind constituted the past of the trance personality calling itself "Gordon Davis." The additional items of information about Davis's house, which would have been acquired through telepathic connection with the more recent history of Davis's mind, would have then been woven into the communication through dramatic artistry.

A serious question for survivalists, if they base at least part of the case for survival on mediumistic messages, is whether cases of the Gordon Davis type discredit the evidential force of all such messages. Ducasse argues that they do not.

> [T]he Gordon Davis case shows only that, since he was still living, the process by which the tone of his voice and his peculiar articulation were reproduced by Mrs. Cooper was not "possession" of her organism by his discarnate spirit. . . . But this mere reproduction of voice peculiarities and of two memories, in the single brief conversation of Dr. Soal directly with the purported Gordon Davis, is a radically different thing from the lively conversational intercourse Hyslop and Hodgson refer to, with its immediate and apposite adaptation of mental or emotional attitude to changes in that of the interlocutor, and the making and understanding of apt allusions to intimate matters, back and forth between communicator and sitter. The Gordon Davis communication is not a case of this at all.[17]

Ducasse's distinction is well taken. Nevertheless, the difference does seem to be one of degree, so that cases of the Gordon Davis type, even though they are few, tend to undermine the evidential force of other messages from mediums.

6. PURPOSES

Cases of this type at least help us refine our criteria. We have thus far examined three of the four criteria suggested by Alan Gauld: memories, intellectual skills, and personal mannerisms. I have suggested that all of these might be explainable in terms of retroprehensive inclusion. More problematic for this hypothesis, however, would be Gauld's fourth criterion: purposes. To be suggestive of continuing existence, they would need to be more than simply purposes that were characteristic of the persons while they were still living: Manifestations of such purposes would be no more evidential than manifestations of the other traits. The purposes instead, to be good evidence of ongoing personal existence, would need to be purposes understandable only as those of the postcarnate individual.

One ability suggesting such purposiveness, in Gauld's view, is the ability to *select*. He makes this point in terms of Mrs. Leonard's book tests, which were illustrated in Chapter 2. In that illustration, "Bim," the communicator, gave a message for Bim's father, telling him the book's location and the page on which there was a reference to beetles, with which his father was obsessed. Gauld discusses the super-ESP hypothesis in terms of the possibility that Mrs. Leonard, through a combination of superclairvoyance and supertelepathy, could have selected the appropriate passage:

> [I]f we grant for the sake of argument that the books were in some sense open to clairvoyant inspection by an agency other than that of the communicator, there remains the problem of how, from this mass of potentially available material, just those passages were so often selected which were particularly appropriate as messages from the communicator to the particular living recipient. *Who selected* for Bim's father the passage about the beetle damaging the trees? To select a passage as appropriate as this, the medium would have had e.g. to tap Bim's father's mind, and then in the light of information telepathically gained from it, select that one of the very numerous book passages clairvoyantly accessible to her which would be most likely to impress Bim's family as a message of a kind he might plausibly address to his father.[18]

This hypothesis is indeed complex. The superpsi explanation becomes much simpler, however, given the idea of retroprehensive inclusion. From this perspective, Mrs. Leonard could have derived the knowledge not only about the father's obsession with beetles but also about the passage in the book directly from the past mind of Bim (who presumably had read that book). She would have needed clairvoyance only to specify where the book was presently located and the number of the page on which the reference to beetles was contained. Accordingly, Mrs. Leonard, thanks to her momentary inclusion of Bim's objectified mind, *could* have selected the passage.

7. PURPOSIVENESS IN THE CROSS CORRESPONDENCES

A much more persuasive *prima facie* demonstration of present purposiveness is to be found in the most extensive and fascinating episode in the history of mental mediumship, which has come to be known as "the cross correspondences." One way to approach this episode, which lasted from 1901 to 1932, is to imagine the task confronting some clever souls who, while living, had been involved in psychical research and now wanted to provide evidence for their own survival that could not be explained away in the usual manner. One way would be to communicate through various mediums at the same time, communicating bits of information to one medium that referred to items communicated through other mediums. These cross correspondences would be especially impressive if the various pieces made sense only when taken together with the others. Although this scenario would not provide absolute proof for life after death, it would at least put additional strains on the superpsi hypothesis. The *prima facie* suggestion, that the various messages were being coordinated by a mind or minds behind the scenes, might appear simpler than any conceivable explanation in terms of ESP and PK among the living.

The episode began shortly after the three most prominent founders of the Society for Psychical Research had died: Edmund Gurney died in 1888; Henry Sidgwick died in 1900; and Frederick Myers, the one who had been most intensely interested in life after death, died five months later, in 1901. The principle mediums involved were women of excellent reputation who were widely separated. One was Mrs. Piper in Boston. A second was Mrs. Fleming (the sister of Rudyard Kipling), who lived in India and carried out this activity under the pseudonym "Mrs. Holland." In England there was Mrs. Verrall, wife of A. W. Verrall, a well-known classical scholar; her daughter Helen Verrall (later Mrs. W. H. Salter); and Mrs. Winifred Coombe-Tennant, who was the first British woman delegate to the Assembly of the League of Nations (and who used the pseudonym "Mrs. Willett"). One interesting feature of the episode is that the apparent cross correspondences in the automatic writings of many of these women were occurring independently for some time before anyone noticed.

The discovery occurred in the following way: After Myers' death in 1901, Mrs. Verrall decided to try to take up automatic writing to enable Myers to demonstrate his survival of death. It was only after several months that scripts with some intelligible meaning (they were mostly in Latin and Greek and were signed "Myers") were produced, but they were cryptic. A year later, Mrs. Piper began to produce scripts, also claiming to come from Myers, with allusions to subjects in Mrs. Verrall's scripts. Then Helen Verrall, before seeing her mother's scripts, was found to be producing allusions to the same subjects. All three then began sending their scripts to Alice Johnson, the secretary of the SPR. Finally, reading Myers' *Human Personality and Its Survival of Bodily Death* in 1903 renewed Mrs. Fleming's interest in her gift of automatic writing. She too began to receive scripts signed "Myers," and one of them instructed her to send it "to Mrs. Verrall, 5 Selwyn Gardens, Cambridge." Although she had read Mrs. Verrall's name in Myers' book, she was very skeptical of her own scripts and did not obey these instructions (although the address was, in fact, correct). She did, however, eventually send the scripts to Miss Johnson, who, having no reason to suspect that these scripts produced by this "Mrs. Holland" in India would be related to those produced by the Verralls and Mrs. Piper, filed them away. It was not until 1905 that she discovered the relation.[19] Eventually over a dozen automaticists were involved, with Mrs. Piper being the only professional medium.

The cross correspondences, unfortunately, do not lend themselves to easy summary. The material is extremely voluminous, consisting of some 3,000 scripts. And many of the allusions, especially those purportedly from Myers (there were finally seven "communicators" involved), who was a classics scholar, are in Latin or Greek and are otherwise too obscure to be unraveled by anyone except another classics scholar. (Among the students of these materials were several classics scholars: J. G. Piddington, A. W. Verrall, and Mrs. Verrall, who doubled as an automatist and investigator.) I will, however, discuss a few of the cross correspondences that are most easily summarizable and therefore best known.

Some of the cases involve simple correspondences, where the same word or idea crops up in two or more of the writings. One of these, which occurred in 1907, involved the idea of death. On April 16, Mrs. Fleming (in India) wrote: "Maurice. Morris. Mors [the Latin word for death]. And with that the shadow of death fell upon him and his soul departed out of his limbs." The next day, April 17, during a sitting that Mrs. Piper was doing in England, the words "Sanatos" and "Tanatos" occurred. (In Greek, which Mrs. Piper did not know, the word for death is "Thanatos.") On April 23, the word "Thanatos" appeared (correctly) in Mrs. Piper's script. On April 29, Mrs. Verrall produced a script with multiple references to death: "Manibus date lilia plenis" (give lilies with full hands), which is a quotation from the *Aeneid* connected with the prediction of Marcellus' death; "Come away. Come away" (which seems to be a reference to "Come away, death," in Shakespeare's *Twelfth Night*); and "Pallida mors aequo pede pauperum tabernas regumque turres" (Pale death with equal foot the huts of the poor and the towers of the rich). At the end, the script said: "But you have got the word plainly written all along in your own writing. Look back." Finally, on April 30, the word "Thanatos" appeared three times in Mrs. Piper's script.[20]

An example of a more complex set of cross correspondences is provided by the "Hope, Star and Browning" case, which occurred earlier that same year (1907). On January 16, Piddington suggested to Mrs. Piper's "Myers" that "he" should indicate when a cross correspondence was being attempted by drawing a circle with a triangle in it. Then, on January 23, Mrs. Verrall's "Myers" wrote: "an anagram would be better. Tell him that—rat, star, tars, and so on." (Myers in life had been addicted to anagrams.) On January 28, Mrs. Verrall's "Myers" wrote "Aster" (Greek for "Star") and "Teras" (wonder), followed by a jumble of quotations from the poetry of Robert Browning, beginning with "The world's wonder." This was followed by a triangle within a circle. On February 3, the "Myers" personality for Mrs. Verrall's daughter, Helen, drew a monogram, a star and a crescent, and then wrote: "A monogram, the crescent moon, remember that, and the star." On February 11, Mrs. Piper's "Myers," who had started the whole thing, asked if Mrs. Verrall had received the word Evelyn Hope (the title of one of Browning's poems), then added: "I referred also to Browning again. I referred to Hope and Browning . . . I also said star . . . look out for Hope, Star and Browning." On February 17, Helen Verrall's "Myers" drew a star and wrote: "That was the sign she will understand when she sees it . . . No arts avail . . . and a star above it all *rats* everywhere in Hamelin town" (Browning, of course, had written a poem on the Pied Piper of Hamelin). This series was concluded with three scripts from Mrs. Piper's "Myers": On March 6, "Myers" told Piddington that "he" had given Mrs. Verrall a circle and a triangle; on March 13, "he" said, after claiming that "he" had drawn a circle and a triangle for Mrs. Verrall: "But it suggested a poem to my mind, hence BHS" (which can be taken to refer to Browning, Hope, Star); on April 8, "Myers" said that "he" had drawn a circle, a star, and a crescent moon.[21]

The most plausible superpsi account of this case would orient the explanation around Mrs. Verrall, who knew both the classical literature and Myers (although she did not know three of the other six communicators). On this account, she would have learned by clairvoyance about the original response by Mrs. Piper's "Myers" to Piddington's suggestion, then produced correspondences in her own script. She then, through psychokinesis (or telepathic influence, if one prefers this language), would have induced correspondences in the script of her daughter, then in those of Mrs. Piper, then again in those of her daughter, and then in the final three scripts of Mrs. Piper. This is—supposing the reality of both ESP and PK—not impossible. But it *is* complex. And, if all the cases in the thirty-year episode are to be explained in like manner, the hypothesis becomes even more complex. Mrs. Verrall would have had to be unconsciously scanning and influencing the scripts of a dozen other automatists, including those in America and India. Also, not all the cross correspondences began in Mrs. Verrall's scripts, and in some of them her scripts were not even involved. After her death in 1916, furthermore, the cross correspondences continued for another sixteen years. So, if an explanation is to be given entirely in terms of superpsi among the living, the ability to monitor and guide the various scripts must be assigned to one or more of the other participants as well.

A reasonable judgment about the cross correspondences cannot be made on the basis of the extremely small amount of material I have summarized. One needs to consult a lengthier study, such as H. F. Saltmarsh's *Evidence of Personal Survival from Cross Correspondences*.[22] My own judgment is that they do provide good (albeit not coercive) evidence of communication from still-active minds of deceased individuals. The reason is that they, better than at least most other mediumistic messages, seem to reflect sustained contemporary purposes, not merely purposes reflective of the earlier concerns of the purported communicator. To be sure, the idea of retroprehensive inclusion would make it more understandable how, say, Myers' general concern with the reality of life after death could have taken the particular shapes shown in the various "Myers" communications. This explanation would require, however, that all the mediums retroprehensively included the past mind of Myers in their own experiences, as well as engaging in the extensive clairvoyance and telepathic influence previously mentioned. Again, this is not impossible, but we all have a boggle-point, at which an explanation becomes too complex to be plausible. Two other factors, besides the complexity of the superpsi explanation of the cross correspondences, affect my judgment here: the fact that life after death does not seem philosophically impossible, and the fact that there seem to be other, somewhat independent, types of evidence for life after death. Before turning to these other types of evidence, however, there is one more phenomenon of mediumistic messages suggestive of contemporary purposes that should be mentioned: the "drop-in communicators."

8. Drop-In Communicators

In most cases of ostensible communications through mediums, the initiative is taken by living persons: The Suttons, for example, asked Mrs. Piper to try to contact their daughter Katherine (Kakie). Once the contact is made, the purported communicator seems quite willing, even anxious, to communicate: In the Sutton case, "Kakie" wanted her brother to know that she was alive and happy, that he should cry for her no more. If, however, the minds or spirits of individuals who have died bodily are indeed still alive and, furthermore, both able and willing to communicate through mediums, we would expect some of them to take the initiative, rather than waiting passively to be contacted. One reason that the cross-correspondences episode seems especially convincing is that it is suggestive of initiative on the side of the departed spirits. In this case, however, there was a circle of mediums with whom Myers and the others were familiar, so the initiative could still be thought to lie with the mediums themselves, at least in their unconscious purposes. (Although Mrs. Fleming in India did seem to have been recruited by "Myers" especially for this episode, she had read Myers' *Human Personality and Its Survival of Bodily Death* before beginning to receive messages purportedly from Myers.[23]) What we should expect, with regard to spirits who do not have a medium among their still-living acquaintances, is that they would sometimes drop in, unexpectedly, in sittings that were arranged for contacting someone else. And, if there were such cases, they would be especially suggestive of contemporary purposes on the part of communicating personalities, because no one at the sitting could be supposed, even unconsciously, to have had the intention of contacting this person, of whom they had never heard.

It turns out that there are indeed, in the records of psychical research, some cases of drop-in communicators. Of course, the mere fact that a coherent personality emerges is, by itself, not evidence for the survival of the mind of a once-living person. (After all, one séance group deliberately created a fictitious personality with its own seemingly autonomous ability to communicate.[24]) The alleged communicator would have to supply information about "his" or "her" own past life that was at the time unknown to anyone involved but that could subsequently be verified.

One such case that has been documented occurred in Iceland in 1941. The medium involved was Hafsteinn Bjornsson, who lived in Reykjavik, which is in the southwest part of Iceland. One January 25, he held a séance for Hjalmar Gudjonsson, who was from eastern Iceland (from which, at the time, communications were poor, being mainly by boat). Although Gudjonsson was anxious to contact various people he had known, the sitting was, to his annoyance, dominated by an intruding communicator, who called himself Gudni Magnusson. This communicator said that he was of average height, with blond hair that was thin on top, although he had been under thirty when he died. Having been a truck driver, he said, he had been driving, alone, over a mountain pass, when his truck broke down. While trying to repair his truck, he had torn or ruptured something in his body. He managed to get home but then died on the boat while a doctor was taking him to another fjord for medical care. "Gudni" addressed himself to Gudjonsson, saying that he had ties with Eskifjordur, which is a remote village in Gudjonsson's part of Iceland, and that his parents were still living.

Two days after the sitting, the woman at whose house it was held told a friend about the drop-in communicator. This friend, Asmundur Gestsson, subsequently (on February 26) wrote to a female cousin who lived in Eskifjordur, asking if there had been a person corresponding to the description provided by the communicator. This cousin, Gudrun Gudmundsdottir, replied on March 14, confirming that a Gudni Magnusson answering the description in Getsson's letter had lived there and had died in the manner described. Her letter also confirmed many of the other details (such as the fact that Reydarfjordur, which "Gudni" had also mentioned, was the town from which he was driving home at the time of his death). Realizing that he had an interesting case, Gestsson then asked Hjalmar Gudjonsson and the hostess to write out—independently, and before they had seen Gudrun Gudmundsdottir's letter from Eskifijordur—their memories of the incident. (A third sitter signed the statement by the hostess.)[25]

The case was later investigated by Erlendur Haraldsson, the Icelandic parapsychologist, and Ian Stevenson (who coined the term "drop-in communicator"). Finding the above-mentioned letters and statements, plus other sources of information, they were able to confirm eighteen of the twenty items provided by "Gudni." They also learned that most of the information could not have been acquired from the obituary or even its writer; that the medium (Hafsteinn Bjornsson) had never been to that part of Iceland (and that he had in no way encouraged the investigation); and that the visitor from that part (Hjalmar Gudjonsson) had no connection with Gudni Magnusson or his family. Haraldsson and Stevenson concluded, in their 1975 report, that the information had been acquired in some paranormal way.[26]

Haraldsson and Stevenson, in reflecting on such cases, point out that the simplest explanation would be in terms of the deceased individuals' retention of their memories and their subsequent communication through the medium. "On the other hand," they add, "sensitives have been known to achieve remarkable feats of deriving and integrating information without the participation of any purported discarnate personality."[27]

Gauld, on whose summary I have based my account, believes that the latter (superpsi) hypothesis would be plausible only if "sensitives operating in a non-mediumistic context can perform [comparable] feats of location and integration of detailed information from discrete sources."[28] However, there may be something distinctive about the mediumistic context that uniquely allows such feats. Also, given the idea of retroprehensive inclusion, the medium's unconscious mind would not need to locate and integrate material from "discrete sources," but would derive it all directly from the past mind of the individual (in this case Gudni Magnusson).

Gauld is correct, however, to argue that drop-in communications are especially suggestive, in that they seem to involve contemporary purposes that cannot be attributed to any of the sitters. And they present special difficulties even for the idea of retroprehensive inclusion. Why, we must wonder, out of all the people who have died, would the medium's mind select that particular past mind for inclusion? We might suppose, to be sure, that Hjalmar Gudjonsson's presence somehow led the medium's unconscious mind to latch onto the past mind of a recently deceased young man from that part of Iceland. But this is a mere possibility, which only shows that this case does not provide conclusive evidence for survival; it does not present an alternative theory that is more plausible. It does not, accordingly, undermine the claim that this case and others like it present good, even if not conclusive, evidence. Drop-in communicators, along with cross correspondences, do provide impressive evidence suggestive of communications from still-experiencing discarnate minds. If this evidence is taken at face value, it then lends additional plausibility to some of the other cases—so that, for example, "Kakie" and "Uncle Jerry" might also be thought to have been what they purported to be.

In my opinion, however, even the most impressive evidence from mediumistic messages would not, by itself, constitute sufficiently strong evidence for life after death. If that were all we had to go on, even in combination with a philosophical worldview that allows for the possibility of life after death, we should probably conclude that, as complex as the superpsi hypothesis must become to account for all the evidence, it is to be preferred to the survivalist hypothesis. Additional credibility may be lent to the evidence from mediumistic evidence, however, by the other types of direct evidence for life after death. I turn in the next chapter to evidence from cases of the possession type.

5

EVIDENCE FROM CASES
OF THE POSSESSION TYPE

Possession is helpfully defined by Carl Becker as "the phenomenon in which persons suddenly and inexplicably lose their normal set of memories, mental dispositions, and skills, and exhibit entirely new and different sets of memories, dispositions, and skills."[1] In this definition, there is no reference to the idea that is usually suggested by the word "possession," which is that of a person, or a person's body, being taken over by an discarnate soul. However, because that notion, which would beg the question at issue, *is* so readily suggested by the term "possession," it is better to speak of "cases of the possession type" (in imitation of Ian Stevenson's reference to "cases of the reincarnation type"). Because that phrase is cumbersome, however, I will often speak simply of possession, or ostensible possession, meaning thereby the phenomenon as described by Becker in neutral language.

Two further delimitations on the topic of this chapter: First, if possession were to be defined as the possession and control of a body by a soul that pre-existed that body, then reincarnation, taken literally, could be considered a form of possession. However, in line with Becker's definition, possession is here limited to cases in which a previous personality is displaced. Although Becker's definition does not specify this, possession usually also has an end as well as a beginning. Cases of the possession type, in other words, involve a *temporary* change. Second, (temporary) possessions can be put into two classes:

voluntary possession, in which the state of possession is cultivated, and involuntary, where it just happens. The emergence of "control" personalities in mediums can be considered cases of voluntary possession. The same is true for shamanistic possession (even though the people who become shamans sometimes do so rather involuntarily, being afflicted by illness until they consent). My discussion here is limited to possession of the involuntary, uncultivated type.

1. The Lurancy Vennum/Mary Roff Case

The most famous case of this type was recounted by a Dr. E. Winchester Stevens in an 1887 book entitled *The Watseka Wonder*, and later summarized by William James in his *Principles of Psychology*. The possessed individual was Lurancy Vennum, who was born in 1864 and from age seven (1871) had lived with her family in Watseka, Illinois. At age thirteen, in July of 1877, Lurancy, who until then had always been healthy, suddenly started seeing persons in her bedroom and hearing them call her (by her nickname) "Rancy! Rancy!" A few days later she began going into cataleptic states lasting for several hours. While in trance she described "angels" or "spirits" of persons who had died, including her own brother and sister. The trances ceased in September, but in November she began experiencing severe pains, and the trances soon returned. Believing she had gone insane, her parents had her examined by local physicians. Their minister wrote to the insane asylum to see if she could be admitted.

In the following January, Dr. Stevens was brought to see Lurancy by Mr. Asa Roff, who had lived about 200 yards away from the house in which the Vennum family had lived for about six months when they first moved to Watseka. The two families had developed only a formal relationship during this brief period. Afterward, the Vennum family never again lived anywhere near the Roffs. The salient fact about the Roff family was that, prior to the Vennum's move to Watseka, they had had a daughter, Mary, who had died in 1865, when Lurancy was about one year old. Mary had had frequent cataleptic fits from the time she was six months old. They had become increasingly severe in her teens. During a despondent mood when she was seventeen, she cut her arm with a knife, then fainted after bleeding profusely. Upon awakening, she was a "raving maniac" for five days, after which she lost the use of all her senses, including her eyesight and yet was able to do everything as if her senses were normal. Tests showed that she was able to read closed books and enveloped letters while heavily blindfolded. Her strange powers were investigated and verified by Watseka's prominent citizens.[2] She died in an insane asylum during a fit at age eighteen.

Mr. Roff had heard of Lurancy's case and of the idea of sending her to an asylum. On the basis of his Spiritualist beliefs, according to which disease has a spiritual origin,[3] he thought that this would be a mistake and sought to intervene. We are not told by Stevens whether Roff had been a Spiritualist all along or only became one after Mary's death; perhaps he was motivated to intervene in part because, having later become a Spiritualist, he had come to believe that he had been mistaken to send Mary to an asylum. In any case, he finally convinced Mr. Vennum to allow him to bring Dr. Stevens, who was a Spiritualist practitioner. Stevens talked for some time with two personalities evidently possessing Lurancy—a sullen, crabbed old woman calling herself Katrina and a troubled young man calling himself Willie. Afterwards, Lurancy fell to the floor, straight and rigid. Employing "magnetic" action and the "laws of Spiritual science," Stevens was "soon in full and free communication with the sane and happy mind of Lurancy Vennum herself, who conversed with the grace and sweetness of an angel, declaring herself to be in heaven."[4]

In the ensuing conversation, she discussed her condition, saying that she regretted the influence of such evil controls. Dr. Stevens suggested that, if she must be controlled, it would be better to find a better control who would prevent the return of the cruel and insane ones. Saying that there were a great number of spirits who would be glad to come, she gave the names and descriptions of several persons long since deceased, some of whom Lurancy had not known, although they were known to other persons present. One of those who wanted to come, she said, is one that the angels wanted to come. "Her name is Mary Roff." Mr. Roff said: "That is my daughter; Mary Roff is my girl. Why, she has been in heaven twelve years. Yes, let her come, we'll be glad to have her come." He told Lurancy that Mary, besides being good and intelligent, had herself been subject to similar conditions. After counsel with the spirits, Lurancy agreed. As Stevens interpreted it, an agreement was made "by which a mortal body was to be restored to health" and "a spirit, unfortunate in earth-life" was "to have an amended earthly experience."[5]

The next morning, Mr. Vennum went to Mr. Roff's office to inform him that the girl, claiming to be Mary Roff, wanted to go home, "wanting to see her pa and ma and her brothers." But the Vennums did not immediately send her to the Roff's home, fearing that this would be a great imposition. They tried to convince the girl that she *was* at home, but "she would not be pacified, and only found contentment in going back to heaven, as she said, for short visits."[6]

After about a week, Mrs. Roff and Mary's sister, Minerva, having heard of the change in Lurancy, went to see her. As they came into sight, "Mary" said, "There comes my ma and sister Nervie!" Stevens's account continues:

> As they came into the house, she caught them around their necks, wept and cried for joy. . . . From this time on she seemed more homesick than before. At times she seemed almost frantic to go home. . . .
> On the 11th day of February, 1878, they sent the girl to Mr. Roff's. . . . On being asked how long she would stay, she said, "The

angels will let me stay till some time in May.". . . The girl, now in her new home, seemed perfectly happy and content, knowing every person and everything that Mary knew when in her original body, . . . recognizing and calling by name those who were friends and neighbours of the family from 1852 to 1865 . . . calling attention to scores, yes, hundreds of incidents that transpired during her [Mary's] natural life.[7]

One illustration of these incidents was recounted to Richard Hodgson, who investigated the case in 1890. Mary's sister told him that one morning "Mary" said, "Right over there by the currant bushes is where cousin Allie greased the chicken's eye."[8] At another time, after Mr. Roff had asked "Mary" whether she recalled moving to Texas (when Mary had been about 10), she said, "Yes, pa, and I remember crossing Red River and of seeing a great many Indians, and I remember Mrs. Reeder's girls, who were in our company." In another incident, when a velvet head-dress that Mary had worn during her last year was put out as a test, the girl, upon seeing it, immediately said, "O, there is my head-dress I wore when my hair was short!"[9]

During this period "Mary" seemed not to recognize any of the Vennum family or any of their friends, and not to remember any of Lurancy's life. She was happy and normal, except that every other day or so she would enter into a trance, which she would describe as "going to heaven." During these periods "other spirits sometimes, by permission, would come and present themselves, and speak freely their own language and sentiments." In other words, Lurancy, or at least her body, was becoming a medium, for which Dr. Stevens had hoped. One time, in fact, "Mary" reported that Dr. Stevens's daughter, Emma, who had died twenty-nine years earlier, had asked if she could borrow the body for a week to go home to Wisconsin with her father to visit the family. Although "Mary" was willing, the Roff's did not consider it advisable. Another unusual thing about "Mary" reported by Stevens was her ability to leave Lurancy's body temporarily and take control of another person's body.

Stevens reports one conversation with "Mary" in which she told about cutting her arm. She started to roll up her sleeve to show him the scar, but then, catching herself, said, "O, this is not the arm; that one is in the ground." She then told him how she had watched it being buried.[10]

After fourteen weeks, in May (as predicted), "Mary" left—albeit reluctantly, because of the affection she had been able to express and receive in relation to the Roff family. When Lurancy returned, she evidently in one sense had no knowledge of what had happened, as she did not recognize the surroundings or the Roffs. She said that it felt as though she had been asleep. And yet she evidently had an awareness of "Mary," speaking of a pain that Mary had felt in her breast and reporting things that "Mary" had told her, such as how Dr. Stevens had helped her. In any case, Lurancy returned home, was healthy from then on, and eventually married, moved to Kansas, and had children. Because of her household responsibilities and the fact that her husband was not a Spiritualist, she seldom practiced mediumship. When the Roffs would visit each year, however, "Mary" would reappear.[11]

Literal Possession or Retroprehensive Inclusion?

This case seems to demand some type of paranormal explanation. Given the fact that the source of the information, Dr. Stevens, was a Spiritualist, one might naturally be suspicious about some of the details of his description. In terms of the general nature of the case, however, fraud seems ruled out by the concurrence of a number of facts: The story was widely reported in the newspapers of the time; Stevens's account is attested to by the Roffs and the Vennums; there are ample testimonials to the integrity of the two principal witnesses, Mr. Roff and Dr. Stevens; the case was investigated by many outsiders, including Richard Hodgson; and the story was accepted by William James and recounted in his *Principles of Psychology*. Also implausible would be the suggestion that Lurancy could have picked up all the information by normal means: She was one year old and living elsewhere when Mary died, and she had never been in the Roff home. Aside from one brief call on Mrs. Vennum by Mrs. Roff, the six-month relationship between the two families consisted of a formal speaking acquaintance between the two men.

The only question seems to be whether to think in terms of literal possession or to posit some sort of superpsi explanation. Again, the notion of retroprehensive inclusion, assuming its possibility, would seem the simplest of the possible superpsi explanations. It would help this explanation if there were a clue as to a possible motivation, even of a subconscious sort, for Lurancy to have developed an altered state of consciousness having Mary Roff's (incarnate) mind as its past. One possibility would be to suppose that the connection to Mary Roff's past life was evoked during Dr. Stevens's examination by the presence of Mr. Roff, who surely had a desire to believe that Mary was still alive and was now healthy and happy. He, indeed, was the one who encouraged "Mary" to "come" to Lurancy when the question came up. On this theory, the motivation would have been his, and he would have played a role similar to that of sitters in a séance hoping to receive word from departed spirits. We could also suppose that Lurancy, in mentioning Mary Roff's name, had subconsciously consented to a prior telepathic suggestion by Mr. Roff that she let Mary's spirit manifest through her as a way to bring about her own healing from temporary insanity. This theory would, of course, leave inexplicable the strange and sudden onset of Lurancy's voices, fits and trances; but, of course, lots of inexplicable things happen in the world of abnormal psychology.

A more serious difficulty for this superpsi explanation than that of motivation is due to the fact that "Mary" for fourteen weeks evidently made not a single slip in speaking of hundreds of incidents experienced by Mary Roff.

The degree of retroprehensive inclusion would have had to be far greater, accordingly, than that needed in any of the mediumistic cases, in which far fewer items of information are usually provided and in which mistakes are usually intermixed with the accurate statements. Still, once the idea of retroprehensive inclusion is allowed, there is no reason not to allow an occasional perfect instance of it. Whether that is more difficult to accept than the idea of literal possession is, of course, a matter of individual judgment.

A (nonsurvivalist) superpsi explanation, of course, would have to consider as fantasy, perhaps archetypal, all of the reports by both Lurancy and "Mary" about being "in heaven." The veridical reports of deceased individuals that neither Mary Roff nor Lurancy Vennum had known could, of course, be explained in terms of knowledge gained through ESP. The same would be true of "Mary's" report of her own funeral, assuming that it contained veridical elements.

Although the question as to which explanatory hypothesis seems most likely is not entirely reducible to the question of motivation, the two issues are closely related. If the motivation behind the possession is thought to have come at least in part from the "other side"—to have been, perhaps, Mary Roff's desire to enjoy a healthy, happy period with her family—the view of literal possession by a discarnate soul is supported. But if the motivation is thought to have been rooted in the living—to have existed, perhaps, in the hidden needs and desires of Lurancy Vennum and Mr. Roff—then a superpsi explanation is supported. Let us examine these questions in relation to a more recent case, which began in the 1970s and has been extensively investigated by Ian Stevenson. This case has added interest because of its dimension of xenoglossy, the ability to use an unlearned language.

2. THE UTTARA/SHARADA CASE

The subject of this case is Uttara Huddar (born in 1941), a part-time lecturer in public administration in Nagpur University, which is in the Maharashtra region of India. She had been introduced to the practice of meditation by her father, and she began regular meditation when she was twenty-four. In her twenties, Uttara had developed respiratory, gynecological, skin, and other physical disorders and in 1970 started being treated by "Dr. Joshi" (pseudonym). Late in 1973, she was admitted into his private hospital. In February, she was initiated by a visiting female ascetic into a new (to her) type of yoga. After being encouraged to let all that was inside her come out, she began to have visions of Bengali alphabets and to hear Bengali sentences. In March, a new personality began emerging at regular intervals, usually on *ashtami* days (the eighth day after either the new or full moon), with the duration ranging from one to forty-three days. Neither personality would recall what the other one had experienced. In May, at the request of "Dr. Joshi" and against her wishes, she was taken back to the home of her parents (with whom she lived, as is customary for unmarried women in India).[12]

The ways in which this new personality was different from the old were various. She called herself "Sharada." Whereas Uttara had sneezed a lot, Sharada did not sneeze at all. She wore her hair loose, rather than in a bun, and wore her sari Bengali style (over her head and face, as a partial veil), rather than Marathi style.[13] Whereas Uttara ate little rice and few sweets, Sharada liked lots of both.[14] Sharada was far more religious in the conventional sense than Uttara had been: Uttara had generally performed worship only when her mother needed a substitute, but Sharada engaged in worship every day. Also, whereas Uttarra's family worshiped Ganesh and Shiva, Sharada worshiped Durga and knew the proper way to do this.[15] Finally, and most strikingly, she spoke Bengali, which her family could not understand.

There was much, besides her sari style and her language, to suggest that Sharada was Bengali. She could not understand Hindi or (unlike Uttara) Marathi and English.[16] She read Bengali books and epics in Bengali.[17] She had a detailed knowledge of the geography of at least certain parts of Bengal.[18] She expressed a desire for various foods that are unique to Bengal, or especially liked there.[19] She was particularly fond of Bengali sweets and could tell the authentic thing from imitations.[20] When she fasted, she would ask for coconut water—and the coconuts in Bengal, unlike those in Maharashtra, have water.[21] In line with her view of herself as a married Bengali woman, she had vermillion applied to the parting of her hair, as do married Bengali women. She strongly desired that the line be drawn from the forehead upward, which corresponds with the Bengali belief that drawing it in the wrong direction may lead to early widowhood. (She would complain to Bengalis, sometimes weepingly, that Uttara's mother drew it the wrong way.)[22]

Several things suggested, furthermore, that she was a Bengali woman *from the early nineteenth century*. She draped herself only in a sari, with no undergarments, which no modern Indian woman would do.[23] Whereas modern Bengali women wear shoes or sandals when they go outside, she went barefoot. She liked a bath, not a shower, and used cold, rather than warm, water. She dried herself with her sari, rather than a towel, and when she had her menstrual period, she asked for a plantain leaf and cotton to use for hygiene. She sat on the floor, instead of on chairs.[24] She knew nothing of postindustrial inventions, such as gas stoves, electricity, electrical lights and fans, tape recorders, telephones, wristwatches, fountain pens, or even glass bottles. (When a portion of a tape recording was played back, she attributed the voice to a witch inside the machine.)[25] She did not like Marathas, calling them "looters" (which corresponds to the widespread opinion of Marathas in Bengal in the nineteenth and late eighteenth centuries).[26] She showed intimate knowledge of Bengali customs. (For example, when one investigator brought her a sari, telling her it was from her aunt, she asked why her aunt had not also sent a shawl; this reaction corresponds to the custom in Bengal in the nineteenth century and earlier to give a sari and a shawl together as a gift.[27]) Sharada's language, finally, contained no English loan words, thereby seeming to be the Bengali of a time before the spread of English, which occurred from the 1830s forward.[28]

With regard to Sharada's description of herself, the following are some of the central items: She said that her grandfather, Ramnath Chattopadhaya, had moved to the village of Bansberia in the Satagram area. Her father, Brajesh Chattopadhaya, had been appointed by the Maharajah of Burdwan to be the priest of the Kankalini Temple in Kanchanager, which is near Budwan. Sharada's mother, Renukha Devi, died when Sharada was about two months old. Her father then married a woman named Anandamoyi, and Sharada was adopted by an aunt (Sharada's mother's sister, Jagadhatri Mukhopadhaya) and her husband, who then, when Sharada was seven, arranged her marriage to his nephew, Vishwanath Mukhopadhaya. The marriage occurred when Sharada was ten. (Child marriages were not uncommon in Bengal at the time.) Sharada's husband was, or became, a physician, traveling by pony from village to village to make his rounds. Ten or eleven years after her marriage, when Sharada was eighteen, her father died. Most of her married life was spent in the Khulna District (which is now in Bangladesh), where her husband was from. When she was twenty-two, however, and five months pregnant (after two miscarriages), she returned to Saptagram to stay with her aunt. While there she wrote to her husband, asking him to come and take her on a pilgrimage, to thank the goddess Tara Devi for a safely completed pregnancy. (Tara is, like Kali, an incarnation of Durga, who is a manifestation of Devi, the wife of Shiva.)[29] But before this could take place, the last event remembered by Sharada occurred: While picking flowers one day—an *ashtami* day in the month of *Magh* (January-February)—when she was seven months pregnant, she was bitten by a snake on her right toe, after which she was carried away before losing consciousness.[30]

The present-day Sharada personality, incidentally, has no sense of having died (which distinguishes her from typical subjects in cases of the reincarnation type, to be discussed in the next chapter). Rather, she believed that her husband had brought her to the Huddars; she would ask to be taken to him or to her aunt, and at least once wrote a letter asking him to come and take her home.[31]

There are some objective bases for considering Sharada actually to be a reemergence of the personality of a woman who had lived in Bengal in the 1810s and 1820s and had had the experiences described by the Sharada personality. With regard to the snakebite: Uttara's mother, while she was pregnant with her, had recurring dreams that a cobra was about to bite her right toe; these dreams stopped after Uttara's birth. Then, during Uttara's infancy and childhood, the only remarkable thing about her, according to her parents, was her phobia of snakes, which was particularly severe between the ages of five and eight.[32] She later outgrew this fear and, in fact, in her teens developed an attraction for snakes. Of interest in this regard is the fact that, during some Sharada phases, her tongue and mouth would become very dark. In one such episode, her eyes were also closed, as if she were intoxicated, and she pointed to her toe—which then had a black area on it—saying: "A king cobra has bitten me." A present-day member of the Chattopadhya family, furthermore, reports hearing that during the time of his great grandmother a female member of the family had died of a snakebite.[33]

With regard to Sharada's story about her thankfulness for her pregnancy, which was nearing term (after two miscarriages), it is interesting that, when asked if she had any children, tears came to her eyes as she said no.[34]

With regard to Sharada's memories of her husband, it is noteworthy that Uttara herself had a recurrent dream, which she reported up to about the age of eight, in which her husband came to her riding on a pony, then caressed her.[35] It is also surely significant that the Sharada personality appeared shortly after Uttara had entered the hospital of "Dr. Joshi," to whom she was strongly attracted.[36] Also, when Sharada first emerged, she seemed to treat "Dr. Joshi" as if he were her husband: One night she burst into the room where he was having dinner with a female assistant and berated him.[37]

Whereas the points in the previous two paragraphs are merely suggestive, Sharada did also provide some verifiable information. Most clear-cut are the nineteen names she gave of relatives. On the basis of the family name and the area, a descendent was found named Satinath Chatterji (an anglicized version of Chattopadhaya), who had a genealogy of his male ancestors. It contained six of the names she gave: those she named as her grandfather (Ramneth), father (Brajesh), two brothers and two uncles (one of whom is a direct ancestor of Satinath Chatterji).[38] The genealogy also confirmed Sharada's statement of the relationships these men would have had to each other. Also, deeds dated in 1827 confirm another name and also tacitly indicate that Brajesh had died by 1827,[39] which, if Sharada had been born about 1809, would correspond with the report of the present-day Sharada that her father died when she was eighteen. (Neither Sharada's name nor that of any other women are mentioned in the genealogy, of course, because it included only male names. And any records that would confirm the names given for Sharada's husband and his family, which would be in Bangladesh, have evidently not yet been sought.)

With regard to whether Uttara could have learned of these names by normal means, investigation discovered that a magazine published in 1907 contained the genealogy of the priests of the rajahs of Bansberia, which contained part of the Chattopadhaya genealogy. However, given the fact that this was a strictly local magazine (which was discontinued in 1909), that it was published over thirty years before Uttara was born, and that it was written in Bengali, it is very unlikely that she would have seen it. Also, it did not contain one of the names Sharada mentioned that was confirmed by the deeds.[40]

Sharada also provided evidential statements about the geography, historic sites, and place names in Bengal, especially those parts in which she claimed to have lived. She correctly said, for example, that the Hansheshwari Temple in Bansberia had thirteen towers (in response to a photograph showing only eleven), and that the temple's idol of the goddess (Durga/Kali) is blue, has four arms, and is made of neem wood.[41] That sort of thing could be learned, of course, from novels about Bengal (which Uttara had read), but Sharada also knew that this temple could be seen from the house of Ramnath Chattopadhaya (whom she called her grandfather).[42] She knew also of the existence of a much more obscure temple (the one to which her father, she said, had been appointed) in Kanchanager, a village that was deserted and overgrown for most of the twentieth century.[43]

Surely the most impressive feature of this case, however, is the apparent xenoglossy (indeed, the case is published in Ian Stevenson's book entitled *Unlearned Language*). The ability to speak Bengali, which appeared suddenly, was remarkable. Unlike some other cases of responsive xenoglossy, in which the vocabulary is quite limited and the speech halting, Sharada could speak fluently. (Most of the native Bengali speakers who had extended conversations with her agreed on this, while two of the three who denied that she spoke fluently, like a native, had only heard some tape recordings.[44]) And yet Uttara had hardly studied Bengali. She had studied with a male classmate for a brief period, at the end of which she had only a very rudimentary knowledge of Bengali: Most said that she could only read a few words, whereas the most extravagant claim, made by her classmate, was that they could "read a Bengali primer."[45] The teacher, furthermore, was not Bengali, could neither read nor speak it himself, and taught the words with Marathi pronunciation. (Uttara did have a Bengali teacher, but she studied English from him, not Bengali.)[46] Uttara *had* studied Sanskrit in high school for four years and had become somewhat proficient. But Sanskrit is related to Bengali, Hindi, and Marathi somewhat the way Latin is related to Italian, French, and Spanish, and, as Stevenson points out, a native French or Spanish speaker could not, by virtue of studying Latin in high school for four years, suddenly begin to speak Italian fluently over a decade later.[47] Stevenson investigated the other normal possibilities—fraud and cryptomnesia—and found them completely implausible.[48] Some sort of paranormal explanation seems necessary. The question, again, is whether the paranormal linguistic ability and experiences can be explained in terms of retroprehensive inclusion, or whether they are better seen as indicative of life after death.

Motivation and Possession/Reincarnation

The case certainly is, *prima facie*, suggestive of some form of literal continuation of a previous life. Thus interpreted, the question would seem to be whether to regard it as a case of possession or of reincarnation. In making this distinction, "possession" is here being used in the literal sense, according to which a discarnate soul enters into the body, taking possession of it. If the case is understood as involving reincarnation, by contrast, the Sharada personality would be thought to have been present, beneath the surface, all along. The problem is that the case does not completely fit the pattern of either the typical possession cases or the typical reincarnation cases. It is like reincarnation cases in that the memories and characteristics of a prior human personality are involved, and it is like *most* reincarnation cases (as we will see in the next chapter) in that there was no memory of experiences between lives. It is like possession cases, however, in that this other personality appeared quite late in life (although there *was* the early snake-phobia) and in that the two personalities alternated, with neither knowing the experiences of the other. It was *unlike* both typical reincarnation and typical possession cases in that the prior personality had no sense of having died. But the fact that the case does not fit neatly into one of the standard forms does not rule out a survivalist interpretation. There is a continuum between paradigmatic reincarnation and possession cases, just as there is a continuum between the latter and paradigmatic mediumistic cases. In any event, the case contains more than enough evidence, as the above summary shows, to be reasonably interpreted as the reemergence of a prior personality.

If it is to be so interpreted, as the real return of a woman named Sharada from the early nineteenth century, however, we should have some inkling as to her *motivation* to return—which is the issue in terms of which this case was introduced. The survivalist interpretation will be more credible if the motivation, and thereby the initiative, behind the reemergence of Sharada's personality seems to have rested in Sharada more than in Uttara. On this question, either answer could be supported.

On the one hand, in terms of any concrete purpose, Sharada did not seem to have any motivation. She had no message to bring, no particular task to carry out, and, therefore, no apparent reason for having come back. She, indeed, had no awareness that she had "come back." However, as we will see in the next chapter, personalities with "unfinished business" are among those that seem to "reincarnate" most often. One could certainly assume that Sharada, as described—given her pregnancy and her preparation for a pilgrimage to fulfill her promise—would have died with a sense of unfinished business. This point, however, raises one of the central unanswered questions about this case: If Sharada had no sense of having died, thinking instead that her husband and relatives were still living, why was she not puzzled as to why she was not still pregnant? A possible answer is that, having had two miscarriages already, she assumed that the cobra bite had caused a third. (The fact that her eyes teared when she was asked if she had any children might suggest this.) But if so, why did she (evidently) not talk about this? In any case, given what we know, it seems that the survivalist interpretation can provide a partly (if only a partly) satisfactory answer to the question of motivation, so that the survivalist interpretation of the case is not ruled out.

Motivation and Retroprehensive Inclusion

On the other hand, there is much to suggest an explanation in terms of retroprehensive inclusion, with the motivation rooted in Uttara's own deep psychological needs. In exploring this alternative, I will build on the suggestions of Stephen Braude, who has argued for the plausibility of a hypothesis combining dissociation and motivated superpsi.[49] My development of this interpretation involves three points: (1) We can understand the emergence of Sharada as an instance of multiple personality motivated by Uttara's problems and needs. (2) We can understand the particular shape of this alternate personality, including its paranormal knowledge and abilities, in terms of retroprehensive inclusion of the life of a previous personality. (3) We can to some extent explain why this particular personality was chosen.

With regard to the first point, there is considerable reason to think that Uttara developed another personality in reaction to deep psychological problems. That she had had severe physical problems for over a decade is clear. It also seems likely that at least some of these problems, such as asthma, menstrual bleeding, and (evidently) eczema, were psychogenic in origin. For example, after reading T. S. Eliot's "The Waste Land," after which she felt that "woman's womanhood had come to an end," leaving "only lust," she suffered heavy menstrual bleeding said by her to be "like abortional bleeding." The next day profuse bleeding occurred again after she taught "The Boy Stood on the Burning Deck" and thought that she should have such a son.[50] Besides being related to her deep desire to fulfill her womanhood, her problems also seemed to be intimately related to unrequited love. This had occurred earlier in relation to the classmate with whom she had taken the Bengali lessons, whom she had hoped to marry. When he did not reciprocate her feelings, being, in fact, interested in another woman, she was so shaken by this rejection that she decided to devote herself wholly to meditation and spiritual development.[51] Then she had some kind of disappointing relationship with "Dr. Joshi." The first time she was touched by him it felt "familiar" and she was drawn to him "like an iron particle to a magnet"; she also claimed (according to him) that she had had a relationship with him in a previous life.[52] When she came to his ashram-hospital, she planned, rather than ever returning to her parents' home, to remain there the rest of her life. She thought of marrying him and adopting an infant.[53] The episode in which she burst into the room where "Dr. Joshi" was having dinner with a female assistant, acting like a jealous spouse, can be taken as a sign that the relationship with him did not work out as she had hoped.

Besides the fact that she had the kinds of problems out of which an alternate personality might have developed as a defense, Uttara also showed signs of being prone to dissociation. She engaged in automatic writing.[54] One day in the early months when a consultant on yoga touched Uttara's forehead, she went immediately into Sharada.[55] When the Sharada phenomenon had first begun, Uttara experienced "a veritable tug of war" and she would sometimes stay awake for several consecutive nights, often gazing at the moon for hours.[56] She would sometimes "feel frightened, hear strange sounds, see a luminous column of air infused with consciousness," and she had repeated visions, including one of someone beating her, after which she felt insulted.[57]

The second point of this alternative scenario is that, assuming that we can understand the motivation for the development of an alternate personality in Uttara's own problems and needs, we can also understand the particular shape it took in terms of retroprehensive inclusion of a past life. Whereas usually (one can assume) the material for the *alter* comes entirely out of the person's own past experiences (including fantasies), in this case, given its paranormal dimensions, much at least of the Sharada personality seems to have been derived from the life of another person, quite likely named Sharada. The paranormal information and xenoglossy were so extensive that, aside from some hybrid form of possession-reincarnation, the only paranormal explanation that seems adequate is that which I have called retroprehensive inclusion. According to this view, Uttara's newly created *alter* acquired a past not by creating one, but simply by taking as its past the life of a nineteenth-century woman up to the time that she lost consciousness after a snakebite. That this nineteenth-century woman's soul had had no intervening existence is consistent with the fact that the Sharada personality reported no intervening memories and, in fact, had no sense of having died. That we can understand the shape of the Sharada personality, with all its paranormal knowledge and abilities, in terms of superpsi is suggested by the fact, emphasized by Braude, that dissociation tends to promote psychic functioning, and also by the fact that Sharada developed a sufficient reputation for paranormal abilities for a small clientele to start coming to her for predictions and advice.[58] Although I agree with Stevenson's axiom that skills, such as linguistic abilities, cannot be communicated normally, I agree with Braude that it does not follow from this axiom that they cannot be communicated paranormally.[59] I do, however, agree with Stevenson that they could not be transmitted by super-ESP as that is usually understood. But retroprehensive inclusion (as defined) is a qualitatively different type of superpsi, in which the present personality has the past personality as its own past, so that it has all its skills and preferences as well as all its memories.

If we can understand the development of the Sharada personality *in principle* in terms of disassociation and retroprehensive inclusion, the third question is whether we can understand why, out of all the billions of lives that were possible candidates, that of Sharada would have been selected. If not, we would be moved back toward the survivalist explanation, according to which the initiative came from Sharada herself (because, perhaps, of unfinished business). But we do have some bases for seeing why Uttara's unconscious mind, using its extrasensory powers, would have settled on this particular past life. In the first place, Uttara, like her father, had a special admiration for the Bengali people. Her father, who took part in the resistance to British rule, thought the Bengalis were the most devoted to independence.[60] Uttara believed that Bengali women were both more feminine and more courageous than other Indian women, and she liked to read Bengali literature (in translation), complaining by contrast that Marathi literature displayed no real heroines.[61] It is no mystery, accordingly, as to why Uttara's unconscious would have narrowed the candidates down to Bengali women. Further narrowing would have occurred through the fact that—given Uttara's obsession with "Dr. Joshi"—the woman had to be married to a doctor and—given her recurrent childhood dream about her husband coming to her on a pony, which started occurring again after she began meditating—the doctor had to ride a pony. This would have tended to limit the Bengali candidates to a particular period in the past. It is also quite likely that the particular period of Bengali history chosen was based on one or more of her favorite Bengali novels; it may have been in them that she especially found the "heroines" she admired. Having the personality of a woman in preindustrial times might, furthermore, have allowed her to engage in some heroic acts—like bathing in cold water! Still another desideratum is that the woman selected should have been one who desperately wanted a child and, preferably, was about to have one—and yet, conveniently, did not actually have one. This woman, furthermore, should not only have been very religious but her religiosity should have been connected with having a child. Finally, given Uttara's childhood phobia of snakes—which on this interpretation would have resulted from picking up her mother's dream telepathically while still in the womb—it was desirable to have a woman who had died of a snakebite. Given all of those desiderata (and surely some others of which we have no clues), the selection by Uttara's unconscious, or by her nascent *alter*, of that particular woman might have been fairly automatic.

It seems to me, accordingly, that in cases of the possession type, in which the subject is psychologically developed enough to have various deep-seated needs, we cannot, even in the best of cases (and I chose the best ones of which I knew), rule out the likelihood that the motivation for the "possession," therefore the initiative behind it, lies in the present subject. And, insofar as the initiative is deemed to be in the present subject, the nonsurvivalist hypothesis of retroprehensive inclusion is supported. This explanation is, to be sure, *prima facie* less plausible for the Lurancy Vennum/Mary Roff case, given the fact that "Mary," by reporting memories of her funeral and of her sojourn in "heaven," gave some evidence of a continuing personality. However, these "memories" could be simply interpreted as fantasies unconsciously created by Lurancy to fill out the account in a way that would meet the Spiritualist expectations of Mr. Roff and Dr. Stevens, under whose influence "Mary" emerged. In any event, I do not claim that this alternative construal of these possession cases is necessarily more plausible than a survivalist construal, only that, when considering these cases by themselves, it is plausible. Whether this theory can remain plausible when the subject is a young child will be the central question of the next chapter.

6

EVIDENCE FROM CASES
OF THE REINCARNATION TYPE

The attitude in the West toward reincarnation has changed dramatically in the past century. Early in the nineteenth century, Arthur Schopenhauer said, in effect, that the best definition of Europe is that it is that part of the world that does not believe in reincarnation.[1] Even at the beginning of the twentieth century, Frederick Myers stated in *Human Personality and Its Survival of Bodily Death* that "for reincarnation there is at present no valid evidence."[2] However, attitudes among both the general public and writers on life after death have been changing. In England, for example, Gallup Polls revealed 18 percent of the population believed in reincarnation by 1969, and that this figure had risen to 28 percent by 1981; in the United States, the figure had risen to 23 percent by 1982.[3] In philosopher C. J. Ducasse's 1961 study, *A Critical Examination of the Belief in a Life after Death*, the final seven chapters were devoted to "Life after Death Conceived as Reincarnation." And books published in 1992 and 1993 on evidence for life after death by Robert Almeder and Carl Becker, respectively, demonstrate a further evolution: They not only include reincarnation as one of the four or five types of phenomena considered, but even place the chapter on reincarnation first.[4]

This change in fortune, both in parapsychological circles and in the general populace, is due to many factors, including the decline in traditional Christian beliefs and a concomitant increase of interest in Asian spiritualities.

Within parapsychological circles, however, the decisive influence has been the work of Ian Stevenson (whose report on the Uttara/Sharada case was discussed in the previous chapter). Whereas Ducasse's book, having been written just prior to Stevenson's first published studies, gave primary attention to the "Bridey Murphy" case, nowadays reincarnation research in the West is virtually synonymous with the work of Stevenson, who has since 1966 published over sixty extensive, meticulously documented studies of what he calls "cases of the reincarnation type," and numerous other less completely documented cases.[5] Recently, other researchers (some of them in other parts of the world), who have been inspired and emboldened by Stevenson's work, have published the results of their own investigations.[6]

1. Bias Against the Idea of Reincarnation

In this chapter I will rely primarily on Stevenson's work. Before summarizing a few of his cases, I will mention some of the more general results of his studies that may be relevant to the extranegative bias with which many readers may approach this material. That is, beyond the bias engendered by late modernity against belief in life after death of any type, there is an additional bias against the notion of reincarnation. Ducasse's 1961 comment, that this conception of survival "seems fantastic and unplausible to the great majority of people today in Europe and America,"[7] would still be largely true today. Alan Gauld, who has presented extensive evidence and argumentation for life after death, probably expresses a widespread attitude in confessing to his "very considerable distaste for the idea of reincarnation."[8]

Some of the prejudice against the idea of reincarnation is due to the association of this idea with the Hindu and Buddhist notion of karma, which (as usually understood) seems, by implying that everyone gets what they deserve, to induce passivity in the face of suffering and injustice. Whatever be the truth and merits of this idea of karma, however, there is no necessary connection between it and the idea of reincarnation: One widespread misconception is that only Hindus and Buddhists believe in reincarnation. But in fact, as the aforementioned quip by Schopenhauer indicated, probably a majority of people on the planet have believed in reincarnation, and many of these have not connected reincarnation with any karmalike notions.[9]

Another reason for reluctance to accept evidence for reincarnation is the widespread assumption, fostered by most believers, that if reincarnation is true in some instances, it must be universally true. Given the dynamics of wishful-and-fearful thinking, this assumption would lead many people—namely, those who have no desire to be reincarnated in the future—to resist the evidence, no matter how compelling, that some particular person is a reincarnation of a prior personality, because such an admission would imply that they themselves not only had lived a human life many times before but would probably do so many times in the future. However, that assumption goes far beyond the evidence. The evidence, at best, suggests only that a *few* people have begun their lives as reincarnations of prior personalities. Even in cultures in which reincarnation is accepted and the reporting of memories of past lives is encouraged, the incidence of reported cases seems to be about one out of every 1,000 inhabitants or, in a few places, about one out of every 500 inhabitants.[10] It is not necessary to assume that, if a few lives involve reincarnations of prior lives, all lives do. The most that one could conclude from the evidence is that reincarnation is a form that life after death sometimes takes.

Another reason for suspicion about reincarnation claims is the assumption that they all take place in cultures in which reincarnation is widely accepted. This assumption creates the suspicion that the claims are all products of fantasy, fraud, and credulity. It is indeed true that there is a much higher incidence of reported cases in cultures in which the belief is accepted. This is, of course, what we would expect, even if the incidence of *actual* cases were the same in all cultures. But it is not true that reported cases appear only in such cultures. Ian Stevenson's files contain, for example, several hundred reported cases from Great Britain and the United States.[11] In any case, the question as to whether all claims are to be dismissed should be settled not in terms of *a priori* suspicions, but on the basis of the evidence. I turn, accordingly, to some of Stevenson's actual cases.

In the typical case, a child between the ages of two and four begins speaking of a prior life, giving, among other things, the name of the prior person and the place where he or she lived. Usually the prior person died within the past five years and lived in a nearby town. The child will typically plead with its parents to take it to its other (or "real") family until they relent. Objective investigators, if involved at all, usually arrive on the scene only after the two families have met. Much of the investigation, accordingly, involves cross-checking testimony to determine exactly what transpired at that first meeting, when identifications of people and objects and verifications of memories were allegedly made. A case is much stronger if the investigators arrive prior to this meeting, so that they can record in advance the child's statements and then witness the meeting. At present, only a small percent of Stevenson's investigated cases have this advantage.[12] I have selected for my main example a case of this type, which Stevenson still considers among the best,[13] from his first book, *Twenty Cases Suggestive of Reincarnation*.

2. The Case of Imad/Ibrahim

This case, in which the child's name is Imad Elawar, occurred among the Druse in Lebanon. In the Druse religion, usually considered an off-shoot from Islam, reincarnation is a fundamental tenet and children are generally not discouraged from speaking of previous lives. The children, perhaps in part for this reason, tend to retain their "memories" of prior lives longer than the average. (In most cultures, these memories typically begin to fade between the ages of five and eight.) This longer retention of memories was true in this case.

Imad Elawar was born in 1958 in Kornayel, a mountain village fifteen miles east of Beirut. Sometime before the age of two, he began speaking of a former life. The life he remembered turned out to correspond to that of Ibriham Bouhamzy, who had died of tuberculosis at the age of twenty-five in 1949, and who had lived in Khirby, a village twenty miles southeast of Beirut, about a twenty-five-mile drive from Kornayel on a winding mountain road. Although Stevenson presents the material in the order of discovery, working from the present back to the past,[14] I will, to make the summary as brief and simple as possible, begin with the salient features about Ibriham Bouhamzy.

Known as a playboy, Ibriham had never married but had a mistress, given the pseudonym "Jamileh" by Stevenson to protect her identity.[15] This name, meaning "beautiful girl" in Arabic, is appropriate because she was famous in the region for her beauty. She was also a classy dresser, having, for example, worn high heels, a practice very unusual for a Druse woman in the villages.[16]

Ibriham's other strong passion was hunting. For guns he had a double-barreled shotgun and a rifle. Because it was illegal for civilians in Lebanon to possess rifles, he had hidden his rifle in a closet.

Whether or not this fact was related to his love of guns, Ibriham had joined the French army, thereby learning French.

Ibrahim lived in a house with his mother, his uncle Salim, his sister Huda, and his three brothers, Fuad being the one to whom he was the closest. (Stevenson does not mention Ibrahim's father, who had evidently died.) This house was about 300 feet from the house of Ibrahim's cousin, Said Bouhamzy.

Perhaps the most traumatic event in Ibriham's life (aside from his own tuberculosis, to be discussed below) was the death of his cousin, Said Bouhamzy, just six years before his own death, in an accident involving a truck. The truck had run over Said, breaking both of his legs and crushing his trunk. After being taken to the hospital, Said had an operation on his abdomen and another on his head, but he died a few hours afterwards. This death of his cousin affected Ibriham deeply.[17]

Ibriham himself was involved in an accident shortly before his own death. His accident involved a bus, which he owned and drove. One day he stepped out of the bus, leaving his assistant inside. The emergency brake slipped, allowing the bus to roll backwards down a slope and turn over, injuring the passengers.[18]

Politically, Ibriham's family belonged to the Joumblati party, and Ibriham was a friend of Kemal Joumblat, the well-known Druse philosopher and politician who was the leader of that party.[19]

The last year of Ibriham's life was spent in a sanitorium because of tuber-culosis. He was greatly enfeebled and was bedridden much of the last six months. He returned home just two days before he died. His bed was placed so that his friends, who could not enter his room for fear of getting the infection, could talk with him through the window. Shortly before his death, his sister, Huda, was with him, but the brother to whom he was the closest, Fuad, had just left. Ibriham, wanting to see him again, said, "Huda, call Fuad," after which Ibrahim died immediately.[20]

There is an interesting postscript to the portion of this story about Said Bouhamzy. He had died in June of 1943. In December of that same year, his sis-ter, of whom he had been very fond, gave birth to a son, who was called Sleimann Bouhamzy. (The sister had married a relative in Syria with the same last name.) At a very young age, reportedly, Sleimann manifested behavior suggestive of the personality of Said. The names of Said's seven children, for example, were virtually the first words he spoke, and he was very possessive of five eggplants and two potatoes to which he had given the names of Said's five sons and two daughters, respectively. He called his mother "sister." He was very afraid of motor vehicles, with the fear of trucks being the last to disappear. He retained a fear of blood and cotton bandages far longer, once fainting when seeing a hospitalized friend's head covered with a white bandage. During Sleimann's first visit to Khriby, he convinced the people there that he was indeed Said Bouhamzy reincarnate: Having been placed in the center of the vil-lage, he found his way to Said's home unaided; he there recognized and gave the names of all the surviving members of the family and several other resi-dents; he was able to identify things that had been Said's; he was able to describe the details of Said's death; and he took a paternal attitude toward Said's sons, even though they were considerably older than he.[21] I mention this episode not as evidential (this meeting had occurred some sixteen years prior to Stevenson's investigation of it), but because the fact that the local people *believed* Sleimann to be the reincarnation of Said is relevant to the case of Imad and Ibriham, as will be seen shortly.

Having given the most salient facts about Ibriham's life, I can now recite the corresponding facts about Imad's life with little comment. Most of these facts, it should be stressed, were written down by Stevenson on March 16 and 17 of 1964, prior to the meeting between the two families, and even prior to the knowledge on the part of Imad's relatives that it was Ibriham Bouhamzy's life to which Imad's memories corresponded.[22]

Imad, who began speaking of his former life as soon as he could speak, indicated that this prior life had occurred in a village called Khriby and that his name was Bouhamzy. He sometimes spoke of someone named Mahboud, but he evidently never used the name Ibriham.

Although Imad's parents were skeptical (especially his father, who scolded him for lying, so that Imad henceforth spoke about it only to his mother and grandparents), Imad's credibility was strengthened by a recognition witnessed by his grandmother: When Imad was about two years old, he saw Salim el Aschkar, a native of Khriby, who had been a neighbor of Ibrahim Bouhamzy's family. (Salim and his wife, who was from Kornayel, were there visiting.) Imad ran to him and threw his arms around him. Salim asked "Do you know me?" and Imad answered: "Yes, you were my neighbor."[23]

After Imad's claims had become more generally known, a woman in the village sought to test his reactions by telling Imad (falsely) that Kemal Joumblat, the Druse statesman whom Imad claimed to have known, had died. Imad became very angry and tried to chase the woman out of the house. (Several years later, incidentally, when Imad was nine, he still identified with the Joumblati party: When a member of his family, which belonged to the Yasbaki party, said something against Kemal Joumblat, Imad said: "Damn your Bashir Elawar," referring thereby to a prominent member of the Yasbaki party from Kornayel.)[24]

At the center of Imad's preoccupations with what he considered his former life, however, was "Jamileh" (I use quotation marks to indicate that this name, unlike the others, is a pseudonym). This was the first word that he clearly articulated. He spoke of "Jamileh's" beauty, indicating that his mother compared unfavorably in that department as well as in that of dress, pointing out, for example, that she did not, unlike "Jamileh," wear high heels. His longing was illustrated one day when he was three and a half years old: Lying on the bed with his mother, he asked her to act as "Jamileh" would.[25]

That Imad was somehow older than his years was also suggested by some other characteristics. He did not like to be with children of his own age, and, when he was, he took a dominant attitude toward them. He also had a fondness for bitter tea and coffee, drinking it already at age two, said his grandfather, like a grown man.[26]

Another distinctive thing about young Imad was his interest in hunting. He would often implore his father to take him hunting. He indicated that in his previous life he had had a double-barreled shotgun (holding two fingers together to show what he meant), as well as a rifle. He also stated that he had hidden his gun.[27]

Imad was precocious in school, especially in French, although neither his parents nor his grandparents spoke it. He was soon able to correct the French of his sister, despite the fact that she, being older, had been studying it longer.[28]

When his baby sister was born, he asked his parents to name her "Huda."[29]

Imad had a phobia of large trucks and buses from his earliest years, running to hide from them even before he could talk. Later, he told stories about two incidents involving large vehicles. In one of these stories, a man was run over by a truck, which broke both of his legs and crushed his trunk. The man went to a "doctor's place" and had an operation. In the other story, Imad said that his own bus had gone off the road, although he himself was not driving at the time. People were killed in the resulting accident. (It will be noticed that Imad here speaks of death with regard to the bus accident, in which [assuming that he is remembering Ibrahim's accident] no death actually occurred, whereas he did not mention death in the truck accident, in which [assuming that he is referring to the accident involving Said] death did actually occur. It is possible [on the assumption that some kind of paranormal memory is really involved here] that there was a fusion of the two stories, either in Imad's accounts or in his parents' memory of these accounts.)[30]

Seemingly related (in his parents' minds) was the great pleasure shown by Imad when he began to walk. "Look, I can walk now," he would say.[31]

On the basis of these statements and behaviors, Imad's parents had concluded the following: In his previous life his name was Mahmoud Bouhamzy; he had a wife named Jamileh; and he had been killed by a truck, which had first broken both his legs. Accordingly, when Stevenson, his interpreter, and Imad's father took Imad to Khriby in March 1964 (when Imad was 5½ years old), they were surprised to find that it was not Mahmoud Bouhamzy, but Said Bouhamzy, who had been killed by a truck. (Mahmoud, who was Ibrahim's uncle, was still very much alive.) Then, assuming that it must have instead been Said's life that Imad was remembering, they were surprised to learn that Said had had no connection with a woman named "Jamileh" and that Said's house did not fit the description given by Imad of "his" former house. What's more, they learned that Sleimann Bouhamzy had already given evidence of being Said reborn that had been found satisfactory by the family and friends.[32] All of these facts are relevant to the common complaint that, in reincarnational claims, the family of the child involved has consciously or unconsciously distorted the child's statements and behaviors to bring them into line with what they know about a prior life. Of course, a determined skeptic could argue that these "mistakes" were deliberately made by this extraclever family to make the case appear more authentic. But there are other factors counting against fraud in this case, which I will summarize later.

In any case, what Stevenson and the family did eventually discover is that Imad's descriptions fit both the house and the life of Ibrahim Bouhamzy. (The apparent memory of not being able to walk, then, would have referred not to having had broken legs but to having been bedridden with tuberculosis.) Besides confirming the details that have already been mentioned, they were able to confirm the correspondence between Imad's memories and Ibrahim's life in relation to a number of other details. (In total, Stevenson considered 51 of 57 items confirmed.)[33] For example, several names that Imad mentioned (Amin, Hehibeh, Adil, Toufic, Salim, and Kemal) corresponded to the names of friends or relatives of Ibrahim. And the following assertions by Imad all turned out to be true of Ibrahim: He had a sheep, a goat with a kid, and a brown dog, and he had beaten a dog. (Ibrahim had beaten a dog that had fought with his.)

He had had, besides the bus, a little yellow automobile and a truck, which he used for hauling rocks. His house had a slope in front of it. The house had two wells—one full, one empty. (Ibrahim's house had two wells that were used to store grape juice; the deeper one would become filled with water during the rainy season, while the water in the shallower one would evaporate.) There was an entrance to the attic with "a sort of round opening" (it is a semicircular opening), at which the car tools were kept. The house had an oil stove (which Imad said in reply to a deliberately misleading question as to whether it had a wood stove). And a new garden with cherry and apple trees was being built at the time of Ibrahim's death.[34]

While at the house (which had been vacant and shut up for many years), Imad was able to make many recognitions. He correctly indicated the area in which the house was located (although he failed to identify the house itself). When asked where the dog had been kept, he pointed to the correct place and correctly stated that the dog was held by a cord (not a chain, as is common in the area). Of the two beds in the bedroom, Imad correctly indicated which had been Ibrahim's, also correctly stating that the bed had been in a different position than it then stood. When asked how he had talked to his friends while he was ill, he pointed to the window and said, "Through there." When asked where he had kept his gun, he pointed to the correct closet. (Ibrahim's mother stated that only she and Ibrahim had known where the rifle was kept.) When Ibrahim's sister asked Imad if he knew who she was, he replied "Huda." He also recognized an oil painting of Fuad and, when asked who a photograph of Ibrahim was of, he said "Me." When asked what he had said just before he died, he said "Huda, call Fuad." He did not, interestingly, recognize Ibrahim's mother (although, after greeting her and being asked if he liked her, he replied, "Yes, a great deal").[35] Perhaps relevant to this failure, fifteen years after Ibrahim's death, to recognize Ibrahim's mother, who was spoken of as "that old lady," is an event that happened six years later, when Imad was eleven. He then met for the first time Ibrahim's uncle, Mahmoud Bouhamzy, and failed to recognize him (although "Mahmoud" had been one of the first words that he had spoken as an infant). But when he was provided an old photograph in which Mahmoud still wore a moustache (which he had since shaved off), Imad said that the photograph was "of my Uncle Mahmoud."[36]

Another evidential event occurred on this occasion. Imad asked Mahmoud's permission to talk with a particular man on the street. Mahmoud, saying that the man was a former soldier, asked Imad why he wanted to talk with him. Imad, giving the man's name, said that the fact that he had been a soldier was precisely why he wanted to speak with him. After Imad had had a long conversation with the man, the latter confirmed to Mahmoud that he and Ibrahim had entered the French army on the same day and had been good friends.[37]

During several follow-up visits between 1968 and 1973, Stevenson found that Imad still seemed to retain his memories of the former life. At age nine, for example, he was still saying that he wanted Ibrahim's rifle—pointing out that he had bought it himself! (During the 1970 visit to Khriby, incidentally, he went hunting with Fuad's sons and was allowed to use Ibrahim's rifle.)[38] And, saying that he wanted to visit and even marry "Jamileh," he stated that he (as Ibrahim) had planned to elope with her and had even had a license, but that his family would not allow it (and tore up the license) because she belonged to the Yazbaki, rather than the Joumblati, party. (By age ten, incidentally, he had decided he would marry "Jamileh's" daughter.)[39] Although in retaining memories of a former life several years after age eight (by which time they have usually faded in children in other cultures), he was typical of Druse children with such memories, the fact that he retained them until at least age fifteen makes his case unusual even among Druses.[40]

After having investigated this case quite extensively, Stevenson has little if any doubt as to its authenticity. Besides the general honesty of the Druses, there are several particular facts about this case that count against the possibility of fraud: Stevenson arrived and wrote down most of Imad's memories prior to their verification; Imad would have had to have been thoroughly coached from the earliest age; a great number of people in both villages would have had to be involved in the conspiracy; both families, which had relatively high standings in their respective communities, would have suffered great embarrassment if the fraud had been discovered, and they knew that Stevenson was going to be cross-checking all the testimony; neither family had anything to gain from the claimed identification (Imad's family surely gained no status from the notion that their son was the reincarnation of a quarrelsome playboy, and Ibrahim's family surely would not have wanted memories of his somewhat scandalous relation to "Jamileh" revived).[41] With fraud considered implausible, there seems to be no "normal" way in which to account for the various facts. The only question, accordingly, seems to be what kind of paranormality was involved—literal reincarnation or some other kind of paranormal relation, such as that which I have called retroprehensive inclusion.

3. General Features of Cases
of the Reincarnation Type

Before dealing with this question, however, we should look more generally at cases of the reincarnation type, to see how the case of Imad/Ibrahim fits into the larger picture. It is important to realize, in evaluating any one case, such as this one, that there are thousands of reports of such cases, and that they come from diverse cultures from many parts of the world. Stevenson has himself published extensive studies of over 65 cases that he has personally investigated (from Alaska, British Columbia, Brazil, India, Lebanon, Sri Lanka, and

Turkey), and he has in his files over 2,600 investigated cases (investigated either by himself or someone in whom he has confidence) that seem authentic, many of which come from still other countries.[42] That cases of the reincarnation type are a "natural kind" is suggested by various features that recur in cases that seem authentic.

1. The children are generally between the ages of two and four when they begin speaking of previous lives, and they usually begin to stop speaking spontaneously of these lives between the ages of five and eight. (In obviously fraudulent cases, the "memories" generally do not appear until later.)[43]

2. There is usually a fairly short interval (from 6 to 48 months) between the birth of the child with the memories and the death of the person whose life is remembered. (In fraudulent cases it is often much longer.)[44]

3. The remembered person usually came from the same culture, from a nearby area, and spoke the same language. (In fraudulent cases, the "remembered" person is often from far away as well as long ago.)[45]

4. The subject's statements about the previous life that are verifiable usually turn out to be between 80 and 90 percent accurate. (In fraudulent cases, the percentage, especially about details that would not be generally known about the person, is far less.)[46]

5. Witnesses to the child's statements of memories, and perhaps of other relevant behavioral patterns, usually include, besides the child's parents, other relatives and even some friends outside the family. (In fraudulent cases, the parents are typically the only ones claiming to have heard the statements.)[47]

6. Neither the child nor the parents typically have anything to gain, whether financially or in social status, from the claimed identification with the past life. (In fraudulent cases, the subjects, the parents, or both typically seek to exploit the claimed identification for personal gain.)[48]

7. Certain types of persons are typically "reincarnated," that is, have their lives remembered. By far the most likely people are those who died violent deaths. (In the cultures studied by Stevenson, the percentage of remembered lives that died violently ranges from 29 percent among the Haida in Alaska and British Columbia to 74 percent among the Alevis in Turkey [whereas in Turkey only 4.5 percent of the deaths in general are from violence].)[49] Among people dying natural deaths, those who died young, quickly (perhaps suddenly), or with obvious "unfinished business" are the most likely to be "reincarnated." Aside from these death-related issues, two other types of people tend to be consciously "reincarnated": wealthy people who

were strongly attached to their possessions and very religious people. (In fraudulent cases, the subjects typically claim identity with some famous figure, or at least some powerful figure within their own family.)[50]

8. In many cases, there will be some other seemingly paranormal characteristics other than memories, namely, *behavioral patterns* that correspond to the past person's life or make sense in terms of that person's mode of death (such as the phobia of large motor vehicles manifested by both Imad and Sleimann Bouhamzy) and *congenital deformities* (birthmarks or defects) that correspond to those of the past person or seem to reflect that person's mode of death. Also, in a few cases in which the previous person spoke a different language, the subject appears to have manifested xenoglossy. (Xenoglossy was illustrated in the previous chapter, in the Sharada case: I will discuss apparently paranormal birthmarks below.)

Culturally Conditioned Differences

The fact that the cases of the reincarnation type share most of these characteristics, Stevenson suggests with some justification, points to their authenticity, meaning that "the reports of them reflect some real human experience that has occurred many times in many different parts of the world."[51] One further similarity among the cases from various parts of the world is, paradoxically, the fact that they also have many culturally specific features. These cultural variations concern, first of all, *beliefs* about reincarnation—for example, whether a person can be reborn as a person of the opposite sex. But these variations are also reflected in the reported cases themselves because, not surprisingly, the beliefs about reincarnation in a given culture tend to correspond closely to the cases in that culture. (This is obviously what would be expected if one assumes the reported cases to be entirely products of fantasy, because people's fantasies would be based on the widespread cultural beliefs. But this correspondence could also be expected by those who take reincarnation literally, because, as Stevenson points out, it could result from the fact that "what we believe will happen to us after we die influences what does in fact happen to us after death and when we are reborn.")[52] Here are some of the culturally conditioned variations:

1. The most general culturally conditioned difference is that the largest percentage of reported cases come from cultures in which reincarnation is generally accepted. There is, however, no one-to-one correspondence. On the one hand, there seem to be far more reported cases in northern than in southern India, although the belief in reincarnation is as widespread and intense in the south.[53] On the other hand, there

are, as I mentioned before, many cases, resembling the others in form, in cultures in which reincarnation is not accepted.[54]

2. Some groups, such as the Druses in Lebanon, the Tlingit Indians in Alaska, and the Alevi Moslems in Turkey, believe that reincarnation involving a sex change is impossible and, not surprisingly, Stevenson has found no reported cases involving two people of different sexes in those cultures. At the opposite extreme, 50 percent of the reported cases among the Kutchin in northwestern Canada involve a "sex change." In Burma and Thailand, the percentages are 20 and 13, respectively, whereas in most places about 5 percent of the cases involve a difference of sex.[55]

3. There are also differences with regard to the interval between the death of the prior personality and the birth of the child. The shortest median interval, which occurs among the Haida of Alaska and British Columbia, is four months. The longest interval, which occurs among the Tlingits of Alaska, is forty-eight months. The median interval is eighteen months for India and Sri Lanka, nine months for the Alevis, and six months for the Druses. (This is a problem for the Druses, given their belief that a soul reincarnates in a baby born at the instant of the prior person's death; they explain the discrepancy by reference to more or less brief intermediate lives.)[56]

4. Differences occur also with regard to reported memories of "intermission experiences" between lives. These reports are more common, for example, in Burma and Thailand than in India, and they are extremely rare among the Druses (which corresponds to their belief that there *are* no such experiences between lives, because rebirth is instantaneous).[57]

5. Great cultural differences exist also with regard to the degree to which subjects can give personal names and other details related to the previous life. Subjects among the Sinhalese Buddhists of Sri Lanka and subjects in the United States, for example, are very poor at this. (With regard to personal names, this incapacity among the Sinhalese Buddhists may be related to the fact that they generally avoid personal names in everyday speech, instead referring to other people in terms of relationships.)[58]

6. Closely related to the prior point is the difference with regard to the percentage of former lives corresponding to the subjects' memories that are discovered. Of the 133 investigated cases among the Alevis, for example, corresponding personalities were identified in 105 of the cases, whereas only 19 of the 80 investigated cases among the Sinhalese Buddhists in Sri Lanka were "solved"; only in the United States, in which identifications have been made in 8 of 40 investigated cases involving children, is there a lower percentage.[59] (This

low incidence of identifications is related, of course, to the fact that the Sinhalese and American subjects usually fail to provide names and other specific details.)

7. In most cultures, it is very rare for the two personalities to be members of the same family. Among the Sinhalese Buddhists in Sri Lanka, for example, Stevenson has found no case in which they were members of the same immediate family, and in only 3 of the 80 investigated cases was there even a distant relationship. But for both personalities to belong to the same immediate family is common among the Burmese, the Eskimos, and especially the Tlingits, in which this occurs in a majority of the cases. (Relevant here is the fact that, among the Tlingits, if a child is recognized at birth as being the reincarnation of a previous person, the child is given the tribal name of that person and receives credit for that person's accomplishments.)[60]

8. Closely related to the prior point is the frequency of "announcing dreams," in which a pregnant woman (or sometimes a relative or friend thereof) has a dream in which a deceased person seems to announce his or her intention to be reborn as her baby. Such dreams are common among the Tlingits (for whom, as we have seen, prompt and proper identification is important), the Burmese, and the Alevis, but less common elsewhere.[61]

9. Closely related is variation with regard to the appearance on the child of congenital deformities (birthmarks or birth defects) that correspond to those of the prior person or to the cause of that person's death. For example, there are corresponding deformities in only about 12 percent of the Druse cases, compared with 50 percent and 62 percent of the Tlingit and Alevi cases, respectively.[62] (Although the birthmarks often correspond to the cause of death of the prior person, such as a bullet or knife wound, the cultural differences are not explainable simply in terms of differences in the incidence of violent deaths among remembered lives. For example, although India and Lebanon are two of the countries with the highest incidence of cases in which the prior personality died violently [46 and 67 percent, respectively], they have a relatively low incidence of cases with congenital deformities.[63])

As Stevenson points out, these variations in the beliefs about reincarnation (and thereby to some extent in the actual cases) provide further support for thinking of it as based on genuine experiences. Just as the uniformities across cultures suggest that experiences of the reincarnation type are spontaneous experiences, not simply induced by cultural beliefs, the variations suggest that the various systems of belief involving reincarnation have not all been derived from one locale, but that at least some of them have arisen independently, on the basis of local experiences.[64]

4. THE THEORY OF RETROPREHENSIVE INCLUSION IN RELATION TO CASES OF THE REINCARNATION TYPE

Given a large number of well-investigated cases from various parts of the world, many of which exhibit about as much evidence of paranormal knowledge as does the case of Imad/Ibrahim, it is hard to deny that some form of paranormal explanation is needed. The only real question is *which kind*—a survivalist or a superpsi explanation. Having introduced earlier the theory of retroprehensive inclusion, which overcomes at least some of the objections to the adequacy of a superpsi explanation for cases of the mediumistic and possession type, I will now examine this theory in relation to cases of the reincarnation type, seeing if it can stand up to the various objections that have been made to the attempt to provide a nonsurvivalist superpsi explanation of all cases of the reincarnation type.

The first objection is one that has already been considered—namely, that although one can acquire information (knowledge *that*) through super-ESP, one could not acquire skills (knowledge *how*). I agree that the acquisition of skills, such as the ability to speak a language, could probably not be acquired by means of super-ESP as usually conceived. As Stephen Braude has argued, however, most discussions consider the superpsi hypothesis "in an unacceptably weak or implausible form."[65] Given the strong form of superpsi that I have called retroprehensive inclusion, I have argued, the manifestation of various unlearned skills provides no insuperable obstacle.

A second objection is that superpsi explanations in cases of the reincarnation type posit a degree of ESP of that *one* past life that goes far beyond any other psychic ability manifested by the subjects.[66] Why, one can ask, should the subject's alleged super-ESP be focused on that one past personality alone? That is indeed a powerful objection against the superpsi hypothesis as usually conceived. In the superpsi theory that I have suggested, however, retroprehensive inclusion is, by hypothesis, a unique form of ESP, which is employed in relation to only one past personality. In this relation, the mind, which consists of a series of experiences, takes *as its past* the series of experiences that constituted the mind of a prior person. It "perceives" those past experiences through that mode of nonsensory prehension that we normally call "memory." It differs from ordinary memory only in that the prior experiences that it remembers occurred in a different body and (by hypothesis) were not connected by a series of experiences to the present. Accordingly, just as it does not follow, from the fact that we retain our skills and consciously remember many of our own past experiences, that we can become consciously aware of the experiences of other people, the fact that a child had retroprehensively included a prior set of experiences as its own past would not imply that it should have an extraordinary telepathic awareness of any other life.

This response to the second objection also answers a third, which is that most things learned through telepathy, super or ordinary, are not manifested as *memories*.[67]

A fourth objection involves the *selection* of the prior personality. In cases of the possession type, as we saw, it is possible to suppose that various deep-seated needs of the subject might explain why the past individual was selected (rather than having to suppose that that past individual, as a still-living agent, took the initiative). In cases of the reincarnation type, however, the behavior, preferences, and memories of the prior person are sometimes manifest before the subject is even two years old. It would be implausible to suppose that the mind of such a young child would (assuming, as the nonsurvivalist theory does, that it is *not* the continuation of a prior mind) have the kinds of deep-seated needs and desires that could explain the selection. I will leave this objection as unanswered for the moment.

A fifth objection would be that, if nothing else does, at least announcing dreams and congenital deformities point to the initiative of the prior soul. Because I have not yet discussed these two phenomena, which occur in many cases, I need to pause to provide some examples.

A case among the Tlingit Indians of Alaska, involving William George, a celebrated fisherman, contains an announcing dream as well as two types of congenital deformities. One day, he told his favorite son, Reginald, and this son's wife, "If there is anything to this rebirth business, I will come back and be your son." He added, "And you will recognize me because I will have birth-marks like the ones I now have," pointing to one mole on his left shoulder and another on his left forearm. Later, when he was about sixty, he gave Reginald his gold watch, telling him to keep it for when he comes back as their son. Telling her what his father had said, Reginald gave the watch to his wife, who put it in a jewel box. A few weeks later, William disappeared from his fishing boat. Shortly thereafter, Reginald's wife became pregnant. During labor, which was barely nine month's after her father-in-law's disappearance, she dreamed that he appeared to her, saying that he was waiting to see his son. When the baby, a boy, came, it had moles on its left shoulder and forearm, at the same locations as those of its grandfather. After William George, Jr., grew up and began walking, his parents noticed that he limped with his right foot turned out-wards, walking thereby with the same gait as his grandfather (who had severely injured his right ankle playing basketball as a young man). One day when young William was not quite five, he wandered into the bedroom while his mother was examining the contents of her jewelry box. Seeing the gold watch, he said, "That's my watch," and clung to it tenaciously. Being firmly convinced that neither they nor anyone else had mentioned the watch to him, the parents were more impressed by this recognition than by the moles—even though young William was the only one of ten children to inherit their grand-father's moles.[68]

Taken in isolation, neither the announcing dream nor the moles plus the characteristic gait would be terribly impressive. They could be dismissed as mere coincidences, which are sure to crop up now and then. However, besides the fact that announcing dreams are often much more explicit, they are also reported in most cultures, with quite high rates in some. In Burma, for example, 107 of Stevenson's investigated 230 cases (47%) contain reports of such dreams.[69] With regard to corresponding congenital deformities (including both birthmarks and birth defects): There are claims about them in about 35 percent of reported cases, and the actual incidence in good cases may be much higher: In 49 cases for which medical documents for the prior person could be obtained, there were clear correspondences in 43 (88%) of the cases.[70] Some of the birth defects, furthermore, are quite dramatic: In one case, a Turkish boy was born with a terribly diminished and malformed right ear. He remembered the life of a farmer who had gone to sleep in a field at the end of the day. A neighbor, hunting at twilight, mistook him for a rabbit and shot him with a shotgun at close range on (as the hospital records show) the right side of his skull.[71]

Although there are hundreds of such accounts in the investigated cases, in which a birth deformity closely corresponds with the cause of death of the prior person whose life is remembered, it might still seem possible to dismiss all the correspondences as mere coincidence. That becomes increasingly difficult, however, when there are *two* congenital deformities that correspond. Stevenson now has, for example, eighteen cases in which two birthmarks, on subjects who recall dying from a gunshot, correspond to entry and exit wounds on the bodies of the prior persons. In fourteen of these, one birthmark is larger than the other, and in nine of these, the smaller and the larger marks clearly correspond to the entry and exit wounds, respectively (exit wounds, of course, are almost always larger). In another case, a Burmese woman, who had as a child remembered the life of a woman who was accidentally killed by a shotgun, has two perfectly round birthmarks in her left chest, one of which is smaller than the other. The shotgun, according to a responsible informant, had contained shot of two sizes.[72] In still another case, reported by another investigator, there are *three* corresponding birthmarks: two that correspond to entry and exit wounds, respectively, on the prior person's body, and one on the crown of the head that corresponds to a congenital birthmark on that prior person's body.[73]

It could be argued that announcing dreams and congenital deformities of this nature confirm the case for literal reincarnation. Do not the announcing dreams point to the agency of the departed and returning soul, which telepathically impresses its intention to be reborn on the dream life of the future mother (or one of her friends or relatives)? Cannot the congenital deformities be explained only in terms of the agency of the returning soul, which impresses on the embryo or fetus it has entered the physical effects of the trauma it had suffered (or, in some cases, a defect corresponding to some injury it had inflicted on someone else)? However, these phenomena might be explainable without supposing the agency of a postmortem soul.

With regard to announcing dreams, the various cases could be handled with one of the following possible explanations: (1) In those cases in which the prior personality while still alive has told the future mother of its desire to return as her child, she could have created the dream apart from any paranormal process. (2) In cases in which the prior personality told the future mother of its desire, but in which the announcing dream is had by some friend or relative to whom this information had not been communicated, this friend or relative could have created the dream after acquiring the information from the future mother telepathically. (3) In cases in which the prior personality desired to return as this woman's child but had not told her or anyone else of this fact, the future mother (or one of her friends or relatives) could have created the dream after learning of this desire through (perhaps retrocognitive) telepathy. (4) In cases in which the prior personality had not specifically desired to return as this woman's child, and perhaps did not even know this woman, the very desire to return as *someone's* child may explain, along with particular (perhaps unconscious) needs of the woman, why she (or one of her friends or relatives) contacted that prior personality, through (perhaps retrocognitve) telepathy, and created a dream on the basis of this paranormal contact. Given the possibility of superpsi combined with the creativity of dreams, accordingly, announcing dreams do not seem to present an insuperable obstacle to the theory of retroprehensive inclusion.

To the contrary, the phenomenon of announcing dreams, by bringing the mother into the picture, actually strengthens the theory by providing a possible solution to the fourth problem, which was left unanswered above, about how the *selection* of the prior personality could be explained in cases of the reincarnation type, in which the child is (by hypothesis) too undeveloped to have deep psychological needs. We could suppose that the so-called announcing dreams are simply an extreme manifestation of something that (by hypothesis) occurs in all cases of the reincarnation type—namely, that it is the mother, with her particular needs, who makes paranormal contact with the mind of the prior personality. She would then, through mother-fetus telepathy (which is rather well-accepted in parapsychological circles), unconsciously connect the mind of the developing fetus to the prior personality. (In cases in which it is a friend or relative who has the announcing dream, we could, perhaps, suppose that this other person has telepathically learned about and brought to [dream] consciousness a paranormal connection that had already been established at the completely unconscious level in the mother's mind.) Having introduced the idea of a paranormal influence of the mother on the fetus, we can then use this explanation in relation to paranormal birthmarks and other deformities. That is, the deformities corresponding to the life of the prior person could be caused by the mother during the course of the pregnancy through "maternal psychokinesis." Besides connecting the fetus's developing mind with that of the prior person, in other words, the mother, having learned about the prior person's physical features and/or actions through retrocognitive clairvoyance, would impress the appropriate physical features onto the body of her embryo or fetus.

Although this theory may seem extremely implausible, because it seems to posit an unparalleled form of psychokinesis, there are three types of paranormal phenomena that can reduce this seeming implausibility. First, as we saw in Chapter 2, minds do in principle seem to have the psychokinetic capacity not simply to make objects move, but to impress patterns on receptive objects, such as photographic film. In some of the demonstrations by Ted Serios, furthermore, the pattern paranormally impressed on the film had itself been learned paranormally. Second, we know through numerous stigmata cases that at least some minds have the capacity to create deformities in their own bodies paranormally. Third, and most important, there is abundant evidence, in the literature on "maternal impressions," of the capacity of at least some women (unintentionally) to produce birthmarks and birth defects on their children.

The apparent examples have been so numerous that at one time the idea of maternal impressions was widely accepted in the medical community. However, it fell into disrepute in recent centuries primarily, evidently, not for lack of empirical evidence but because of the lack of any physical (neuronal) connection capable of transmitting effects from the mother's mind to the fetus, combined with the widespread assumption that a paranormal explanation—that is, in terms of "maternal psychokinesis"—was impossible. Recently, however, the theory has been revived, with impressive documentation, by a medical doctor who has no a priori reason to object to the paranormal explanation—Ian Stevenson.[74] He analyzed fifty-two cases involving deformities ranging from common moles and birthmarks to missing ears, toes, fingers, hands, and even a penis!

In these "normal" cases of maternal impressions, the mothers acquired the image of the deformity through normal means—usually through some frightening or otherwise traumatic experience or through long-term exposure. If the idea of maternal psychokinesis is extended to deformities in cases of the reincarnation type, the only difference would be that the image of the deformity would usually be acquired by the mother unconsciously, by paranormal means. Given the capacity of a Ted Serios psychokinetically to impress images on film that he acquired clairvoyantly, however, the double paranormality that this theory involves seems to provide no insuperable obstacle. To the extent that this alternative explanation seems plausible, those who dislike the idea of literal reincarnation, belief in which has become far more widespread in the West through the work of Ian Stevenson, can thank Stevenson himself for reviving the evidence for maternal impressions, which supports this alternative explanation. (Stevenson himself mentions maternal psychokinesis as a possible explanation,[75] but not [to my knowledge] the idea—which alone could make this explanation adequate—that the mother may have learned of the defects paranormally.) Given this alternative explanation of the congenital deformities, what would otherwise be a serious difficulty for the theory of retroprehensive inclusion might be overcome.

To make this alternative explanation plausible, however, rather than simply a possibility in principle, some psychological studies on the mothers of subjects with congenital deformities would have to be carried out. The task would be to see if in a majority of a representative sample one could come up with a plausible scenario, something like that suggested above in the Sharada case, as to why the mother would have chosen (unconsciously) to make her child be, in a sense, a continuation of that particular past life. This would be an exemplification of the kind of study for which Stephen Braude has called.[76] My own guess would be that the chance for success in many cases would be slim. But something like this kind of investigation needs to be carried out if the superpsi alternative to literal reincarnation is to be fully evaluated.

In any case, even assuming that the theory of retroprehensive inclusion (or some other superpsi explanation) could survive the first five objections, there are still more. To prepare the way for these, I will explain a little more fully the theory of retroprehensive inclusion and its implications. According to this theory, a kind of "reincarnation" does occur, in that the previous mind, which was a series of occasions of experience that continued up to the person's death, would begin having new experiences in a new body. This account would, in fact, come close to Buddhist accounts of reincarnation, according to which there is no enduring soul (atman) that reincarnates but only a historic series of experiences (sometimes imaged in terms of a series of torches, each of which lights the next one). This account would differ from the usual understanding of reincarnation, including most Buddhist understandings, however, in implying that there would be no discarnate experiences after death: There would be "life after death" only if and insofar as one's mind, as a historic route of experiences, is retroprehensively included and consciously remembered by some subsequent human being. As we have seen, even in cultures in which the reporting of memories of previous lives is encouraged, only (roughly) one person in a thousand seems to report such memories. This would mean, accordingly, that for most people there would be *no* life after death in any sense.

With this clarification, I turn now to the sixth objection presented by cases of the reincarnation type for the theory of retroprehensive inclusion. This objection involves the theory's prediction that there would be no genuine "intermission memories," that is, no genuine discarnate experiences between the physical death of the prior person and the retroprehensive inclusion of that prior person's (incarnate) experiences as the past of some living person. And, in fact, most subjects say that they have no memories of experiences between incarnations.[77] As mentioned earlier, however, some subjects, especially in Burma and Thailand, do report such experiences. (In Burma, there were such reports in 52 of 230 [23%] of Stevenson's adequately investigated cases; in Thailand, 21 of 38 [55%] cases contained such reports.) The memories typically involve such things as viewing the previous personality's funeral rites, hanging around the burial sites, encountering a "man in white" who serves as a guide, viewing events in the lives of the previous and new families, and appearing in "announcing" (or, among the Burmese, given their habitual politeness, "petitioning") dreams.[78]

Although most such reports are not susceptible of either verification or falsification, some of the statements in a few cases have indicated veridical knowledge of events that occurred between the subject's birth and the death of the remembered life. For example, in India, Veer Singh, while four and a half years old, correctly reported on many events that had occurred in the family of the previous personality, Som Dutt Sharma, during the eleven years that passed between the death of Som Dutt and the birth of Veer. These events included lawsuits, the purchase of a female camel, the breaking of a swing (which he claims to have caused), and the birth of another son and two more daughters (the names of whom he gave and the faces of whom he recognized on meeting them).[79]

In Sri Lanka, Disna Samaraisnge, at age five, correctly reported that Babanona, the woman whose life she gave good evidence of remembering, had been buried near an anthill. (The gravesite had been selected by Babanona's family after her death,[80] so knowledge about it would not have been among the "memories" that Disna would have acquired by means of retroprehensive inclusion of Babonona's [incarnate] life.)

In Burma, Protomwan Inthanu, at age twenty (at which time the memories of a previous life first arose while she was meditating), provided convincing evidence of remembering the life of a baby girl who died when three months old (such as the name of her father and the fact that he had played a xylophone to soothe her).[81] Besides giving the name of the part-time undertaker who had buried the infant's body, she also correctly stated that the body had been buried outside the cemetery, rather than inside. (The gravesite was unmarked and the undertaker had told no one about his dereliction of duty; he said that he had buried the body outside because of fear of tigers from the jungle adjacent to the cemetery.) Protomwan also correctly described the house to which the parents had moved some time after the infant's death.[82]

In Thailand, Ratana Wongsombat, while still about two years old, made many verified statements about the life of Kim Lan Prayoon Supamitr, a deeply religious Chinese woman who had died less than two years before Ratana's birth and had bequeathed her body for use by medical students, stipulating that her remains be deposited under the Bo Tree at the meditation center she had entered near the end of her life. Ratana correctly stated that Kim Lan's ashes had been scattered around the tree, rather than being buried under it as directed. (Kim Lan's daughter said that there were too many roots under the Bo Tree to fulfill her mother's wishes, so she had simply scattered the ashes instead—a fact that she had told no one.)[83]

In a less well-documented case, that of Maung Yin Maung in Burma, the subject reports having been seen while he was between bodies and this subjective report corresponds to a reported apparition of him at that location.[84]

Although these accounts (except possibly the last one) are impressive, especially when read within the context of each case as a whole, they do not necessarily prove that the persons were actually having "intermission experiences." Given the range of superpsi that we have allowed as possible, we could suppose that the subjects, besides retroprehensively including the souls of the prior personalities as their own, also, by means of retrocognitive telepathy and clairvoyance, learned about various events that occurred between the two lives, then created fantasized "memories" of these events. (For example, in the next to the last example, Ratana, having identified with the life of Kim Lan, might have learned through retrocognition that her ashes had been scattered instead of buried.) Accordingly, although verified intermission memories do strengthen the case for literal reincarnation, with continued existence between incarnations, they do not provide absolute proof, because they can perhaps be accommodated by a superpsi alternative to the survivalist interpretation.

This nonsurvivalist alternative, however, faces a related difficulty, which constitutes a seventh objection: It predicts not only that there would be no discarnate experiences between lives, but that there would be no discarnate experiences whatsoever. Any evidence for out-of-body experiences of any sort, accordingly, would threaten the superpsi alternative and give support to the survivalist interpretation of cases of the reincarnation type. This topic will be the subject of Chapter 8.

An eighth objection to the adequacy of the theory of retroprehensive inclusion is based on the following two corollaries of the theory: (1) The reason the soul of a prior person is "reincarnated" is not that it chooses to do so (because it is no longer an active agent), and (2) the fact that this soul is "reincarnated" in one person would not prevent its being "reincarnated" in others (because its being retroprehensively included by one person does nothing to reduce its availability to be so included by others). With regard to the first of these corollaries: The idea that the soul does not actively choose to be "reincarnated," but is chosen by subsequent subjects out of a vast number of available past lives, suggests that there was something about this soul making it especially likely to be retroprehensively included. To be sure, as we saw in the Sharada case, we can probably assign some of the reasons to the present subject, especially when this subject is an adult. This would seem *prima facie* impossible when the subjects are very young children; but even in these cases, I suggested, we might be able to attribute the motivations behind the selection partly to the mother. Nevertheless, even if these suggestions are plausible, much of the reason as to why a particular past life was selected would surely lie in the nature of that life—including its death. This supposition does, indeed, fit with the facts as reviewed above. That is, persons who are "reincarnated" tend to be persons of a particular type—those who are intensely materialistic and possessive, or intensely religious—or persons who have died in a particular manner: violently (or at least suddenly), while still young, or with strongly felt "unfinished business." The crucial factor, accordingly, seems to be the *intensity* with which that person lived, died, or wanted to continue living.

If we combine this point with the second corollary (that being "reincarnated" in one person would not prevent a soul from being "reincarnated" in others), it follows, even more in reincarnation cases than in possession and mediumistic cases, that a particular past personality *would often be "reincarnated" in more than one present subject.* That is, the reason why that past personality was selected by one present subject was, to a significant extent, that personality's peculiar intensity. Its especially intense existence (in life, death, or both) constituted, as it were, a standing invitation to be "picked up" as the past life of present persons in the making. And the fact that it is "picked up" by one nascent individual does not prevent its being selected by others. If the theory of retroprehensive inclusion is the correct explanation of cases of the reincarnation type, accordingly, we should expect many cases in which there are multiple more-or-less simultaneous reincarnations of the same personality.

This explanation, however, does not seem borne out by the evidence. There are, to be sure, a few cultures that *believe* in the possibility of multiple reincarnations, such as the Gitxsan Indians of British Columbia, the Igbo of Nigeria, and (as popularized by the movie *Little Buddha*) the Tibetan Buddhists. Stevenson, however, has said (in personal correspondence):

> So far as I have looked at them, all the cases of double or triple candidacy to be someone reincarnated lack authenticity either for all of the candidate subjects or for all but one of them.[85]

Stevenson has published a brief report of one such case, involving two boys born in Turkey, both of whose parents considered them to be reincarnations of John F. Kennedy; one of the boys, indeed, was given the surname "Kenedi." In neither case were there any evidential memories.[86]

Somewhat more impressive cases have been published by an anthropologist, Antonia Mills, who has studied one of the cultures believing in multiple simultaneous reincarnations, the Gitxsan Indians. In the most impressive case, the prior personality was a Susan Albert, who died at about the age of 77, at a time when a granddaughter, a great-granddaughter, and a third woman raised by the family were all pregnant. All three resulting baby girls were, on the basis of dreams interpreted as announcing dreams, identified by their parents as reincarnations of Susan Albert. One of the three, Rhonda, did indeed give signs— memories, blond hair (Susan had said she would be blond in her next life), a birthmark (a curving brown line on her right waist reminiscent of a tattoo of an *S* Susan had had there), and an extremely strong sense of identification with some of her grandmother's possessions—suggesting that she is, in some sense, a reincarnation of Susan Albert. One of the other girls had a suggestive birthmark (where Susan had broken her arm) and had a patch of white hair in her otherwise black hair. But neither she nor the third girl made any statements suggestive of memories of Susan Albert's life.[87] At this time, accordingly, Stevenson's evaluation, that there are no known cases providing convincing evidence of multiple simultaneous reincarnations, apparently stands.

Even if a few good cases should show up, furthermore, this would not necessarily disprove the theory of literal reincarnation, and this for two reasons. On the one hand, such cases would be patient of various interpretations; for example, literal reincarnation might be thought the correct interpretation for one of the subjects and retroprehensive inclusion for the other(s); or some theory of multiple personality or of soul-splitting might be advocated. On the other hand, if the theory of retroprehensive inclusion were the correct explanation for most cases of the reincarnation type throughout the world, multiple simultaneous reincarnations should be extremely common. Indeed, because the very fact that a previous personality has been "picked up" by one subject would mean that it had the kind of intensity and other characteristics that made a life liable to being retroprehensively included, multiple reincarnations should be more the rule than the exception. Because this is evidently not the case, the theory of retroprehensive inclusion seems inadequate to the facts.

A ninth and final problem faced by the theory of retroprehensive inclusion (and any other superpsi alternative to literal reincarnation) follows from the fact that death, by hypothesis, should not first make a soul available for "reincarnation." That is, the theory, at least as I have articulated it, presupposes that each mind or soul is a temporal strand of momentary occasions of experience. After bodily death, by hypothesis, it has no subsequent experiences, unless it somehow gets "reincarnated." A mind that has been reincarnated, or retroprehensively included, did not, at the death of the body with which it was associated, in any sense "break free" of that body so as suddenly to become a candidate for reincarnation. Rather, according to the theory of retroprehensive inclusion, the mind that is reincarnated is precisely that past mind while it was associated with its body. There is no reason in principle, accordingly, why a mind as it has existed up to some particular moment, which we can call "moment X," could not be retroprehensively included as the past of some child. To be sure, the occurrence of a particular kind of death, such as a violent or otherwise sudden death, may give that strand of experiences that we call the mind a climactic intensity that it would otherwise not have had, thereby making it an especially likely candidate for reincarnation. Many of the previous lives in cases of the reincarnation type, however, do not fit that pattern. In any case, the moment of death as such, according to the theory of retroprehensive inclusion, does not bring about some structural change that first allows the soul to animate another body. The occasions of experience constituting the mind of some new body could equally well, at moment X, retroprehensively include as its past life that mind as it existed up to that moment.

If this type of dynamic can account for cases of the reincarnation type, we should expect, accordingly, that many souls—especially ones that had lived a particularly intense existence up to moment X—*would be "reincarnated" by children while the "past person" is still alive and having his or her own new experiences.* We would expect, in other words, many reincarnation-type analogues of the "Gordon Davis" case, in which the apparently deceased Gordon Davis personality spoke through the medium while the actual Gordon Davis was still alive. We would expect, furthermore, that *several* people would sometimes seem to themselves and others to be the reincarnation of the same still-living person.

There seems, however, to be even less evidence for this expectation than there is for the previous one. There are, to be sure, cultures in which it is *believed* that the spirit of an elderly person can animate a child prior to the elderly person's death;[88] but there seems to be little if any evidence to support this belief; and whatever evidence there is seems to the people involved to be compatible with literal reincarnation. Antonia Mills does report a case from India containing good evidence for reincarnation (strongly evidential memories plus three corresponding birthmarks), in which two dates, a year apart, have been given for the birth of the child, Titu, the earlier of which would put the birth about eight months prior to the death of the previous personality.[89] My own reading of the evidence, however, makes the later date (four months after the death) seem the more likely one.* In any event, apart from the details of this particular case, the absence of strong and abundant evidence for pre-mortem reincarnations counts strongly against the theory of retroprehensive inclusion as a general theory for cases of the reincarnation type: If it were the correct theory, such "reincarnations" of still-living personalities should be quite common. The fact that all the good evidence for reincarnation involves souls whose bodies have died suggests rather convincingly that bodily death brings about a change that makes it possible for a soul to become reincarnated. And this lends support to some theory of literal reincarnation, according to which the soul continues to have experiences after separation from the physical-biological body, over against all superpsi theories, including that of retroprehensive inclusion.

5. SUMMARY

The theory of retroprehensive inclusion, as apparently the strongest superpsi alternative to literal reincarnation, can quite easily handle the first three objec-

_____

* For example, Titu's parents, who had assumed the later date to be correct until learning that the hospital records had the earlier date, recall him as having begun to talk when he was only one and a half years old, thereby earlier than his siblings. If the earlier of the two birthdates were correct, he would have been rather late, not early, in beginning to talk.

tions. It can also perhaps handle the fourth, fifth, and sixth objections, even if the explanations must become rather convoluted. The eighth and ninth objections, however, seem to be insuperable (even though more data are needed before any definitive judgment can be made). Whether the nonsurvivalist interpretation is further undermined by the seventh objection—the fact that out-of-body experiences, which it implies should not occur, are widely reported—will be examined in Chapter 8. First, however, we will look at evidence for life after death from apparitions.

7

EVIDENCE FROM APPARITIONS

Another kind of evidence for life after death is provided by apparitions (which in earlier days were sometimes called "phantasms"). Although this is the fourth of the five kinds of evidence that I am examining, it was the first to be systematically investigated by the Society for Psychical Research at the end of the nineteenth century.

The results of these investigations are found primarily in *Phantasms of the Living* (1886),[1] written primarily by Edmund Gurney with the assistance of Frederick Myers and Frank Podmore, the "Report on the Census of Hallucinations" (1894), written primarily by Eleanor Sidgwick,[2] and a lengthy section on "Phantasms of the Dead" in Frederick Myers' *Human Personality and Its Survival of Bodily Death* (1903). The primary purpose of the first of these publications, *Phantasms of the Living*, was to provide evidence for telepathy. Such evidence was provided insofar as some of the apparitions turned out to be veridical—that is, to provide correct information that the percipient had no normal way of knowing. Some of these veridical cases, however, seemed to provide evidence for life after death, because the evidence provided paranormally by the apparition was *that*, and sometimes *how*, the person who appeared—to be called "the apparent"—had just died. That is, the telepathic agent seemed to be the mind of a recently deceased individual. (The title, *Phantasms of the Living*, was somewhat misleading, in that Gurney included under this category not only apparitions of people who were clearly alive at the time, but also all those apparitions of dying people that occurred within twelve hours of the death.*) The main purpose of the "Report on the Census of Hallucinations" was to show that it was extremely unlikely that most of the apparitions that closely coincided with the death of the apparent could be explained in terms of chance.[3] Myers' discussion drew on these publications plus some more cases that were reported in the journals.

After these extensive surveys, investigations, and publications, it was generally felt that little more would be gained from further work. Also, with the discovery of Mrs. Piper, mental mediumship became the Society's primary focus of attention. Accordingly, when in 1942 George N. M. Tyrrell delivered his Myers Memorial Lecture, subsequently published as *Apparitions*,[4] he drew largely on the same body of evidence as had Myers himself back in 1903. Likewise, since the time of Tyrrell's study there has been only a little more empirical data gathered about apparitions, as those few psychical researchers who have devoted extensive attention to evidence for life after death have been focusing on other areas, such as cases of the reincarnation type and near-death experiences. Contemporary treatments of the evidence from apparitions, therefore, must still draw primarily upon old case material.

The fact that most of the investigated evidence for apparitions is old, however, does not mean that it should be dismissed.[5] Besides being investigated quite thoroughly, this evidence was also evaluated by critical standards. Cases were rejected as evidence for telepathy (whether from the living or the dead) if the reports could be explained in terms of fraud, misperception, faulty memory, cryptomnesia, or some other normal explanation. For example, one rejected case involved a Mrs. Barter, whose husband was in India. During the time of the Indian Mutiny, she dreamed that her husband was wounded in the leg, that he bound his leg with a puggaree (the cloth band wrapped around the crown of a hat or helmet), and that he was then carried away by four men. The case was rejected as evidence for telepathy because, although Mrs. Barter was correct about everything else, her husband had actually bound his leg with a silk necktie instead of a puggaree, and because she had also had a dream about her husband that was not veridical.[6] With regard to taking apparitions as evidence for life after death, the Society's investigators were especially critical, generally leaning toward nonsurvivalist explanations where possible.[7] Before turning to this issue, however, the kinds of apparitions and their general characteristics need to be discussed.

---

* Gurney justified this extension to twelve hours after death with a theory of "telepathic deferment," according to which the information received telepathically might not rise to consciousness in the form of an apparition until many hours later, when the subject was in a receptive state of mind (George N. M. Tyrrell, *Apparitions* [1953; New Hyde Park, N.Y.: University Books 1961; published in one volume with *Science and Psychical Phenomena*], 44).

1. Types of Apparitions

Although there are various ways to classify apparitions, I find most helpful a simple threefold classification: (1) apparitions of the living, which can be further divided into spontaneous and intentional (or experimental) cases; (2) apparitions of the dying, understood as occurring at about the time of the apparent's death; and (3) postmortem apparitions, understood as occurring at a time clearly after the apparent's death. In this third category, I am including here only apparitions that appear but once, or at most a few times; I am excluding, in other words, those long-term, recurrent phenomena usually called "haunting apparitions" or simply ghosts.

Three other classifications of apparitions have special importance. First, some apparitions are "veridical," which, to repeat, means that the apparition provided correct information that the percipient could not have known about through normal means. A veridical apparition, in other words, involves paranormal influence of some sort. My focus is on veridical apparitions, although some of the general characteristics listed below apply to nonveridical apparitions as well. Second, many cases involve "crisis apparitions," in which the apparition coincides with some crisis being undergone by the apparent. Apparitions of the dying belong to this type by definition, but some apparitions of the living also qualify. Third, some apparitions are "multiple" or "collective," meaning that more than one person experiences them.

2. Characteristics of Apparitions

With regard to the general characteristics of veridical apparitions, one point to be made about them is that, even if they should be categorized as "hallucinations" of a sort, they are quite distinct from hallucinations of the insane: Most people reporting them never experience another apparition in their lives; apparitions are not correlated with illness or morbidity on the part of the percipients; and telepathic apparitions are usually visual in nature (in distinction from hallucinations of the insane, which are primarily auditory).[8] These differences from pathological hallucinations belong to a more general point, which is that veridical apparitions seem to form a "natural kind." That is, there are reports of them from (at least virtually) every culture, and they tend to have a number of characteristics in common. These common characteristics can most helpfully be classified into two groups: those suggesting that the apparitions are "objective" and those suggesting that they are, nevertheless, *not* "physical" (at least in the usual understanding of that term).

On the side of their apparent objectivity are the following characteristics: They can appear to be as real as the sight of a real person before one's eyes. They usually seem to occupy ordinary space and usually obscure the space behind them. They obey the laws of perspective.[9] When they move about, their visibility tends to vary with that of the lighting.[10] They disappear from view if one shuts, screens, or averts one's eyes, just as a physical object does, and then will often still be where they were when one looks again.[11] They are often perceived by more than one person and sometimes even by animals.[12] Although they are primarily visual, they are sometimes auditory and occasionally tactual as well. They are sometimes reflected in mirrors.[13] They generally appear to be aware of the physical surroundings—for example, making use of doors and stairs and moving around furniture.[14] They often seem to be trying to achieve a particular purpose. And—to conclude with one of the most important characteristics of veridical apparitions—they occur most often by far at times that coincide with crises in the lives of the apparents.

Because apparitions are so similar to sensory perceptions of ordinary physical bodies, one might be led to assume that apparitions simply *are* physical—that is, that the sensorylike image arises from sensory perceptions of a "physical object," as that term is usually understood. There are, however, several features of apparitions that count against this assumption: They sometimes do *not* appear to be real but may be partially or totally transparent. Even when they do appear fully real for part of the time, they may fade into existence, out of existence, or both. They often appear in, and disappear from, rooms with locked doors. They may walk through walls. They usually do not cast shadows. They usually do not touch and hardly ever can *be* touched. They only sometimes produce sounds and even more rarely do they speak.[15] In collective cases, in which more than one person sees the apparition, some persons present and looking at the "right place" might not see it.

3. VERIDICAL APPARITIONS AND THE QUESTION OF INTERPRETATION

Given these general characteristics of apparitions, the question is: how to explain them. The second set of characteristics, which counts against their physicality, lends support to the dominant view of them in modern intellectual circles, which is that they are purely subjective hallucinations, meaning that they are completely the product of the brain and/or mind of the percipient, with no "objective" element that corresponds to something external. So understood, they would not necessarily be signs of psychopathology, but they also would not be taken as veridical—that is, as somehow arising from anything objective to the percipient and providing knowledge thereof. The problem with this blanket view of all apparitions, however, is that many of them *are* veridical. I will illustrate in terms of a few actual cases, thereby making clearer what is meant by "veridical" apparitions.

One case, which was reported in the *Herald* newspaper of Dubuque, Iowa, on February 11, 1891, concerned one Michael Conley, a farmer from the town of Ionia, who had been found dead in the outhouse of the place he had been visiting in Dubuque. The coroner's preparation of his body for shipment home involved a change of clothes: Conley's clothes, which were covered with filth from the outhouse, were thrown outside the morgue, and Conley's body was dressed instead in black clothes, with a white shirt and felt slippers. After Conley's son brought the body home, one of his sisters, on being told of her father's death—but without seeing the body—fell into a swoon, in which she remained for several hours. When she was finally revived, she said: "Where are father's old clothes? He has just appeared to me dressed in a white shirt, black clothes, and felt slippers, and told me that after leaving home he sewed a large roll of bills inside his gray shirt with a piece of my red dress, and the money is still there." Although the rest of the family considered this a purely subjective hallucination (none of them had seen more than the face of the father's body through the coffin lid), their physician advised them to go get the clothes, which she was demanding, as he thought that this might, by setting her mind at rest, help her come out of the deathly ill state into which she had fallen. The son, accordingly, telephoned the coroner, found that the clothes were still there, and arranged to come to fetch them. Upon arriving, he reported the daughter's statement to the coroner, who said that her description of the burial clothes, including the slippers, was accurate. The men then, upon examining the gray shirt, found a large roll of bills sewed in it with a piece of red cloth.[16]

The daughter's apparition, accordingly, was doubly veridical, in that it contained two items of true information that she could not have known normally: how her father was dressed for burial and that his old shirt had the money sewed in it with (presumably) a piece of her red dress. This case (assuming its veracity) does not, however, necessarily imply that the apparition was somehow evoked by the postmortem agency of the father's mind: The information about both the money and the burial clothing could have been picked up unconsciously by the daughter through ordinary clairvoyance, then brought to consciousness by means of a dramatic apparition.

Another case involving hidden material and counting against a purely subjective interpretation of all apparitions, but not necessarily for a survivalist interpretation, is the oft-cited "Chaffin will" case, reported in 1927, shortly after its occurrence. The case involved the estate of James L. Chaffin, a farmer in North Carolina, who made a will in 1905 leaving his farm to his son Marshall and nothing to his wife and other three sons. When he died in 1921, the will was not contested. In 1925, however, one of the other sons, James P. Chaffin, evidently began having vivid dreams of his father appearing at his bedside. In the earlier dreams, according to his account, the apparition did not speak, but in a later dream his father, wearing his familiar black overcoat, said, "You will find my will in my overcoat pocket." The next morning, young James (according to the account) learned from his mother that this coat had been given to his brother John, who lived twenty miles away. A few days later, he went to John's house and found the coat. Stitched inside the inside pocket, he found a little roll of paper with, in his father's handwriting, the statement: "Read the 27th chapter of Genesis in my Daddie's old Bible." Then, accompanied by his wife and daughter, a neighbor, the neighbor's daughter, and the testator's wife, James returned to his mother's house to look for the old Bible. Upon finding it and turning to the 27th chapter of Genesis, they found another will, in the father's handwriting, dated January 16, 1919. It declared that, after having read Genesis 27, he wanted his property divided equally among his four children, and that they were to care for their mother. Although this will, unlike the first one, was not witnessed, it was legally valid because it was judged to be wholly in the father's handwriting, and it was admitted to probate.[17]

Most people reading about this case will rightly be suspicious, in that the person reporting the apparition was one of the financial beneficiaries of its purported message. Without knowing more about the story, one will naturally suspect that young James, perhaps along with other disinherited members of the family, concocted the whole story, forging the note and the second will and then inserting them, respectively, into the coat and the Bible. But assuming that this explanation (which surely would have occurred to Marshall and his attorney) was ruled out by investigators at the time and that there really was a veridical apparition, do we have good reason to think that the apparition is best explained as caused in terms of the postmortem activity of the father's still-living soul? This has often been claimed on the grounds that the apparition had a clear purpose, which suggests that the motivation for the apparition was on the father's side, not the son's. However, given the fact that the son had been read out of the father's first will, he likely would have been highly motivated to discover that there was a second will, and might have even suspected this. This motivation could have well created a state of mind ready to put in dramatic form knowledge acquired, through clairvoyance, retroprehensive telepathy, or both, that a second will had indeed been written.

We can, in fact, extend this reasoning back to the prior case, adding to what was already said the point that the (unconscious) desire for the remaining members of the family to learn about the hidden money could have been in the mind of Michael Conley's daughter, not that of the father. It is far less likely in the Conley case, to be sure, in that the apparition appeared so quickly after the daughter had learned of her father's death, when financial concerns were not likely to have been paramount. It is, nevertheless, possible. Accordingly, even if both of these cases be accepted as authentic, neither one provides strong evidence for life after death.

Another case that suggests, at least *prima facie*, that the purpose behind the apparition must have been in the mind of the sender is that of Captain G. F. Russell Colt. He reports that in 1855, his eldest brother, Oliver, who was then nineteen years old and a lieutenant in the military, was in low spirits prior to a major offensive. Russell reports that he had written to Oliver, whom he loved dearly, that he was to cheer up, but that, if anything did happen to him, he was to let him (Russell) know by appearing in his room. Shortly thereafter, Russell awoke suddenly one night and saw Oliver kneeling. Thinking it must be some trick played by the moonlight, he looked away. When he looked again, however, Oliver was still there, looking at him "lovingly, imploringly, and sadly." Shutting his eyes, Russell walked through the apparition to the door, but, before leaving the room, he looked back. "The apparition turned round his head slowly and again looked anxiously and lovingly at me, and I saw then for the first time a wound on the right temple with a red stream from it." Russell then went into a friend's room, staying on the sofa the rest of the night, telling the friend why. He also told others in the house, but his father ordered him not to repeat such nonsense, especially not to his mother. About two weeks later, the family learned that Oliver had been killed on the night in question—by a bullet that struck him in the right temple. They also learned that he had fallen among heaps of other dead bodies, and that he had been found "in a sort of kneeling posture (being propped up by other dead bodies)." From a clergyman, furthermore, Russell learned that Oliver had indeed received his letter asking Oliver to appear in Russell's room if he were to be killed.[18]

This case, which is a good example of a "crisis apparition," certainly provides evidence of paranormal influence. It does not, however, clearly suggest postmortem activity: One could, of course, argue that the timing of the apparition and the apparent purpose (to fulfill his brother's request) point to Oliver as the source of the apparition. But one could also point out that Russell, being apprehensive about his brother's welfare and being asleep (which tends to make one more receptive to extrasensory information), was in the perfect state to learn, through clairvoyance, of his brother's death and of the appearance of his dead body. The production of the apparition would then have been the means to bring this unconsciously received knowledge to consciousness.

A somewhat more suggestive case is the following, which is reported by a young man whose sister had died of cholera at the age of eighteen at home in St. Louis. A year or so later he had become a traveling salesman, and it was in 1876, eleven years after his sister's death, that the apparition appeared to him. He had just had a very successful time in St. Joseph, Missouri, and had gone to his room to send in his unusually large orders. He was in a very happy state of mind, thinking about how pleased his company would be at his success.

I had not been thinking of my late sister, or in any manner reflecting on the past. The hour was high noon, and the sun was shining cheerfully into my room. While busily smoking a cigar and writing out my orders, I suddenly became conscious that someone was sitting on my left, with one arm resting on the table. Quick as a flash I turned and distinctly saw the form of my dead sister, and for a brief second or so looked her squarely in the face; and so sure was I that it was she, that I sprang forward in delight, calling her by name, and, as I did so, the apparition instantly vanished. Naturally I was startled and dumbfounded, almost doubting my senses; but the cigar in my mouth, and pen in hand, with the ink still moist on my letter, I satisfied myself I had not been dreaming. I was near enough to touch her, had it been a physical possibility, and noted her features, expression, and details of dress, etc. She appeared as if alive. Her eyes looked kindly and perfectly natural into mine. Her skin was so life-like that I could see the glow or moisture on its surface.

He was so impressed with this "visitation" that he took the next train home to tell his parents, which he did in the presence of some friends. His father, "a man of rare good sense and very practical," was inclined to ridicule his son's credulity. But attitudes changed when the son later added one more detail:

I told them of a bright red line or *scratch* on the right-hand side of my sister's face, which I distinctly had seen. When I mentioned this my mother rose trembling to her feet and nearly fainted away, and as soon as she sufficiently recovered her self-possession, with tears streaming down her face, she exclaimed that I had indeed seen my sister, as no living mortal but herself was aware of that scratch, which she had accidentally made while doing some little act of kindness after my sister's death. She said she well remembered how pained she was to think she should have, unintentionally, marred the features of her dead daughter, and that unknown to all, how she had carefully obliterated all traces of the slight scratch with the aid of powder, etc., and that she had never mentioned it to a human being from that day to this. . . . So strangely impressed was my mother, that . . . she . . . told me *she knew* at least that I had seen my sister. A few weeks later my mother died, happy in her belief she would rejoin her favorite daughter in a better world.[19]

It is easy to see why this story is often repeated as evidence for survival. The *effect* of the apparition was twofold: It got the son to return home to see his mother one more time before she died, and it allowed his mother to die happy. From these quite predictable effects it would not be unreasonable to infer the *motivation*. From a survivalist standpoint we could infer, accordingly, that the daughter, realizing that her mother was about to die, produced the apparition in order to bring about these effects. That is not the only possible inference, however. We could also suppose that the son, learning unconsciously, through clairvoyance, of his mother's failing health, also unconsciously learned, through telepathy or retrocognitive clairvoyance, of the scratch on his dead sister's face, then produced the apparition as a means of bringing this unconscious knowledge to consciousness in such a way as to produce the desired effects.

This superpsi explanation may seem somewhat more artificial than in the previous cases, but it does not seem beyond the bounds of possibility.

Neither this case nor any of the previous ones, therefore, provides irresistable evidence for survival. They do, to be sure—assuming that we accept the authenticity of at least some of them or some of the thousands of similar cases—refute the assumption that all apparitions can be dismissed as purely subjective hallucinations: These veridical cases contain an objective element, which can only be accounted for by some kind of paranormal process. But these cases, because they can be explained in terms of fairly straightforward (albeit fairly super-) telepathy and/or clairvoyance, do not, by themselves at least, provide conclusive evidence for postmortem agency.

One reason why the above cases lend themselves to superpsi explanations is that the percipient in each case was someone with a strong attachment to the person appearing in the apparition. We can suppose, accordingly, that some kind of "telepathic bond" existed between them, through which the apparition can be assumed to have arisen. In some cases, however, people see apparitions of people that they did not know, and whose identity they discover only later. In one such case, some people had rented the second floor of a house, the ground floor of which was occupied by an invalid lady. This lady died one day, and the next night one of the women awoke and saw, at the foot of her bed, "an old gentleman with a round, rosy face, smiling, his hat in his hand, dressed in an old-fashioned coat (blue) with brass buttons, light waistcoat and trousers." The woman was quite astonished the next day to learn, after describing this apparition to her niece, that her description exactly fit that of the deceased lady's husband, who had himself died three years earlier.[20]

This case is difficult to explain in terms of any telepathic bond between the apparent and the percipient, because she had known nothing of him. We could, however, suppose that the very fact of having been in the invalid lady's house had created, unconsciously, some kind of bond with her which, in turn, created some kind of bond with her husband, so that, after learning of the lady's death, the woman produced an apparition of him on the basis of unconscious clairvoyant knowledge. Alternatively, we could suppose that the percipient, through telepathy, unconsciously received the lady's "deathbed vision" of her husband, then brought this vision to consciousness the following night as an apparition. Some readers may find such explanations of this and similar cases more implausible than those in which postmortem agency is involved. But it must be admitted that, however complex, such explanations are not impossible.

4. Multiple Appearances

One reason why the prior cases lend themselves to somewhat straightforward superpsi explanations is that the apparitions were seen by only one person.

Many times, however, the apparition is seen by more than one person. In some of these cases, the apparition appears to the various people individually, at different times. A classic multiple case of this sequential type is that of Eldred Bowyer-Bower, who was an airman shot down over France early on the morning of March 19, 1917. That same day, his half-sister, who was in Calcutta, India, and did not know that he was in combat, saw him:

> At that time I was either sewing or talking to my baby. . . . The baby was on the bed. I had a very strong feeling that I must turn round; on doing so I saw my brother, Eldred W. Bowyer-Bower. Thinking he was alive and had been sent out to India, I was simply delighted to see him, and turned round quickly to put baby in a safe place on the bed, so that I could go on talking to my brother; then turned again and put my hand out to him, when I found he was not there. I thought he was only joking, so I called him and looked everywhere I could think of looking. It was only when I could not find him I became very frightened and the awful fear that he might be dead. . . . Two weeks later I saw in the paper he was missing.[21]

On the morning of the same day, another sister's daughter in England, who was not quite three years old, came into her mother's room, saying, "Uncle Alley Boy is downstairs."[22]

Nine months later, incidentally, both Eldred's mother and his fiancée saw apparitions of him, but this was long after his death was known, and no new information came through, so these apparitions cannot be considered veridical. In any case, the virtually simultaneous apparitions seen by Eldred's half-sister and his very young niece, neither of which had reason to be especially anxious for his life on that day, provide a stronger basis than the prior cases for supposing that the apparition reflected postmortem agency. Even a case such as this one, however, *can* be explained without positing such agency. We can simply assume that both the half-sister and the niece were sufficiently attuned to Eldred, and sufficiently telepathic, to pick up extrastrong impressions of him due to his crisis, which they then turned into momentary apparitions.

5. COLLECTIVE APPARITIONS

Matters become more complex, however, when we turn to *collective* apparitions, in which two or more persons see the apparition *at the same time*. One case that is particularly interesting, because eight people witnessed the apparition, is reported by Charles Lett, a military man.

> On the 5th April, 1873, my wife's father, Captain Towns, died at his residence. . . . About six weeks after his death my wife had occasion, one

evening about nine o'clock, to go to one of the bedrooms in the house. She was accompanied by a young lady, Miss Berthon, and as they entered the room—the gas was burning all the time—they were amazed to see, reflected as it were on the polished surface of the wardrobe, the image of Captain Towns. It was barely half figure, the head, shoulders, and part of the arms only showing . . . The face appeared wan and pale, as it did before his death, and he wore a kind of grey flannel jacket, in which he had been accustomed to sleep. Surprised and half alarmed at what they saw, their first idea was that a portrait had been hung in the room, and that what they saw was its reflection; but there was no picture of the kind.

Whilst they were looking and wondering, my wife's sister, Miss Towns, came into the room, and before either of the others had time to speak she exclaimed, "Good gracious! Do you see papa?" One of the housemaids happened to be passing downstairs at the moment, and she was called in, and asked if she saw anything, and her reply was, "Oh miss! The master." Graham—Captain Towns' old body servant—was then sent for, and he also immediately exclaimed, "Oh, Lord save us! Mrs. Lett, it's the Captain!" The butler was called, and then Mrs. Crane, my wife's nurse, and they both said what they saw. Finally, Mrs. Towns was sent for, and seeing the apparition, she advanced towards it with her arm extended as if to touch it, and as she passed her hand over the panel of the wardrobe the figure gradually faded away, and never again appeared.[23]

The problem created by cases such as this for the superpsi, nonsurvivalist theories of apparitions is how to account for the fact that two or more see the same apparition, at the same time, and from their own perspectives. The reason why this is such a difficulty is that, by hypothesis, there is nothing "out there" external to the perceivers: The apparition is said to be produced by the perceiver's mind and then projected onto that region of space. In veridical cases, to be sure, we are assuming that the apparition is not created out of whole cloth, but, in part at least, out of telepathic perceptions, clairvoyant perceptions, or both. The object of those perceptions, however, is not, by hypothesis, now there in the room, but somewhere else, in the past, or both. How, then, would we explain why two or more people would happen to perceive just the same apparition of the apparent at the same time and at the same place?

One theory involves the notion of "telepathic contagion." According to this view, Mrs. Lett, in the present case, would have created the apparition of her father, simultaneously inducing this apparition in Miss Berthon. Then Mrs. Lett, or perhaps the two of them, would have induced the same apparition in Miss Towns, when she entered the room. The same apparition would have then been spread, by psychic contagion, to the other five people, as they entered the room.

This theory has several difficulties. One is the very notion of psychic contagion: We have little if any evidence that such contagion ever occurs. Also, we know, as documented in Chapter 2, how difficult it is to evoke a clear image in someone else's mind telepathically. Even in quite successful cases the percipient receives a somewhat distorted image, and the resulting report involves a mixture of "hits" and "misses." The explanation of collective apparitions in terms of telepathic contagion, by contrast, requires that the image be transmitted with complete exactitude, because the people invariably report seeing the same thing, down to the fine details. In the present case, furthermore, the image would have had to be transferred with exactitude not just to one other person, but to seven! Finally, Mrs. Lett would have had to cause the others to project their telepathic hallucinations onto exactly the same region of space, so that it would appear to all of them to be on the wardrobe.

A further problem is that of the timing: The various people usually agree not only on the content of the apparition, but on *when* it is there. In this case, they all saw it fading out of existence at the same time. The theory of psychic contagion would have to attribute to Mrs. Lett not only the power to provide the same data to all the others, but also to cause it to rise to consciousness in the form of an apparition just as they entered the room and looked at the wardrobe, and then for it to fade from consciousness in all the people simultaneously.

Perhaps the most difficult feat, however, would be that of getting everyone to see the apparition *from their own perspective*. That problem is not so obvious in the Lett-wardrobe case, because the apparition was not three dimensional and the various people evidently saw it from approximately the same location. In most collective cases, however, the apparition is three dimensional, and is seen from various locations. In one such case, two brothers sharing a cabin in a naval ship were sleeping in cots hung parallel to each other. They both woke suddenly to see the figure of their father standing between them. As they stared in amazement, it raised one hand and pointed to its own eyes, which were closed. Their father, they later learned, had died at about that time.[24] By the theory of psychic contagion, the one brother would have learned of the father's death telepathically, then awakened the other brother telepathically while creating an apparition and telepathically inducing it into the brother's mind as well. The apparition created in the brother's mind could not, however, be simply a duplicate of his own apparition, because the one brother would have to see it from the left side, the other from the right side. For example, the hand that was raised to point to the eyes would have been the near hand for the one brother, the far hand for the other. So, in reality, two apparitions would have to be created. In other cases, three, four, or eight (or even, in one well-documented case,[25] some 100) apparitions would have to be created, all with just the right perspective.

The theory of psychic contagion could be amended, to try to handle these problems, by supposing that the apparition is the joint product of all the people involved. The basic idea would come from the original percipient, but the other percipients would then make their contributions, so that the final product, with its timing, location, and various perspectives, would be produced by all. This theory, however, becomes hopelessly complex when one tries to apply it in detail,[26] and it still leaves unclear how the various percipients would all see the apparition from their respective perspectives.

The difficulty created for the theory of apparitions as hallucinations, even telepathically induced hallucinations, by collective apparitions should not, on the assumption that reports of collective apparitions are rare enough to be dismissed as anomalies, hoaxes, or fantasies, be supposed to be a minor difficulty. For example, in the 1886 Census of Hallucinations, there were at least two persons present in 283 of the 1,087 cases of visual apparitions, and 95 of these 283 cases involved collective apparitions. In a 1956 study by Hornell Hart in America, the sample contained 46 cases in which a second person was in a position to be a percipient, and the apparition was collective in 26 of these 46 cases (56 percent of them).[27] The evidence suggests, accordingly, that when two or more persons are in a position to be a percipient, the apparitions are likely to be collective one third to one half of the time. No theory can be considered adequate if it cannot deal satisfactorily with this fact. The view that at least some apparitions are due to the postmortem agency of the apparent could certainly provide the simplest explanation.

There is, however, another possible theory that does not require postmortem agency. This theory would supplement super-ESP with super-PK, at least in collective cases. The new idea would be that, in projecting the hallucinated image outward, thereby creating the apparition, the primary percipient creates a quasi-physical entity. As quasi-physical, it would be physical enough to stimulate the sensory (primarily the visual) organs of some people, but not necessarily physical enough to stimulate those of all people. This would explain why, among those sensitive enough to see the apparition, there would be detailed agreement about its details, location, and timing, while also explaining why some people would not see it. This quasi-physical view of apparitions would seem more plausible, furthermore, for those cases in which the apparition is also evidently seen by a dog or some other animal. The chief problem for this theory would be to explain why the apparition would be physical enough to appear completely real and alive to some people while being nonphysical enough to be completely invisible to others. This would be a very strange kind of physicality, affecting human sensory organs in a way seemingly without parallel. That problem might not, however, be insuperable. A second problem with this theory is that it requires attributing, to thousands of people who otherwise manifest no capacity for conscious ESP and especially for conscious PK, the once-in-a-lifetime ability to manifest not only super-ESP but also super-enough-PK to produce quasi-physical apparitions of exquisite lifelikeness.

In addition to those problems, there is yet another problem for any theory, including this one as well as the psychic contagion theory, that attributes the initiative behind collective apparitions to an intimate bond between the primary percipient and the apparent. This problem is created by the fact that, in some cases involving collective apparitions, the primary percipient did not know the apparent.

One such apparition was reported by a woman as having occurred on Christmas Eve of 1869, just two years after she had gotten married. After she and her husband, Willie, had gone to bed, and as she was about to extinguish the lamp, she saw a man, dressed as a naval officer, standing at the foot of the bed. Being too astonished to be afraid, she touched the shoulder of her husband, who was turned away from her, saying, "Willie, who is this?" Her husband, after looking in astonishment, shouted, "What on earth are you doing here, sir?" The figure, which had been leaning on its arms, drew itself upright and said in a commanding, reproachful voice, "Willie, Willie!" The figure then moved slowly toward the wall. "As it passed the lamp, a deep shadow fell upon the room as of a material person shutting out the light from us by his intervening body, and he disappeared, as it were, into the wall." When her husband then put his arms around her, asking if she knew what they had seen, she replied that she feared that it might have been the spirit of her brother, who was in the navy and on a voyage to India. Her husband said, "Oh! no, it was my father." Willie's father, who had been a naval officer in his youth and had been dead fourteen years, had never been seen by Willie's wife. Willie later revealed to her that, having been in great financial difficulty, he was about to take a man's advice that would have led him to ruin, and that the apparition of his father led him to reject that advice.[28]

Although this report is interesting in several respects, including the fact that the apparition not only spoke audibly but also cast a shadow, both of which are rare, the most important feature for our purposes is that it did not appear first to Willie. Had it done so, we could attribute the initiative behind it to his anxiety about his intended financial decision in conjunction with his (presumed) more-or-less conscious sense that his father would not approve. But because it first appeared to his wife, a more complex assumption would be necessary, if we are to avoid attributing the initiative to the spirit of Willie's father. We would presumably need to suppose that his wife, having telepathically picked up his anxieties and his thoughts about his father, and also having learned of his father's appearance and manner of speaking telepathically from Willie or by means of retrocognitive clairvoyance, created the apparition herself. She then would have telepathically induced the apparition in Willie, or, by our alternative theory (which would fit better the report that the apparition created a shadow when passing before the lamp), created a quasi-physical apparition, which Willie would then have perceived, in part, by means of his eyes.

Although neither of these nonsurvivalist theories is completely beyond the pale of possibility, they do both face extremely difficult problems, which they can solve only by becoming extremely complex and by moving to really superpsi. The natural question to raise at this point, accordingly, is whether a survivalist theory would be less implausible.

6. THEORIES INVOLVING POSTMORTEM AGENCY

The mere decision to include postmortem agency certainly does not by itself suggest a plausible theory. Edmund Gurney, for example, held the view of psychic contagion, which I explained above, except that he supposed veridical apparitions of the dead to originate from telepathic influence exerted by the postmortem spirit. This supposition avoided the need to attribute super-ESP to the primary percipients to explain their acquisition of the new information, but it left intact the various other problems faced by the nonsurvivalist version of this theory mentioned above. The characteristics of many apparitions are such that no account of them as simply hallucinations can be adequate, even if the hallucinations are thought to result in part from an idea provided by the agency of a postmortem soul.

At the opposite extreme is the view of veridical apparitions as resulting simply from sensory perceptions of the apparent's "subtle" or "astral" body, in which the soul is said to be embodied after biological death. The standard objection to this view is the fact that apparitions usually are not naked but clothed (most often in clothing characteristic of the apparent while living or the clothes in which he or she died). Apparitions also often include jewelry, canes, and even vehicles, which appear just as real as the human bodies. Are we to assume that all of these things have astral copies as well?

A fully adequate theory, if one is ever developed, will surely be somewhere in between these two extremes. A few such theories have been developed. Frederick Myers suggested that the postmortem soul, or some element thereof, produces quasi-physical effects in the region of space at which the apparition is seen. His view seemed to be that in some cases these effects are physical enough to be detected by our sensory organs (which could account for those cases in which *everyone* present sees the apparition), but that often they can only be detected extrasensorily (which could account for those cases in which only some people present see the apparition). Some version, or modification, of this type of theory would seem the most promising. In such a theory, the quasi-physical effects created by the discarnate soul could include any type of image (just as a Ted Serios can produce any type of image on a film), which would account for the fact that apparitional bodies are usually clothed and often accompanied by other things as well. Such a theory would seem to be fully compatible with all those features of apparitions that reveal them not to be physical in the ordinary sense.

The upshot of the foregoing discussion is that an adequate theory of apparitions, especially for collective cases, would seem to require the assumption of postmortem agency. It would be unfortunate, however, if such a momentous and controversial conclusion had to rest solely on such an inferential basis. The conclusion would seem much less tenuous if there were some more direct reason to suppose that veridical apparitions, at least sometimes, reflected the agency, and even presence, of discarnate souls. And, it turns out, some students of the subject have provided such a reason. Their argument requires that we examine apparitions of the living, including the type that are called "reciprocal."

7. APPARITIONS OF THE LIVING

Although a good number of the cases in *Phantasms of the Living*, as I indicated earlier, should have been classed as postmortem cases (because they occurred up to 12 hours after the death of the apparent), some of the cases clearly involved apparitions of the living. Such apparitions are of two basic types: spontaneous and intentional (sometimes called "experimental").

Some of the spontaneous type are "arrival cases," in which an apparition of the person arrives sometime before the person actually arrives. One well-known nineteenth-century case involved two brothers, Robert and Clement Coe, who had married two sisters and lived about a mile and a quarter apart. One day, at about four o'clock, Robert suddenly said to his wife, "Let's go to Clement's." Shortly thereafter, a mutual friend staying at Clement's place (who was the source of this report) looked out the window and said, "Here is your brother coming." Clement came to the window and said, "Oh, yes, here he is; and see, Robert has got Dobbin out at last"—referring thereby to Robert's horse, which had been unused for several weeks because of an accident, but was now seen pulling the carriage. Clement's wife then looked out and said, "And I am so glad, too, that my sister is with him. They will be delighted to find you here." But then the couple's vehicle went right on by and disappeared. Clement then exclaimed, "Why, what can be the matter? They have gone on without calling, a thing they never did in their lives before." Five minutes later, Robert's daughter, about twenty-five, came in, pale and excited, and said, "Oh, aunt, I have had such a fright. Father and mother have passed me on the road without speaking. I looked up at them as they passed by, but they looked straight on and never stopped nor said a word." (She reported that when she had left home a quarter hour before, her parents had been sitting by the fire.) Then, ten minutes later, the visitor looked up the road and said, "But see, here they are, coming down the road again." Clement replied, "No, that is impossible, because there is no path by which they could get on to this road, so as to be coming down it again. But sure enough, here they are, and with the same horse!"[29]

This spontaneous case is interesting in several respects. With regard to our previous concerns, it further illustrates the inadequacy of explanations of apparitions solely in terms of astral bodies, given the horse and carriage, and of explanations of collective apparitions in terms of psychic contagion, given the fact that the first person in the house to see it was the visitor, not one of the siblings, and the fact that the apparition was also seen, at a different time and from a quite different perspective, by the niece down the road. The most important feature of this apparition for our present purposes, however, is that, although it was not consciously created by Robert or his wife (or, we can presume, their horse), *it did appear at Clement's house at a time when they were planning to go there.* We can suppose, accordingly, that although they did not intend to create an apparition as such, the apparition was "intentional" in a broader sense, in that it was produced by their intention to travel to Clement's place. Yet another important feature of this apparition is that neither Robert nor his wife had any sense of being there where they were first perceived by the others.

8. Reciprocal Cases

Some apparitions of the living, however, are *reciprocal*, meaning that each person, the one who is there physically and the one who is not, seem to be aware of the other. Perhaps the best known of such cases is that involving Mr. and Mrs. S. R. Wilmot in 1863. Mr. Wilmot was returning to America from Europe by ship, sharing a cabin with his friend W. J. Tait. The upper berth, which Tait had, was not directly above the lower berth, but extended further back. After a week of bad weather, Wilmot was finally getting a good night's sleep, during which, toward morning, he dreamed that he saw his wife, in her night-dress, come to the door. "At the door she seemed to discover that I was not the only occupant of the room, hesitated a little, then advanced to my side, stooped down and kissed me and after gently caressing me for a few moments, quietly withdrew." Upon waking, Tait said, "You're a pretty fellow, to have a lady come and visit you in this way." Asked what he meant, Tait described what he had seen, while awake, and this description corresponded to Wilmot's dream. When Wilmot returned home, his wife asked, "Did you receive a visit from me a week ago Tuesday?" Wilmot indicated that such a visit would have been impossible, because he was out to sea. "I know it," she replied, "but it seemed to me that I visited you." She then recounted that, because of the severity of the weather and the fact that another ship had been reported lost, she had become very anxious. The morning in question she had been lying awake thinking about her husband, and at about four o'clock it seemed that she went out to seek him. She crossed the sea, came to a low, black steamship, went up the side, descended into the cabin, and passed through it until she came to his stateroom. "Tell me," she said, "do they ever have staterooms like the one I saw where the upper berth extends further back than the under one? A man was in the upper berth looking right at me, and for a moment I was afraid to go in, but soon I went up to the side of your berth, bent down and kissed you and embraced you and then went away." Mrs. Wilmot and her sister both signed Mr. Wilmot's testimony.[30]

A more recent case has been reported in 1957 by a young woman in Plains, Illinois, writing under the pseudonym of "Martha Johnson." In the early morning of January 27 of that year, she reports, she dreamed that she had floated to her mother's home in northern Minnesota. "After I entered, I leaned up against the dish cupboard with folded arms. . . . I looked at my Mother who was bending over something white and doing something with her hands. She did not appear to see me at first, but she finally looked up. I had a sort of pleased feeling and then after standing a second more, I turned and walked about four steps." She recorded that she awoke from her dream at 2:10 A.M. Her mother's account of the experience was given in letters of January 29 and February 7, from which the following statement has been extracted:

I believe it was Saturday night, 1:10, 26 January, or maybe the 27th. It would have been 10 after two, your time. I was pressing a blouse here in the kitchen. . . . I looked up and there you were by the cupboard just standing smiling at me. I started to speak and you were gone. . . . I think the dogs saw you too. They got so excited and wanted out—just like they thought you were by the door—sniffled and were so tickled. Your hair was combed nice—just back in a pony tail with a pretty roll in front. Your blouse was neat and light—seemed almost white."

The daughter later confirmed that this was how she appeared during her "trip."[31]

In both the Wilmot and the "Johnson" cases, it is not clear that the women intended to make themselves appear at the scene; it seems, rather, that they simply found themselves going (in a dream in the latter case). However, in some "experimental" cases, the person deliberately tries to make the other person aware of his or her presence. And some of these cases turn out to be reciprocal, even if only imperfectly so. One such case is reported by Edith Maughan (later Mrs. G. Rayleigh Vicars). She reports that, after reading some cases of "astral projection" in 1888, she decided to see if she could accomplish a projection of herself "by force of will-concentration." Remarking that the room next to hers was occupied by a long-time friend, Ethel Thompson, she said: "I perfectly recall lying back on my pillow with a resolute but half-doubtful and amused determination to make Miss Thompson see me. The candle was burning on a chair at the side of my bed, and I heard only the ticking clock as I 'willed' with all my might to appear to her. After a few minutes I felt dizzy and only half-conscious." Upon returning to a fully conscious state, she blew out the candle, assuming that she had failed. At that moment, however, she heard Miss Thompson's slightly raised voice and then, after hearing her own clock strike two, fell asleep. The next morning Miss Thompson, who looked rather tired, asked Edith whether she had gone into her room to frighten her. She said that Edith had seemed to come in and bend over her and then disappear. The time seemed to have been between 1 and 2 A.M.[32]

Although this can be considered a "reciprocal" case in the weak sense, in that the woman was perceived at the time and place that she intended to be, other experimental cases are reciprocal in the stronger sense, in which (as in the case of "Martha Johnson") the projector seems to herself or himself to be subjectively present at the location. For example, a Dr. Alfred Backman of Sweden reported an experiment involving a woman called Alma, who was able to engage in "traveling clairvoyance" at will. Without any prearrangement, he told Alma to "go" to the home of the Director-General of Pilotage at Stockholm and report what she saw. Upon reporting that the man was writing at his table in his study, on which lay, among other things, a bunch of keys, she was told by Dr. Backman to seize the keys and shake them and to put her hand on the Director-General's shoulder. She repeated these actions two or three times, finally declaring that he had observed her. When subsequently asked about his experience on that occasion, the Director-General said that, while being fully occupied with his work, he suddenly, for no reason, turned his attention to the bunch of keys lying on the table. He wondered why the keys were there instead of where he usually put them. While reflecting on this issue, he caught a glimpse of a woman. He assumed he had seen the maid-servant until the occurrence was repeated, at which time he learned that no woman had been in the room.[33] The success of this experiment, obviously, was only partial: The percipient did not see or hear the keys rattling, did not feel the hand on his shoulder, caught only brief glimpses of the apparition, and evidently did not see it as right next to him. The case is significant, nonetheless, in suggesting that some apparitions coincide with the subjective presence of the soul from which the apparition arises.

SUMMARY AND CONCLUSION

Having provided a few illustrations, it is now time to draw out the main points to be made about apparitions of the living in relation to apparitions of the dead. One point involves timing: On the one hand, most apparitions of the dead or dying occur within an hour of the death of the apparent (this was confirmed for over 60% of the cases in "Phantasms of the Dead," produced primarily by Eleanor Sidgwick).[34] On the other hand, apparitions of the living, as we have seen, occur most often when the apparent is thinking or dreaming about the place in question and perhaps even trying to be there, or at least to be perceived there. A second point of comparison involves the appearance and behavior of apparitions: In the aforementioned 1956 study, Hornell Hart, on the basis

of a systematic comparison of apparitions of the dead and dying with reciprocal apparitions of the living, concluded that they were "so closely similar . . .
that the two types must be regarded as belonging to the same basic kind of
phenomena."[35] The natural conclusion to draw from these two points, which in
fact is the main point of Hart's study, is that in at least some apparitions of the
dead the apparitions are produced, at least partly, by the intentional activity
and/or presence of the still-conscious minds of the apparents.

This conclusion, that apparitional phenomena provide evidence for life
after death, would be given additional support if there were empirical evidence
to support the view that minds or souls can indeed have experiences outside of
biological bodies. In the discussion above, I have provided, to be sure, some
reports of people who have *felt* like they were out of their bodies when they
were being perceived, but this is not terribly strong evidence. It is interesting,
furthermore, to recall that in a few cases of the reincarnation type, there are
accounts of reciprocal apparitions during the period in which the soul in question was "between bodies," but such accounts also do not provide strong evidence. What is needed is verifiable evidence supporting the belief of some
people that they really do sometimes briefly exist apart from their bodies. Such
evidence would supply support for the conclusion of this chapter, that what are,
from without, "apparitions" are sometimes, from within, "out-of-body experiences." Whether such evidence exists is the concern of the next chapter.

8

EVIDENCE FROM
OUT-OF-BODY EXPERIENCES

The term "out-of-body experience" is ambiguous. It could be taken to mean either (1) an experience had while one was out of one's body or (2) an experience of being out of one's body (whether one really was or not). The latter is what is meant. Susan J. Blackmore, for example, begins a book on the subject by defining an out-of-body experience (OBE) as "an experience in which a person seems to perceive the world from a location outside his physical body." She then stresses, in agreement with John Palmer, that "the *experience* of being out of the body is not equivalent to the *fact* of being out."[1] The question of whether persons (or their minds or souls) are *really* out of their bodies when they are having OBEs, at least sometimes, is at the center of the critical discussion of these experiences.

1. THE EXTRASOMATIC AND INTRASOMATIC HYPOTHESES

The contrast between these two views, that one's mind really *is* or *is not* out of the body, has been expressed with various terminologies. The former view has been variously called the *separation*, the *ecsomatic*, and the *extrasomatic* hypothesis. The latter view has been variously termed the *psychological*, the *imaginal*, and the *hallucination* hypothesis. None of these contrasts is adequate. For one thing, the terms *imaginal* and *psychological* do not adequately reflect those views that reject the extrasomatic hypothesis in terms of a primarily physiological theory. And the term *hallucination* has psychopathological connotations that are not necessarily intended. Another problem with these standard contrasts—although it is really another way of making the same point—is that they are not true contraries: What is needed are parallel terms, each of which is the contrary of the other. Much better, therefore, is the contrast between *objectivist* and *subjectivist* hypotheses.[2] This contrast is problematic, however, for another reason: The so-called objectivist hypothesis is also subjectivist in a sense, in that it holds that the person's subjectivity is outside his or her body. Also, the terms *ecsomatic* and *extrasomatic* have been employed so frequently as to be virtually standard usage by now, so it seems necessary to choose between them for the view that the mind is really outside the body. A contrast between *ecsomatic* and *ensomatic* hypotheses, however, would lead too easily to misreading errors.

I propose, accordingly, the contrast between *extrasomatic* and *intrasomatic* hypotheses.* All *extrasomatic* hypotheses hold that something (consciousness, mind, soul, spirit, double, astral body, spiritual body, or whatever) actually leaves the physical body and perceives from an extrasomatic locus. All *intrasomatic* theories hold that nothing of the sort really happens, because the "mind," however it be understood, remains right there in the body where it always is. The task, accordingly, is to explain the illusion that it does leave.

The relevance of this controversy to the issue of life after death is obvious: During an OBE one *seems* to be feeling, perceiving, thinking, deciding, and acting while being apart from one's body, including one's brain. This experience gives strong *prima facie* support to the idea that, when the body dies, this core of the person will continue to experience. Indeed, surveys show that about two-thirds of those who have had an OBE say that it convinced them that they would survive bodily death.[3] The extrasomatic hypothesis lends support to this "natural" interpretation, agreeing with the out-of-body experiencers (OBErs) that they did indeed leave their bodies. The intrasomatic hypothesis does not support it, saying instead, in Susan Blackmore's words: "Nothing leaves the body in an OBE and so there is nothing to survive."[4]

---

* One virtue of this proposed terminological contrast is that it allows for a third parallel term, *transsomatic*, for a third view. According to this view, consciousness or the mind is not properly described as normally "in" the body. Indeed, the body may be said to be in the mind (see Michael Grosso, *The Final Choice: Playing the Survival Game* [Walpole, N.H.: Stillpoint, 1985], 106–12). In any case, it would be misleading, from this viewpoint, to say that during an OBE the person's conscious mind has left the body. But it would be even more misleading to subsume this position under the intrasomatic hypothesis—which not only says that the mind is in the body during an OBE but also generally denies that there is any aspect of the person that could survive bodily death—because transsomatic interpreters generally believe in life after death.

2. TYPES OF OBES

There are various ways to classify different types of OBEs. One classification is in terms of how they come about.* The most important distinction of this type is between spontaneous (or involuntary) and deliberate (or voluntary). Although most OBEs occur spontaneously, a few people have developed the ability to induce them deliberately. This fact allows for the possibility of experiments; indeed, this type of OBE is sometimes called "experimental."†

Within the category of spontaneous OBEs there is a distinction of great importance: OBEs that occur when persons are physically near death, or at least believe that they are, and those that occur in other circumstances. The former, which perhaps constitute about 10 percent of the OBEs,[5] are commonly called near-death out-of-body experiences (ND OBEs). In many treatments of evidence for life after death, near-death experiences (NDEs) and OBEs are treated separately.‡ And, indeed, not all NDEs involve OBEs (estimates range from 31 to 77 percent),[6] and there are several aspects of typical NDEs that are not necessarily or even usually involved in OBEs as such; I will briefly discuss some of

---

* Another distinction that has been much discussed, especially in the older literature, is that between OBEs in which the persons seem to themselves in their out-of-body state to have a body of sorts (often called a "spiritual" or "astral" body) and those in which they do not. The two views are termed *parasomatic* and *asomatic* OBEs by Celia Green (*Out-of-the-Body Experiences* [London: Hamish Hamilton, 1968], 30–36). In Green's study, 80 percent of the subjects reported asomatic OBEs, although other surveys show a much higher incidence of parasomatic experiences (Susan J. Blackmore, *Beyond the Body: An Investigation of Out-of-the-Body Experiences* [1982; Chicago: Academy Chicago Publishers, 1992], 64–67).

† Robert Crookall, *The Study and Practice of Astral Projection* [London: Aquarian Press, 1961] and *More Astral Projections* [London: Aquarian Press, 1964], distinguished between "natural" and "enforced" cases. Natural OBEs included those of people who nearly died, were very ill, or were exhausted, as well as people in good health. Enforced OBEs were those brought on by anesthetics, by suffocation, by falling, or deliberately (by hypnosis). This distinction seems to involve considerable arbitrariness. Could not, for example, an OBE brought on by nearly dying be considered "enforced"? The distinction between spontaneous (or involuntary) and experimental (or voluntarily-induced) OBEs, which I am employing, has been stressed by Celia Green, *Out-of-the-Body Experiences*, 22, 23, 73–75.

‡ My decision not to treat them separately reflects my belief that most, at least, of the evidence for life after death provided by NDEs is provided by the ND OBE, insofar as it provides evidence for true out-of-body existence. As I suggest in the final part of this chapter, I suspect that most of the other features of many NDEs often taken as evidential, such as the similarity of the elements found in the transcendental dimension, are explainable in archetypal (collective unconscious) terms. One aspect of some NDEs that *can* (in my opinion) be regarded as somewhat evidential is the vision of deceased relatives and other persons, especially when the subject did not previously know that they were deceased. However, such visions, especially when they occur prior to the subject's death, would most properly be treated under the heading of apparitions. For one of the early treatments, see Sir William Barrett, *Death-Bed Visions: The Psychical Experiences of the Dying* (1926; Wellingborough, England: The Aquarian Press, 1986). For an excellent recent cross-cultural study, see Karlis Osis and Erlendur Haraldsson, *At the Hour of Death* (New York: Avon Books, 1977).

these other features of NDEs at the end of this chapter. References to these "other features" brings up another common distinction: that between OBEs in which what is experienced is one's own body and/or other features of ordinary reality (sometimes called *autoscopic, mundane,* or *naturalistic* OBEs) and those in which the content includes visions of deceased individuals, religious figures, and extraordinary sights and sounds, whether heavenly or hellish (sometimes called *supernaturalistic* or *transcendental* OBEs). This chapter, until the brief treatment of NDEs as such at the end, is devoted solely to the former.

In any case, besides being central to many NDEs themselves, OBEs are central to the *discussion* of NDEs (because, as we will see, the main argument against most intrasomatic explanations of NDEs is based on veridical perceptions that occurred from an out-of-body perspective while the person was behaviorally unconscious). I will, in fact, orient my discussion of OBEs primarily around ND OBEs, for three reasons: They have been at the center of the recent discussion; they thereby provide a number of *recent* examples; and some of these examples present the most difficult cases for the various intrasomatic theories.

3. COMMON FEATURES OF OBEs

To see what the various intrasomatic theories are up against, we need to look at various features of OBEs, at least most of which seem, at least *prima facie,* to count against intrasomatic views and thereby to support an extrasomatic interpretation.

The Feeling of Being Out of the Body

This first feature, of course, is the one that gives the phenomenon its name. People report that they were having experiences from a locus other than that of their physical bodies. Quite often, evidently in about 60 percent of the cases, they report having seen their own bodies from a position outside of it,[7] which is why this type or phase of OBE is sometimes termed "autoscopic." In a typical description, one subject wrote: "While in bed at night, I found myself 'outside myself' looking down at my own body. I seemed to be about 2 ft. above the bed, at the side, slightly at the back, looking down at myself." Another wrote: "I had a clear view from my position in the top right-hand corner of the window (I was in no doubt at all as to where I was) of my body lying on the bed." Still another reported: "The part of me that was out of my body was the real me, as I knew it, the part that sees, thinks, and feels emotionally."[8]

The Conviction That this Experience Was Real

OBEers are virtually unanimous in saying that the experience was real, in distinction from being either a dream or a hallucination. Dreams and hallucinations may, of course, seem real at the time; but in retrospect people can usually recognize them for what they were. OBErs, by contrast, almost always find their experiences to be real not only at the time but also on reflection. And this is a point about which they are often emphatic. For example, one subject said: "It's reality. I know for myself that I didn't experience no fantasy. There was no so-called dream or nothing. These things really happened to me. It happened. I know. I went through it." Another subject said: "I *know* it was real. I *know* that I was up there. I *know* that. And I *know* that I seen me down there. I could swear on a Bible that I was there. I seen things just like I see them now." Another emphatic subject said: "That was real. If you want to, I'm perfectly willing for you to give me Sodium Pentothal. . . . It's real as hell."[9] (We can hope that he is wrong about the presupposition expressed in the last point.)

Greatly Altered Emotional State

OBErs often make comments such as the following: "Then I suddenly felt filled with the utmost joy and happiness. I felt such great freedom, like a bird just being let out of the cage for the first time in life." "Both occasions were so happy, ecstatic almost, that I have never stopped wishing that I could repeat them. . . . There was a quality of extreme joy."[10] In one study of OBErs, by Emilio Tiberi, 35 percent said that emotions were the main feature of their OBEs. Of these emotions, the most prevalent seems to be serenity-tranquillity, with 72 percent reporting it. Emotional state, incidentally, seems to be one of the respects in which ND OBEs are somewhat different than other OBEs, as seren-ity/tranquillity was reported by 92 percent of the ND OBErs but only 64 percent of the others, whereas anxiety was reported, at least sometime during the experience, by 52 percent of the others but only 20 percent of the ND OBErs.[11]

Absence of Pain

Most subjects (about 90% in the study just mentioned) report that they felt no pain during their OBE.[12] This fact is most striking, of course, in accident victims or in hospital patients being subjected to painful procedures without anesthesia. For example, one man, whose case will be described more fully below, said that the doctor's "pounding on the chest . . . didn't hurt even though it cracked a rib. I felt no pain." In reporting on watching the efforts to restart his heart with electrical shocks to his chest, he said, "I could see myself jolt, but . . . it didn't hurt like an electric shock should hurt."[13] This absence of pain might be thought explainable in terms of endorphins or some other kind of "natural anesthetic" provided by the body, except that the subjects report that the pain returned the moment that they returned to their bodies.

Normal or Better-Than-Normal Visual Perception

Most OBErs report that they could see. It is, in fact, this experience of seeing things, including often one's own body, from a perspective apart from one's body that is primarily responsible for the experience of actually being outside of one's body. Most subjects, furthermore, report that their visual images are normal or even more vivid than normal.[14] In Tiberi's study, 70 percent described them as vivid, while only 17 percent described them as faded or obscure. With regard to *color* perception, only 15 percent called it faded while the rest called it either normal or brilliant.[15] These statistics should not lead us, to be sure, to ignore the fact that in many OBEs, especially of the voluntary type, blurry, distorted, and even erroneous visual perception occurs. An adequate theory of OBEs, however, must account for the fact that this is evidently not always the case, and may not even be true for a majority of the cases.

Normal Hearing

The other sensory-type perception that is common is hearing, with between 30 to 60 percent of the OBErs reporting that they had at least normal hearing.[16] The fact that fewer people report auditory than visual images is interesting, given the fact that hearing is the last of the senses to go as one becomes unconscious. If OBEs that occur when people are behaviorally unconscious were due, as some suggest, to the fact that they are really not *fully* unconscious and are creating their experiences from bits of information acquired from residual hearing, we would expect auditory imagery to be the most prevalent.

Veridical Perceptions

This term refers to perceptions during the OBE that not only were accurate but were of things that could not have been normally perceived by the person, given his or her position, closed eyes, and behavioral unconsciousness. In the light of what was said about hearing in the previous point, these reports are most impressive if they involve *visual* images of things that occurred while a patient was behaviorally unconscious, with eyes closed. The following account, in which a woman tells what happened to her in the hospital after she called nurses because of a severe pain in her chest, illustrates this and several of the previous points.

> I heard the nurses shout, "Code pink! Code pink!" As they were saying this, I could feel myself moving out of my body and sliding down between the mattress and the rail on the side of the bed. . . . Then, I started rising upward, slowly. On my way up, I saw more nurses come running into the room—there must have been a dozen of them. My doctor happened to be making his rounds in the hospital so they called him and I saw him come in, too. I thought, "I wonder what he's doing here." I drifted on up past the light fixture—I saw it from the side and very distinctly—and then I stopped floating right below the ceiling, looking down. . . . I watched them reviving me from up there! . . . I heard one nurse say, "Oh, my God! She's gone!", while another one leaned down to give me mouth-to-mouth resuscitation. I was looking at the *back* of her

head while she did this. I'll never forget the way her hair looked; it was cut kind of short. Just then, I saw them roll this machine in there, and they put the shocks on my chest. When they did, I saw my whole body just jump right up off the bed, and I heard every bone crack and pop. . . . As I saw them beating on my chest and rubbing my arms and legs, I thought, "Why are they going to so much trouble? I'm just fine now."[17]

This account, which is reported by Raymond Moody, contains eleven items that were potentially veridical, the most important being the report of the doctor's presence (assuming that, as it seemed, it was unexpected) and the description of the back of the one nurse's head (assuming that the woman had not seen her before or after this episode). Although Moody did not in fact provide any corroboration for these items from witnesses or the medical report,* this case does illustrate the kinds of accounts that are quite common. For most people, it is this aspect of OBEs that gives the strongest support to the extrasomatic interpretation.[18]

Clarity of Thought

Besides the fact that most people (over 80 percent in Tiberi's study[19]) report that they could think clearly during their OBE , many of them say that they could think even more clearly than usual. Some representative comments are: "I was as clear thinking as at any time in my life." "The mind is clear as a bell." "I

---

* In Moody's first book, from which the above case was taken, he says, in response to the question of whether he has investigated the medical records of his subjects: "In so far as possible, I have. In the cases I have been invited to investigate, the records have borne out the assertions of the persons involved. In some cases, due to the passage of time and/or the death of the persons who carried out the resuscitation, records are not available. The reports for which substantiating records are not available are no different from those in which records are available. In many instances when medical records have not been accessible, I have secured the testimony of others—friends, doctors, or relatives of the informant—to the effect that the near-death event did occur" (*Life After Life* [1975; New York: Bantam, 1976], 146). Later in this same book, in defending the reality of the experiences, he refers to "the fact that independent corroboration of a kind exists for certain of the reports of out-of-body episodes" (176). Unfortunately, however, besides not publishing this corroborating evidence, Moody does not even tell us *which* of the cases he was able to verify to his own satisfaction, so we do not know, for example, whether the case cited above is one of those. In this book (176) and his next one, Moody defends his practice of not giving names and identifying details on the grounds that people have told him their stories with the assumption that they would remain anonymous. That is certainly legitimate, but Moody errs when he adds that publishing the names of the subjects "would not make my study more credible from a scientific point of view" (*Reflections on Life After Life* [1977; Bantam, 1978], 82). Such identification would allow other researchers to corroborate the accounts. Moody, who rightly receives much of the credit for opening up research on near-death experiences, is fully justified in restricting his work to that role, leaving it to others to carry out the more scientific research. Others, fortunately, *have* taken up this task, so that there are now cases, some of which are cited below, that have been somewhat corroborated, even if the documentation is still not as rigorous as desirable. We need studies of veridical perceptions in OBEs that are as carefully researched and meticulously documented as Ian Stevenson's studies of cases of the reincarnation type.

have never been so wide awake."[20] This is certainly not what should be expected, on the intrasomatic interpretation, with regard to those ND OBEs that occur when the person is behaviorally unconscious, especially in cardiac cases in which the brain is not receiving the normal amount of oxygen and in cases in which the EEG registers little brain activity.

Transforming Effects

This is one of the most discussed features, especially of ND OBEs—the fact that they usually result in remarkable changes in people's values, beliefs, mood, and behavior. Many studies of near-death experiences, in fact, give primary attention to these transforming effects.[21] It is surely the case that these effects to a significant extent derive from the transcendental aspect of the NDE, not the OBE as such. But in his study of "Extrasomatic Emotions," Emilio Tiberi, while granting the tendency of NDErs to emphasize more positive and powerful aftereffects than do other OBErs, suggests that "many of the behavioral changes often described as consequences of an NDE . . . may be attributable to the out-of-body experience" as such.[22] The transforming effects seem to arise primarily from the strong emotions (usually positive but sometimes negative) experienced during the OBE combined with the certainty of life after death produced by the OBE. (Although this belief has widely been credited to the NDE, Glen Gabbard and Stuart Twemlow point to evidence suggesting that "the perception of the existence of consciousness as separate from the body may be the key factor influencing belief change, rather than any specific NDE characteristics.")[23] These transforming effects provide for many interpreters strong support for the extrasomatic interpretation of the experience. As Tiberi puts it, "no mere dream could stimulate such radical and lasting changes."[24]

Significantly Altered Sense of Time

Although some interpreters and even some OBErs speak of "timelessness," this is a misleading exaggeration, in that the reports almost always speak of a sequence of events, with some experiences happening after other experiences.* But the reports do commonly suggest that during the OBE the temporal nature of existence is often much less keenly felt, that time feels far less important. As one experient put it repeatedly, "I felt I had all the time in the world."[25]

---

*For example, right after saying, "Time became of no more importance," one of Margot Grey's subjects said: *"Next* I was drawn into total darkness. *Then* I stopped. . . . I asked. . . . He answered. . . . I believed him" (Margot Grey, *Return from Death: An Exploration of the Near-Death Experience* [London & Boston: Arkana, 1985], 62; italics added). Grey herself, in spite of recognizing that references to timelessness and linear time are often paradoxically conjoined (62), proclaims that "there is no such thing as time (as we understand it) on the 'other side'" (181). The tendency to describe these experiences as "timeless" goes back to philosopher-turned-physician Raymond Moody, whose statement that timelessness is said by most NDErs to characterize the out-

Similarity and Universality

Although this point is sometimes exaggerated, there *is* a remarkable sameness to reports of OBEs from various people from different times and places, regardless of sex, age, religion, culture, occupation, the circumstances under which the OBE occurred, or any other variable. Explaining this similarity is one of the main tasks for intrasomatic theories, according to which the experience is not what it seems to be. These theories must also account for the virtual universality of the belief that at least some people have experiences while out of their bodies. One study showed 51 of 54 cultures holding this belief.[26]

Variability in Conditions

In spite of the similarities in the basic nature of the OBE in a majority of cases, there is great variability in the conditions under which OBEs occur. I have already mentioned two—that most are spontaneous but some are deliberately induced, and that among spontaneous OBEs some occur near death whereas others occur in a variety of other circumstances. There are several other variables: Some occur during sleep, others in the twilight zone between sleeping and waking, and some others during waking hours. Some occur when people are ill and taking medication, others while people are in good health. These and other variables make it very difficult for intrasomatic theorists to come up with an explanation as to why and how OBEs occur that will cover even a majority of the cases, let alone all of them, because these explanations must also explain the OBErs' illusion of being out of their bodies.

The High Incidence

Surveys indicate that about 10 percent of the population have at least one OBE during their lives. Even more striking is the incidence of ND OBEs among persons who have been in near-death conditions. This was one of the big surprises to the medical profession. For example, when cardiac physician Michael Sabom first read Moody's accounts in *Life After Life*, he assumed that it was a work of fiction and, in fact, considered it "ridiculous."[27] When he began asking his own patients, accordingly, he was amazed to learn not only that they gave very similar accounts, but also that 27 percent of those who had a near-death

---

of-body state (*Life After Life*, 47) seems to be drawn less from the statements themselves (see 47–51, 57, and 172) than from Plato, who, Moody says, "points out [not simply *says*] that time is not an element of the realms beyond the physical, sensible, world" (116). Janice Miner Holden, in "Unexpected Findings in a Study of Visual Perception During the Naturalistic Near-Death Out-of-Body Experience" (*Journal of Near-Death Studies* 7/3 [Spring 1989], 155–63), reports that, in contrast with the emphasis by several interpreters on the sense of timelessness, or the meaningless of time, during the ND OBE, subjects in fact describe their experiences in temporal sequence and make references to the passage of time. A majority of the respondents in her study, furthermore, were even willing to estimate the duration of their (naturalistic near-death) OBEs (156–57).

crisis had had a NDE.[28] It is in part this high incidence that has made it difficult for reports of ND OBEs and other OBEs to be off-handedly dismissed, as they were previously, as fabrications or aberrations of deranged brains.

4. MATERIALISM AND INTRASOMATIC THEORIES

In spite of all these features of OBEs, at least most of which *prima facie* suggest the truth of the extrasomatic interpretation, the intrasomatic interpretation is held by many psychologists, physicians, and other intellectuals who have thought about OBEs. This is not surprising, of course, given the pervasiveness within intellectual, and perhaps especially medical, circles of materialistic views, according to which the mind is identical with the brain or at least totally dependent on the brain for all its experiences. Such views make the idea of the mind's existence outside the body nonsense. For example, although both Raymond Moody and Michael Sabom were Christians, they both report that, prior to their study of near-death experiences, they assumed that death meant extinction.[29] It is widely thought that only an intrasomatic interpretation could be "scientific." This is illustrated by an exchange between Sabom and another physician, Richard S. Blacher. Blacher had written a commentary in the *Journal of the American Medical Association* describing the NDE as a "fantasy of death" and warning physicians against "accepting religious belief as scientific data." Sabom wrote a response, arguing that none of the proposed medical-scientific explanations given thus far could fully account for the NDE, adding that "equal caution should be exercised in accepting scientific belief as scientific data."[30] In his rebuttal, Blacher said:

> Dr. Sabom takes me to task for describing the episodes as "fantasy." By using this word, I locate the phenomenon with the patient's psyche. . . . The alternative to the intrapsychic* location would be one of something (the soul?) leaving the person in reality and hovering over the table. I do not think one has to apologize for scientific belief if one does not accept the ideas of spirits wandering around the emergency room.[31]

Blacher's ridicule of the extrasomatic interpretation illustrates how fully the late modern view of the person has been equated with the "scientific" view.† Given

---

* In using the term "intrapsychic," Blacher really means intrasomatic: Everyone agrees that the psyche's experiences occur within the psyche. The issue is whether the psyche is really still within the body while it is having an out-of-body experience.

† Another example is provided by Susan Blackmore. In *Beyond the Body: An Investigation of Out-of-the-Body Experiences* (see the footnote on page 231, above), several statements (on 55, 133, 229, 231, and 235) suggest that she leans toward a materialistic view of the mind-body relation. Her later book, *Dying to Live: Near-Death Experiences* (Buffalo: Prometheus Books, 1993),

this materialistic view, of course, some version of the intrasomatic hypothesis *must* be true. The question is whether any version of it can do justice to the facts.

Those intrasomatic theories that are consistent with materialism can be most conveniently classified under two headings: primarily cultural-psychological theories and primarily physiological theories. I follow Harvey Irvin in using the modifier "primarily," thereby recognizing that each basic type may draw elements from the other in trying to develop a complete theory.[32] It is widely agreed that none of these theories is even close to adequate. (Of course, each theorist thinks more kindly of his or her own theory, but its weaknesses are readily apparent to others.) Not being able to discuss these various theories here at any length, I will simply point to the obvious weaknesses that have been discussed, indicating in the endnotes where the interested reader can turn for more thorough discussions.

Primarily Cultural-Psychological Theories

The most obvious explanation of this type, of course, is that the people reporting the OBEs are simply lying, expecting to be rewarded for supporting belief in life after death in a culture that values it. This suggestion, however, flies in

---

leaves no doubt of this and her identification of this view with science. Having identified the view that we have a soul that may survive death with religion, she says: "Of course, this comforting thought conflicts with science. Science tells us that death is the end and, as so often, finds itself opposing religion" (xi). Then, having given her opinion that the idea of evolution is the "most beautiful in all of science," she adds: "The problem with evolution is . . . that it leaves little room . . . for an individual soul" (xi). (That this is not necessarily true, unless materialism be *presupposed*, is shown by my discussion in Chapter 3, above, in which I presuppose a [naturalistic] evolutionary worldview and suggest that the capacity of the human soul to survive apart from its physical body may be one of the emergent powers developed in the course of its evolution.) Whereas these statements seem simply to equate science, materialism, and truth, she shows awareness elsewhere that it is not so simple. Defining materialism as the view that "mental phenomena depend upon, or are an aspect of, brain events," she says, "Scientists *for the most part* assume some form of materialism" (47; italics added), thereby acknowledging that not *all* scientists hold this view. And she even acknowledges that the materialistic majority may be wrong: Citing some previous errors of scientific orthodoxy, she says: "Our current materialism and its rejection of the idea of a spirit or soul may be just another great falsity" (48). However, the fact that she really believes that an explanation, to be "scientific," must be materialistic is shown by her statements that a "scientific account" of NDEs would be impossible if paranormal events were genuine (135, 262). The problem with genuine extrasensory perception (which is the kind of "paranormal event" she has in mind) is that it would violate the materialistic view that *all* "mental phenomena depend upon, or are an aspect of, brain events." The degree to which she accepts a reductionistic, materialistic version of neo-Darwinism (combined with a neo-Buddhist psychology) is illustrated by her statement that "our minds have evolved to crave purposefulness and cling to the idea of a self because that will more efficiently keep alive the body and perpetuate its genes" (xii). This statement, in combination with her treatment of evidence for paranormal vision in OBEs (see subsequent footnotes), illustrates perfectly how our wishful-and-fearful thinking, in combination with paradigmatic thinking, leads us to go to extreme lengths to deny the reality of claimed facts that contradict our worldviews while being quite uncritical of ideas that are in harmony with them.

the face of several facts. First, subjects usually do not anticipate being rewarded but, to the contrary, suspect that other people will consider them "crazy"—an anticipation that, at least in the past, has often been fulfilled (by their pastors as well as their physicians). Second, it would be difficult to explain the profound, positive changes that usually result if we assume that the experiences did not really occur. Third, given the similarity of OBEs, it would be hard to explain how people in widely different times and places have managed to tell approximately the same lies. Finally, the idea that OBEs are fabrications cannot account for the veridical perceptions often reported in them.

A second theory is that OBEs, especially those with religious visions, are fantasies fulfilling religious and cultural expectations. However, besides the fact that this explanation suffers from the third and fourth weaknesses of the lie-theory, it also is not supported by empirical data: The form of the experiences (as distinct from some of the content, especially of the transcendental aspects) is not affected by religious or even more broadly cultural beliefs.[33] This theory is also in tension with growing evidence of OBEs in very young children.[34]

Another view is that the OBE, especially the ND OBE, is an unconscious psychological defense against the dread of death. This theory is also strained by the fact that ND OBEs, contrary to earlier flat denials, occur in children, by the fact that perhaps as many as 90 percent of the OBEs do not occur in near-death situations, and by the fact that personality inventories do not show OBErs to have any higher concern with death than the rest of the population.[35] Furthermore, this theory, like the previous ones (I will not keep repeating this point in relation to the succeeding theories), cannot account for the veridical perceptions. Finally, even if OBEs did result as a defense against the dread of oblivion, this would say nothing about whether the OBE should be given an intrasomatic or an extrasomatic interpretation. After all, a life-threatening event just might frighten one out of one's skin! The point here is that theorists often confuse two different types of "explanation." One interesting question is *why*, and *when*, and *to whom* OBEs occur; this is the question most scientific investigations seek to answer. Another question is ontological: What actually occurs during an OBE? Does the mind really leave the body or not? To be sure, some of the answers to the first question, if they were to prove adequate, would lend more-or-less weighty support to the intrasomatic answer to the second question (although they could not be said to *prove* it). But many of the proposed answers to the first question, such as the present one, would, even if accepted, provide *no* support for either position on the second question.

Another theory regards the OBE as a dream. However, many OBEs occur while the people are wide awake. Almost all OBErs, moreover, insist that their experience was not like a dream. Physiological studies involving experimental OBEs, furthermore, support this contention, showing that the bodily state during voluntary OBE periods is not similar to a dream state.[36]

Another view sees the OBE as a version of the phenomenon of "autoscopy," in which people report seeing a double of themselves. This theory, of course, arises from the fact that viewing one's own body is a central feature of mundane OBEs, and that this viewing is often called "autoscopy." However, even if we had an explanation for autoscopy in the traditional sense of the term, which we do not,[37] it would hardly explain the kind of "autoscopy" that occurs in OBEs, as they are very different. Traditional autoscopic visions are apparitions: One sees them from the point of view of one's physical body, and they often mimic one's real body. In the OBE, however, one is viewing the physical body from beyond it, and it is usually not moving.

The fact that one sees one's body from without, often also being quite unconcerned about it, has led to the view that the OBE is a form of "depersonalization." But this view also is inconsistent with many facts. First, depersonalization is more common among women than men, nonexistent among children, and rare among people over forty; none of this is true for OBEs. Also, in depersonalization one seems to be a stranger to oneself, whereas in OBEs one's sense of self (often called one's "true self," in distinction from one's body) is enhanced. Further, although one may be unconcerned with one's body (especially in ND OBEs), one does not, as in depersonalization, usually fail to realize that the body is one's own.[38] One problem at the root of this theory is that it was based upon subjects who were psychologically, but not physically, near death; those who were physically near death were found to be significantly different.[39]

One of the most widespread casually held views among psychologists and psychiatrists is that OBEs are hallucinations resulting from schizophrenic-like states. However, psychotic hallucinations are extremely varied from person to person, showing nothing like the kind of consistency evidenced in OBEs. They also tend to be primarily auditory, whereas OBEs are primarily visual. Personality inventories, furthermore, do not reveal any similarities between OBErs and the mentally ill, and psychiatric patients do not have a high incidence of OBEs.[40]

There are still other psychological theories. Insofar as they are not simply of the off-handed "OBEs-must-be-nothing-but" type, they seek to show a statistically significant correlation between OBErs and some trait, such as the capacity for imagery of a certain type or for absorption in one's activities. But even if such correlations were considerably more impressive than they are, they would still fail to provide anything like a complete theory, insofar as a significant portion of the OBE population was merely average or even below average with regard to that variable. Finally, as I said above, answers about *who*, *when*, and *why*, even if convincing, would not necessarily say anything about *what* the OBE is, that is, whether it is really, as it seems to be, an experience had while out of the body.

Primarily Physiological Theories

Within the medical profession, the dominant assumption has probably been that OBEs, insofar as they could not be dismissed in one of the above ways, are to be explained in primarily physiological terms. One of the most mentioned possibilities is that they result from hypoxia (or anoxia), or inadequate oxygen reaching the brain due to cardiac arrest. The idea is that this loss of oxygen leads the brain to produce various hallucinogens and neuronal discharges that produce the imagery. This suggestion, however, faces various difficulties: Most OBEs do not occur under such circumstances; there is no evidence that OBEs are accompanied by neural states similar to those that produce hallucinations; and the loss of oxygen produces a muddled state of mind, not the clarity of thought reported by most OBErs.[41]

Others have suggested that the OBE imagery results not so much from the hypoxia following upon cardiac arrest as from the hypercarbia, meaning the elevated level of carbon dioxide. Experiments have indeed shown that hypercarbia can produce experiences similar to those found in OBEs, especially in their transcendental phases, such as bright lights, ecstasy, and revival of past memories.[42] This theory, however, is likewise undermined by the fact that most OBEs, even those with vivid transcendental imagery, do not occur in hypercarbic situations. Indeed, Sabom has one case in which a patient's oxygen level was *above* average and carbon dioxide level was *below* average during the OBE. (The subject is the one, discussed below, who saw the doctor giving him what he took to be a "shot in the groin"; the doctor was actually drawing blood for a blood-gas analysis.)[43] Hypercarbia also produces a range of experiences that are dissimilar to OBEs, such as "stained-glass window effects," animated fantasized objects (such as moving musical notes), seeing everything in duplicate or triplicate, and feelings of horror.

Another assumption is that the imagery of the OBE is produced by drugs administered to the patient, such as ketamine, which does produce a vision of light. However, most OBEs, even most ND OBEs, occur to people who have not taken drugs.[44] Also, OBE visions seldom if ever have the kind of bizarre imagery that occurs in drug-induced hallucinations, and the latter are recognized as unreal at the time, or at least in retrospect, while OBEs are taken to be real both during their occurrence and in retrospect.[45]

Still another idea is that the OBE is something like an epileptic reaction, resulting from a temporal lobe seizure. The main connection here is with the life-review that occurs in some OBEs, especially in the transcendental phase. An immediate problem with this attempted explanation, however, is that the reliving of memories caused by malfunctions of the temporal lobe are usually limited to a single event of no special significance; it is nothing like the life-review of myriad events of great significance. Also, these neurological hallucinations typically involve taste and smell, which are usually absent in OBEs; the perception of the immediate environment is often distorted; and subjects experience forced thinking.[46]

A final suggestion, based primarily on the pleasant emotions and absence of pain reported in OBEs, is that they are produced by a release of endorphins.

However, injections of endorphins produce sleepiness, not the hyperalertness reported in OBEs. Also, an endorphin injection gives relief from pain for many hours (from 22 to 73), whereas OBErs, as mentioned earlier, report that their pain returns suddenly as soon as they reenter their bodies.[47]

In sum, Irwin's assessment, that "the physiological approach has yet to generate a viable account of the OBE,"[48] seems justified.

5. VERIDICAL PERCEPTIONS IN OBES

In addition to the various specific inadequacies these various theories suffer, there are several problems that they all have in common, including that of accounting for the similarity of the OBEs and the strong feeling of being out of the body. Probably the most difficult problem for intrasomatic theories, at least insofar as they remain within a materialistic, sensationistic framework, is that they cannot do justice to the veridical perceptions reported in many OBEs. Whereas these theories all say, in one way or another, that the OBEs are illusions, these veridical perceptions show that something other than illusion is occurring. Although there was a time when one could perhaps plausibly claim that a theory of OBEs did not have to explain such perceptions, because all the reports were purely anecdotal without corroborating investigation, this has been increasingly untrue since 1982, when Michael Sabom published *Recollections of Death*, in which he included several cases in which the claimed veridical perceptions were confirmed by checking the medical reports, interviewing witnesses, or both. In the intervening years, several other researchers have published other cases in which such reports have been confirmed.*

---

* Susan J. Blackmore's *Beyond the Body: An Investigation of Out-of-Body Experiences* (1982; Chicago: Academy Chicago Publishers, 1992) was first published in the same year as Sabom's book (1982) and thereby before his confirmation of several cases involving veridical perceptions was known. When she was writing her book, accordingly, there was no strong evidence against her claim that "paranormal effects found during OBEs are terribly small" (238). This claim is important to her case, because she develops a "psychological" intrasomatic theory, according to which "psychic events of any kind are not expected during the OBE" (251). From this viewpoint, she regards the question of whether ESP occurs in the OBE as perhaps "the most important question about the OBE . . . because a purely psychological theory of the OBE cannot directly account for paranormal phenomena" (68–69, 243). This perspective tempts her in the direction of explaining away all reports of such phenomena: "I find the evidence for paranormal events during the OBE limited and unconvincing. . . . I think it is possible that all the claims for ESP and PK in OBEs are groundless. . . . [In relation to several cases,] it is true, I would have to argue that the witnesses or investigators were lying or mistaken; but I do not think this is impossible, nor do I think there is actually very much evidence which has to be 'explained away' in this fashion" (242–43). Her hope and prediction is that the question of how to account for such claims will not have to be answered because "the question of paranormal phenomena will quietly be dropped" (243). At the same time, she is not dogmatic about the absence of significant paranormal phenomena in OBEs. She in one place admits that she cannot explain away all claims (135) and, after predicting that the

One of Sabom's cases involved a man who had had a massive heart attack in 1973, when he was thirty-nine years old. In his interview with Sabom five years later, he described various things that he witnessed, including hearing "Code Blue" on the intercom and seeing the following: nurses and Dr. A running into his CCU room, an injection into his IV line, his body being lifted onto the plywood, Dr. A pounding on his chest ("and it didn't hurt even though it cracked a rib. I felt no pain"), and the replacement of the oxygen nose tube with a light-green face mask. After the description of those details, the interview went like this (A = Author [Sabom], S = Subject):

A: Do you remember any of the other details that went on in the room?
S: I remember them pulling over the cart, the defibrillator, the thing with the paddles on it. I remember they asked for so many watt-seconds or something on the thing, and they gave me a jolt with it.
A: Did you notice any of the details of the machine itself or the cart it was sitting on?
S: I remember it had a meter on the face. . . . It was square and had two needles on there, one fixed and one which moved.
A: How did it move?
S: It seemed to come up rather slowly, really. It didn't just pop up like an ammeter or a voltmeter or something registering.
A: And how far up did it go?
S: The first time it went between one-third and one-half scale. And then they did it again, and this time it went up over one-half scale, and the third time it was about three-quarters.
A: What was the relationship between the moving needle and the fixed needle?
S: I think the fixed needle moved each time they punched the thing and somebody was messing with it. And I think they moved the fixed needle and it stayed still while the other one moved up. . . .
A: What did the rest of the machine look like?

---

question of paranormal phenomena will be dropped, she adds that "some new discovery may at any time prove me quite wrong" (243). In the light of all this, it is puzzling and disappointing that in the new edition's "Postscript," written in 1990, she makes no mention of Michael Sabom's book, even though she refers to many other relevant publications that had appeared in the intervening years. This omission is especially puzzling in the light of the fact that Sabom's book has been repeatedly cited in books and articles as having provided (thus far) the best documentation of paranormal perceptions in ND OBEs (e.g., Mark B. Woodhouse, "Five Arguments Regarding the Objectivity of NDEs," *Anabiosis: The Journal for Near-Death Studies* 3/1 (June 1983), 63–75, at 70; Michael Grosso, *The Final Choice: Playing the Survival Game* [Walpole, N.H.: Stillpoint Publishing, 1985], 143). In any case, in her 1993 book, *Dying to Live*, she does finally refer to some cases provided by Sabom and others that suggest paranormal vision during ND OBEs. Her treatment of this evidence (as discussed in subsequent footnotes), however, seems to reflect less a genuine interest in them than simply her wish that they would go away.

S: It had a bunch of dials on it. It was on wheels with a little railing around the thing, and they had stuff on it. And they had the two paddle affairs with wires attached.

A: How did they operate?

S: They held one in each hand and they put it across my chest, and they seemed like they were squeezing both of them simultaneously.

A: Did you see how they made the machine discharge?

S: With the squeezing or pushing a button top; I think it was like a handle with little buttons on it. . . .

A: What did it look like when they discharged the machine?

S: I could see myself jolt, but again, it didn't hurt like an electric shock should hurt. . . .

A: And this happened how many times?

S: Three.

A: Did they do anything else in the room that you can recall?

S: He was pounding on my chest sort of like a sharp blow.

A: In the sequence of things, where did this occur?

S: He gave the shock first, then he pounded, and then they gave a shock, he pounded again, and they gave another shock. . . .

A: Did you notice any other details?

S: Dr. A had on his air force uniform, the dark-blue pants with the light-blue shirt, and the nurses had on regular whites that they wear. I remember a bunch of people were looking in from what they call the fishbowl. They had a big window between the nursing station and actual ICU itself and there was a little door right around the corner that came into it.[49]

After commenting that this description accurately describes what would occur in such a situation, Sabom says:

I was particularly fascinated by his description of a "fixed" needle and a "moving" needle on the face of the defibrillator as it was being charged with electricity. The movement of these two needles is not something he could have observed unless he had actually seen this instrument in use. These two needles are individually used (1) to preselect the amount of electricity to be delivered to the patient ("they moved the fixed needle and it stayed still") and (2) to indicate that the defibrillator is being charged to the preselected amount ("[the moving needle] seemed to come up rather slowly, really. It didn't just pop up like an ammeter or a voltmeter or something registering"). This charging procedure is only performed immediately prior to defibrillation. . . . Moreover, the meters of the type described by this man are not found on more recent defibrillator models, but were in common use in 1973, at the time of his cardiac arrest.[50]

Because the medical report was too brief and general to confirm or disconfirm any of the details of this man's report, and because Sabom did not otherwise verify the details through interviews, we might suspect that the man put together this account from operations he had seen on television and things he had learned about his own operation after the fact.* One thing counting against the idea that the man was simply lying is that he is one of the small minority of people with ND OBEs who are not especially impressed by their experiences. Although he realized he was seeing things that he could not have seen from that position ("the only way I could have seen would have been straight up, 'cause I was lying on my back"), he dismissed the experience by saying that "the brain still functions even though it is partially dead, or starving from oxygen. . . . [Y]ou are still perceiving things even when you can't talk or move. . . . It hasn't changed my thinking about life, death, the hereafter or anything else. It's one of the facts of life you can't explain."[51]

But if he was not consciously lying, might he have observed these CPR (cardio-pulmonary resuscitation) procedures on television (although he said that he had not) and then fantasized the experience? Counting against this interpretation are the results of a comparison of the reports from thirty-two patients like this man, who reported OBEs, with constructed accounts of a control group of twenty-five seasoned cardiac patients. This control group was asked to describe in visual detail what they would expect to see if they were watching a medical team revive a person whose heart had stopped beating. Of these twenty-five patients, two said they were not able to give any account, three gave correct but very limited descriptions (with nothing like the detail provided in the above account), while each of the other twenty imaginary descriptions contained at least one major error. By contrast, there were no detectable errors in any of the accounts of the thirty-two patients who reported OBEs. Of these, twenty-six were not able to recall specific details of the procedure (generally because they were focused on their amazement at the experience itself and its pleasant qualities), but their general accounts corresponded to the customary procedures. And the reports of the six patients who *were* able to give specific details were free of any detectable errors.[52] It seems unlikely, accordingly, that the above report could have been consciously or unconsciously constructed on the basis of general knowledge of the procedures in question.[†]

---

* Susan Blackmore, who selects this as one of the cases given by Sabom to examine, takes this approach (*Dying to Live*, 118–19).

† Blackmore, believing that realistic visual imagery can be created out of information received from the still-functioning senses of touch and hearing (*Dying to Live*, 124, 125), argues that the control group's less accurate reconstructions are understandable because they had less information (120). This is a valid point (assuming that the senses of hearing and touch are still functioning). The remaining questions would be (1) whether the vivid visual imagery sometimes expe-

In other cases, furthermore, Sabom did verify some of the specific details. One such case involved a sixty-two-year-old mechanic whose OBE following a heart attack had occurred somewhat over a year before Sabom's interview with him in 1979. This man said:

[A]ll of a sudden it seemed like I moved up. . . . Just like getting up out of the bed, just about. I was above myself looking down. . . . It was an unusual feeling. I could see them working on me and then I realized it was me they were working on. . . . They gave me a shot in the groin.[53]

Sabom comments:

According to his medical records, arterial blood was drawn from his left femoral artery during CPR to measure the amount of oxygen in his blood. This procedure is accomplished by inserting a small needle and syringe into the groin area to obtain the blood. If observed from a distance, it could easily be mistaken as the administration of a "shot."[54]

The man's account continues:

Dr. B came up and decided to put one in my left—well, not in my armpit, but on my side. Then he changed his mind and went to the other side, next to the heart. . . . [Later] when Dr. B seen me, he told me I had a close call and died and all that stuff. I told him, "Dr. B, I couldn't have died. I knew everything that went on." I told him when he came up under my right armpit and changed his mind and went to the other side. He said it was impossible and that I couldn't have possibly seen that, and that I was legally dead at that time. . . . And I asked, "Am I right?" He said, "Yes, you're right!". . . . I felt like I was alive. It was just as though I was standing there talking to you.[55]

Sabom comments:

[T]his man's description of additional "shots" . . . is a portrayal of attempts by his doctor to enter the subclavian vein, which is located on both sides of the chest under the collarbone. This is a frequently used procedure to gain access to the central venous system for the administration of drugs during a cardiac arrest or to insert pressure-monitoring

---

rienced is plausibly understood as constructed from relevant sensory data deriving from auditory and tactile receptors, and, even if so, (2) whether in *all* the cases relevant data were thereby supplied for *all* the veridical details of the visual imagery. Because a definitive answer may be impossible for the first question and also for the second question in cases involving details in the vicinity of the person's body, a careful scrutiny of cases involving events out of hearing range is especially important.

catheters. . . . Many times it is difficult to find the subclavian vein, deep in the chest, during the rushed circumstances of a cardiac arrest, and the usual procedure here is to attempt it first on one side, then on the other.[56]

The observant reader, incidentally, may have noticed that the man's first account of this procedure was confused: He said that the doctor first tried the left side but then went to "the other side, next to the heart," whereas the heart, of course, is on the left side. In the report of his conversation with Dr. B, however, he told it the other way, as he did again later in the interview: In response to Sabom's question, "Could you tell me about how they were trying to stick a needle in your armpits?" the subject said: "It looked like he started to come in under the right armpit and then he changed and come in on the left side." This same left-right confusion may have occurred in relation to the "shot in the groin," discussed above.* Later in the interview, the man said: "They gave me those shots first in the groin down there somewhere. . . . My right side."[57] Sabom comments:

> A discrepancy arises here, . . . since the man claims that this "shot" was given in his right groin, whereas the arterial blood gas laboratory slip identifies the site of the puncture as "LF"—left femoral. It is of no medical significance which side of the body the blood was obtained from, which raises the possibility that the lab slip is in error. On the other hand, the man may have been suffering from a right-left confusion. If he had looked down on his body from the foot of his bed, the right side of his physical body might well have been on his left.[58]

Sabom reports that he later interviewed the man's wife and then his physician. The wife said that her husband had told her and their daughter about the NDE the day after the cardiac arrest, that he has retold the story only a few times (which fits with his own statement), and that each of these retellings has been consistent with the original description.† The physician ("Dr. B") could not recall this particular case (which by the time of the interview with him was over two years in the past), but added that he had had several patients who told him of such experiences and that this could have been one of them.[59]

Since Sabom's pioneering effort to verify some of the claimed veridical perceptions (besides the two cases I have summarized here, he presents seven

---

* Blackmore, countering Sabom's claim that the patient would have been unlikely to confuse a withdrawal of blood for a "shot" if he had gotten the information from hearing (rather than extrasomatic vision), says that he could have gotten it from touch. This explanation, however, would fail to explain the left-right confusion.

† Blackmore, in treating this case as uncorroborated, fails to mention this corroboration by the patient's wife and her indication that it could also be corroborated by their daughter. As a last resort, of course, Blackmore could claim that they are all lying.

other cases in similar detail*), others have contributed to the effort. Kenneth Ring and Madelaine Lawrence, for example, have published an article titled "Further Evidence for Veridical Perception During Near-Death Experiences," in which they summarize three cases submitted by nurses at Hartford Hospital (in Connecticut). One of the nurses, Joyce Harmon, reports being astonished when a female patient, whom she had helped resuscitate the day before, said upon seeing her something like, "Oh, you're the one with the plaid shoelaces." Her reason for astonishment was that she *had* been wearing plaid shoelaces the day before, that being her first day back at work after a vacation, during which she had purchased the shoelaces. When nurse Harmon registered her astonishment, the patient replied that she had seen the shoelaces while she was watching what was happening from above after she died.[60]

Whereas there is now a growing number of somewhat verified accounts of veridical perceptions of events in the patient's hospital room,[61] some interpreters, like the first of Sabom's subjects quoted above, believe that such perceptions must somehow be explainable in terms of residual brain functioning. More impressive, accordingly, would be *verified reports of perceptions occurring beyond the immediate vicinity of the body*. The older OBE literature does contain reports of this nature (sometimes under the rubric of "traveling clairvoyance"),[62] but such stories can always be dismissed as unconfirmed or at least old. Now, however, the list of confirmed recent cases of this type is growing.

One of Sabom's cases contains such an element. A man who had had a third heart attack during his stay in the hospital in 1976 described the attempts to resuscitate him, then said:

> I kept going up and up. . . . I couldn't hear anything. Not one peep. . . . And I remember seeing them down the hall just as plain as could be. The three of them were standing there—my wife, my oldest son and my oldest daughter and the doctor. . . . I knew damn well they were there.[63]

His wife corroborates this account, saying that in three days, as soon as her husband had regained his orientation, he told her about witnessing the operation and seeing the three of them at the end of the hall. She told Sabom: "He couldn't have seen us. . . . He swore he'd seen us, and I said he couldn't have."[64]

Lying behind her astonishment were the following facts: First, the man had been on the ambulatory floor that day, anticipating discharge the next day, so his wife had not been planning to visit that evening. Second, the couple

---

* Given her own statement that her position rests on the assumption that *none* of these cases will stand up to scrutiny, it is disappointing that Blackmore chose not to examine these remaining cases.

had six grown children, and each visit to the hospital during the weeks he was there always involved a different combination. Third, that evening, after the eldest son and the eldest daughter happened to come by to visit their mother, they all decided to surprise the father with a visit. Fourth, when they arrived, they noticed "a lot of commotion" in the hallway outside his room and then were stopped by a nurse "at least ten rooms down." Fifth, the woman saw doctors and nurses working on a man lying on a bed in the hallway. Although his face was pointed away from her, so that she could see only the top of his head, she recognized her husband's gray hair. Sixth, he was then taken directly to the intensive care unit on another floor without passing by her and the children.[65] This seems, accordingly, to be a case of paranormal vision of people at some remove from the subject's body.*

Perhaps the most well-known case of this type is that reported by Kimberly Clark, a professor at the School of Medicine at the University of Washington and a critical care social worker at the Harborview Medical Center in Seattle. Prior to the case in question, she had had no encounter with NDErs. This case involved a migrant worker named Maria, who had had a severe heart attack while visiting friends in Seattle. A few days after being admitted to the hospital, she suffered a cardiac arrest, from which she was resuscitated rather quickly. When Clark went to visit her, Maria was anxious to tell her about "the strangest thing." She reported that, while the doctors and nurses were working on her, she found herself looking down on them from the ceiling. Although she described who was there and what they were wearing and doing, Clark was unimpressed, figuring that, because hearing is the last sense to go and because Maria had had time to observe many things beforehand, she could have constructed the story from things learned normally. But then Maria reported that, having been distracted during her OBE by something over the emergency room driveway, she found herself out there. Even Maria's description of this area did not impress Clark greatly, as she assumed that at some period Maria's bed may have been by the window. But then Maria reported that, being further distracted by an object on the third-floor ledge on the north end of the building, she "thought her way" up there and found herself "eyeball to shoelace" with a tennis shoe. Maria gave several details, including the fact that there was a worn place in the little-toe area of the shoe and that the lace was stuck under the heel. Maria then asked Clark to confirm that the tennis shoe was really out there, to validate her OBE.

"With mixed emotions," Clark consented. Looking up from outside, she reports, revealed nothing. She continues:

---

*Blackmore says that she is always on the lookout for claims of paranormal vision during ND OBEs that can be corroborated (Dying to Live, 134–35). However, although Sabom says that this case was corroborated by the patient's wife, it is one of several cases given by Sabom that Blackmore passes over in silence.

> I went up to the third floor and began going in and out of patients' rooms and looking out their windows, which were so narrow that I had to press my face to the screen just to see the ledge at all. Finally, I found a room where I pressed my face to the glass and looked down and saw the tennis shoe![66]

From that perspective, however, she could not see the worn place, the lace under the heel, and other details provided by Maria. "The only way she would have had such a perspective was if she had been floating right outside and at very close range to the tennis shoe." Clark confirmed those details when she retrieved the shoe to take to Maria.*

Interestingly, one of the three accounts from nurses at Hartford Hospital published by Kenneth Ring and Madelaine Lawrence also involved a shoe. Kathy Milne wrote to Ring about her 1985 conversation with a woman who had recently been resuscitated.

> She told me how she floated up over her body, viewed the resuscitation effort for a short time and then felt herself being pulled up through several floors of the hospital. She then found herself above the roof and realized she was looking at the skyline of Hartford. . . . [O]ut of the corner of her eye[†] she saw a red object. It turned out to be a shoe. . . . I was relating this to a (skeptical) resident who in a mocking manner left. Apparently, he got a janitor to get him onto the roof. When I saw him later that day, he had a red shoe and became a believer, too.

Ring, incidently, subsequently learned that Kathy Milne had not heard of Kimberly Clark's story about Maria's shoe.[67]

6. CHOOSING BETWEEN PARAPSYCHOLOGICAL HYPOTHESES

Given the growing number of accounts of veridical perception that have been confirmed by medical professionals, including accounts in which the perceived

---

* Although Blackmore points out that her position is most threatened by cases of claimed paranormal vision of events at some remove from the patient's body (because such apparent observations could not be explained in terms of residual touch and hearing), the only case she mentions (other than an embellished, sensationalized newspaper story that no serious researcher would cite as evidence [*Dying to Live*, 126–27]) is this one involving Kimberly Clark and Maria—and her treatment of it is dismissive. Saying that it is one of those cases about which she has been "unable to get further information," she puts it aside as "fascinating but unsubstantiated" (128). She does not make clear, however, what further substantiation, beyond the written testimony of a health-care professional, would be needed.

† Some OBErs report, as I mentioned earlier, having had bodies of a sort. In the present case, however, I suspect that the reference to her "eye" was just a manner of speaking.

objects or people were not in the immediate vicinity of the body,[68] any theory of OBEs, to be adequate, must be able to accommodate paranormal perception.* This means that all theories articulated on the basis of a materialistic metaphysic, and thereby a sensationist theory of perception, are inadequate. But does it also mean that all intrasomatic theories are ruled out, so that the extrasomatic hypothesis is proved? This conclusion has often been expressed. For example, Raymond Moody has said:

> Such experiences are perhaps the best answer to people who think NDEs are the brain playing tricks on itself. After all, on the surface it is entirely possible that the brain, while in great distress, could calm itself by creating tunnel experiences and Beings of Light to put the person to rest. But NDEers who can tell you what was going on in other rooms while having their episodes are truly having out-of-body experiences.[69]

Returning to this point later in the same book, Moody says:

> How is it that patients can give such elaborate and detailed accounts of resuscitations, explaining in their entirety what the doctors were doing to bring them back to life? How can so many people explain what was going on in other rooms of a hospital while their bodies were in the operating room being resuscitated? To me, these are the most difficult points for NDE researchers to answer. In fact, so far they have been impossible to explain except with one answer: they really occurred.[70]

In a similar vein, physician Melvin Morse has said that "giving accurate details of one's own cardiac arrest [is] virtually impossible to explain if we do not believe in a conscious separation from our bodies."[71]

The truth of the extrasomatic interpretation of OBEs, however, does not follow automatically from the fact of paranormal perceptions occurring during

---

*Blackmore, to be sure, does not agree. Having suggested that some of the cases could be explained by residual touch and hearing, others by lucky guesses, others by faulty memory and fabrication, and that the remainder are not sufficiently corroborated, she concludes: "the suspicion must be, rightly or wrongly, that there may be no properly corroborated cases that cannot be accounted for by the perfectly normal processes of imagination, memory, chance, and the use of the remaining senses" (*Dying to Live*, 128). However, even if that were granted, it would be at least equally true that "the suspicion must be" that there *may* be several properly corroborated cases that *cannot* be thus explained away, and the evidence suggests that this suspicion is far more likely than the one on which she gambles (she admits that the documentation of truly paranormal events in ND OBEs would overthrow her theory [262]). She says that it is her "impression" that paranormal perception in NDEs "probably never does happen. Certainly I have found no evidence, yet, that convinces me that it does" (135). But her conclusion, I submit, says less about the quality of the available evidence than about her own worldview combined with wishful-and-fearful thinking, which together would probably make it very difficult for her to find *any* evidence convincing.

them. That several people involved in the interpretation of ND OBEs seem to think otherwise is in part due to the fact that most of the people involved in research on NDEs have not been parapsychologists, but medical professionals with little if any acquaintance with parapsychological literature. (In his 1991 survey of parapsychology, Richard Broughton refers to NDE research as "the one that got away."[72]) Those interpreters who do know about parapsychology, however, point out that the veridical perceptions, while demanding a paranormal explanation, do not necessarily require an extrasomatic one.[73] All the perceptions could perhaps be explainable in terms of clairvoyance, exercised by the still incarnate mind, which was still alert even though the person was receiving no sensory input and was behaviorally unconscious, due to the brain's greatly reduced level of activity. Indeed, some (reasonably) suggest, it is the very reduction of brain activity and the loss of all sensory and proprioceptive data that explains the extraordinary clairvoyance that sometimes occurs in near-death patients.

With this discussion, we have introduced what is often called a third type of intrasomatic theory, beyond the physiological and the cultural-psychological, namely, the parapsychological. Such theories require that the materialistic view that all the mind's experiences are totally dependent upon the body be modified sufficiently to allow for extrasensory perceptions, but many interpreters find this limited admission of the paranormal at least more palatable than extrabodily existence, which would allow for the possibility of life after death. In any case, one problem with speaking of "the parapsychological theory" is that, although it is often listed as a third type of theory, it is in practice usually used only as an addendum to a basically physiological or especially a psychological theory, to account for the veridical perceptions. A second problem is that the extrasomatic hypothesis is also a "parapsychological theory." With these caveats, I will discuss the so-called parapsychological theory.

One difficulty faced by the (intrasomatic) parapsychological theory is that, as we have seen, the clarity and the accuracy of the extrasensory perceptions that are reported in OBEs greatly exceed anything ever verified in intrasomatic clairvoyance (or remote viewing), whether in experimental or spontaneous cases. This difference in quality (along with the feeling of being out of the body and of actually perceiving things from that perspective) seems more understandable if the mind really is out of the body, so that its capacity for nonsensory perceptions is not at all interfered with by influences from the brain. Of course, I mentioned above how the intrasomatic parapsychological theory might respond to this point: by saying that in near-death patients the mind may receive little more influence from the brain than if the mind really were outside the body. One serious problem for this explanation, however, is that ND OBEs constitute perhaps only about one-tenth of all OBEs. Most OBEs occur when the brain is functioning perfectly normally, and some of these other reported OBEs, especially spontaneous ones, rival ND OBEs for clarity and accuracy of perception. Even with the addition of the parapsycho-logical dimension, accordingly, it seems difficult for the intrasomatic hypothe-sis to do justice to the extrasensory perception that occurs in many OBEs.

Effects Produced during OBEs

Another paranormal dimension that evidently occurs in at least a few OBEs is the production of effects by the mind at a distance from its body. One example of this phenomenon was discussed in the section on apparitions: In reciprocal cases, apparitions of the persons are seen at the same time that the persons seem to themselves to be out of their bodies and at the location at which they are perceived. In 1954, Hornell Hart published a study on "ESP Projection," by which he meant an out-of-body experience in which veridical (paranormal) knowledge was acquired. Out of 288 published cases located in the literature, 99 were found to be evidential (meaning that the OBEr reported the details before receiving evidence of veridicality). Of these 99 cases, at least 55 were reciprocal (meaning that an apparition of the OBEr was seen). Of these recip-rocal cases, 30 were spontaneous OBEs, while 25 were intentional, produced by concentration or more complex methods.[74] One purpose of this study was to encourage more rigorous experiments. Since that time there has been at least one rather successful laboratory experiment to see if an OBEer could be detected.

This experiment, which occurred in 1973, involved Keith Harary, who had been having OBEs most of his life and was able to induce them at will. The intended detector was a kitten named Spirit, who was quite fond of Harary. In the experiment, Harary was on a bed in the psychophysiology laboratory of Duke University Medical Center. He was, at times designated by his experi-menter, to leave his body and go to the laboratory of the Psychical Research Foundation, about a quarter of a mile away. At that lab, Robert Morris was ready to record the behavior of Spirit, who was in a long, narrow box, the floor of which was divided into numbered squares for quantifying Spirit's movements. There were to be eight OBE sessions, during which Harary would try to go to the other lab and make his presence felt by Spirit, and eight control sessions, during which Harary would chat with his experimenter and not think about Spirit. Neither Morris nor anyone else in the lab with Spirit would know at the time, of course, which of the sessions, each of which lasted 100 sec-onds, was which. The results were quite striking. During what turned out to be the control periods, Spirit walked around the box quite actively and meowed often—a total of thirty-seven times in the eight control periods. During the eight OBE sessions, Spirit usually sat quietly and never meowed once.

On several occasions, furthermore, researchers at the lab reported sensing Harary's presence at just the times he felt he was there and even at the exact places. During one session, for example, John Hartwell, who usually was the experimenter with Harary, was instead operating television equipment at the lab that Harary was to visit. He reported strong impressions of Harary's presence on four occasions, all of which turned out to correspond with OBE sessions. In one of these sessions, he noted on his record sheet that he had seen an image of Harary on the television screen. This recorded sighting was in the very corner of the room, it was later learned, that Harary was attempting to visit at just that time.[75]

If people during OBEs can induce changes in humans and animals, the next question would be whether they can affect physical things. Controlled experimentation has thus far proved inconclusive, if suggestive.[76] But there are anecdotal reports that suggest that such effects may sometimes be possible. Perhaps the best-known account is the case involving Lucian and Eileen Landau, which he (Lucian) reported in 1963. He says that, one night in 1957, before they were married and were sleeping in separate rooms, she managed, during an OBE in which she was seen by him as an apparition, to bring a rubber toy dog, weighing slightly more than 100 grams, into his room.[77]

More recently, philosopher Michael Grosso reports an incident involving an anthropology student, Mrs. Elizabeth Sebben of Belleville, New Jersey. After she told Grosso that she often felt like she was out of her body and that, once out she had some control over where she went, he suggested that she come to visit him sometime. One morning a few weeks later he went to the living room, as usual, to practice his flute. But he found that his music stand, instead of being by the bookcase where he always kept it, was in the middle of the room. Because no one else had been in the house, he was quite puzzled. His report continues:

> Within an hour, I received a telephone call from Mrs. Sebben. Without my mentioning the music stand, she recounted the following. The night before—it was well past midnight—she found herself in the out-of-body state and thought of "visiting" me. She did this merely by concentrating on me; suddenly she found herself observing me reading in the kitchen. (I was, in fact, reading in the kitchen at that time.) My out-of-body guest hovered nearby but was unable to make any impression on me. She then wondered how she could leave her mark; after straying through the house, she came upon the music stand and took hold of it in her OBE "hands," appearing to herself to succeed in moving it to the center of the living room. She then "returned" to her normal bodily self in Belleville.*

---

*Grosso, *The Final Choice*, 99–100. Of course, alternative explanations, as Grosso knows, are always possible. Perhaps he moved the stand absentmindedly or while sleepwalking, then Mrs. Sebben learned of this fact during her OBE, or simply through clairvoyance, and fantasized or fabricated the rest; perhaps she was in the neighborhood (bodily), broke into his house during the night, moved the stand, then made up the story of the OBE; or perhaps the two of them simply

Now, if at least some of the reports are true, do they prove the truth of the extrasomatic interpretation of OBEs? Anyone who has read the discussion of psychokinesis in Chapter 2 knows that they do not. Keith Harary, one could say, used PK to cause his "presence" to be felt, and even an apparition of him to be created, in the distant lab while he, through the use of ESP, imagined himself to be there. Any effects in physical detectors could also be explained by PK at a distance. Perhaps even Grosso's two-pound music stand could have been spotted clairvoyantly by Mrs. Sebben and then moved psychokinetically. Such effects can conclusively prove the truth of the extrasomatic interpretation of OBEs no more than can veridical perceptions.[78]

The Question of the Most Probable Interpretation

The proper question, however, is not about conclusive proof but about the most probable interpretation. Empirical data can seldom provide absolute proof of any theory, due to the fact that alternative possible interpretations are usually conceivable. Once this is realized, the question then becomes: How do we determine which interpretation is most probable? And this question, of course, brings us back to the way, discussed earlier, in which estimates of probability are based not simply on empirical evidence but also on worldview and wishful thinking. Those who have imbibed the late modern worldview find the idea of experience outside the body antecedently so improbable that they conclude that, because the extrasomatic interpretation of OBEs cannot be absolutely proved by the evidence, it can be rejected. Likewise, because they believe the intrasomatic interpretation to be antecedently so probable, the fact that none of the intrasomatic interpretations thus far come close to accounting for OBEs does not dissuade them from their conviction that some version of the intrasomatic view *must* be true.

In discussing the mind-body problem in Chapter 3, however, we have seen that there is little reason to assign to the materialistic view a high degree of probability, even apart from the evidence for ESP and PK. We have also seen that this evidence for paranormal functioning further undermines the assump-

---

agreed to fabricate the story. The question, as always, is whether these normal, or at least more normal, explanations are more or less believable than the straightforward, exceedingly paranormal, account, and on this question people will differ, for a variety of reasons. In my own case, knowing Michael Grosso personally, I do not believe that he would have fabricated the story, so I would have to choose among the other options, all of which are problematic. One difficulty with the story as told is why, if Mrs. Sebben was able to move Grosso's (two-pound) music stand, she was not able simply to tap him on the shoulder. A similar feature occurs in the Landau case, as the woman was reportedly supposed to bring in Mr. Landau's small diary (weighing 38 grams) but brought in the toy dog instead. In that case, however, there was an explanation, as she said: "As a child, I had been told never to handle other people's letters or diaries, so probably for this reason I did not want to touch this one" (Charles Tart, *Psi: Scientific Studies of the Psychic Realm* [New York: E. P. Dutton, 1977], 181). It is conceivable that there might be some analogous psychological explanation as to why Mrs. Sebben would, in that extraordinary state, not be able to affect a man in his house in the wee hours of the night even though she could, out of his sight, move a physical object.

tion that the materialistic view of the mind-body relation should have any privileged status in interpreting phenomena such as the out-of-body experience. Even apart from these other considerations, furthermore, we have seen that the evidence provided by some OBEs themselves show that no purely materialistic viewpoint can do justice to them, insofar as materialism entails a sensationist view of perception. The only intrasomatic theories that could possibly be correct are ones that allow for a very strong degree of very accurate clairvoyance. Once this concession is made, however, materialism is rejected: The mind is admitted to have the capacity to perceive information that does not come to it through the body. Likewise, if the capacity for psychokinesis of a rather impressive sort is allowed, in order to account for effects on people, animals, and perhaps even physical objects, then the mind has been credited with power to act without employing the physical body as an instrument. With this modification of the materialist position, the assumed antecedent improbability of extrasomatic experience is considerably reduced. The mind now seems more like the sort of thing that might be able to have experiences outside its body.

This idea, of course, makes many people nervous, because they assume that the extrasomatic interpretation would involve dualism, which they (rightly) assume to be untenable. And, indeed, many interpreters of ND OBEs who have rejected the intrasomatic hypothesis, including Michael Grosso, Michael Sabom, and Emilio Tiberi, have explicitly endorsed "dualism."[79] All that they need mean by using this term, however, is interactionism, and, as I argued at length in Chapter 3, we can have interactionism without dualism. Indeed, I argued, a nondualistic interactionism is the only defensible kind. One can entertain the possibility of genuinely out-of-body experiences, accordingly, without the bug-a-boo of dualism.*

Strengths of the Extrasomatic Hypothesis

If the interpretation of OBEs is approached with an attitude approaching neutrality, according to which the extrasomatic and intrasomatic hypotheses are regarded as antecedently about equally probable, the extrasomatic hypoth-

---

*Part of Blackmore's reason for rejecting the extrasomatic interpretation of OBEs seems to be that she assumes that the only view of the mind-body relation that would allow for it would be Cartesian dualism. And she rightly regards it as problematic. Although much of her criticism of dualism seems to presuppose a somewhat materialistic-behavioristic view of the person (*Beyond the Body*, 228–31, 234–36), she also raises the question of how consciousness can interact with the brain if it is without spatial extension and hence "apparently everywhere" (236). This criticism is based on a widespread, but false, understanding of Descartes' position; see my "Dualism, Materialism, Idealism, and Psi: A Reply to John Palmer," *Journal of the American Society for Psychical Research* 88 (January 1994), 23–39, at 23–24). Even if that criticism is misplaced, however, dualism is conceptually incoherent for other reasons, as I argued in Chapter 3. Her position illustrates the importance of adopting a clearly nondualistic form of interactionism.

esis, it seems to me, can do far more justice to the facts. To return to the 13 features listed earlier: (1) The extrasomatic hypothesis can explain the OBErs feeling of being out of the body, obviously, by saying that they were. (2) It can likewise explain the conviction that the experience was real, rather than a dream or hallucination, by agreeing that it was. (3) The greatly altered emotional state can be explained as resulting from a twofold consequence of being apart from the body: One is free from the sensory and proprioceptive influence from the body and thereby more able to bring nonsensory perceptions, including the prehension of God, to consciousness. (4) The absence of pain is explained, of course, simply by the fact that the mind or soul is not contiguous with the brain, to which the feelings from pain receptors are channeled. (5) The normal or even above-normal visual perception can be regarded as resulting from the fact that, once sensory data from the body are no longer forcing themselves onto the mind and into consciousness, the data received nonsensorily from the same objects can be formed into visual images of the same or even better quality than sensory-based images.* The fact that the images are created out of nonsensory perceptions would explain, incidentally, why OBErs report being able to see in the dark or, alternatively, that things seem to be lit from within or from some nonlocalized source of light.[80] (6) The ability to hear would be explained in the same way: Just as the data that result in visual images in sensory perception are not different in kind, but only in degree, from those that result in auditory perceptions, so the data received nonsensorily can be turned into auditory as well as visual perceptions. (I do not have an explanation as to why visual images are more common than auditory in OBEs, or why both of these are more common than images corresponding to the other modalities.) (7) The veridical per-

---

* The fact that vision is often blurred, distorted, or even erroneous (as mentioned earlier) creates no problem for the extrasomatic hypothesis, assuming that a naively passive view of perception in general is not held. In the view that I am presupposing, all conscious perception involves a complex constructive process, in which creation and projection as well as reception are involved, with elements from all of these sources being intricately intertwined in the final product. In what we consider normal (incarnate) visual perception, the received data arise not only from the optic system but also from other bodily organs, memories, and (through ESP) the rest of the past universe. Although there is a tendency, especially in the mode of consciousness that has been gaining ascendency over the past few millennia, for data received through the physical senses largely to determine our sensory projections onto contemporary regions (see John B. Cobb, Jr., *The Structure of Christian Existence* [1967; Lanham, Md.: University Press of America, 1990], Chs. 2–5), there is no inevitability about this. Material from memories, extrasensory perception, unconscious symbolization, or all of these may be combined with the sensorily derived data to produce distortions and even complete hallucinations. In an out-of-body state, the material welling up from memories and unconscious symbolization would no longer be kept from rising to consciousness so often by sensorily derived data. Nonsensory perceptions would be the only source of information about the contemporary (or, precisely, the just-past) world. That the final product does not always correspond to this world should be no source of surprise. What is amazing is that out-of-body vision does evidently often give a picture so close to that which normal eyesight would provide.

ceptions sometimes reported in OBEs would need no special explanation beyond that given in the previous two points. (8) The increased clarity of thought often reported, especially in ND OBEs, would follow from the fact that the mind is free from any confusing, disorienting feelings and information from the brain.* (9) The transforming effects would result from the intense emotions that are usually felt in the OBE, combined with the (reasonable) inference that this experience is a foretaste of what one will probably experience after death. (10) The altered sense of time during the OBE can be explained by the fact that, actually being outside one's body, one would temporarily not be receiving the subliminal, but constant, influences from the rhythmic processes of one's bodily members. (11) The similarity and universality of the reports about OBEs require no elaborate explanation but would follow simply from the fact that the various people were reporting what really happened. (12) The fact that this similarity in the basic phenomenology of OBEs is combined with great variability in the circumstances under which OBEs occur is not, as it is for intrasomatic theories, a problem: Explanations as to why OBEs happen when they do need not also serve to explain the phenomenological features of the out-of-body experience itself; the fact of being out of the body handles this latter issue. (13) The incidence of OBEs, which is evidently much higher than earlier assumed (both in near-death and other circumstances), is no embarrassment for the extrasomatic hypothesis, because it does not imply that OBErs are borderline psychotic or that they at least suffer from a very serious illusion not affecting other people—namely, that they have, at least once, actually been outside their bodies.

The extrasomatic hypothesis, accordingly, provides an extremely parsimonious explanation for a wide range of data. Of course, advocates of the intrasomatic hypothesis also consider the principle of parsimony (according to which one should, all other things being equal, adopt the simplest, or most parsimonious, hypothesis) to be on their side. This confusing situation exists because there are at least two meanings to the principle of parsimony (or simplicity). One meaning involves the number of entities: One should not multiply entities beyond those necessary to explain all the phenomena. The second meaning involves explanatory principles: One should try to explain all the phenomena with the fewest explanatory principles, which implies that those principles that explain the greatest number of phenomena are, all other things being equal, to be preferred. When advocates of the extrasomatic hypothesis point to parsimony, they have the second meaning in mind.[†] Advocates of the intrasomatic hypothesis, especially insofar as they base it on a materialistic

---

* Blackmore, in support of her "dying brain hypothesis" (*Dying to Live*, 3–4), suggests that it may be that, "as the brain dies, less [*sic*] thoughts are possible and so the few that remain seem clearer . . . by comparison" (44). This seems a rather desperate suggestion.

[†] Harvey Irwin (*Flight of Mind*, 229) concedes that in this sense the extrasomatic hypothesis "has the notable merits of conceptual parsimony and explanatory breadth."

equation of mind and brain, are thinking of the first meaning. This ambiguity does not mean that we have a standoff with regard to the principle of parsimony, because the first meaning is that no *unnecessary* entities are to be posited, and, as I argued in Chapter 3, it is necessary, to account for a wide range of data (including, but by no means restricted to, parapsychological data), to posit a numerical distinction between mind and brain, thereby regarding them as different entities (albeit not ontologically different *types* of entities). The law of parsimony, accordingly, insofar as it supports either one, supports the extrasomatic hypothesis.

One might suspect that, in giving the list of 13 features of OBEs, I stacked the deck in favor of the extrasomatic hypothesis, because all 13 features give support to, or are at least clearly compatible with, this hypothesis. I left out, one might suspect, all those features of OBEs that favor the intrasomatic over the extrasomatic hypothesis. However, the fact is (at least to the best of my knowledge) that there *are* no such features. The only thing that favors the intrasomatic hypothesis is philosophical prejudice: the assumption, based on the late modern worldview, that (to use Richard Blacher's words) "the idea of spirits wandering around the emergency room" is simply too absurd to take seriously, and certainly too "unscientific" to profess or even to entertain in public. The only real argument against the extrasomatic hypothesis, accordingly, is purely philosophical; all the empirical evidence about OBEs, at least in relation to the better cases, favors the extrasomatic hypothesis. Most scientists favoring the intrasomatic hypothesis, fancying themselves to be empiricists, would, of course, hate to admit this.

This is not to say, to be sure, that there are no facts that can be construed as support for a particular intrasomatic theory. Susan Blackmore, for example, puts much emphasis on the tunnel experience (which is often transitional between the mundane and transcendental aspects of full-fledged OBEs, especially ND OBEs), portraying it as a very common feature of OBEs,* and even looking for evidence, against earlier studies, that it is experienced by OBErs in diverse cultures.† She uses this (alleged) universality of the tunnel experience, combined with her assertion that it is explainable in physiological terms, as support for the intrasomatic hypothesis. The universality of the tunnel experience,

---

* Although in her 1990 "Postscript" to *Beyond the Body* she suggests that a physiological explanation of the tunnel "provides the answer about OBEs" (279), she had earlier cited, without demurrer, Ring's study in which under 10 percent of the OBErs described anything like a tunnel (147).

† Susan J. Blackmore, "Near-Death Experiences in India: They Have Tunnels Too," *Journal of Near-Death Experiences* 11/4 (Summer 1993), 205–17. Even given the results of her study and a couple others suggesting that something like 38 percent of NDErs experience tunnels (215), it is hard to see how a physiological explanation of the tunnel experience, even assuming its adequacy, could provide the key to the OBE itself, as it would leave about 62 percent of the OBEs without an explanation. Furthermore, the incidence of tunnel experiences surely runs higher in ND OBEs than in OBEs as such, so the figure of 38 percent is probably too high for OBEs in general.

however, would be equally consistent with an extrasomatic view—one that held that there really is a tunnel connecting this world with the next one, or one that regards the tunnel as a universal archetype that is liable to impress itself on an out-of-body mind. And the same is true, as far as I can see, with any of the other common features of OBEs that may be taken as support for this intrasomatic theory or that: They are equally compatible with an extrasomatic hypothesis. The inclusive argument for the extrasomatic hypothesis, accordingly, is that, philosophical prejudices aside, some of the empirical features of OBEs support it over the intrasomatic hypothesis and the remaining features are equally compatible with it.

7. THE TRANSCENDENTAL ASPECT OF OBEs

This conclusion concerns the mundane OBEs (or the mundane phase of OBEs that also have a transcendental aspect), on which I have thus far focused. When the transcendental aspect is considered as well, however, there *is* an argument that could count against the extrasomatic hypothesis. This argument, which is at least implicit in the discussion by some intrasomatic theorists of OBEs, especially ND OBEs, can be put thus:

(1) Veridical perceptions in the mundane phase of OBEs are used by many extrasomatic theorists to argue that the visions in the transcendental phase—the tunnel, the light at its end, the deceased relatives and friends, the being of light, the other religious figures, the heavenly scenes, the beautiful music, and the personal messages—are also literally true perceptions.*

(2) This idea, however, is incredible. Although most of the visions of this other world are indeed similar in many respects, they are also quite different in several respects. Very few people experience all the standard items, and most of these standard items are reported by only 10 to 50 percent of the accounts, which argues against the idea that the visions correspond to an objectively real "other world." Furthermore, some of the NDEs are painful, some even hellish, rather than heavenly, and we have learned in recent years that these are evidently far more common than "near-death orthodoxy"[81] had averred, perhaps constituting more than a tenth of the NDEs.[82] If the visions of "heaven" are literally true, are we to

---

*I am here presupposing basic familiarity with the transcendental phase that is characteristic of many near-death experiences. Those unfamiliar with it could read Raymond Moody's *Life after Life* (New York: Bantam, 1976) or *The Light Beyond* (with Paul Perry) (1988; New York: Bantam, 1989), Kenneth Ring's *Life at Death* (New York: Coward, McCann and Geoghegan, 1980) or *Heading Toward Omega* (New York: William Morrow, 1984), or Margot Grey's *Return from Death: An Exploration of the Near-Death Experience* (London & Boston: Arkana, 1985).

conclude that there is also a literal hell—created, presumably, by the God who radiates unconditional love in the heavenly experiences? Finally, historical studies of NDEs suggest that these transcendental visions are culturally conditioned to a significant extent.[83]

(3) It makes more sense, accordingly, to conclude that the NDE in its entirety is imaginal, with the veridical perceptions in the mundane phase being imagination based on ESP.

The second step of this argument, it seems to me, has considerable merit. I do not think, however, that it need be taken as an argument against the extrasomatic interpretation of (at least some) OBEs. There are ways in which the probable truth in this argument about the transcendental aspect of (especially) NDEs can be combined with the extrasomatic view of OBEs. Although I cannot here launch into a full-scale discussion of NDEs as such, I will suggest that the transcendental dimensions of NDEs should usually be regarded as a creative synthesis of nonsensory, archetypal, cultural, and individual elements. Genuine nonsensory perceptions could account for veridical experiences of relatives or other people that the percipient did not previously know to have died. The experience of overwhelming love, which is often reported, could be based upon a genuine experience of God. The experience of the void, or emptiness, which sometimes occurs prior to, or instead of, the experience of any religious figures could be understood as a direct experience of what Whitehead calls "creativity," Buddhists call "emptiness," Hindus call "nirguna Brahman," and others call simply the interdependence of all events. Being out of one's body, thereby free from sensory perceptions and the rather clear boundary between oneself and others that embodiment creates, might open up one's conscious experience to this dimension of reality as well as to the divine presence. Many other of the more-or-less universal elements of the transcendental dimension of heavenly NDEs, such as the noise, the tunnel, the light at the end, the people of light, the being of light, the beautiful scenery, the border, the message, and the life-review, could be considered archetypal elements, meaning that they tend to be experienced because countless previous NDErs have experienced them.[84] The hellish NDE, with its various common elements, would be the other basic archetype. Cultural influences would account for those elements that are common to NDErs in a specific culture but not truly universal, such as the perception of the being of light as Jesus, or Mary, or Krishna. Individual experiences, finally, would account for those factors that are unique to the individual, such as the particular deceased individuals seen and the details of the life review.

With some such understanding, the above argument does not count against the extrasomatic interpretation of ND OBEs. One can agree, in other words, that the transcendental aspect of the OBE is largely imaginal without concluding that the apparent perceptions reported in mundane OBEs are really imaginal, rather than perceptual, in nature. The negative moral of this account is that the veridical perceptions that sometimes occur in mundane OBEs should *not* be used to argue for the veridical nature of most aspects of the transcendental visions.

Summing Up OBEs

I have argued that the extrasomatic hypothesis about OBEs is supported because the intrasomatic view is grossly inadequate, at least for the best cases, in which, besides several other features problematic for the intrasomatic hypothesis, there are corroborated veridical perceptions, including perceptions of things at some distance from the person's body. Some might be tempted to argue that a theory should not be based on what are considered the "best cases" from the extrasomaticist's point of view, but on the more ordinary cases, constituting the majority. So to argue, however, would be to forget that the (philosophical) issue at hand is precisely whether the intrasomatic hypothesis, which seeks to explain away the subjects' experience (that they really were out of their bodies), can do justice to *all* the facts in *all* the cases, and we can test this hypothesis only by looking at those cases that are the most difficult from the point of view of that hypothesis, which means, of course, those that are the best from the point of view of the extrasomatic hypothesis. The fact that these "best cases" constitute a minority of the cases (in part, at least, because most cases involving potentially veridical perceptions are not adequately investigated and documented) can provide no support for an exclusively intrasomatic approach to OBEs, given the logical point that it takes only one white crow to prove that all crows are not black. It would take only one good case to disprove the universal claim behind the intrasomatic approach, which is that the mind never leaves the body—although, of course, we have far more than one, and the numbers are growing annually. OBEs, even if understood as truly extrasomatic experiences, do not, of course, provide proof that there is indeed life *after* biological death, because even those who return to report ND OBEs have, obviously, not suffered death, at least if we accept the definition of death as an irreversible condition. But OBEs do provide direct experiential support of an affirmative answer to the chief question at issue, which is simply whether the person (the mind or the soul, with or without some kind of nonphysical body) can exist apart from the physical body.

8. Five Types of Evidence for Life After Death: Summary and Conclusion

The main reason for the decline in belief in life after death in the late modern world, especially among intellectuals, I have argued, is not lack of evidence but a worldview that strongly discourages any serious examination of this evidence, especially publicly. It is, to be sure, not simply the philosophical worldview as such that prevents this examination but an interlocking set of correlative intellectual habits, social conventions, reward-and-punishment systems, and learned senses of what hypotheses are intellectually respectable. Because of the late modern worldview, in this broad sense of the term, probably not one intellectual in a thousand, including college and university professors, is conversant with the kinds of evidence discussed in these five chapters.

I have also argued, however, that if this evidence *is* seriously examined, the examiners will confront the following dilemma: On the one hand, if they do not accept the reality of ESP and PK, and even of *super*-ESP and *super*-PK, they will be confronted with a massive amount of evidence that, unless it is dogmatically rejected or simply set aside as anomalous, provides virtual proof of life after death. On the other hand, if they do employ the notion of superpsi in order to provide a nonsurvivalist interpretation of all this evidence, they will in effect have accepted a view of the mind as distinct from the brain and as having the power both to perceive and to act without the brain's mediation. They will thereby have rejected the modern reasons for assuming that the mind is not the kind of reality that could survive bodily death. Once this antecedent improbability of survival is rejected, there is no reason why a superpsi explanation of the data should be considered antecedently preferable to a survivalist interpretation.

I have not, however, argued that the evidence does indeed provide coercive proof for life after death. Having accepted the reality of both ESP and PK and the possibility that the scope of each may be very extensive, I have argued that superpsi explanations of at least most of the evidence are conceivable. The question, however, should not be posed in terms of absolute proof, as such is not possible: One cannot prove either the truth or the falsity of the belief in life after death. The question should be posed instead in terms of the most plausible theory, Plato's "most likely account." In terms of this question, I have suggested that there is formidable evidence for life after death, some of which can be given a superpsi explanation at best with considerable difficulty and can be more naturally and simply explained in terms of a survivalist hypothesis.

Having looked at five kinds of evidence, I found that four of them contained phenomena that were in themselves strongly suggestive of survival. The exception involved cases of the possession type: In these cases, it seemed, one could explain the phenomena, impressive as they are, in terms of retroprehensive inclusion, with the selection of the particular prior life understandable in terms of motivations of the living. (This is not to say that some cases, such as the Lurancy Vennum/Mary Roff case, should not be given a survivalist interpretation, *if* one has already, on other grounds, decided for survival. My point is only that possession cases by themselves would not provide sufficient reason to accept survival.) The other four types of evidence, however, each contained some phenomena that do not seem best explainable in terms of incarnate superpsi.

With regard to mediumistic messages, the most impressive phenomena were judged to be the cross correspondences and the drop-in communicators, both of which seem to point to contemporary purposes of postcarnate individuals.

In cases of the reincarnation type, a crucial difference from possession cases is that the motivation behind the selection of the prior life can hardly be ascribed to the present subject, given the appearance of suggestive phenomena at a very young age or even at birth. Cases of this type were taken to be especially impressive when, besides memories, attitudes, phobias, tastes, and other behavioral patterns, the child also has multiple birthmarks corresponding closely to birthmarks or wounds on the prior personality's body. Although it might he possible to attribute the selection of the prior life to the mother, who would somehow bring about the retroprehensive inclusion of the prior soul, and the birthmarks to her "maternal psychokinesis," we do not at this time have any psychological studies to test whether attributing the motivation to the mothers' needs is plausible. Besides the antecedent improbability (in my view) that such studies, when produced, will support the assignment of the motivation to the mothers involved, there are two further counts against superpsi explanations of reincarnation cases: Such explanations seem to entail that multiple reincarnations of the same personality should be common and, in fact, that reincarnations of individuals while they are still in the prime of life should be common. Neither of these expectations is supported by the evidence. I take the nonfulfillment of these two predictions to be the most decisive disconfirmation of the theory of retroprehensive inclusion, which seems to be the only superpsi explanation that could otherwise handle the evidence.

With regard to apparitions, two phenomena tip the scales in favor of an explanation in terms of postmortem agency. One is the phenomenon of collective apparitions, which are made all the more difficult for superpsi explanations when the apparent was not known by the first percipient. The second phenomenon is the similarity between apparitions of the living and those of the dead, which gives rise to an argument: Apparitions of the living are usually attributable in part to the agency of the apparent (who may be dreaming or thinking about the place in question, intending to go there bodily, trying to be perceived there as an apparition, or even, in reciprocal cases, having an OBE of being there); and the similarity of apparitions of the living and of the dead suggests that the latter, too, are attributable in part to the apparents. This argument is given added support by the fact that the majority of such apparitions occur within an hour of the death of the apparent.

OBEs, as we have seen, have numerous features that render the extrasomatic hypothesis far more adequate than the intrasomatic, which really has nothing to commend it, at least with regard to the stronger cases, except philosophical prejudice. OBEs thereby, while not providing direct evidence of life after death as such, do provide strong evidence that the self can exist, feel, perceive, think, decide, and even sometimes (to a more or less limited extent) influence other actualities while apart from its physical body. OBEs thereby provide strong evidence against the primary assumption behind the rejection of belief in life after death.

Whereas mediumistic messages, cases of the reincarnation type, apparitions, and OBEs all individually provide strong evidence for belief in life after death, taken together they provide an even stronger case. This is for three reasons. The first is the principle of parsimony or simplicity: Whereas the non-survivalist interpreter must come up with a variety of hypotheses to handle the various kinds of data (perhaps retroprehensive inclusion for mediumistic messages and cases of the reincarnation [as well as the possession] type, another theory for apparitions, and still another for OBEs), the survivalist can use one hypothesis—survival with (limited) agency—to explain the basic features of all the phenomena.

The evidence taken collectively is stronger, second, because each of the kinds of evidence increases the antecedent probability of a survivalist interpretation of the others. This elementary point is often overlooked. Those few intellectuals who take the time to examine one kind of reputed evidence for life after death, such as ND OBEs, assume that the appropriate "background" on the basis of which to estimate the antecedent probabilities of the competing hypotheses is constituted by the kinds of facts that support the nonsurvivalist interpretation, especially those that seem to show the complete dependence of conscious experience on bodily state. And, if it is commonly assumed that this background does not even include the evidence for ESP and PK, all the more is it assumed not to include the other kinds of reputed evidence for life after death other than the one being considered. (As I pointed out in the section on OBEs, for example, most of the discussion of NDEs has been carried on without benefit of familiarity with the relevant parapsychological literature.) But the background, in reality, should be taken to be *all* the evidence other than that directly relevant to the issue at hand. The background for a discussion of reputed evidence for reincarnation, accordingly, should include the evidence for survival provided by mediumistic messages, apparitions, OBEs, and cases of the possession type. As a result, the sense of the antecedent probability of a survivalist interpretation with which one approached the evidence would be considerably higher.

The third reason why the argument for life after death is strengthened when the five kinds of phenomena are taken collectively is that some of them provide support for elements of the others. This is most true of the relation between OBEs and the other kinds of evidence. OBEs, especially those in which the OBErs make others aware of their presence, support the survivalist interpretation of (some) apparitions by suggesting that what is an apparition from the perspective of the percipient may be an OBE from the perspective of the apparent. This was the main point of Hornell Hart's 1956 study of apparitions. He argued, first, that "conscious ESP projections," which are OBEs in which paranormal knowledge is acquired and remembered, "provide internal views of the phenomena observed externally in connection with [some] apparitions of the living."[85] He then marshaled considerable data to show that "conscious projections of living persons are in most respects essentially indistinguishable from apparitions of the dying" and of those who have been dead for hours, "days, months, or years."[86] (In this regard, he points out that, if consciousness were dependent on the living physical brain even during an OBE, as some maintain, then, because at least some apparitions of the living are an external view of OBEs, there should be a sharp alteration in the character and behavior of apparitions after the point of death is passed. "But *no such alteration is evident in the data*—except such as might be expected from the alterations of purpose which death would produce in the appearer."[87] From these two points he concludes that "some of the most frequent types of apparitions of the dead presumably carry with them the memories and purposes of the personalities which they represent, and thus constitute evidence of survival of personality beyond bodily death."[88]

In relation to mediumistic messages and cases of the reincarnation type, OBEs undermine the main reason for preferring some superpsi explanation (such as retroprehensive inclusion) by providing evidence for discarnate existence with consciousness, perception, and (limited) agency. With regard to reincarnation cases in particular, furthermore, OBEs support the literal truth of the reports of "intermission experiences," which should not occur if a nonsurvivalist theory were correct. These reports of intermission experiences can then, in return, be taken as examples of out-of-body experiences that occurred unambiguously after (irreversible) physical death.

Mutual reinforcement is even provided by a feature of OBEs that has been taken as a problem in providing experimental evidence for the extrasomatic interpretation of them, to which I have referred parenthetically above: the fact that the ability of OBErs to *exercise agency*, in the sense of exerting causal influence on other things, is usually quite limited in comparison with their ability to *perceive* other things. They usually cannot even make themselves visible to others, and they still more rarely can affect physical objects or speak audibly. These facts correspond exactly with the phenomenology of apparitions and with the reports of reincarnational intermission experiences. They also lend some antecedent credibility to at least some mediumistic messages by explaining why many deceased individuals with important things to communicate to the living have done so only after they were contacted by a "medium." These facts, finally, lend support to belief in life after death by suggesting an answer to the question as to why, if all people survive bodily death, so few convey information about this fact.

9

PARAPSYCHOLOGY AND POSTMODERN SPIRITUALITY

I am using the term "spirituality" rather than "religion" not because of any personal hostility to the latter word. Indeed, my professional job-description indicates that I teach "philosophy of religion." I have noted informally, however, as sociologists of religion have more systematically, that many people today say that they are spiritual but not religious. Upon questioning, this distinction usually turns on the institutional connotations that the word "religion" has for them. The professional student of religion can point out, to be sure, that this distinction can be regarded as purely arbitrary. Furthermore, for many in the Roman Catholic tradition who had a legalistic form of spiritual discipline imposed upon them, "spirituality" is the bad word and "religion" the good word. Nevertheless, this distinction is so widespread that we should, rather than belittling it, seek to understand its significance. My reflection about it has led me to suspect that the distinction often being expressed is similar to my own distinction between two different stances within theistic religions: one based on supernaturalistic theism, the other on naturalistic theism.

According to supernaturalistic theism (as I am using the term), God has the power to interrupt the normal causal processes of the world. The types of extraordinary events often called "miracles" provide, of course, the chief examples of this kind of intervention, but supernaturalists have believed in other forms as well. In a notorious example in the history of science, Newton believed that God intervened occasionally to adjust the orbits of the planets. (It was on the basis of better calculations that the French astronomer Pierre Laplace was supposed to have said, when Napoleon asked him where God fit into his astronomy, "I have no need of that hypothesis.") Other examples are related to our discussion of dualism in Chapter 3. The form of dualism known as "vitalism" accepted a mechanistic account of "inanimate" nature but believed that life involved the sudden appearance of a new, teleological principle (an elàn vital). Many vitalists used this as evidence of supernatural intervention. Many supernaturalists also pointed to the human mind as an emergence requiring a supernatural cause. These and other examples contributed to the scientific community's eventual consensus that "God is not a scientific hypothesis." Given the equation of the term "God" with supernaturalistic theism, that conclusion is arguably justified. The basic presupposition of the "natural sciences," which is that all events are interconnected in an unbroken causal nexus, is threatened by the idea of a being outside this nexus that can intervene in it now and then.

In any case, the widespread reaction against (institutionalized) religion can be seen as an analogous response, as a negative reaction to a religion based on supernaturalistic premises. These premises give religious institutions a basis for portraying themselves as the One True Way. Given the supernaturalistic view of deity, God can be said to have chosen one people, to have established one religion, as *the* vehicle of divine revelation and salvation. This religion's scriptures can be declared to be infallibly inspired. If that is not enough—because multiple readings are possible—God can be said to have made one institution the infallible interpreter of the infallible book. The institution can then say that there is no salvation outside its doors, that it alone has been given the "keys to the kingdom." God is love, to be sure, but everyone not baptized in this institution, not believing its doctrines, and not dying in a state of grace (meaning, in good standing with this institution) will be excluded from salvation. Given the supernaturalistic view of divine power—as destructive as well as creative, as coercive as well as persuasive—this "exclusion from salvation" can be portrayed as a damnation to an eternity of divinely inflicted torments, an added inducement to join the One True Church. Those who are outside this church, furthermore, can be seen as enemies of God—either as ones who have willfully refused God's gracious invitation (perhaps through the institution's missionaries, who came to convert the heathen) or as ones God has deliberately given over to reprobation. In either case, being God's enemies, they are enemies of God's chosen people as well. Those who are inside the church, the saints, furthermore, often show few signs of saintliness. Being "religious" is often equated with believing the right dogmas, praying in a perfunctory way, and avoiding a limited number of types of action, primarily of a sexual nature. Little if any encouragement is given for spiritual growth. Spending an eternity with such people would hardly seem like "heaven"; the answer to this, however, is that *God* will transform them after death into fit subjects for eternity.

In these and related ways, religions teach a universal creator but promote a bigoted exclusivism; they teach that God is Truth but reject truths that contradict ideas in a book thousands of years old; they teach that God is love but say that all the horrors of this life happen because God caused, or at least permitted, them to happen; they preach love but promote indifference and hate; they preach peace but promote war.

It is something like this attitude toward religion, all too amply justified by some of the facts, that lies behind, I suggest, the widespread rejection of "religion" by those who are interested in "spirituality." Just as scientists came to reject supernaturalistically based science because, they came to see, it contradicted the very nature of what science should be, so many deeply spiritual people have come to reject supernaturalistically based religion because it contradicts the very nature of what religion should be: a spiritual adventure through which our souls continuously increase in wisdom, compassion, loving kindness, joy, beauty, peacefulness.

The theistic religious traditions could overcome their negative and destructive tendencies and become vehicles for promoting life as a spiritual adventure, I suggest, by changing their foundation from a supernaturalistic to a naturalistic theism. Given naturalistic premises, there would be no basis for believing that God could have, by overriding anyone's power of self-determination, infallibly inspired any book, council, or office. The scriptures of all religious traditions, accordingly, could be assumed to be mixtures of divine inspiration and human ignorance and perversity. There would be no basis for an externalistic view of salvation, according to which it is something done *to* one, if one has believed and done the right things. Salvation would be seen as a process of becoming whole, a process in which divine inspiration and human response cooperate. Those in other religious traditions would be seen as fellow travelers, from whom one can learn and with whom one can share. Because divine power is not the power to prevent and to destroy, the calamities of life would not be viewed as punishments or trials inflicted by God, not even as events God "permitted" while having the power to prevent. The Holy Power of the universe could be viewed as wholly good, wholly supportive of everything fine. The idea of divine vengeance would become self-contradictory. The religious life would be based entirely on attraction toward the true, the good, and the beautiful, not partly on fear of punishment. And so on.

Of course, this change has already been made, to some degree, in some institutions. Quite often, however, this transition has not been carried out in an explicit and thoroughgoing way. Members are left with an inconsistent and confusing mixture of the old and the new. Even more problematic, the transition is often seen as, and indeed often is, more a diminishment than an enlargement. The focus is on "what we, unlike those foolish others, no longer believe"; at best it is on "what we can still believe." The new, naturalistic basis often fails, accordingly, to ground a religion that even approximates the robustness that the "old-time religion," for all its problems, had. This has often led either to a drift away from religion altogether, or, by reaction, to a rejection of "liberal" religion in favor of a return to a conservative or even fundamentalist form of religion.

We seem to be faced with a trilemma. On the one hand, supernaturalistic religion has been robust but terribly destructive, arguably as harmful as helpful. On the other hand, naturalistic religion has overcome most of these destructive features but has usually been too tepid to retain, let alone attract. On the third hand, to introduce a new point, civilization seems to need a religious or spiritual orientation as never before for its very survival. If a mode of human life oriented around material satisfactions—around the "domination of nature," around the control, possession, and exploitation of the planet's physical resources for human consumption—continues to spread, there is little hope for avoiding virtual or complete extinction, preceded by unprecedented misery. We evidently need a spiritual orientation that is both naturalistic *and* robust.

It is at this point that parapsychological evidence has its greatest potential importance. On the one hand, it undermines one of the main traditional bases for supernaturalistic theism. On the other hand, it supports not only a naturalistic theism but also a spiritual life no less robust, challenging, and satisfying than that supported by supernaturalistic theism at its best.

In the following discussion, I will focus on the ways in which parapsychological evidence supports the various presuppositions for a life understood primarily as a spiritual journey, involving both self-discipline and adventure. In passing, I will point out how, in doing this, it simultaneously supports a naturalistic rather than supernaturalistic understanding of the Holy Power of the universe.

1. THE REALITY OF THE SELF-DETERMINING SOUL

The basic presupposition of a spiritual life is the existence of a mind or soul, in the sense of a center of experience that is not simply the brain or an impotent by-product thereof. My argument for an interactionist position in Chapter 3 was based primarily on other than parapsychological evidence, partly to counter the view that this evidence provides the only or even the primary basis for affirming interactionism. This evidence does, nevertheless, provide important support. The fact that extrasensory perception occurs and cannot be understood in terms of physical fields suggests that we have a receptive center other than the brain and its sensory organs. The fact that psychokinesis occurs and cannot be understood in terms of brain waves suggests a center of activity that transcends the brain. Given the reality of the soul as distinct from the brain, our presupposition that we have a degree of self-determining freedom can be taken at face value.

2. The Power of the Soul

The idea of the soul's existence and freedom would not suffice to support spiritual discipline as very important if the soul's power were thought to be limited to its power to determine its own states, as some forms of epiphenomenalism have held. The importance of spiritual discipline is even minimized if we assume that the soul, while having power to affect other things, does not have very much, and that what direct power it does have is limited to its power to influence its motor-muscular system through its brain. While psychosomatic phenomena show that it has the power to influence much more of its body, and sometimes dramatically (as in stigmata and psychosomatic healing), thought-transference and psychokinesis show that the soul's power can be exerted directly on actualities beyond one's own body, both "physical" things and other souls. This power can, in relation to living matter, either promote or discourage growth, either bless or curse. The fact that psychokinesis sometimes has large-scale effects shows, moreover, that this power to bless or curse is not necessarily trivial, that a significant amount of power, either healing or destructive, may be radiating from one's soul. The fact, furthermore, that large-scale psychokinetic effects tend to be the result less of conscious than of unconscious processes, as in "poltergeist" cases, suggests that most of whatever direct causal influence we exert on the extrasomatic world results less from our conscious aims than from simply the state of our soul. For these reasons, the soul's self-discipline is extremely important.

3. The Reality of God

The possibility and importance of the soul's self-discipline are necessary conditions for a life devoted to spiritual growth, but not sufficient. Another necessary twofold presupposition is that there are values in terms of which the soul *should* be disciplined and that the soul has access to these values. We saw in Chapter 3 that the capacity for nonsensory perception, which parapsychology supports, provides a necessary presupposition of access to such values, if such there be. A prior question, however, is how the existence of things such as normative values—of things that are real but not physical, not even actual in any sense—is possible. This brings us to the question of God.

Many people interested in spirituality or even "religion" in a non-Western sense may see no necessary connection between religion and belief in "God." Does not Buddhism get along quite well without belief in God? Does not Hinduism say that the supreme reality, Brahman, transcends the gods, which are finally illusory? Answering these questions—or, rather, indicating the direction an answer would take—will help bring out how naturalistic theism differs from the supernaturalistic form of theism (which most people still identify with "belief in God") and why theism of the naturalistic sort is important.

It would be a great mistake, from the idea that "Buddhism is atheistic," to conclude that its worldview is similar to that of modern Western atheism. The latter, as Nietzsche, Heidegger, and Weber have seen, implies nihilism, because it means that there is no other realm, beyond the causal nexus of finite, temporal events, in which transtemporal values can abide. This means that there are no norms, no standards, according to which life should be lived. Values are chosen or invented, not discovered.[1] Nothing inherent in the nature of things, accordingly, says that one way of life is better than another. On this basis, incidentally, Heidegger notoriously pledged allegiance to Hitler, calling him the wave of the future.[2]

Buddhism is not atheistic in this sense. In the first place, there are two major types of Buddhism, Theravada and Mahayana, with Mahayana having far more adherents. The Mahayana universe is filled with spiritual beings of various levels, and the "Dharmakaya," or the most inclusive of the "three bodies of Buddha," plays a role in the universe not unlike that of the Western God understood naturalistically. Even in Theravada Buddhism, furthermore, the "atheism" is a rejection of a very particular idea of God: a being who created the world *ex nihilo* and who, thereby, exists absolutely independently, outside the universal web of "dependent origination." This is precisely the supernaturalistic idea of God that is rejected here. The rejection of a creator in this sense has not left Theravada Buddhists with a nihilistic worldview comparable to that of modern Western atheists. They definitely believe in the objectivity of various values that serve as ethical norms, and they even, arguably, understand their own spiritual efforts, in spite of their insistence on their "own power," as supported by a salvific power inherent in the nature of things.

With regard to Hinduism, there are, as with Buddhism, many different forms. The form of Hinduism referred to above, which says that the ultimate reality is Nirguna Brahman—Brahman without attributes—is Advaita Vedanta, based on the teachings of Shankara. Although it is well known in the West, much more followed than Shankara in India is Ramanuja, who portrayed Brahman with attributes, a personal deity to whom devotion (bhakti) is appropriate.[3] In any case, whether or not the name of Ramanuja or one of the other theistic Hindu philosopher-theologians is known, Hindu religion is overwhelmingly oriented around deity—whether one, many, or many and (ultimately) one.

Even Shankara's teaching, furthermore, could not be compared with that of Western nontheism. In the first place, the idea that the personal God (Ishvara) is "illusory" (maya) cannot be understood in our modern sense of illusion—as if there were something else, such as "molecules in motion," that were more real. In the second place, while said to be "devoid of qualities," Nirguna Brahman is also said to be characterized by "existence-consciousness-bliss" (*sat-chit-ananda*). This is a far cry from atheism Western-style. The universe supports the spiritual quest.

One might well agree, however, that the spiritual life requires a supportive universe, but wonder why that requires belief in some form of deity. Why is it not sufficient to believe that the universe contains objective values which we, through nonsensory perception, can directly apprehend? By thinking of such objective values as "Platonic forms," why could the spiritual life not be adequately supported by such a purely Platonic religion? (I use the term "Platonic" for this view only for convenience; Plato himself, at least in some of his writings, spoke of an actual deity.)

There are two problems with this type of Platonic religion. In the first place, as intimated above, the idea that the forms, ideals, or norms as such, having a purely ideal existence, could exist on their own is dubious. There has been a widespread agreement, shared by thinkers as diverse as Whitehead and Thomas Aquinas, that they can exist only as entertained by something actual, by a mind. We can believe that values exist objectively (to the human mind), then, only if they exist *subjectively*—as entertained by a cosmic subject. Such a subject of cosmic scope is what is here meant by "God." Whitehead's suggestion, furthermore, is not only that values exist in "the primordial mind of God," but that they exist there as *appetitions*. God prehends truth, beauty, and goodness with the appetition that they be actualized in the world of finite beings. This is Whitehead's explanation as to why we feel these values *as ideals*, that is, as *important*, as possibilities that *should* be actualized.[4] We do not, therefore, with our nonsensory perception simply prehend these values directly; we prehend them by prehending God. Whitehead says, accordingly, that our "experience of ideals—of ideals entertained, of ideals aimed at, of ideals achieved, of ideals defaced . . . is the experience of the deity of the universe."[5]

A second problem with the attempt to have a purely Platonic religion is that the fundamental religious desire is the desire to be in harmony with the supreme power of the universe. It is hard to see the trinity of Truth, Beauty, and Goodness, for all its grandeur, as the supreme power of the universe. We can accept as the supreme power only that which is the source of the stars above and the earth below as well as the call to truth, beauty, and goodness within. The supreme power can only be that which is responsible for the fine-tuned order of the physical constants of the universe, for the emergence of life, and for the human form of life.

For these two reasons, the kind of religion proposed by John Dewey in *A Common Faith* or Donald Cupitt in *Taking Leave of God*,[6] according to which we use the term "God" for a cluster of values we have chosen to honor, will not work. We need to believe that the values we serve are discovered, not invented, and therefore we need an actual, not merely an ideal or "as-if," God.

Parapsychological evidence is relevant to this twofold presupposition of the spiritual life as well. In the first place, by supporting the interactionist view of the mind-body relationship, it provides an analogy for the God-world relationship. Just as a materialistic view of the person generally supports an atheistic view of the universe, an interactionist view of soul and body is assumed by most forms of theism. In the naturalistic theism proposed here, which is panentheism, God is the soul of the universe. God relates to the world in somewhat the same way we are related to our bodies. God is thereby the dominant member of the universal society, providing the overall order, and the supreme recipient of value, feeling both the delights and the pains of the creatures.

4. THE POWER OF GOD

Psychokinesis supports, beyond the bare existence of a Universal Soul, the idea that this Soul is the creator of the universe, thereby the supreme power of the universe toward which our religious life is naturally attracted. The idea of God as creator has tended to fade as epiphenomenalist and materialist views of the mind spread, because they provided no analogy for thinking of "downward causation" from superior to inferior beings. The general reductionism of the late modern worldview, according to which all causal action goes upward or sideways, has made the idea of causal influence from God in the evolutionary process seem completely out of place. This is one reason that the late modern worldview, in rejecting God as a scientific hypothesis, excludes not only supernaturalistic theism but any kind of divine influence. Understanding our own souls in terms of their psychokinetic potential, thereby moving away from epiphenomenalism or perhaps a form of interactionism near the epiphenomenalist end of the spectrum, we have an anological basis for seeing the supreme power of the universe as a Universal Soul through whose downward causal influence the various levels of order in our universe, from atoms to human, have been built up.

The idea suggested here is that of "continual creation." This idea does not exclude the possibility of a decisive event, a "big bang," at or at least near the beginning of our particular universe (what Whitehead calls "our cosmic epoch"). But we should not suppose that everything that now exists was implicit in the laws and particles extant at that time. In what sense could life and consciousness, including the Beethoven piano concertos and the Sermon on the Mount, be said to have been implicit in those early particles and laws, ready to be simply rolled out? (The word "evolution" did, in fact, originally have this meaning, but this conception of evolution has long been rejected.) That kind of big-bang deism is not only incoherent but also unnecessary. We can assume that the same cosmic mind that instilled the mathematical forms that we call the laws of physics into the process at the beginning could instill new forms, including not only the purely objective forms of mathematics but also the subjective forms involved in feeling and consciousness, all along the way, as they become relevant.

This kind of theistic evolutionism, with its idea of continual creation, has seemed impossible to the late modern mind. Even prior to the acceptance of the evolutionary account of the world, the idea of ongoing divine "providence" had already been widely given up, far more widely than in that small group of eighteenth-century thinkers labelled "deists." One of the major reasons for the decline in the sense of ongoing providential guidance was the mechanistic view of nature. This ontology produced a mind-body problem writ large: How could a Cosmic Mind exert causal influence on insentient matter, matter that can conceivably be moved only by the impact of other bits of matter? Given the sensationist theory of perception, furthermore, it was even impossible to assume that the emergence of life provided a window of opportunity for the divine influence: All living things were windowless monads except for their sensory equipment geared to detect other physical things. In this context, philosophers and theologians had to struggle to find some point of contact between the divine reality and the human mind, perhaps the "moral law within" (Kant) or the "feeling of absolute dependence" (Schleiermacher). Some such fragile connection being the only conceivable point of contact between God and the world, the idea of divine providential activity throughout nature withered. When the evolutionary perspective became accepted in scientific circles, philosophers and theologians had no conceptual tools for modifying Darwin's purely deistic conception, according to which the process proceeded mechanistically after God had created molecules and the laws of nature. With no way to see God as active in the evolutionary process, even the deistic conception of God came to seem otiose.

Parapsychological evidence helps overcome this centuries-old problem by giving additional support to a panexperientialist view of the universe. As we saw, a comparison of the evidence for telepathy and that for clairvoyance suggests that the mind-mind relation and the mind-matter relation are the same kind of relation. This suggests in turn that what we know from within as "mind" and what we know from without as "matter" are not, in themselves, different in kind. The fact that the mind's outgoing paranormal causal influence includes both thought-transference and psychokinetic changes in "inanimate matter" suggests the same thing. These parapsychological-based considerations are not, to be sure, the only or even the primary basis for accepting panexperientialism. Indeed, the case for it in Chapter 3 was made without reference to these parapsychological considerations. However, the prejudice in favor of the view of the elementary units of nature, and even living cells, as insentient is so great that the panexperientialist viewpoint can use all the help it can get. This evidence from parapsychology might be especially significant for data-led minds, for whom empirical evidence is more important than purely theoretical considerations.

In any case, with this panexperientialist view we can again see the world as led by divine providence as well as resulting from divine creation. More precisely, given the continual emergence of novel forms in cosmic, geological, chemical, biological and cultural evolution and in individual growth, we can identify these two doctrines, seeing providence as simply continuing creation.

With this conception, we can see the universe itself as a spiritual adventure, what Whitehead called the "Adventure in the Universe as One."[7] As a colleague's book title puts it, *God Has a Story Too*.[8] This gives us an even stronger basis for seeing our life as a spiritual journey. We can see our own spiritual adventure as part of the adventure being lived out by the Soul of the Universe.

The analogical basis for thinking of a divine creator offered by parapsychology goes beyond that provided by simple psychokinesis, in which locomotion is induced in inanimate things, as when strings or matchsticks are made to move. More suggestive is psychic photography, or "thoughtography," in which a complex pattern in the mind of the agent is impressed upon photographic film. Jule Eisenbud has suggested: "Perhaps God, to paraphrase those who would have him a mathematician, is the supreme thoughtographer."[9] Even more suggestive yet, of course, is full-out materialization, in which a material object is created.

At this point, however, it may seem that the psychokinetic power of the mind has supported more, by analogy, than is desired. Does not materialization involve creation out of nothing? Does it not by analogy, therefore, support an *ex nihilo* doctrine of the original creation of the universe? And does that not take us right back to the supernaturalistic form of theism, with all its problems?

It is certainly the case that the idea the universe was created *ex nihilo*, in the sense of an absolute absence of any realm of finite beings, events, or processes, leads back to supernaturalism. This idea of *creatio ex nihilo* can, in fact, be considered the fundamental support of the supernaturalistic idea of God. Only if God created our world from absolutely nothing would God have absolute control over this world. If God had instead created our world by, say, bringing order out of a pre-existing chaos of events, the more complex creatures formed out of the entities in the chaos might be thought to have a power of their own. There might be, furthermore, certain principles descriptive of the way finite things could be ordered that would set limits to what is really possible. In other words, the creator might, as Plato suggested, confront a certain "necessity" inherent in the nature of things so that divine creative agency would be persuasive, not coercive. The doctrine of *creatio ex nihilo* rejects this idea that the creator only does the best that can be done, given the recalcitrance of the world. God simply speaks, or wills, and it is done, exactly as God desired. Because all was created from nothing—and "nothing" cannot resist—there are no inherent finite powers and principles leading to a nexus of cause and effect that God cannot interrupt. If materialization suggested the possibility of creation *ex nihilo* in the absolute sense, then it would indeed provide aid and comfort to supernaturalists.

Materialization, however, does not imply this, but rather the creation of one kind of order out of another. For example, in settings where materializations have appeared, it is common for people to report feeling cold spots in the room. The information we have about this is anecdotal. The point is, however, that what evidence we do have does not support the idea that creation out of nothing is possible.

Besides not providing positive support for supernaturalistic theism, furthermore, psychokinesis undermines the remaining of its two major bases.

One of the traditional bases for the assumption that the Supreme Power of the universe has the overwhelming coercive power attributed to God by supernaturalism was the nonevolutionary view of the universe. When it was assumed, as it was in Jewish, Christian, and Islamic thought, that the world had been created in essentially its present form all at once, or at most in six days, it would have been impossible to have attributed exclusively persuasive power to the creator. Loving persuasion could not in six days have turned chaos into an atom or an apple, let alone an Adam and an Eve. The evolutionary picture of the world's origin, opened up by the subtle methods of modern science, has changed the situation dramatically. The six days have been turned into something like 15 billion years, which means that the creator had almost 100 billion times longer than had traditionally been thought. This is one place where a quantitative difference, a difference in degree, betokens a qualitative difference, a difference in kind. The evolutionary picture suggests that the creator's power is persuasive, evocative power, not coercive, controlling, all-determining power.

Some thinkers (such as Plato) and traditions (such as Hinduism and Buddhism) had, to be sure, already come to an evolutionary view of the formation of our universe without waiting for scientific developments of the 19th and 20th centuries. These scientific developments have, however, put those earlier intuitions on a solid basis. The question of how the process occurred, and even the question of how long it took, are not settled. But the fact that the process took many billions of years is no longer open to reasonable doubt. The inference from the creation to the coercive omnipotence of the creator is no longer cogent.

The other major basis for supernaturalism was the occurrence of "the miraculous." In medieval times, miracles were technically defined in terms of the scheme of primary and secondary causes. God was the primary cause of all events. Secondary causes were what are now called natural causes. The primary cause of conception, for example, was God; the secondary cause was the insemination of the mother by the father. All events had their primary causation from God, and most events had their secondary causation as well. Some few events, however, were caused directly by God's primary causation without the use of secondary causes. God could, for example, directly cause a virgin to become pregnant.

It is often argued that people in earlier times, including biblical times, did not have this concept of a "miracle" as an interruption of the natural causal nexus. It is true that they did not think in terms of the medieval scheme of primary and secondary causes and did not have the modern sense of the universe as an interconnected network of causes and effects. This should not be taken to mean, however, that these extraordinary events were not seen as signs of divine omnipotence, especially in the biblical tradition. For example, it was in relation to the story of an elderly woman's becoming pregnant that we get the fateful rhetorical question, "Is anything too hard for Yahweh?" (Genesis 18:14). (It matters not for the present discussion whether or not that particular event happened. The point is that the passage shows that events of the type that can without anachronism be called "paranormal," because they stood outside the normal causal patterns, were used as evidence of divine omnipotence.) Another well-known example from the Hebrew Testament is the story of the contest between Elijah and the prophets of Baal on Mount Carmel (I Kings 18:17-40). After the prophets of Baal had called on their God for many hours in vain, Elijah called on Yahweh and his offering was consumed by fire, even after having been soaked with water. This was taken as proof that Elijah's God, Yahweh, was the true God. In the Christian Testament, the idea that miraculous events are special divine interventions is pervasive. Usually the inference from the event to divine power is implicit but occasionally it is explicit. For example, both Mary, who had no husband, and her kinswoman Elizabeth, who was in her old age, could both become pregnant because "with God nothing will be impossible" (Luke 1:37).

It is surely difficult for us today, given either our belief that events of this nature did not happen or our parapsychological explanation of them, to realize the role they have played in Western thought. For most Christians, the miracles of Jesus, and especially the resurrection, have been taken as *the principle* evidence that he was divine, or at least God's anointed, and that Christianity was designated by God as the One True Religion. As we saw in Chapter 1, the fact that certain philosophies flourishing in the early seventeenth century allowed action at a distance as a fully natural phenomenon, thereby affording a naturalistic explanation of the Christian miracles, was a major motivation beyond the adoption of the mechanistic philosophy. Had the appeal to miracles been undermined, the chief cornerstone in the edifice of Christian apologetics would have crumbled.

An illustration from this period involving the Duke of Braunschweig-Luneberg, John Frederick, should be of particular interest to philosophers, because he was Leibniz's patron. Perhaps the best-known recurring miracles of the age were the levitations of Saint Joseph of Copertino. Joseph, an extremely pious young man from Copertino, Italy, became a monk in the Order of St. Francis in 1625. Reportedly, while rapt in prayer, he would sometimes, in broad daylight and in places where he could be observed by many people, levitate several feet off the floor or ground. Having heard of this phenomenon, John Frederick journeyed to Italy in 1649 in hopes of observing it with his own eyes. John Frederick evidently observed two of Joseph's levitations. On this basis, he converted from Protestantism to Catholicism, becoming convinced by this event that the Catholic branch of Christianity is the one that God sanctions.[10] If Leibniz's sponsor had heard instead about some such phenomenon in India and had travelled there and observed it, how might Western thought and history have differed?

In any case, given our present understanding of paranormal events—that they have occurred in virtually every time and place and often in connection with people who could hardly be considered special representatives of the deity—the second traditional basis for the supernaturalistic understanding of divine power has been undermined. This is perhaps parapsychology's chief negative importance, that it, in conjunction with knowledge of the evolutionary origin of our world, removes the grounds for the conceit of many of the religious traditions that they, their dogmas, and their rites have a supernatural origin and protection from error.

It could be said that there was yet another traditional reason for accepting divine omnipotence, the belief in infallible revelation and inspiration, and that this belief was undermined by the historical-critical study of the scriptures. It is true that the belief in supernaturalism and infallible deliverances are closely connected, as I said earlier, and also that the historical-critical study of the scriptures, by discrediting their infallibility, cast doubt on divine omnipotence, or at least on the belief that this divine omnipotence operated in history after the original creation of the world. (Deists held that it did not.) However, belief that the scriptures and their heroes were infallibly inspired was primarily an effect of the belief in divine omnipotence, rather than primarily a conclusion derived directly from studying the scriptures. Insofar as the scriptures themselves did seem to suggest their own supernatural inspiration, or at least that of their heroes, it was because of the miracles associated with the lives of these heroes (in the Christian Testament, primarily Jesus, Peter, and Paul). The decisive factor in discrediting divine omnipotence in relation to the production of the scriptures has, accordingly, been the rejection of miraculous events, either by rejecting the actual occurrence of the events themselves or by reinterpreting them as *paranormal* events. The former way of rejecting the miraculous has thus far been the dominant one in intellectual circles. It is unstable, however, because events of that nature keep happening. This fact, plus the late modern assumption that events of that nature would imply supernatural intervention if they did happen, allows supernaturalism to retain one of its bases. This basis will be finally undermined, allowing a naturalistic approach to all phenomena, only when the paranormal interpretation is widely accepted.

Christianity (as well as the other theistic traditions that do not already do so) should now, I am suggesting, take the route that it, partly by means of encouraging the adoption of the mechanical philosophy as the framework for natural science, explicitly rejected in the 17th century. It should see its miracles as extraordinary but not supernatural events, not different in kind in relation to divine causation from similar events in other traditions. This means giving up every pretense, even with regard to the resurrection of Jesus, that its originating events prove its uniquely divine origin. It should base its claim to truth—partial truth, of course—on its fruits, not its alleged roots. Its fruits can be spiritual, social, and philosophical effectiveness—in giving birth to transformed lives, in giving birth to a transformed social and international order in which the biblical vision of a world of justice and peace finally obtains, in giving birth to a philosophical description of the universe that can be commended in terms of its self-consistency, adequacy, and illuminating power. This focus on fruits instead of roots is an epistemic, not an ontological, point. That is, not resting the claim to truth on origins need not mean a lack of conviction that the divine reality was somehow especially present in the founding events of Christianity. The point is that this conviction should be supported in terms of the intrinsic merits of Christian belief and practice, not by appeals to external signs of that special divine presence.

By taking the opposite route in the 17th century, Christianity took, in effect, an all-or-nothing approach. With regard to the human soul: Christian thought sought to guarantee its immortal nature *a priori* by defining it as absolutely different in kind from the rest of creation, thereby risking the possibility, already foreshadowed in Hobbes, that the existence of the soul would be denied altogether, which came about through the combined effect of conceptual incoherence and empirical disproof (through evidence of evolution). With regard to God: Being unwilling to live with the consequences of a naturalistic theism, as offered by the pantheistic and especially the panentheistic options of the day, Christian thought insisted on a God absolutely omnipotent over the universe, thereby risking disproof, which came about through the historical-critical study of the scriptures, evidence of evolution, and the problem of evil. With regard to paranormal phenomena in both biblical and contemporary times: Christianity sought, by defining nature and human perception so as to make such phenomena impossible naturally, to use them to prove the unique divine origin of (and, for Catholics, continued divine attestation to) Christianity, thereby risking the possibility that the reality of such phenomena would be denied altogether, which, of course, also occurred. This led to the further discrediting of the Christian scriptures (as filled with "myth") and of various religious practices, such as spiritual healing. Christianity in the 17th century, through those founders of the modern worldview who, in terms of our present distinctions, were theologians and philosophers as well as scientists, took a big gamble and lost. Of course, the losers have been Christians and the world in general in the following centuries. It is time, now that we realize what happened, belatedly to take the road rejected then. Parapsychology can be decisive in this change of course.

Parapsychology, by helping to overcome the supernaturalistic form of theism, aids the cause of theism itself. As mentioned above, one of the major reasons for the transition from supernaturalism to atheism was the problem of evil. If God were all-powerful as well as all-good, there would be no genuine evil in the world. Leibniz's answer, that there *is* no genuine evil—that this is "the best of all possible worlds"—was simply a rephrasing of the orthodox Christian position that had obtained at least since Augustine. In the 18th century, however, it would no longer wash: The "Enlightenment" meant that doctrines could no longer be defended on the basis of authority and with appeals to "mystery" whenever a contradiction arose; they had to commend themselves on the basis of reason and experience. Voltaire's merciless parody of Leibniz's position in *Candide* was, while in one sense unfair (Leibniz had never denied that lots of rotten things happen), in another sense appropriate: It represented the refusal to agree to a dogma whose falsity we all inevitably presuppose in practice, the dogma that everything that happens is for the best, all things considered. By helping undermine the idea of divine omnipotence, parapsychology helps us reconcile theism with the fact of genuine evil, a fact that no one can consistently deny. It allows us to do this, furthermore, without following the route taken by many recent thinkers, including Carl Jung, which is to compromise the perfect goodness of God. With a naturalistic theism, we can affirm without qualification the two dimensions implied in our idea of a Holy Reality: perfect in goodness as well as supreme in power.

5. OUR EXPERIENCE OF GOD AND VALUES

A fifth presupposition of the view of human life as a spiritual journey, beyond the existence and power of both the soul and God, is the capacity of the soul to experience both God and divinely-rooted values.

One of the major reasons for doubting the reality of genuine religious experience—genuine in the sense of involving real contact with a Numinous Reality—has been the assumption that all perception of realities beyond ourselves is through our physical senses and is thereby limited to physical things. As John Bowker has shown in *The Sense of God*,[11] the major sociological, anthropological, and psychological theories of religion in late modernity— those of Feuerbach, Marx, Comte, Durkheim, and Freud—have been based on the assumption that all so-called religious experience must be inauthentic. Given that assumption, these thinkers had a major problem: how to explain why people in every time and place have been religious. These thinkers, or at least their followers, could have disabused themselves of this assumption—if they had wanted to be so disabused—by examining the evidence for extrasensory perception. (Actually, as mentioned earlier, Freud did, after having been hostile to the possibility of extrasensory perception [a conflict over the paranormal was evidently one of the main reasons for the break between Freud and Jung], eventually come to accept it;[12] his view of religion, however, had long since been settled.) The sensationist doctrine of perception led also, as we have seen, to the denial of genuine moral and aesthetic experience—genuine in the sense of involving real contact with objectively existing moral and aesthetic values. This denial lies behind the widespread moral and aesthetic subjectivism and relativism of our age. With this development, our lives cannot even be seen as moral or aesthetic journeys, in which we could become more appreciative of, and more conformed to, higher values, because no objective distinction between higher and lower values is thought to exist.

Early modernity did not intend, as mentioned in Chapter 1, to lead to a denial of the possible truth of religious and axiological assertions. One of the motives behind the sensationist epistemology was, to be sure, to rule out "enthusiasm," the claim made by Quakers, Ranters, and others to be directly filled by God (en-thused). The denial of this possibility by John Locke, for example, did not seem to him, given his supernaturalism, to threaten the doctrine of the incarnation: Jesus did not need to have religious experience of God; Jesus *was* God. We did not need religious experience to know religious truth because we could read in the New Testament the revelation provided by Jesus. Even deistic thinkers, such as Thomas Jefferson, who could not accept Locke's view of a divine intervention in history in Jesus, could be sanguine about the possibility of knowing objective values, in spite of the sensationist veto on a direct "intuition" of them, given their retention of a supernatural creator. They could explain our obvious knowledge of values, implicit in our judgments of some things as morally better or more beautiful than other things, on the assumption that God had implanted in our souls an innate knowledge of values.[13]

The death of God—of the supernatural creator—and therefore of this God's supernaturally created human soul led to the widespread relativism and nihilism of the late modern period. All the traumas, both individual and civilizational, that have resulted from these developments followed significantly from the decision, made in the 17th and 18th centuries, to rule out *natural* religious, moral, and aesthetic knowledge.

We cannot, of course, change the past. What we can do, however, is finally to realize that our religious, moral, and aesthetic knowledge, like our scientific knowledge, is based on direct perception.

The fact that religious, moral, and aesthetic knowledge is based primarily on nonsensory perception should not make it seem less empirical (experientially based) than scientific knowledge, for two reasons. First, nonsensory perception is our *fundamental* mode of perception, so that science, insofar as it is based on sensory perception, is based on a derivative mode of perception. Second, science is also directly based on nonsensory perception, in two ways. On the one hand, insofar as science is based on both mathematics and logic, it is based on things whose status in the nature of things is similar to that of moral and aesthetic values and principles and must be known in the same way: through nonsensory perception—which we often call "intuition." (I hereby side with the position that mathematical as well as logical truths are discovered, not invented—which is fairly obvious once one has no metaphysical prejudice against the idea that nonphysical objects can truly exist and be apprehended.) On the other hand, although natural science's explicit data (aside from its mathematical data) are based on sensory perceptions, the categories it uses to interpret them—such as an actual world, causality, and time—are based on nonsensory perception, as pointed out in Chapter 3. Accordingly, in terms of nonsensory and sensory perception, the difference between theology (or philosophy of religion), ethics, and aesthetics, on the one hand, and the natural sciences, on the other, is only a difference of degree. (I leave aside the question of the social or human sciences, in which the difference is still less.)

This constructively postmodern way of overcoming the absolute difference between the natural sciences and the humanities should be preferred by most, I would think, to the way proposed by deconstructive postmodernists. Richard Rorty, for example, dislikes late modern scientism, according to which science alone is cognitive (capable of being true or false), whereas everything else, such as literary theory (with which he is especially concerned), is noncognitive. Rorty's way of putting science on all fours with the humanities is to declare that scientific assertions are also noncognitive, simply a matter of taste. One of his moves is to reject the correspondence theory of truth, so that "truth" is simply that which we find useful.[14] I mention this drastic solution to pose a question to people who want to overcome late modernity's invidious distinction between the sciences and the humanities but may still be nervous about appealing to nonsensory perception. I am asking which alternative they prefer (assuming that they cannot come up with a viable third).

In any case, parapsychology, by giving evidence of nonsensory perception, sometimes quite dramatic evidence, provides scientific disconfirmation of the sensationist theory of perception, which has been one of the two major bases for assuming that we can have no perceptual knowledge of values (the other basis being the assumption that values have no objective existence in the nature of things). Parapsychology thereby proves itself to be not only, as J. B. Rhine suggested, religion's science,[15] but ethics' science and aesthetics' science as well.

To accept parapsychology's help here, I should perhaps remind the wary reader, one need not accept the reliability of all, or a majority, or even 10% of the evidence generally put forth by advocates of parapsychology as reliable. William James's point about crows—made precisely in relation to the sensationist dogma—still stands: It takes only one white crow to prove that all crows are not black. Can a person honestly examine a sizable amount of the evidence and conclude that not a single case suggests the reality of nonsensory perception? If not, then a revolution in thought should be in order.

I have suggested, in agreement with Whitehead, that we experience moral and aesthetic values by means of our prehension of God. We should not, however, reduce the importance of our experience of God to this dimension of it, in spite of its extreme importance. The direct experience of God is important in its own right, as experience of the Holy Reality *as* Holy. Many people have given testimony to having had what can be called a religious experience in the strong sense, namely, an overwhelming experience of a numinous presence, of the presence of something described as totally loving. Well-known collections of such testimonies have been published by William James in *The Varieties of Religious Experience* and Richard Maurice Bucke in *Cosmic Consciousness.*[16] (Both James, a world-renowned psychologist, and Bucke, a prominent professor of psychiatry, argued against the fashionable reductionist view that such experiences could be dismissed as psychopathic.) Testimonies to this kind of experience have become common again in recent decades in reports of out-of-body experiences, especially those that occur in near-death situations.

The possibility that we could have a direct experience of the mind or soul of the universe is supported, by analogy, by the evidence for telepathy. (In our experience of God, however, there would be no "distance" involved, assuming, as do both traditional theism and panentheism, the all-pervasiveness of God.) Such experiences support the conception of one's life as a spiritual journey. They not only reinforce the belief in the bare existence of a Holy Power we can call God. They also provide direct experiential support for the conviction that this power is truly *Holy*, that is, of infinite intrinsic worth, and therefore that it is *the* reality in relation to which it is appropriate to order one's life. These experiences thereby elevate the importance of spiritual issues, in relation to egoistic and materialistic concerns, making it seem appropriate to understand one's identity *primarily* as a person on a spiritual journey. This new understanding lies at the heart of the transformative effects so often reported after near-death experiences.

Parapsychology, besides helping to provide a basis for taking such experiences seriously rather than as signs of psychiatric disorder, also provides an analogy for suspecting that they represent merely an extreme form of experience that is being enjoyed all the time. As suggested in Chapter 3, we probably are having, at an unconscious level, direct prehensions of other extrasomatic things, including other human minds, all the time. What is usually called "extrasensory perception," accordingly, is probably unusual only in that occasionally this constant direct nonsensory prehension of other minds or things rises to the conscious portion of one's experience. By analogy, we would be having direct experiences of the Holy Reality all the time. Those very rare experiences in which we have a religious experience in the strong sense, a numinous experience, would be unusual only in rising, in those rare moments, to consciousness. The constant but generally unconscious experience of God could account, then, for our presupposition, even if we consciously affirm otherwise, that there is something of ultimate intrinsic worth. This idea, incidentally, would fit with James' thesis that the kinds of experiences reported in *The Varieties of Religious Experience* are simply extreme versions of experiences common to everyone.

This experience of the divine experience, analogous to telepathic experience of other finite minds, may also be important for moral experience beyond the way mentioned above. There I spoke of our prehension of God's appetitive envisagement of values, what Whitehead called God's "primordial nature." Abraham Heschel has suggested that the Hebrew prophets spoke out of an experience of the divine "pathos," God's suffering with the poor and oppressed.[17] This idea corresponds with Whitehead's suggestion that we can also have a prehension of God's "consequent nature," which is God's sympathetic response to the world: God's delight in the joys of the creatures and compassion with their sufferings. Parapsychology can allow us to take Heschel's suggestion more seriously than we otherwise might. On the basis of this suggestion, furthermore, we can understand conceptually the claim by Christian liberation theologians that Christ is especially present among the poor. "Christ" here would refer to God as revealed by Jesus, especially on the cross: God as suffering love.

6. OUR CONTINUING JOURNEY

Another reason the conception of human life as a spiritual journey has faded in modern times is the decline in belief in life beyond bodily death. It is very difficult to believe that this life itself should be conceived as a spiritual journey if this journey is to come to an end so soon. Because of our awareness of the tremendous gap between the real and the ideal—between what we are now and what we sense we should be—it is hard to orient this life around a movement toward the ideal if this life be all we have. Why start out on a journey if it in all likelihood we will not traverse even one-tenth of the distance? The quip "God give me patience, and give it too me right now!" expresses, beyond the humor, the sense that this life is far too short in comparison with the number of virtues we would have to incarnate to make any significant movement toward sanctification, or what Eastern Orthodoxy calls "deification."

Besides the psychological problem of motivation, there is the conceptual problem of belief. We may not accept Kant's formulation of the good life in terms of a match between virtue and happiness, and we may not accept his argument for immortality based thereon: that unless we can believe that dutiful souls obedient to the moral law will eventually enjoy the happiness they deserve, we cannot believe in the moral law itself. We can, nevertheless, agree with the intuition behind the argument: Unless we can believe that lives lived as spiritual journeys will have time to reach their destination, we probably cannot believe that the universe in any sense intends them to be spiritual journeys.

We have seen, in Chapters 3 through 8, that a postmodern philosophical account of the mind-body relation, combined with empirical evidence, both direct and indirect, can overcome the late modern conviction that life after death is impossible or at least highly improbable. That argumentation and evidence need not be rehearsed. Two other kinds of objections, however, require discussion.

One objection to the idea that our journey in this life continues after separation from the physical body, an objection that can be based on several considerations, is that any such existence of the soul would be timeless.

One possible basis for this idea is the conception of God as eternal in the sense of timeless. That view, however, is rejected in the panentheism advocated here. God's "primordial nature" can be considered eternal, to be sure, but it is merely an abstract aspect of God. God as a whole, which Whitehead calls God's "consequent nature," is not eternal but everlasting. The temporal process is real for God.

A second basis on which some have assumed that a discarnate existence would be timeless is the idea that time is the result of physical processes. A widespread idea has been that the "arrow of time" is derived from entropy, which presupposes the existence of atoms in a highly organized state. Once we are free from the body with its entropic decay, this argument goes, we will be free from time. The truth, however, is almost the opposite. As discussed in Chapter 3, if atoms were truly devoid of experience, no real time would be involved in their activities. The so-called arrow of time provided by entropic processes is not irreversible in principle, therefore not time in the real sense of the word. The temporal distinctions of past, present, and future are functions of experience, with its "now" dividing the settled past and the still-to-be settled future. The existence of a discarnate soul, accordingly, would be fully temporal. It may well be true, as I suggested in relation to out-of-body experiences in Chapter 8, that we in a discarnate state might have a significantly altered sense of time, in that we would no longer be subconsciously experiencing the rhythms of our various bodily members. But that is completely different from literal timelessness.

A third basis for assuming that postcarnate existence, if actual, would be nontemporal has been so-called precognitive experiences. A widespread assumption among believers in true precognition has been that such experiences provide revelatory glimpses of the real nature of reality: as timeless. Such experiences have probably, in fact, played a decisive role in the history of thought, both East and West. Just as psychokinetic events have been a major reason for attributing omnipotence to God, ostensible precognitive experiences have been a major reason for thinking that God—or Brahman, or the Tao, or Ultimate Reality—is timeless. This idea, combined with the (dubious) assumption that separation from the body will mean a sudden breakthrough from Appearance to Reality, has contributed to the belief that post-bodily existence would be post-temporal. As we have seen in Chapter 2, however, besides the fact that true precognition is an incoherent idea, there are many ways to interpret the experiences without compromising the reality of time. Such experi-

ences provide no good basis, accordingly, for assuming that reality is not ultimately temporal.

The objections addressed thus far to the idea of a continuing journey
past bodily death have all been ontological and epistemological objections,
those raised by our rational and empirical concerns. Much of the animus against
belief in life after death in modern times, however, has been rooted in fearful
thinking: the conviction either that life after death itself is undesirable or that
belief in it is harmful. This basis for rejecting belief in life after death, mentioned only in passing in Chapter 3, will be addressed briefly here.

One reason that some people hope that there is no life after death is that
they have a negative picture of it. Life after death may seem *aesthetically* unattractive, especially when thought of as continuing forever, as when people suspect that "heaven" would be boring, or as when Karl Popper considers the
prospect of immortality "utterly frightening."[18] Or life after death may seem
morally repellent. Many moralists have rightly been offended by the suggestion
that the main reason to be moral is the anticipation of rewards and punishments after death. Another source of moral repulsion has been the idea that
those who did not believe or do the right things in the present life, perhaps
through no fault of their own, will be condemned to everlasting torment. Such
views, besides being morally repellent, have often added an inordinate fear of
death to the already difficult task of living.

There is, however, no necessary connection between the idea of life after
death as such and any particular conception of it, such as the view that it
involves rewards and punishments. Many other ideas of life after death, without
those unattractive features, have been envisaged, often on the basis of purported empirical evidence. The idea of life after death, furthermore, does not
necessarily imply *immortality*, in the sense of a form of existence that would
continue literally forever. There might be, for example, truth in the idea that it
is karmic activity, activity with desire, that is self-perpetuating. It might be, in
other words, that we would continue to exist only as long as we still had unful-
filled desires. The point here, however, is not whether this idea is true, but
only that the idea of a continuing life as such should not be bound to any ideas
with which it has contingently been associated.

An objection to *belief* in life after death is that it has given power to
dubious organizations. The classical example is the idea that the Christian
Church has been given the "keys to the kingdom," so that being in good standing with the church is a precondition for being consigned to heaven instead of
hell. A more contemporary example is the power that certain televangelists
have acquired over people's consciences—and pocketbooks—with their preach-
ing of the One And Only Way To Heaven.

Again, the reply is similar: There is no necessary connection between life
after death and the idea that some particular organization or theology is the
gateway to this afterlife.

Another objection to the belief in life after death is that it has served as an opiate: Whether the belief system has said that God at the last judgment will punish the wicked and vindicate the oppressed or that reincarnation with its law of karma explains why some are fortunate and others unfortunate in this life, the belief in a future life has undermined the passion to achieve justice here and now.

Again, there is no necessary connection between belief in life after death and any of these conceptions of rewards and punishments. Indeed, as Ian Stevenson has shown in *Cases of the Reincarnation Type*, there is not even any necessary connection between belief in reincarnation and acceptance of the so-called law of karma: Many peoples have accepted reincarnation without thinking in terms of karmic rewards and punishments.[19]

A more recent objection to belief in life after death is that it makes people complacent about the fate of the earth in the face of threats to its continued viability through nuclear or more gradual ecological destruction. People who believe in God and an afterlife, it is said, think that the earth is dispensable: If we destroy this world, God can simply create another one, and, in any case, our real life will be in an immaterial heaven.

There has certainly been too much of this kind of thinking around. This view was expressed by a person who occupied, of all offices, that of the Secretary of the Interior of the United States (James Watt). It may have even been held by the president who appointed him (Ronald Reagan). In any case, this consequence, while following from some ideas of God and a future life, by no means follows from all of them.

Most of these objections, in fact, presuppose the supernaturalistic idea of a deity who unilaterally and arbitrarily determines things, overriding any power that the creatures may have. This is clearly true of the idea of a last judgment with consignment to heaven or hell, the idea that God has given a particular institution the keys to the afterlife, the idea that the next life will consist of rewards and punishments, and the idea that God could simply create a new world if this one is destroyed. Even the law of karma is often presented less as a law of natural consequences than as a law of imposed rewards and punishments. Accordingly, by undermining the reasons for holding a supernaturalistic form of theism, we have already undermined at least most of the objections that have been voiced against either the idea of life after death as such or the belief in it.

Besides the fact that the reasons for rejecting belief in life after death based on fearful thinking can be countered, reasons for favoring the belief can also be given.

The belief can help overcome the inordinate fear of death that has been characteristic of the late modern world.

The belief can help give people the courage to fight for freedom, social justice, and ecologically sustainable policies. The Marxist argument can in a sense be turned upside down: The state, or any group with superior force at its disposal, has coercive power over our bodies. The belief that we *are* our bodies, at least that our identities are inextricably tied up with the fate of our bodies, gives the state and other military organizations power over our identities. People who believe otherwise have a basis for seeing that they, in their essential identities, are not subject to any earthly power.

The belief in a continuing journey after biological death can help people develop a greater love for the universe through the conviction that the great unfairness characteristic of the present life, especially for human beings, is not the final word. Those who had their lives ended prematurely, or for some other reason had little chance in this life, will have further opportunities to develop their potentialities and experience happiness.

The belief in life after death can help individuals and our civilization as a whole overcome the extremely materialistic view of life that has characterized the modern world, especially the late modern world. This materialistic view, with its belief that the very meaning of life is tied up with the control, possession, and use of material goods, has contributed greatly to the ecological destruction of nature and will lead to increasing militarism as resource wars become ever more the focus of international relations.

Finally, the belief that we are on a spiritual journey, a journey in which there will be sufficient travel time to reach our destination, can motivate us to think creatively about things we can do now, socially and even internationally as well as individually, to help ourselves move closer here and now to what we should be. The doctrine that the way we now behave reflects our essential nature has been the basis for political "realism," the dominant political philosophy of our time. The idea that human beings are *by nature* selfish, greedy, and power-hungry, and therefore always will be, has been the basis for the "realist" dogma that war and its threat are permanent features of the international order. The idea that human sanctification will never progress far enough to make a world without war possible has been a central ingredient in the "Christian realism" of Reinhold Niebuhr. The idea that we are not headed towards sanctification, in other words, has served to block creative thinking. The idea that what we are now is what we essentially are has left political thinkers content with the present system. If we were as a culture, however, to come to the belief that our present lives are simply small parts of a longer journey, a journey in which we will become transfigured, then we might be motivated to find an international order that would enable us to live more in harmony with the peaceable selves we are ultimately destined to be. This is, of course, one version of the argument for the political relevance of utopian thinking.

These final two considerations, together, have become central in my own thinking. I believe the human race now faces the greatest challenge in its history. If it continues on its present course, widespread misery and death of unprecedented proportions is a certainty within the next century or two.

Annihilation of human life, and of millions of other species as well, is probable. This is so because of polluting technologies, economic growth-mania, out-of-control population growth, global apartheid between rich and poor nations, rapid depletion of nonrenewable resources, and proliferation of nuclear weapons combined with a state of international anarchy that makes war inevitable and sufficient measures to halt global ecological destruction impossible. What is needed is the creation of a new international order that can address the above problems quickly enough. There will be tremendous obstacles, especially in the rich and powerful nations. The rich would have to give up their "right" to remain so much richer than the poor. The powerful would have to give up their "right" to intervene militarily, whether overtly or covertly, in the affairs of the weak. All would have to give up the ideology of the domination of nature for short-term human benefit in favor of a sustainable harmony. That we will find the wisdom and the courage to do this is highly questionable.

What seems clear, however, is that such a transition in world *order*, if it is to occur, will have to be accompanied by a widespread shift in world*view*, one that would lead to a new sense of adventure, one replacing the modern adventure of unending economic growth based on the technological subjugation of nature and the military and/or economic subjugation of weaker peoples. Only, I am convinced, if we come to see human life as primarily a spiritual adventure, an adventurous journey that continues beyond this life, will we have a chance of becoming sufficiently free from destructive modern motivations to effect a transition to a sustainable global order. Here, of course, I have only stated my belief; an argument for all this will have to wait for a subsequent book.[20]

NOTES

1. Parapsychology and Postmodern Philosophy

1. See C. D. Broad, *Religion, Philosophy, and Psychical Research* (New York: Humanities Press, 1969) and *Lectures on Psychical Research* (London: Routledge and Kegan Paul, 1962).

2. John W. Godbey, Jr., "Central-State Materialism and Parapsychology," in Jan Ludwig, *Philosophy and Parapsychology* (Buffalo: Prometheus Books, 1978), 401–04 (reprinted from *Analysis* 36 [1975], 22–25).

3. C. E. M. Hansel, *ESP: A Scientific Evaluation* (New York: Scribner's, 1966); *ESP and Parapsychology: A Critical Reevaluation* (Buffalo: Prometheus Books, 1980).

4. The address for the *Journal of the American Society for Psychical Research* is 5 West 73rd Street, New York, NY 10023. The address for the *Journal of the Society for Psychical Research* is 49 Marloes Road, London W8 6LA, England.

5. For good surveys of the results of parapsychological investigations, see Richard S. Broughton, *Parapsychology: The Controversial Science* (New York: Ballantine Books, 1991); John White and Edgar D. Mitchell, ed., *Psychic Exploration: A Challenge for Science* (New York: G. P. Putnam's Sons, 1974); Benjamin Wolman, ed., *Handbook of Parapsychology* (New York: Van Nostrand Reinhold, 1977); Hoyt Edge, Robert Morris, John Palmer, and Joseph Rush, *Foundations of Parapsychology* (Boston and London: Routledge and Kegan Paul, 1986); and Stanley Krippner, *Advances in Parapsychological Research* (6 vols.), 1977, 1978, 1982, 1984, 1987, 1990.

6. Most of the main extant journals in English are mentioned in notes 4 and 8; another is the *European Journal of Parapsychology* (Department of Psychology, University of Edinburgh, 7 George Square, Edinburgh EH8 9JZ, Scotland). Parapsychology is also one of the central concerns of the *Journal of the Society for Scientific Exploration* (Pergamon Press, Fairview Park, Elmsford, NY 10523).

7. See Walter Franklin Prince, *The Case of Patience Worth* (1927; New Hyde Park, N.Y.: University Books, 1964), and Irving Litvag, *Singer in the Shadows: The Strange Story of Patience Worth* (New York: Macmillan, 1972).

8. The address for the *Journal of Parapsychology* is Box 6847, College Station, Durham, NC 27708.

9. J. R. Ravetz, "The Varieties of Scientific Experience," *The Sciences and Theology in the Twentieth Century*, ed. Arthur Peacocke (Notre Dame, Ind.: University of Notre Dame Press, 1981), 197–206, at 200–01 (italics added).

10. Mary Hesse, *Forces and Fields: The Concept of Action at a Distance in the History of Physics* (Totowa, N.J.: Littlefield, Adams, and Co., 1965), 118, 125, 291.

11. Richard Westfall, *Never at Rest: A Biography of Isaac Newton* (Cambridge and New York: Cambridge University Press, 1980), 15–16.

12. Ibid., 381.

13. Brian Easlea, *Witch Hunting, Magic and the New Philosophy: An Introduction to the Debates of the Scientific Revolution 1450–1750* (Atlantic Highlands, N.J.: Humanities Press, 1980), 93–95, 108–15, 121, 132, 135.

14. Westfall, *Never at Rest*, 390.

15. Ibid., 464.

16. Ibid.

17. Ibid., 505.

18. Robert E. Schofield, *Mechanism and Materialism: British Natural Philosophy in an Age of Reason* (Princeton: Princeton University Press, 1970), 115–24.

19. Westfall, *Never at Rest*, 644.

20. Keith Thomas, *Religion and the Decline of Magic* (New York: Charles Scribner's Sons, 1971), 577–78; Hugh Trevor-Roper, *The European Witch Craze of the Sixteenth and Seventeenth Centuries and Other Essays* (New York: Harper & Row, 1969), 132–33; Moody Prior, "Joseph Glanvill, Witchcraft and Seventeenth-Century Science," *Modern Philosophy* 30 (1932–1933), 167–93.

21. Easlea, *Witch Hunting* 94–95, 108–15, 138, 158, 210; James Jacob, *Robert Boyle and the English Revolution* (New York: Franklin, Burt Publishers, 1978), 162–76.

22. Robert Lenoble, *Mersenne ou la naissance du méchanisme* (Paris: Librairie Philosophique J. Vrin, 1943), 133, 157–58, 210, 375, 381.

23. Alan Kors and Edward Peters, *Witchcraft in Europe 1100–1700* (Philadelphia: University of Pennsylvania Press, 1972).

24. Easlea, *Witch Hunting* 1, 196–201; Lenoble, *Mersenne*, 18, 89–96.

25. Eugene Klaaren, *Religious Origins of Modern Science: Belief in Creation in Seventeenth-Century Thought* (Grand Rapids, Mich.: William B. Eerdmans, 1977), 173–77; Alexandre Koyré, *From the Closed World to the Infinite Universe* (Baltimore, Md.: Johns Hopkins Press, 1968), 178–84, 210–13.

26. Jacob, *Robert Boyle*, 172; Easlea, *Witch Hunting*, 113, 234–35; Klaaren, *Religious Origins*, 173–77; Koyré, *From the Closed World*, 178–84, 210–13.

27. *The Notion of Nature*, Vol. IV of *The Works of the Honorable Robert Boyle* (London: Miller, 1744), 363.

28. C. D. Broad, *Religion, Philosophy and Psychical Research* (see note 1), 7–26.

29. Ibid., 9.

30. Jane Duran, "Philosophical Difficulties with Paranormal Knowledge Claims," *Philosophy of Science and the Occult*, ed. Patrick Grim (Albany: State University of New York Press, 1982), 192–206, at 202.

31. Keith Campbell, *Body and Mind*, 2d ed. (Notre Dame: University of Notre Dame Press, 1984), 55.

32. John J. McDermott, ed., *The Writings of William James* (New York: Random House, 1967), 787.

33. William James, "Address of the President before the Society for Psychical Research (1896)," in James, *Essays in Psychical Research* (Cambridge: Harvard University Press, 1986), 127–37, at 131.

34. Campbell, *Body and Mind*, 135.

35. Ibid., 131.

36. Ibid., 132.

37. I owe this term to Susan Haack, "Double-Aspect Foundherentism: A New Theory of Empirical Justification," *Philosophy and Phenomenological Research* LIII/1 (March 1993), 113–28, at 116n.8.

38. McDermott, *The Writings of William James*, 787.

39. Reported by W. F. Barrett, "Address by the President," *Proceedings of the Society for Psychical Research* 18 (1904), 323.

40. Alfred North Whitehead, *Modes of Thought* (New York: Free Press, 1968), 3.

41. Eugene Taylor, ed., *William James on Exceptional Mental States* (Amherst: University of Massachusetts Press, 1984), 109; quoted by Marcus P. Ford, "William James," in *Founders of Constructive Postmodern Philosophy: Peirce, James, Bergson, Whitehead, and Hartshorne*, by David Ray Griffin, John B. Cobb, Jr., Marcus Peter Ford, Pete A. Y. Gunter, and Peter Ochs (Albany: State University of New York Press, 1993), 91–92.

42. Crookes's statement is quoted by Stephen E. Braude in *The Limits of Influence: Psychokinesis and the Philosophy of Science* (New York and London: Routledge and Kegan Paul, 1986), 86.

43. See Carl G. Jung, *Memories, Dreams, Reflections*, recorded and edited by Aniela Jaffe, rev. ed. (New York: Vintage Books, 1965), 150.

44. William James, *The Will to Believe* (Cambridge: Harvard University Press, 1979), 19; quoted by Ford, "William James," 107.

45. See James W. McClendon, Jr., and James M. Smith, *Understanding Religious Convictions* (Notre Dame, Ind.: University of Notre Dame Press, 1975).

46. See Jule Eisenbud, *The World of Ted Serios* (New York: Morrow, 1967) and *Parapsychology and the Unconscious* (Berkeley: North Atlantic Books, 1983). Braude's accolade is on the back cover of the latter book.

47. John G. Taylor, *Superminds: An Enquiry into the Paranormal* (London: Macmillan; New York: Viking, 1975).

48. Taylor, *Science and the Supernatural* (London: T. Smith; New York: Dutton, 1980), 164.

49. Ibid., 6.

50. Ibid., 165.

51. Ibid., 4.

52. William James, "What Psychical Research Has Accomplished," *Essays in Psychical Research*, 89–106, at 90.

53. See Herbert Thurston, S. J., *The Physical Phenomena of Mysticism* (London: Burns Oates, 1952); D. Scott Rogo, *Miracles: A Parascientific Inquiry into Wondrous Phenomena* (Chicago: Contemporary Books, 1983), which, besides covering much of the same material as Thurston's book, also adds some more recent examples; and Michael Murphy, *The Future of the Body: Explorations into the Further Evolution of Human Nature* (Los Angeles: Jeremy Tarcher, 1992).

54. See the books cited above in n. 5.

55. James, "What Psychical Research Has Accomplished" (a partly different essay from the one with the same name cited in n. 52), *William James on Psychical Research*, ed. Gardner Murphy and Robert O. Ballou (New York: The Viking Press, 1960), 25–47, at 25, 26.

56. James, *The Will to Believe*, 236; quoted by Ford, "William James," 111.

57. C. D. Broad, *Religion, Philosophy and Psychical Research*, 9.

58. A few philosophers who have expressed this view are D. M. Armstrong, *A Materialist Theory of Mind* (London: Routledge & Kegal Paul, 1968), 364; Herbert Feigl, "Mind-Body, *Not* a Pseudoproblem," *Dimensions of Mind*, ed. Sydney Hook (New York: New York University Press, 1960), 24–36, at 28–29; and Keith Campbell, *Body and Mind*, 33, 91–96.

59. This interpretation of precognition is given by, for example, J. G. Pratt, *Parapsychology: An Insider's View of ESP* (New York: Doubleday, 1964), 167, and Bob Brier, *Precognition and the Philosophy of Science* (New York: Humanities Press, 1974), 174.

60. Whitehead, *Science and the Modern World* (1925; New York: Free Press, 1967).

61. Whitehead, *Process and Reality: An Essay in Cosmology* (original ed. 1929), corrected edition, ed. David Ray Griffin and Donald W. Sherburne (New York: Free Press, 1978).

62. *Science and the Modern World*, vii.

63. On Whitehead as postmodern philosopher, see my introduction and Cobb's chapter on Whitehead in Griffin et al., *Founders of Constructive Postmodern Philosophy*.

64. Whitehead, *Essays in Science and Philosophy* (New York: Philosophical Library, 1948), 129.

65. Whitehead, *Science and the Modern World*, 114.

66. Whitehead, *The Function of Reason* (1929; Boston: Beacon Press, 1958), 61.

67. *Essays in Science and Philosophy*, 227.

68. *Science and the Modern World*, 184–86.

69. Ibid., 157.

70. Whitehead, *Adventures of Ideas* (1937; New York: Free Press, 1967), 224.

71. Ibid., 225.

72. Ibid., 280.

73. *Science and the Modern World*, 150.

74. *Process and Reality*, 162.

75. Ibid., 308.

76. *Adventures of Ideas*, 186.

2. WHITE CROWS ABOUNDING: EVIDENCE FOR THE PARANORMAL

1. *William James on Psychical Research*, ed. Gardner Murphy and Robert O. Ballou (Clifton, N.J.: Augustus M. Kelley, 1973), 40–41.

2. Ibid., 41.

3. Richard S. Broughton, *Parapsychology: The Controversial Science* (New York: Ballantine, 1991), 299.

4. This statement occurs in a chapter titled "The Nature of Evidence in Matters Extraordinary" in Edmund Gurney, *Tertium Quid* (London: Kegan, Paul, Trench & Co., 1887), Vol. I: 227–73, at 264.

5. Henry Sidgwick, "President's Address," *Proceedings of the Society for Psychical Research* 1 (1883), 7–12.

6. Henry Sidgwick, *The Methods of Ethics* (London: Macmillan, 1874).

7. C. D. Broad, *Religion, Philosophy and Psychical Research: Selected Essays* (1953; New York: Humanities Press, 1969), 86.

8. Ibid., 94.

9. Ibid., 87, 108–09.

10. Quoted in ibid., 97.

11. Ibid., 115.

12. Ibid., 114.

13. *William James on Psychical Research*, 31–32.

14. Ibid., 310.

15. Ibid., 40.

16. Ibid., 41.

17. Ibid., 317, 322.

18. Ibid., 108–10.

19. Ibid., 321.

20. Ibid., 209.

21. Ibid., 310.

22. Alan Gauld, *The Founders of Psychical Research* (New York: Schocken Books, 1968), 115–16, 139, 182, 186–93, 255–56, 267–68, 275, 337–38.

23. Stephen E. Braude, *The Limits of Influence: Psychokinesis and the Philosophy of Science* (New York and London: Routledge & Kegan Paul, 1986), 85–86.

24. Ray Hyman, cited in Broughton, *Parapsychology*, 128.

25. For a summary, see Robert L. Van de Castle, "Parapsychology and Anthropology," in Benjamin B. Wolman, ed., *Handbook of Parapsychology* (New York: Van Nostrand Reinhold, 1977), 667–86.

26. See Michael Murphy, *The Future of the Body: Explorations into the Further Evolution of Human Nature* (Los Angeles: Tarcher, 1992), 478–82. Murphy expresses his deep appreciation of, and indebtedness to, Herbert Thurston, S. J., *The Physical Phenomena of Mysticism* (Chicago: Henry Regnery, 1952).

27. See Murphy, ibid., 478–526.

28. See note 63, below.

29. Alan Gauld, *Mediumship and Survival: A Century of Investigations* (London: Granada [Paladin Books], 1983), 32.

30. Gauld, *Founders*, 253.

31. Ibid., 254.

32. Ibid., 256.

33. I have derived this account from Gauld's versions in *Founders*, 257, and *Mediumship*, 42–43.

34. Gauld, *Founders*, 258.

35. Ibid., 256–61.

36. Gauld, *Mediumship*, 259.

37. Ibid., 34–35.

38. Gauld, *Founders*, 261.

39. Ibid., 361–63.

40. Gauld, *Mediumship*, 47–48.

41. Ibid., 48.

42. Braude, *The Limits of Influence*, xi. (See n. 23, above. A revised edition is to be published by the University Press of America in 1997.)

43. Ibid., 60.

44. Ibid., 75–76.

45. E. Jenkins, *The Shadow and the Light: A Defence of Daniel Dunglas Home the Medium* (London: Hamish Hamilton, 1982), 37–49.

46. Braude, *The Limits of Influence*, 32.

47. Ibid.

48. Ibid., 32–33.

49. Ibid., 33.

50. Ibid., 29, quoting C. J. Ducasse, "Physical Phenomena in Psychical Research," *Journal of the American Society for Psychical Research* 52 (1958), 3–23, at 22.

51. Braude, ibid., 90.

52. Ibid., 89.

53. Ibid., 95–97.

54. Ibid., 91–95.

55. Ibid., 87.

56. Ibid., 87–88.

57. Ibid., 33.

58. Ibid., 88.

59. Ibid., 284–85.

60. Two recent books that have tried to cast doubt on the genuineness of Home's phenomena are R. Brandon's *The Spiritualists* (New York: Alfred A. Knopf) and T. H. Hall's *The Enigma of Daniel Home* (Buffalo: Prometheus Press, 1984). Stephen Braude says that, although these books may appear to uninformed readers to be scholarly and unbiased, "they are to serious psychical research what the *National Enquirer* is to serious news reporting" (*The Limits of Influence*, 34). In a review of Brandon's book (*Journal of the Society for Psychical Research* 52 [1983], 209–12), Brian Inglis calls it "deplorable." Braude, who has written a review of Hall's book (*Journal of the Society for Psychical Research* 53 [1985]: 40–46), calls it "equally shoddy" (*The Limits of Influence*, 34).

61. See Thurston, *The Physical Phenomena of Mysticism*, 1–31.

62. Braude, *The Limits of Influence*, 108–60.

63. Erlendur Haraldsson, *Modern Miracles: An Investigative Report on Psychic Phenomena Associated with Sathya Sai Baba* (New York: Fawcett Columbine [Ballantine Books], 1987), 216.

64. Nandor Fodor, *Encyclopaedia of Psychic Science* (New Hyde Park, N.Y.: University Books, 1966), 352.

65. Jule Eisenbud, *The World of Ted Serios: "Thoughtographic" Studies of an Extraordinary Mind* (New York: Simon & Schuster [Pocket Books], 1968), 14.

66. Jule Eisenbud, "Paranormal Photography," in Wolman, ed., *Handbook of Parapsychology*, 414–32, at 419.

67. Eisenbud, *The World of Ted Serios*, 100–10.

68. Ibid., 103.

69. Eisenbud, "Paranormal Photography," 421.

70. Ibid., 419, 422.

71. The article in question, "An Amazing Weekend with the Amazing Ted Serios," by David B. Eisendrath and Charles Reynolds, was published in the October 1967 issue of *Popular Photography*. This article and related events are discussed by Eisenbud in the Epilogue to the second edition of *The World of Ted Serios* (Jefferson, N.C. and London: McFarland & Co., 1989), 222–26.

72. See Eisenbud, ibid., 226–28; Curtis Fuller, "Dr. Jule Eisenbud *vs* the Amazing Randi," *Fate*, August, 1974: 65–74; and Jule Eisenbud, "Correspondence: On Ted Serios' Alleged 'Confession,'" *Journal of the American Society for Psychical Research* 69 (1975), 94–96. For more on the credibility of Randi (and of CSICOP, of which he is the most well-known member), see Broughton, *Parapsychology*, 84–85.

73. Eisenbud, *The World of Ted Serios*, 110.

74. Broughton, *Parapsychology*, 144.

75. Ibid., 145.

76. Ibid., 145–46.

77. Arthur S. Berger and Joyce Berger, *The Encyclopedia of Parapsychology and Psychical Research* (New York: Paragon House, 1991), 233.

78. Broughton, *Parapsychology*, 146–47.

79. On stigmata, see Thurston, *The Physical Phenomena of Mysticism*, 32–129.

80. Ian Stevenson, *Telepathic Impressions: A Review and Report of Thirty-Five New Cases* (Charlottesville: University Press of Virginia, 1970), 10–11.

81. Ibid., 56–61.

82. Ibid., 60–61.

83. Ibid., 61–64.

84. Ibid., 1, referring to L.E. Rhine, "Psychological Processes in ESP Experiences. Part I. Waking Expriences," *Journal of Parapsychology* 26 (1962), 88–111.

85. Ibid., 185.

86. Broughton, *Parapsychology*, 217.

87. William G. Roll, *The Poltergeist* (New York: New American Library, 1974), 92.

88. Broughton, *Parapsychology*, 218.

89. Ibid., 216.

90. Ibid., 218; Roll, *The Poltergeist*, 92.

91. Broughton, *Parapsychology*, 218–19.

92. William G. Roll, "Poltergeists," in Wolman, ed., *Handbook of Parapsychology*, 383–413.

93. Ibid., 386.

94. Ibid., 386–87.

95. Ibid., 401.

96. See Ian Stevenson, "Are Poltergeists Living or Are They Dead?" *Journal of the American Society for Psychical Research* 66 (1972), 235–52; see also the final chapter—with the same title, borrowed from Stevenson—of Alan Gauld and A. D. Cornell, *Poltergeists* (London & Boston: Routledge and Kegan Paul, 1979).

97. Roll, "Poltergeists," 387.

98. Ibid., 389.

99. Hans Bender, "New Developments in Poltergeist Research: Presidential Address," *Proceedings of the Parapsychological Association* 6 (1969), 81–102, at 96.

100. Roll, "Poltergeists," 390.

101. Roll, *The Poltergeist*, 118.

102. Ibid., 109.

103. Ibid., 104–07.

104. Ibid., 110.

105. Ibid., 113.

106. Ibid., 117.

107. Ibid., 108.

108. Ibid., 122.

109. Ibid., 130.

110. Ibid., 133.

111. Ibid., 153.

112. Ibid., 154–55.

113. Ibid., 156–57.

114. See notes 87 and 96, above.

115. Broughton, *Parapsychology*, 69; Hoyt L. Edge, Robert L. Morris, John Palmer, and Joseph H. Rush, *Foundations of Parapsychology: Exploring the Boundaries of Human Capability* (Boston and London: Routledge & Kegan Paul, 1986), 162.

116. Edge, et al., ibid., 168.

117. Ibid., 171.

118. Broughton, *Parapsychology*, 91.

119. Edge, et al., *Foundations of Parapsychology*, 175.

120. Broughton, *Parapsychology*, 95.

121. Ibid., 115–16.

122. Ibid., 120; Edge et al., *Foundations of Parapsychology*, 178–79.

123. Broughton, *Parapsychology*, 121. Although Broughton's summary does not make clear that Schlitz was not privy to the target pool, and this is not even explicitly stated (but simply presupposed, as part of standard remote-viewing procedure) in the original report (Marilyn Schlitz and Elmar Gruber, "Transcontinental Remote Viewing," *Journal of Parapsychology* 44 [December 1980], 305–17), it is explicitly stated in the report of a replication (Marilyn J. Schlitz and JoMarie Haight, "Remote Viewing Revisited: An Intrasubject Replication," *Journal of Parapsychology* 48 [March 1984], 39–48, at 41. See also "Transcontinental Remote Viewing: A Rejudging," *Journal of Parapsychology* 45 (September 1981), which deals with a potential weakness in the first study.

124. Broughton, ibid., 122.

125. Ibid., 95–96; Edge et al., *Foundations of Parapsychology*, 127.

126. Broughton, *Parapsychology*, 101.

127. Ibid., 285; Edge et al., *Foundations of Parapsychology*, 179.

128. Broughton, *Parapsychology*, 286.

129. Ibid., 287.

130. Ibid., 287.

131. Ibid., 324.

132. James A. Alcock, "Parapsychology as a 'Spiritual' Science," in Paul Kurtz, ed., *A Skeptic's Handbook of Parapsychology* (Buffalo: Prometheus Books, 1985), 537–65, at 562.

133. Broughton, *Parapsychology*, 291, 322–24.

134. Ibid., 288.

135. Ibid., 112.

136. Ibid., 113.

137. Ibid., 295.

138. Ibid., 286, 296.

139. Ibid., 170–71, 177.

140. Edge et al., *Foundations of Parapsychology*, 254.

141. Broughton, *Parapsychology*, 289.

142. Ibid., 290.

143. Ibid., 291.

144. Edge et al., *Foundations of Parapsychology*, 248.

145. Ibid., 248; Broughton, *Parapsychology*, 332.

146. Edge et al., *Foundations of Parapsychology*, 248; Broughton, *Parapsychology*, 332.

147. Bernard Grad, "Experiences and Opinions of an Unconventional Scientist," in Rosemarie Pilkington, ed., *Men and Women of Parapsychology: Personal Reflections* (Jefferson, N.C., and London: McFarland & Co., 1987), 146–60, at 151, 154.

148. Broughton, ibid., 334.

149. Ibid., 166–68.

150. J. B. Rhine, *The Reach of the Mind* (New York: William Sloane, 1947), 66.

151. "Comment by Antony Flew," in Ray Hyman, *The Elusive Quary: A Scientific Appraisal of Psychical Research* (Buffalo: Prometheus Books, 1989), 268.

152. Antony Flew, "Parapsychology: Science or Pseudoscience?", Paul Kurtz, ed., *A Skeptic's Handbook of Parapsychology* (Buffalo: Prometheus Books, 1985), 519–36, at 529.

153. Quoted by Flew, ibid., 528.

154. Ibid., 532.

155. Flew, "Parapsychology Revisited: Laws, Miracles, and Repeatability," Jan Ludwig, ed., *Philosophy and Parapsychology* (Buffalo: Prometheus Books, 1978), 263–69, at 264.

156. Flew, "Parapsychology: Science or Pseudoscience?," 533.

157. Stephen Braude, *The Limits of Influence*, 261–74.

158. Rhine, *The Reach of the Mind*, 82.

159. David Ray Griffin, "Parapsychology and Philosophy: A Whiteheadian Postmodern Approach," *Journal of the American Society for Psychical Research* 86/3 (July 1993), 217–88, at 270–75.

160. It was suggested by A. Tanagras in "The Theory of Psychobolie," *Journal of the American Society for Psychical Research* 43 (1949), 151–54, and in *Psychophysical*

Elements in Parapsychological Traditions (New York: Parapsychology Foundation, 1967). It has also been developed by William Roll in "The Problem of Precognition," *Journal of the Society for Psychical Research* 41 (1961), 115–28; by Jule Eisenbud in *Paranormal Foreknowledge: Problems and Perplexities* (New York: Human Sciences Press, 1982), passim, and *Parapsychology and the Unconscious* (Berkeley: North Atlantic Books, 1983), 44–46, 87–98, 137–45; and by Stephen Braude in *The Limits of Influence*, 256–77.

161. Robert Morris, "Assessing Experimental Support for True Precognition," *Journal of Parapsychology* 46 (1982), 321–36, at 334.

3. THE MIND-BODY RELATION AND THE POSSIBILITY OF LIFE AFTER DEATH

1. Frederick W. H. Myers, *Human Personality and Its Survival of Bodily Death* (London: Longmans, Green and Co., 1903).

2. I have reviewed Nielsen's book *God, Scepticism, and Modernity* in the *Journal of the American Academy of Religion* 59/1 (Spring 1991), 189–90.

3. Kai Nielsen, "God and the Soul: A Response to Paul Badham," in Stephen Davis, ed., *Death and Afterlife* (London: Macmillan, 1989), 53–64, at 61.

4. C. D. Broad, *Lectures on Psychical Research* (New York: Humanities Press, 1962), 430.

5. See my *God and Religion in the Postmodern World* (Albany: State University of New York Press, 1989), 98–108.

6. Bruce R. Reichenbach, *Is Man the Phoenix? A Study of Immortality* (Grand Rapids, Mich.: Christian University Press, 1978), 84–85.

7. John Searle, "Minds and Brain Without Programs," in Colin Blakemore and Susan Greenfield, ed., *Mindwaves: Thoughts on Intelligence, Identity, and Consciousness* (Oxford: Basil Blackwell, 1987), 209–33, at 215.

8. John Searle, *The Rediscovery of the Mind* (Cambridge: MIT Press, 1992), 17.

9. Ibid., 17–18.

10. Ibid., 48.

11. Alfred North Whitehead, *Process and Reality: An Essay in Cosmology*, Corrected Edition, ed. David Ray Griffin and Donald W. Sherburne (New York: Free Press, 1978), 151.

12. Ibid., 12.

13. Searle, *The Rediscovery of the Mind*, 8.

14. Whitehead, *Process and Reality*, 47.

15. See *Unsnarling the World-Knot: Consciousness, Freedom, and the Mind-Body Problem* (Berkeley and Los Angeles: University of California Press, 1997), Ch. 3.

16. John A. Passmore, *Philosophical Reasoning* (London: Duckworth, 1970), 55.

17. See Gilbert Ryle, *The Concept of Mind* (London: Peregrine, 1963).

18. John Cottingham, trans., *Descartes' Conversation with Burman* (Oxford: Clarendon, 1976), 28; Desmond Clark, *Descartes' Philosophy of Science* (University Park: Pennsylvania State University Press, 1982), 27. See also "Correspondence Between Princess Elisabeth and Descartes," in Donald Wayne Viney, *Questions of Value: Readings for Basic Philosophy* (Needham Heights, Mass.: Ginn Press, 1989), 103–11.

19. I have discussed Berkeley's view in *God, Power, and Evil: A Process Theodicy* (Philadelphia: Westminster, 1976), 231–39.

20. Thomas Reid, *Essays on the Intellectual Powers of Man* (Cambridge, Mass.: MIT Press, 1969), 96–97, 99, 110, 118, 123, 220, 240, 318.

21. Diderot's statement is quoted in David Lorimer, *Survival? Body, Mind and Death in the Light of Psychic Experience* (London: Routledge and Kegan Paul, 1984), 105.

22. Karl R. Popper, *Of Clouds and Clocks* (St. Louis: Washington University Press, 1966), 15; italics his.

23. Karl R. Popper and John C. Eccles, *The Self and Its Brain: An Argument for Interactionism* (Berlin: Springer-Verlag, 1977), 16, 37, 494–95.

24. Ibid., 105.

25. Ibid., 483, 499, 510.

26. Ibid., 494–95.

27. John C. Eccles, *Facing Reality* (Heidelberg: Springer-Verlag, 1970), 162.

28. Ibid.

29. Eccles, "Cerebral Activity and Consciousness," in Francisco J. Ayala and Theodosius Dobzhansky, *Studies in the Philosophy of Biology* (Berkeley: University of California Press, 1974), 87–107, at 100; *The Self and Its Brain*, 514, 545.

30. C. Wade Savage, "An Old Ghost in a New Body," in Gordon G. Globus, Grover Maxwell, and Irwin Savodnik, ed., *Consciousness and the Brain: A Scientific and Philosophical Inquiry* (New York: Plenum Press, 1976), 125–53, at 131.

31. John Eccles, "Cerebral Activity and Consciousness," 98 (italics added).

32. C. J. Ducasse, *A Critical Examination of the Belief in a Life After Death* (Springfield, Ill.: Charles C. Thomas, 1961), 112, 116, 117.

33. Ibid., 102.

34. C. J. Ducasse, "Minds, Matter and Bodies," in J. R. Smythies, ed., *Brain and Mind* (London: Routledge and Kegan Paul, 1965), 85.

35. Ibid., 83. A similar position is taken by Hywel D. Lewis in *The Elusive Mind* (London: George Allen and Unwin, 1969), 26–29, 123, 173.

36. Paul Badham, "God, the Soul, and the Future Life," in Stephen T. Davis, ed., *Death and Afterlife* (London: Macmillan, 1990), 36–52, at 44–45. The problem of dualistic interaction is also not addressed in Badham's *Christian Beliefs About Life After Death* (London: Macmillan, 1976) or in his *Immortality or Extinction?* (London: Macmillan, 1982), which was coauthored with Linda Badham.

37. This move is made by W. D. Hart, *The Engines of the Soul* (Cambridge: Cambridge University Press, 1988), 62–64, 127, 149, 152, 178, 186n.

38. See note 58 of Chapter 1.

39. Paul Badham, "God, the Soul, and the Future Life," 48–49.

40. H. H. Price, "Psychical Research and Human Personality," in J. R. Smythies, ed., *Science and ESP* (London: Routledge and Kegan Paul, 1967), 33–45, at 38. David Lorimer, who cites this discussion by Price, accepts this view as well (*Survival?*, 149).

41. Daniel Dennett, *Consciousness Explained* (Boston: Little, Brown, and Co., 1991), 31, 41.

42. Searle, *The Rediscovery of the Mind*, 130.

43. Thomas Nagel, *The View from Nowhere* (New York: Oxford University Press, 1986), 50.

44. Dennett, *Consciousness Explained*, 23, 458.

45. Searle, *The Rediscovery of the Mind*, 130.

46. William Seager, *Metaphysics of Consciousness* (London & New York: Routledge, 1991), 188.

47. Searle, *The Rediscovery of the Mind*, 54, 48.

48. Owen Flanagan, *Consciousness Reconsidered* (Cambridge: Cambridge University Press, 1992), 5–6.

49. Nagel, *The View from Nowhere*, 123.

50. Ibid., 29; *Mortal Questions* (London: Cambridge University Press, 1979), 182, 190, 211.

51. *The View from Nowhere*, 110–17; quotation is on 112.

52. Searle, *The Rediscovery of the Mind*, 112.

53. Colin McGinn, *The Problem of Consciousness: Essays Toward a Resolution* (Oxford: Basil Blackwell, 1991), 17n.

54. George Santayana, *Scepticism and Animal Faith* (1923; New York: Dover, 1955), 15–20.

55. Ibid., 15–20.

56. Searle, *The Rediscovery of the Mind*, 55.

57. Ibid., 14, 125.

58. Seager, *Metaphysics of Consciousness*, 179.

59. Searle, *The Rediscovery of the Mind*, 125.

60. Nagel, *Mortal Questions*, 176.

61. McGinn, *The Problem of Consciousness*, 1–2, 7.

62. William S. Robinson, *Brains and People: An Essay on Mentality and Its Causal Conditions* (Philadelphia: Temple University Press, 1988), 29.

63. Seager, *Metaphysics of Consciousness*, 195.

64. This point has been made by Charles Hartshorne in "Physics and Psychics: The Place of Mind in Nature," *Mind in Nature: Essays on the Interface of Science and Philosophy*, ed. John B. Cobb, Jr., and David Ray Griffin (Washington, D.C.: University Press of America, 1977), 89–96, at 90, and in *Creative Synthesis and Philosophic Method* (London: SCM Press, 1970; Lanham, Md.: University Press of America, 1983), 9.

65. Herbert Feigl, "Mind-Body *Not* a Pseudoproblem," *Dimensions of Mind*, ed. Sydney Hook (New York: New York University Press, 1960), 24–36, at 32, 33.

. 66. For the debates generated by Descartes' position, see Leonora Cohen Rosenfield, *From Beast-Machine to Man-Machine* (New York: Oxford University Press, 1940).

67. See Adolf Grünbaum, *Philosophical Problems of Space and Time* (New York: Knopf, 1963); "The Anisotropy of Time," *The Nature of Time*, ed. Thomas Gold (Ithaca, N.Y.: Cornell University Press, 1967), 149–86; *Modern Science and Zeno's Paradoxes* (Middletown: Wesleyan University Press, 1967).

68. J. T. Fraser, *The Genesis and Evolution of Time: A Critique of Interpretation in Physics* (Amherst: University of Massachusetts Press, 1982), 132.

69. J. J. C. Smart, "Sensations and Brain Processes," in C. V. Borst, ed., *The Mind-Brain Identity Theory* (London: Macmillan, 1979), 52–66, at 53. Where Smart's text had "sensations" I inserted "states of consciousness" (which Smart tends to use synonymously) to bring out his point more clearly.

70. Michael E. Levin, *Metaphysics and the Mind-Body Problem* (Oxford: Clarendon, 1979), 87.

71. Ibid., 92.

72. McGinn, *The Problem of Consciousness*, 212–13; Nagel, *Mortal Questions*, 172, 188, 201, and *The View from Nowhere*, 7, 15–16, 25; Seager, *Metaphysics of Consciousness*, 31; Searle, *The Rediscovery of the Mind*, 3, 11, 51.

73. Eccles, *Facing Reality*, 83.

74. Popper and Eccles, *The Self and Its Brain*, 29.

75. Ibid., 69–71, 87.

76. J. J. C. Smart, "Materialism," in C. V. Borst, ed., *The Mind-Brain Identity Theory*, 159–70, at 168–69.

77. Thomas Nagel, *Mortal Questions*, 189.

78. Sewall Wright, "Panpsychism and Science," in Cobb and Griffin, ed., *Mind in Nature*, 79–88, at 82.

79. Eccles, *Facing Reality*, 173.

80. Popper and Eccles, *The Self and Its Brain*, 560.

81. McGinn, *The Problem of Consciousness*, 17n.

82. Ibid., 46.

83. Ibid., 45.

84. Ibid., 212.

85. Searle, *The Rediscovery of the Mind*, 55.

86. Ibid., 3.

87. Geoffrey Madell, *Mind and Materialism* (Edinburgh: The University Press, 1988), Preface (n.p.).

88. Ibid., 2.

89. Ibid., 140–41.

90. Ibid., 135.

91. Ibid., 9.

92. Searle, *The Rediscovery of the Mind*, 49.

93. Ibid., 14, 26, 54.

94. C. V. Borst, ed., *The Mind-Brain Identity Theory*, 14.

95. John Hick, *Death and Eternal Life* (San Francisco: Harper, 1976), 112.

96. James R. Jacob, *Robert Boyle and the English Revolution* (New York: Franklin, Burt, 1978), 172; Brian Easlea, *Witch Hunting, Magic and the New Philosophy* (Atlantic Highlands, N.J.: Humanities Press, 1980), 113, 235–45.

97. Hick, *Death and Eternal Life*, 126.

98. See, e.g., Donald R. Griffin, *The Question of Animal Awareness: Evolutionary Continuity of Mental Experience* (New York: Rockefeller University Press, 1976), 14, 23.

99. Julius Adler and Wing-Wai Tse, "Decision-Making in Bacteria," *Science* 184 (June 21, 1974), 1292–94; A. Goldbeter and D. E. Koshland, Jr., "Simple Molecular Model for Sensing and Adaptation Based on Receptor Modification with Application to Bacterial Chemotaxis," *Journal of Molecular Biology* 161/3 (1982), 395-416.

100. Popper and Eccles, *The Self and Its Brain*, 55.

101. Charles Hartshorne, "The Compound Individual," *Philosophical Essays for Alfred North Whitehead*, ed. Otis H. Lee (New York: Longmans, Green, 1936), 193–220; reprinted in Charles Hartshorne, *Whitehead's Philosophy: Selected Essays 1935–1970* (Lincoln: University of Nebraska Press, 1972), 41–61. For a discussion, see John B. Cobb, Jr., "Overcoming Reductionism," in *Existence and Actuality: Conversations with Charles Hartshorne*, ed. John B. Cobb, Jr., and Franklin I. Gamwell (Chicago: University of Chicago Press, 1984), 149–63.

102. Hartshorne, "Physics and Psychics," 95; *Creative Synthesis and Philosophic Method*, 90; *The Logic of Perfection* (Lasalle, Ill.: Open Court, 1962), 213.

103. Milič Čapek, *The New Aspects of Time: Its Continuities and Novelties* (Dordrecht and Boston: Kluwer Academic, 1991), 135, 205.

104. Popper and Eccles, *The Self and Its Brain*, 10.

105. See Nagel's discussions in *Mortal Questions*, 181–95, and *The View from Nowhere*, 49–51.

106. Seager, *Metaphysics of Consciousness*, 241–42n. However, just before correcting proofs, I learned that Seager had recently developed a version of panpsychism ("Consciousness, Information, and Panpsychism," *Journal of Consciousness Studies* 2/3 [1995], 272–88), having decided that its *prima facie* implausibility could be ameliorated (283n.14).

107. McGinn, *The Problem of Consciousness*, 2n.

108. Ibid., 28n.

109. Ibid., 2n.

110. See, e.g., Geoffrey Madell, *Mind and Materialism*, 3, and Nicholas Humphrey, *A History of the Mind* (London: Chatto and Windus, 1992), 193.

111. McGinn, *The Problem of Consciousness*, 2.

112. See the book referred to in note 15, above.

113. Henri Bergson, *Time and Free Will* (London: Allen and Unwin, 1950).

114. This move away from dualism is described in Pete A. Y. Gunter's chapter on Bergson in Griffin et al., *Founders of Constructive Postmodern Philosophy*, and in Milič Čapek, "Bergson's Theory of the Mind-Brain Relation," in *Bergson and Modern Thought: Towards a Unified Science*, ed. A. D. Papanicolaou and P. A. Y. Gunter (New York: Harwood Academic Publishers, 1987), 129–48.

115. Ralph Barton Perry, *The Thought and Character of William James* (Boston: Little, Brown and Co., 1935), vol. II: 745; see also James, *A Pluralistic Universe* (London: Longmans, Green and Co., 1912), 292.

116. James, *Varieties of Religious Experience* (New York: Colliers, 1961), 387. This statement and the passages cited in note 115 are quoted by Marcus Ford, who extensively documents James's affirmation of panpsychism in his chapter in Griffin et al., *Founders of Constructive Postmodern Philosophy*, 89–132. See also Ford's book *William James's Philosophy: A New Perspective* (Amherst: University of Massachusetts Press, 1982).

117. William McDougall, *Body and Mind: A History and a Defense of Animism*, 5th ed. (New York: Macmillan, 1920), x.

118. Ibid., 192.

119. Ibid., x, 366; cf. 192.

120. See Arthur Danto, *Analytical Philosophy of Action* (Cambridge: Cambridge University Press, 1973), 28–115.

121. Darwin's argument is discussed in Lorimer, *Survival?*, 109–11.

4. Evidence for Life After Death:
Mediumistic Messages

1. Alan Gauld, *Mediumship and Survival* (London: Granada, 1983), 15.

2. Ibid., 7.

3. Ibid., 23.

4. John Hick, *Death and Eternal Life* (San Francisco: Harper & Row, 1976), Ch. 7.

5. David Lorimer, *Survival? Body, Mind and Death in the Light of Psychic Experience* (London: Routledge & Kegan Paul, 1984).

6. Richard Broughton, *Parapsychology: The Controversial Science* (New York: Ballantine Books, 1991), 272.

7. Gauld, *Mediumship and Survival*, 8, 31.

8. Ibid., 43.

9. C. J. Ducasse, *A Critical Examination of the Belief in a Life After Death* (Springfield, Ill.: Charles C. Thomas, 1961), 179.

10. Gauld, *Mediumship and Survival*, 40–41.

11. Ibid., 41.

12. Ibid., 41–42.

13. Idem.

14. James H. Hyslop, "A Further Record of Observations of Certain Trance Phenomena," *Proceedings of the Society for Psychical Research* 16 (1901), 1–649, at 293 (quoted by Ducasse, *A Critical Examination*, 181).

15. Richard Hodgson, "A Further Record of Observations of Certain Phenomena of Trance," *Proceedings of the Society for Psychical Research* 13 (1897–1898), 284–582, at 328 (quoted by Ducasse, 181). Hyslop's essay with the same title, cited in the previous note, was evidently intended as a continuation of Hodgson's work.

16. Ducasse, *A Critical Examination*, 183, 197–98; Hoyt L. Edge, Robert L. Morris, John Palmer, and Joseph Rush, *Foundations of Parapsychology* (Boston & London: Routledge & Kegan Paul, 1986), 339.

17. Ducasse, *A Critical Examination*, 197–98.

18. Gauld, *Mediumship and Survival*, 49.

19. Rosalind Heywood, *Beyond the Reach of Sense: An Inquiry into Extra-Sensory Perception* (1959; New York: E. P. Dutton, 1971), 60–62; Alice Johnson, "Report on the Automatic Writing of Mrs. Holland," *Proceedings of the Society for Psychical Research* 21 (1908–1909), 166–391.

20. George N. M. Tyrrell, *Science and Psychical Phenomena* (1938; New Hyde Park, N.Y.: University Books, 1961 [published in one volume with *Apparitions*]), 236–37.

21. Gauld, *Mediumship and Survival*, 81–83.

22. H. F. Saltmarsh, *Evidence of Personal Survival from Cross Correspondences* (London: Bell, 1938).

23. Arthur S. Berger and Joyce Berger, *The Encyclopedia of Parapsychology and Psychical Research* (New York: Paragon House, 1991), 138.

24. See Iris M. Owen and Margaret Sparrow, *Conjuring Up Philip* (New York: Harper & Row, 1976), which is important in spite of its many flaws. (For the latter, see Richard Reichbart's review, "Group Psi: Comments on the Recent Toronto PK Experiment as Recounted in *Conjuring Up Philip*," *Journal of the American Society for Psychical Research* 71/2 (April, 1977), 201–12.

25. Gauld, *Mediumship and Survival*, 64–65.

26. Erlendur Haraldsson and Ian Stevenson, "A Communicator of the 'Drop in' Type in Iceland: The Case of Gudni Magnusson," *Journal of the American Society for Psychical Research* 69 (1975), 245–61, at 161.

27. Erlendur Haraldsson and Ian Stevenson, "A Communicator of the 'Drop in' Type in Iceland: The Case of Runolfur Runolfsson," *Journal of the American Society for Psychical Research* 69 (1975), 33–59, at 57.

28. Gauld, *Mediumship and Survival*, 73.

5. EVIDENCE FROM CASES OF THE POSSESSION TYPE

1. Carl B. Becker, *Paranormal Experience and Survival of Death* (Albany, N.Y.: State University of New York Press, 1993), 11.

2. E. W. Stevens, *The Watseka Wonder: A Narrative of Startling Phenomena Occurring in the Case of Mary Lurancy Vennum* (Chicago: Religio-Philosophical Publishing House, 1887 [bound together with Rev. Wm. S. Plummer, *Mary Reynolds: A Case of Double Consciousness*]), 11.

3. Ibid., 4.

4. Ibid., 7.

5. Ibid., 7–8.

6. Ibid., 9, 13.

7. Ibid., 13–14.

8. Gauld, *Mediumship and Survival*, 158.

9. Stevens, *The Watseka Wonder*, 16.

10. Ibid., 17, 8, 18, 23, 24, 21.

11. Ibid., 19–21, 27–28, 18, 30, 36–37.

12. The information for this case is taken primarily from Ian Stevenson, *Unlearned Language: New Studies in Xenoglossy* (Charlottesville: University Press of Virginia, 1984), with supplemental information from V. V. Akolkar, "Search for Sharada: Report of a Case and Its Investigation," *Journal of the American Society for Psychical Research* 86/3 (July 1992), 209–47. The information for this first paragraph is from Stevenson 73, 75, 82, 106–08, 110, 115, and Akolkar 210, 215, 221.

13. Stevenson, *Unlearned Language*, 74, 99, 152.

14. Ibid., 102, 103.

15. Ibid., 82, 100.

16. Ibid., 75, 134.

17. Ibid., 100.

18. Ibid., 94.

19. Ibid., 103–04.

20. Ibid., 102–03.

21. Ibid., 100.

22. Ibid., 99.

23. Akolkar, "Search for Sharada," 226.

24. Idem.; Stevenson, *Unlearned Language*, 99–101, 114.

25. Ibid., 104–05.

26. Ibid., 90–91.

27. Ibid., 101.

28. Ibid., 119, 124–25.

29. Ibid., 86–87; Akolkar, "Search for Sharada," 210, 233. According to Akolkar, Sharada put her age at 24, rather than at 22.

30. Stevenson, *Unlearned Language*, 86–87, 106; Akolkar, "Search for Sharada," 210.

31. Stevenson, ibid., 114.

32. Ibid., 80.

33. Ibid., 112; Akolkar, "Search for Sharada," 240.

34. Stevenson, ibid., 114.

35. Ibid., 81, 147.

36. Ibid., 74, 105, 151.

37. Ibid., 74, 105.

38. Ibid., 88–89. Akolkar ("Search for Sharada," 231) reports finding that the genealogy contained the names of six of the men Sharada had mentioned, not only five, as Stevenson had reported. In particular, the genealogy does contain the name of Srinath, whom she had referred to as one of her stepbrothers. This seems to be the only serious discrepancy between the two reports. Otherwise, Akolkar's independent investigation serves to support the accuracy of Stevenson's.

39. Ibid., 88–89.

40. Ibid., 90.

41. Ibid., 91.

42. Ibid., 88, 95.

43. Ibid., 92.

44. Ibid., 120–33.

45. Ibid., 139, 146n; Akolkar, "Search for Sharada," 214–15.

46. Stevenson, ibid., 139, 141.

47. Ibid., 118–19, 136.

48. Ibid., 134–35, 137–38, 140, 146.

49. Stephen Braude, "Dissociation and Survival: A Reappraisal of the Evidence," in Lisette Coly and Joanne D. S. McMahon, eds., *Parapsychology and Thanatology* (New York: Parapsychology Foundation, 1995), 208–28, at 210, 223.

50. V. V. Akolkar, "Search for Sharada," 216.

51. Ibid., 217.

52. Ibid., 217, 221.

53. Ibid., 218.

54. Ibid., 222.

55. Ibid., 221.

56. Idem.

57. Ibid., 220–221. According to the survivalist interpretation, this vision would be regarded as a memory: Sharada reported that sometimes, when she would get tired of doing the chores, her husband would beat her, and she would feel insulted (ibid., 233).

58. Stevenson, *Unlearned Language*, 113.

59. Ibid., 146, 159–61; Stephen E. Braude, "Survival or Super-Psi?" *Journal of Scientific Exploration* 6/2 (1992), 127–44, at 138.

60. Stevenson, *Unlearned Language*, 79–80.

61. Ibid., 81.

6. EVIDENCE FROM CASES OF THE REINCARNATION TYPE

1. Arthur Schopenhauer, *Parerga and Paralipomena: Short Philosophical Essays*, trans. E. F. J. Payne (Oxford: Clarendon, 1974), II: 368–69.

2. Frederick W. H. Myers, *Human Personality and Its Survival of Bodily Death*, ed. (and abridged into a one-volume edition) by Susy Smith (New Hyde Park, N.Y.: University Books, 1961), 294.

3. George Gallup, Jr., with William Proctor, *Adventures in Immortality* (New York: McGraw-Hill, 1982), 137.

4. For Ducasse's and Becker's books, see Ch. 4 n.9 and Ch. 5 n.1, respectively. Robert Almeder's book is *Death and Personal Survival: The Evidence for Life after Death* (Lanham, Md.: Rowman & Littlefield, 1992).

5. For Ian Stevenson's extensively documented studies, see *Twenty Cases Suggestive of Reincarnation* (1966; 2nd ed., revised and enlarged, 1974), *Cases of the Reincarnation Type, I: Ten Cases in India* (1975), *Cases of the Reincarnation Type, II: Ten Cases in Sri Lanka* (1977), *Cases of the Reincarnation Type, III: Twelve Cases in Lebanon and Turkey* (1980), *Cases of the Reincarnation Type, IV: Twelve Cases in Thailand and Burma* (1983), all of which are published by the University Press of Virginia (Charlottesville). For less fully documented cases, see Stevenson, *Children Who Remember Previous Lives: A Question of Reincarnation* (Charlottesville: University Press of Virginia, 1987), and Stevenson and Godwin Samararatne, "Three New Cases of the Reincarnation Type in Sri Lanka with Written Records Made Before Verifications," *Journal of Scientific Exploration* 2/2 (1988), 217–38.

6. See Karl Muller, *Reincarnation Based on Facts* (London: Psychic Press, 1971); K. N. Jayatilleke, *The Message of the Buddha* (New York: Free Press, 1974); Guy Lyon Playfair, *The Indefinite Boundary* (New York: St. Martin's, 1976); Antonia Mills, "A Replication Study: Three Cases of Children in Northern India Who are Said to Remember a Previous Life," *Journal of Scientific Exploration* 3 (1989), 133–84; Erlendur Haraldsson, "Children Claiming Past-Life Memories: Four Cases in Sri Lanka," *Journal of Scientific Exploration* 5 (1991), 233–61; Jürgen Keil, "New Cases in Burma, Thailand, and Turkey: A Limited Field Study Replication of Some Aspects of Ian Stevenson's Research," *Journal of Scientific Exploration* 5 (1991), 27–59; Satwant Pasricha, *Claims of Reincarnation: An Empirical Study of Cases in India* (New Delhi: Harman Publishing House, 1992).

7. Ducasse, *A Critical Examination*, 207.

8. Gauld, *Mediumship and Survival*, 187.

9. Stevenson, *Cases*, III: 7, 186.

10. Stevenson, *Twenty Cases*, 274 n.8; D. R. Barker and S. Pasricha, "Reincarnation Cases in Fatehabad: A Systematic Survey in North India," *Journal of Asian and African Studies* 14 (1979), 231–40.

11. See Stevenson, "American Children Who Claim to Remember Previous Lives," *Journal of Nervous and Mental Disease* 171 (1983), 742–48, and *Children Who Remember Previous Lives*. The fact that far fewer American cases are solved (meaning that a prior personality corresponding to the claims is found) suggests that, if anything, claims by children in America, where reincarnation is not culturally accepted, are more likely to be pure fantasy. In fact, Stevenson has told me (personal correspondence, May 16, 1994) that he does not recall having in the United States, outside of Alaska, a single solved "long-distance case," meaning one in which the two families concerned had no contact with each other before the case developed.

12. "Three New Cases" (see n. 5, above), 219.

13. Personal correspondence, May 16, 1994.

14. *Twenty Cases* (see n. 5, above), 273–79, 319.

15. Ibid., 281n.

16. Ibid., 286.

17. Ibid., 290, 281.

18. Ibid., 291, 303.

19. Ibid., 292.

20. Ibid., 281, 300, 301.

21. Ibid., 305–08.

22. Ibid., 271, 275, 279–80.

23. Ibid., 276, 298.

24. Ibid., 302, 317.

25. Ibid., 113.

26. Ibid., 305.

27. Ibid., 292, 304.

28. Ibid., 305.

29. Ibid., 289.

30. Ibid., 303, 290–91.

31. Ibid., 303.

32. Ibid., 280.

33. Ibid., 285.

34. Ibid., 286–97.

35. Ibid., 300–01.

36. Ibid., 318.

37. Ibid., 318.

38. Ibid., 316, 318.

39. Ibid., 316, 317.

40. Ibid., 128.

41. Ibid., 309, 311.

42. "Ian Stevenson: An Omega Interview" (conducted by Robert Kastenbaum), *Omega: Journal of Death and Dying* 28/3 (1993–1994), 165–82, at 170.

43. Stevenson, *Cases*, III: 10, 344.

44. Ibid., 344.

45. Gauld, *Mediumship and Survival*, 175.

46. Stevenson and Samararatne, "Three New Cases," 235.

47. Stevenson, *Cases*, III: 344.

48. Idem.

49. Ibid., 356.

50. Stevenson, *Cases*, III: 358, 344.

51. Ibid., 358–59.

52. Ibid., 353.

53. *Cases*, II: 62.

54. Stevenson, *Twenty Cases*, 349–50; "Ian Stevenson: An Omega Interview," 171, 175.

55. *Cases*, III: 352.

56. Ibid., 10.

57. *Cases*, I: 64; IV: 6–8, 210, 224.

58. *Cases*, III: 8–9.

59. *Cases*, II: 7; III: 118–19.

60. *Cases*, II: 7–9.

61. *Cases*, I: 67–68.

62. *Cases*, III: 12.

63. *Cases*, I: 68; III: 13, 356.

64. *Cases*, III: 358, 180.

65. Stephen Braude, "Dissociation and Survival" (see n. 49 for Ch. 5, above), 209.

66. Stevenson, *Twenty Cases*, 353–54.

67. Ibid., 349.

68. Ibid., 232–34, 240.

69. *Cases*, III: 215.

70. Ian Stevenson, "Birthmarks and Birth Defects Corresponding to Wounds on Deceased Persons," *Journal of Scientific Exploration* 7/4 (Winter 1993), 403–16, at 405. These phenomena will be discussed much more extensively by Stevenson in a two-volume study, *Reincarnation and Biology: A Contribution to the Etiology of Birthmarks and Birth Defects*, scheduled to be published by the Greenwood Publishing Group in 1997.

71. Ibid., 411 (with photograph on 412).

72. Ibid., 408, 410–11.

73. Antonia Mills, "A Replication Study: Three Cases of Children in Northern India Who Are Said to Remember a Previous Life," *Journal of Scientific Exploration* 3/2 (1989), 133–84, esp. 159, 168–69.

74. Ian Stevenson, "A New Look at Maternal Impressions: An Analysis of 50 Published Cases and Reports of Two Recent Examples," *Journal of Scientific Exploration* 6/4 (Winter 1992), 353–73.

75. Stevenson, "Birthmarks and Birth Defects," 415.

76. Braude, "Dissociation and Survival," 225–27.

77. *Cases*, I: 63–64; IV: 6.

78. *Cases*, IV: 6–7, 224.

79. *Cases*, I: 322–24, 327, 329, 331.

80. *Cases*, II: 97, 105.

81. *Cases*, IV: 151, 143, 154–55.

82. Ibid., 143, 154–55.

83. Ibid., 19–21, 27.

84. Ibid., 280, 288–89.

85. Ian Stevenson, personal correspondence, May 16, 1994.

86. Ian Stevenson, Satwant Pasricha, and Godwin Samararatne, "Deception and Self-Deception in Cases of the Reincarnation Type: Seven Illustrative Cases in Asia," *Journal of the American Society for Psychical Research* 82/1 (January 1988), 1–31, esp. 22–26.

87. Antonia Mills, "A Preliminary Investigation of Cases of Reincarnation among the Beaver and Gitksan Indians," *Anthropologica* XXX (1988), 23–59, esp. 35–39; "Gitxsan and Witsuwit'en Experience of the Boundaries of the Self: Body-Bounded or Spirit Bound?" (forthcoming in *Ethos*); and personal correspondence, June 8, 1994. (She changed the spelling from Gitksan to Gitxsan for the latter article.)

88. Mills, "Gitxsan and Witsuwit'en Experience," 11 (ms.).

89. Mills, "A Replication Study: Three Cases of Children in Northern India Who Are Said to Remember a Previous Life," 156–72.

7. Evidence from Apparitions

1. Edmund Gurney, Frederick W. H. Myers, and Frank Podmore, *Phantasms of the Living*, 2 vols. (London: Trübner, 1886).

2. Henry Sidgwick, Eleanor M. Sidgwick, and Alice Johnson, "Report on the Census of Hallucinations," *Proceedings of the Society for Psychical Research* 10 (1894), 25–422.

3. Alan Gauld, *The Founders of Psychical Research* (New York: Schocken Books, 1968), 182–84.

4. George N. M. Tyrrell, *Apparitions* (1953; New Hyde Park, N.Y.: University Books, 1961 [published in one volume with *Science and Psychical Phenomena*]).

5. See Richard Broughton's judgment, cited in the text in relation to n. 6 of Ch. 4.

6. Gurney, et al., *Phantasms of the Living* I: 337 (cited in Tyrrell, *Apparitions*, 26).

7. Ibid., Case 127 (cited in Tyrrell, *Apparitions*, 26).

8. Tyrrell, *Apparitions*, 22.

9. Ibid., 78.

10. Ibid., 61, 78.

11. Ibid., 62, 78.

12. Ibid., 76.

13. Ibid., 63.

14. Ibid., 60.

15. Ibid., 77–80; Becker, *Paranormal Experience and the Survival of Death* (see Ch. 5 n.1, above), 47.

16. Frederick W. H. Myers, *Human Personality and Its Survival of Bodily Death* (see Ch. 6 n. 2), 228–29.

17. Ducasse, *A Critical Examination* (see Ch. 4 n. 9), 157–58.

18. Myers, *Human Personality*, 230–31.

19. Ibid., 222–24.

20. Tyrrell, *Apparitions*, 137.

21. Ibid., 36.

22. Ibid., 139; W. H. Salter, *Ghosts and Apparitions* (London: G. Bell & Sons, 1938), 53.

23. Myers, *Human Personality*, 243.

24. Tyrrell, *Apparitions*, 71.

25. The apparition of Lydia Blaisdell is reported in Abraham Cummings, *Immortality Proved by Testimony of the Sense* (Bath, Me.: J. C. Tobbley, 1826).

26. Even Tyrrell's version of this theory, which allows for telepathically received information from the discarnate soul, becomes extremely complex; see Tyrrell, *Apparitions*, 93–97, 100–03, 109–15, 147–49, 155–58.

27. Alan Gauld, *Mediumship and Survival*, 240.

28. Myers, *Human Personality*, 218–19.

29. Tyrrell, *Apparitions*, 67, 129.

30. Ibid., 116–17.

31. Gauld, *Mediumship and Survival*, 222–23.

32. Myers, *Human Personality*, 204.

33. Tyrrell, *Apparitions*, 122–23.

34. Becker, *Paranormal Experiences*, 51.

35. Ibid., 52.

8. EVIDENCE FROM OUT-OF-BODY EXPERIENCES

1. Susan J. Blackmore, *Beyond the Body: An Investigation of Out-of-the-Body Experiences* (1982; Chicago: Academy Chicago Publishers, 1992), 1, 10.

2. See Mark B. Woodhouse, "Five Arguments Regarding the Objectivity of NDEs," *Anabiosis—The Journal for Near-Death Studies* 3/1 (June 1983), 63–75, esp. 64.

3. Glen O. Gabbard and Stuart W. Twemlow, *With the Eyes of the Mind: An Empirical Analysis of Out-of-Body States* (New York: Praeger, 1984), 138; Emilio Tiberi, "Extrasomatic Emotions," *Journal of Near-Death Studies* 11/3 (Spring 1993), 149–70, at 158.

4. Blackmore, *Beyond the Body*, 251.

5. Gabbard and Twemlow, *With the Eyes of the Mind*, 136.

6. Harvey J. Irwin, *Flight of Mind: A Psychological Study of the Out-of-Body Experience* (Metuchen, N.J., & London: Scarecrow, 1985), 12.

7. Whereas Blackmore (*Beyond the Body*, 93) and Tiberi ("Extrasomatic Emotions," 153) give figures of about 60 percent, Celia Green (*Out-of-the-Body Experiences* [London: Hamish Hamilton, 1968], 42) says that about eighty percent of her subjects reported autoscopy.

8. These quotations are from Green, *Out-of-the-Body Experiences*, 46, 85.

9. These quotations are from Michael Sabom, *Recollections of Death: A Medical Investigation* (New York: Harper & Row, 1982), 16.

10. These quotations are from Green, *Out-of-the-Body Experiences*, 86, 87.

11. Tiberi, "Extrasomatic Emotions," 156–57.

12. Ibid., 155.

13. Sabom, *Recollections of Death*, 31.

14. Ibid., 28; Blackmore, *Beyond the Body*, 93.

15. Tiberi, "Extrasomatic Emotions," 154, 155.

16. Ibid., 155; Blackmore, *Beyond the Body*, 68.

17. Quoted in Raymond Moody, *Life After Life* (1975; New York: Bantam, 1976), 35–36.

18. See, e.g., ibid., 18, 146, 169–70, 176, and Woodhouse, "Five Arguments Regarding the Objectivity of NDEs," 71.

19. Tiberi, "Extrasomatic Emotions," 231; see also Sabom, *Recollections of Death*, 22.

20. Green, *Out-of-the Body Experiences*, 81, 83.

21. See Kenneth Ring, *Life at Death: A Scientific Investigation of the Near-Death Experience* (New York: Coward, McCann and Geoghegan, 1980) and *Heading Toward Omega: In Search of the Meaning of the Near-Death Experience* (New York: William Morrow, 1984); Margot Grey, *Return from Death: An Exploration of the Near-Death Experience* (London and Boston: Arkana, 1985); Charles P. Flynn, *After the Beyond: Human Transformation and the Near-Death Experience* (Englewood Cliffs, N.J.: Prentice-Hall, 1986) and "Meanings and Implications of Near-Death Experience Transformations," in *The Near-Death Experience: Problems, Prospects, Perspectives,* ed. Bruce Greyson and Charles P. Flynn (Springfield, Ill.: Charles C. Thomas, 1982), 278–89; Rosalie D. Newsome, "Ego, Moral and Faith Development in Near-Death Experiences: Three Case Studies," *Journal of Near-Death Studies* 7/2 (Winter 1988), 73–105; Phyllis M. H. Atwater, *Coming Back to Life* (New York: Dodd, Mead, 1988); David Lorimer, *Whole in One: The Near-Death Experience and the Ethic of Interconnectedness* (London: Arkana, 1990); Melvin Morse (with Paul Perry),

Transformed by the Light: The Powerful Effect of Near-Death Experiences on People's Lives (New York: Villard Books, 1992); and Cherie Sutherland, *Transformed by the Light: Life after Near-Death Experiences* (Sydney, Australia: Bantam, 1992).

22. Tiberi, "Extrasomatic Emotions," 164.

23. Gabbard and Twemlow, *With the Eyes of the Mind*, 138.

24. Tiberi, "Extrasomatic Emotions," 166.

25. Margot Grey, *Return from Death*, 49.

26. D. Sheils, "A Cross-Cultural Study of Beliefs in Out-of-the-Body Experiences," *Journal of the Society for Psychical Research* 49 (1978), 697–741.

27. Sabom, *Recollections of Death*, 3, 156; Sabom's statement about having considered Moody's book ridiculous is in Moody (with Paul Perry), *The Light Beyond* (1988; New York: Bantam, 1989), 140.

28. Sabom, *Recollections of Death*, 56.

29. Ibid., 2; Moody, *The Light Beyond*, 3.

30. Richard S. Blacher, "Commentary: To Sleep, Perchance to Dream . . . ," *Journal of the American Medical Association* 242 (Nov. 23, 1979), 2291; Michael Sabom, *Recollections of Death*, 153 (citing his response in the July 4, 1980 issue of *JAMA*).

31. Blacher, "Near-Death Experiences" (letter), *JAMA* 244 (1980), 30.

32. Irwin, *Flight of Mind*, 238, 245.

33. Sabom, *Recollections of Death*, 58–59; Gabbard and Twemlow, *With the Eyes of the Mind*, 129.

34. See Melvin Morse (with Paul Perry), *Closer to the Light: Learning from Children's Near-Death Experiences* (New York: Villard Books, 1990).

35. Irwin, *Flight of Mind*, 249.

36. Blackmore, *Beyond the Body*, 125–31.

37. Moody, *Life After Life*, 169.

38. Irwin, *Flight of Mind*, 246–47.

39. Sabom, *Recollections of Death*, 163.

40. Irwin, *Flight of Mind*, 245.

41. Gabbard and Twemlow, *With the Eyes of the Mind*, 131; Sabom, *Recollections of Death*, 175–76.

42. Sabom, ibid., 176.

43. Ibid., 178.

44. Irwin, *Flight of Mind*, 234.

45. Idem.

46. Sabom, *Recollections of Death*, 173–74.

47. Ibid., 171–72.

48. Irwin, *Flight of Mind*, 244.

49. Sabom, *Recollections of Death*, 100–02.

50. Ibid., 104.

51. Ibid., 105.

52. Ibid., 83–87.

53. Ibid., 106.

54. Ibid., 109.

55. Ibid., 105–06.

56. Ibid., 110.

57. Ibid., 107.

58. Ibid., 109.

59. Ibid., 110–11.

60. Kenneth Ring and Madelaine Lawrence, "Further Evidence for Veridical Perception During Near-Death Experiences," *Journal of Near-Death Studies* 11/4 (Summer 1993), 223–29, at 227.

61. For some more of these, see Sabom, *Recollections of Death*, 64–74, 98–99; Morse, *Closer to the Light*, 24–26, 165; Ring and Lawrence, "Further Evidence," 227–28.

62. See, e.g., the short chapter on "Travelling Clairvoyance" in Green, *Out-of-the-Body Experiences*, 126–30.

63. Sabom, *Recollections of Death*, 111.

64. Ibid., 112–13.

65. Idem.

66. Kimberly Clark, "Clinical Interventions with Near-Death Experiences," Greyson and Flynn, *The Near-Death Experience*, 242–55, at 242–43.

67. Ring and Lawrence, "Further Evidence," 226–27.

68. For other accounts, see Morse, *Closer to the Light*, 3–7, 153. For some interesting, albeit not corroborated, accounts, see Moody, *The Light Beyond*, 18–20, 170–71, 173, and Green, *Out-of-the-Body Experiences*, 121.

69. Moody, *The Light Beyond*, 18.

70. Ibid., 169–70.

71. Morse, *Closer to the Light*, 169.

72. Richard S. Broughton, *Parapsychology: The Controversial Science* (New York: Ballantine Books, 1991), 259.

73. Irwin, *Flight of Mind*, 251–55, 313; Blackmore, *Beyond the Body*, 129, 136, 138–39, 238, 251; Gabbard and Twemlow, *With the Eyes of the Mind*, 223–24.

74. Hornell Hart, "ESP Projection: Spontaneous Cases and the Experimental Method," *Journal of the American Society for Psychical Research* 48/4 (October 1954), 121–46, esp. 125–35.

75. Broughton, *Parapsychology*, 249–51.

76. Ibid., 254; Blackmore, *Beyond the Body*, 222–23; Robert Almeder, *Death and Personal Survival* (see Ch. 6 n.4, above), 185–94.

77. L. Landau, "An Unusual Out-of-the-Body Experience," *Journal of the Society for Psychical Research* 42 (1963), 126–28; reprinted in D. Scott Rogo, ed., *Mind Beyond the Body: The Mystery of ESP Projection* (New York: Penguin, 1988), 307–09; and summarized in Charles T. Tart, *Psi: Scientific Studies of the Psychic Realm* (New York: E. P. Dutton, 1977), 179–82.

78. See Blackmore, *Beyond the Body*, 223; Irwin, *Flight of Mind*, 233–34; Michael Grosso, *The Final Choice: Playing the Survival Game* (Walpole, N.H.: Stillpoint, 1985), 111.

79. Grosso, *The Final Choice*, 106–07; Sabom, *Recollections of Death*, 182–83; Tiberi, "Extrasomatic Emotions," 168.

80. Green, *Out-of-the-Body Experiences*, 75–78; Blackmore, *Beyond the Body*, 68.

81. This expression was used by Nancy Evans Bush in her review of Phyllis Atwater's *Coming Back to Life* in the *Journal of Near-Death Studies* 7/2 (Winter, 1988), 121–28, at 127.

82. Morse, *Closer to the Light*, 169.

83. See Carol Zaleski, *Otherworld Journeys: Accounts of Near-Death Experience in Medieval and Modern Times* (New York & Oxford: Oxford University Press, 1987), and Ioam Culiano, *Out of this World: Other-Worldly Journeys from Gilgamesh to Einstein* (Boston: Shambhala, 1991).

84. I have discussed this interpretation of collective archetypes in my introduction to David Ray Griffin, ed., *Archetypal Process: Self and Divine in Whitehead, Jung, and Hillman* (Evanston, Ill.: Northwestern University Press, 1989), 1–76, esp. 39–44.

85. Hornell Hart, "Six Theories About Apparitions," *Proceedings of the Society for Psychical Research* 50 (May 1956), 153–239, at 177.

86. Ibid., 235.

87. Idem.

88. Idem.

9. PARAPSYCHOLOGY AND POSTMODERN SPIRITUALITY

1. See Martin Heidegger, "The Word of Nietzsche: 'God is Dead,'" in *The Question Concerning Technology: Heidegger's Critique of the Modern Age*, trans. William Lovitt (New York: Harper & Row, 1977), and Stephen P. L. Turner and Regis A. Factor, *Max Weber and the Dispute over Reason and Value: A Study in Philosophy, Ethics, and Politics* (London: Routledge & Kegan Paul, 1984), 38, 65, 96, 97, 183.

2. On Heidegger's embrace of Nazism, see Richard Wolin, *The Politics of Being: The Political Thought of Martin Heidegger* (New York: Columbia University Press, 1990), Michael E. Zimmerman, *Heidegger's Confrontation with Modernity: Technology, Politics, and Art* (Bloomington: Indiana University Press, 1990), or Tom Rockmore, *On Heidegger's Nazism and Philosophy* (Berkeley: University of California Press, 1992).

3. See John B. Carman, *The Theology of Ramanuja: An Essay in Interreligious Understanding* (New Haven: Yale University Press, 1974).

4. Alfred North Whitehead, *Modes of Thought* (New York: Free Press, 1968), 102–13.

5. Ibid., 103.

6. John Dewey, *A Common Faith* (New Haven: Yale University Press, 1934); Donald Cupitt, *Taking Leave of God* (New York: Crossroad, 1981).

7. Whitehead, *Adventures of Ideas* (New York: Free Press, 1967), 295.

8. James A. Sanders, *God Has a Story Too* (Philadelphia: Fortress Press, 1979).

9. Jule Eisenbud, *Parapsychology and the Unconscious* (Berkeley: North Atlantic Books, 1983), 126.

10. Herbert Thurston, *The Physical Phenomena of Mysticism* (Chicago: Regnery Co., 1952), 16.

11. John Bowker, *The Sense of God: Sociological, Anthropological and Psychological Approaches to the Origin of the Sense of God* (Oxford: Clarendon, 1973).

12. For the evolution of Freud's views, see Robert Aziz, *Jung's Psychology of Religion and Synchronicity* (Albany: State University of New York Press, 1990), 93–110, and Ernest Jones, *The Life and Works of Sigmund Freud*, vol. II (New York: Basic Books, 1957), 375–407. Freud's most forthright statement of his acceptance of telepathy, "Psychoanalysis and Telepathy," was published only posthumously, in 1941 (in German). The English translation appeared in George Devereux, ed., *Psychoanalysis and the Occult* (New York: International Universities Press, 1953). It is reprinted in Raymond Van Over, ed., *Psychology and Extrasensory Perception* (New York: New American Library [Mentor Books], 1972). It can also be found in James Strachey, ed., *The Standard Edition of the Complete Psychological Works of Sigmund Freud* (London: Hogarth and the Institute of Psychoanalysis), XVIII: 177–93.

13. Francis Hutcheson's theory that we were endowed by God with a moral sense, which influenced Adam Smith and Thomas Jefferson, is discussed by Garry Wills in Chapter 13 (". . . endowed by their creator . . .") of his *Inventing America: Jefferson's Declaration of Independence* (New York: Vintage Books, 1978).

14. See Richard Rorty, *Philosophy and the Mirror of Nature* (Princeton: N.J.: Princeton University Press, 1979), 174, 190–91; *Consequences of Pragmatism* (Minneapolis: University of Minnesota Press, 1982), xvii, xxiv, xliii, xlvi, 140, 191–92, 204.

15. J. B. Rhine, "Parapsychology and Religion," *Journal of Parapsychology* 9 (1945), 1–4; *New World of the Mind* (New York: William Sloane, 1953), 220; *The Reach of the Mind* (New York: William Sloane, 1947), 202. This idea has been developed by J. Shoneberg Setzer in "Parapsychology: Religion's Basic Science," *Religion in Life* 39 (1970), 595–607.

16. William James, *The Varieties of Religious Experience* (New York: Longmans, Green and Co., 1902); Richard Maurice Bucke, *Cosmic Consciousness: A Study in the Evolution of the Human Mind*, 9th ed. (New York: E. P. Dutton, 1940).

17. Abraham J. Heschel, *The Prophets* (New York: Harper and Row, 1962), 308, 313, 314. See also John C. Merkle, *The Genesis of Faith: The Depth Theology of Abraham Joshua Heschel* (New York: Macmillan, 1985).

18. For a discussion of life after death as a continuing journey, written from a Whiteheadian perspective, see the epilogue, "Adventure and Immortality," of Bruce G. Epperly, *At the Edges of Life: A Holistic Vision of the Human Adventure* (St. Louis: Chalice, 1992), 159–72.

19. Karl Popper and J. C. Eccles, *The Self and Its Brain* (Heidelberg: Springer Verlag, 1977), 556.

20. Ian Stevenson, *Cases of the Reincarnation Type, III: Twelve Cases in Lebanon and Turkey* (Charlottesville: University Press of Virginia, 1980), 6–7, 186.

21. I refer to a work in progress, tentatively titled *The Divine Cry of Our Time*.

NOTE ON SUPPORTING CENTER

This series is published under the auspices of the Center for Process Studies, a research organization affiliated with the Claremont School of Theology and Claremont University Center and Graduate School. It was founded in 1973 by John B. Cobb, Jr., Founding Director, and David Ray Griffin, Executive Director; Mary Elizabeth Moore and Marjorie Suchocki are now also Co-Directors. It encourages research and reflection on the process philosophy of Alfred North Whitehead, Charles Hartshorne, and related thinkers, and on the application and testing of this viewpoint in all areas of thought and practice. This center sponsors conferences, welcomes visiting scholars to use its library, and publishes a scholarly journal, *Process Studies*, and a newsletter, *Process Perspectives*. Located at 1325 North College, Claremont, California 91711, it gratefully accepts (tax-deductible) contributions to support its work.

INDEX

Action at a distance, 16–25
Adler, Julius, 310n. 99
Aesthetic experience, 4, 284
Akolkar, V. V., 313n. 12, 314nn. 29, 38
Alcock, James, 84, 303n. 132
Almeder, Robert, 184, 316n. 4
Announcing dreams, 196, 198–200
Anomaly, 34, 97
Antecedent probability, 256–57, 264, 266
Apparent, 209
Apparitions, 209–28; collective, 211, 218–23, 265; crisis, 211; experimental, 224–25; multiple, 211, 217–18; reciprocal, 224, 225–27, 228; spontaneous, 224–25; veridical, 209, 211–17; as hallucinations, 211, 221; of the dead, 211, 265; of the dying, 211; of the living, 211, 224–25, 265
Aquinas, St. Thomas, 275
Armstrong, D. M., 296n. 58
Atheism, 1, 2, 3, 274
Atkinson, Richard, 84n
Atkinson, Rita, 84n
Atwater, P.M.W., 322n. 21
Augustine, St., 283
Automatic writing, 54, 162–64
Autoscopy, 232, 240–41, 322n. 7
Ayala, F., 306n. 29

Badham, Linda, 307n. 36
Badham, Paul, 110, 112, 307n. 36
Balfour, Arthur, 13

Ballou, Robert, 296n. 55
Barker, D. R., 306n. 10
Barrett, W., 13, 26, 231, 295n. 39
Barth, Karl, 146
Basic actions, 144–45
Becker, Carl, 169, 184, 313n. 1, 316n. 4
Beloff, John, 15n, 112
Bem, Daryl, 84n
Bender, Hans, 72, 74, 302
Bentley, Richard, 19, 22
Berger, Arthur and Joyce, 301n. 77, 312n. 23
Bergson, Henri, 13, 138, 140, 143, 311nn. 113, 114
Berkeley, Bishop, 106, 109, 134–35
Birthmarks, 196, 198–200, 265
Bjornsson, Hafsteinn, 166–67
Blacher, Richard, 238, 260, 323nn. 30, 31
Blaisdell, Lydia, 321n. 25
Blake, William, 13
Blakemore, Colin, 305n. 7
Bohm, David, 13
Bolten, Frances, 13
Book tests, 55, 161
Borst, C. V., 308n. 69, 309n. 94
Bouhamzy, Ibriham, 187–92
Bowker, John, 283, 326n. 11
Boyle, Robert, 1, 15, 131
Brain, 143, 150, 238, 272
Brandon, R., 300n. 60
Braude, Stephen, 30, 49, 56, 91, 180, 181, 197, 202, 295n. 42, 296n. 46, 300n. 60, 305n. 160, 315n. 49, 315n. 59

331